European Music in the
Twentieth Century

Chapters by

EVERETT HELM
ERIC WALTER WHITE
BERNARD STEVENS
WALTER AND ALEXANDER GOEHR
NORMAN DEL MAR
IAIN HAMILTON
ANTHONY MILNER
REGINALD SMITH BRINDLE
DAVID DREW
BO WALLNER
HOWARD HARTOG
JOHN G. PAPAIOANNOU

European
Music in the
Twentieth
Century

EDITED BY HOWARD HARTOG

GREENWOOD PRESS, PUBLISHERS
WESTPORT, CONNECTICUT

Library of Congress Cataloging in Publication Data

Hartog, Howard, 1913-   ed.
    European music in the twentieth century.

    Reprint of the ed. published by Routledge and Paul,
London.
    Includes index.
    1. Music--History and criticism--20th century.
2. Music--Europe--History and criticism. 3. Composers.
I. Title.
[ML197.H27 1976]   780'.94   75-45461
ISBN 0-8371-8680-3

First published 1957 by Routledge & Kegan Paul Ltd.

Reprinted with the permission of Routledge & Keegan
Paul Ltd.

Reprinted in 1976 by Greenwood Press,
a division of Williamhouse-Regency Inc.

Library of Congress Catalog Card Number 75-45461

ISBN 0-8371-8680-3

Printed in the United States of America

APR 7 1978

Contents

v

CONTENTS

Contributors

EVERETT HELM, American composer, musicologist and broadcaster, has had various works performed in Europe and the U.S.A., including a Piano Concerto, a Symphony for Strings, a radio opera, etc., etc.

ÉRIC WALTER WHITE is the author of *The Rise of English Opera 1951, A Monograph of Benjamin Britten* and two studies of Stravinsky and his music. In the 1930's he collaborated with Lotte Reiniger in her silhouette films. He is now Assistant Secretary to the Arts Council of Great Britain.

BERNARD STEVENS is a well-known composer, and a Symphony, Cello Concerto and chamber music have reached concert programmes.

WALTER GOEHR, born in Berlin, was a pupil of Arnold Schönberg. He is a conductor, composer, musicologist (editions of Bach and Monteverdi) and lives in London.

ALEXANDER GOEHR, a composer, was born in Berlin. He is a pupil of Richard Hall and Oliver Messiaen.

NORMAN DEL MAR, conductor, born in London, is also a composer and broadcaster and teaches at the Guildhall School of Music.

IAIN HAMILTON, composer, born Glasgow, 1922, has also broadcast and written numerous contributions on musical subjects. He is a lecturer at Morley College.

ANTHONY MILNER, born Bristol, 1925, is a composer and journalist and lecturer at Morley College.

REGINALD SMITH BRINDLE was born in the industrial north in 1917 but has lived in Florence since 1943. He studied music in Wales and under Pizzetti and Dallapiccola. Among his compositions are a Symphony, Variations on a Theme of Dallapiccola, etc. He has been a music critic and broadcaster.

DAVID DREW, musicologist, is at present preparing a book on Kurt Weill and has contributed to various musical journals.

CONTRIBUTORS

DR. BO WALLNER, Swedish musicologist, has a keen interest in contemporary music and is actively concerned with furthering same both as an administrator and as a writer in Stockholm.

HOWARD HARTOG, born London, 1913, has broadcast and written on musical subjects. He works with a firm of music publishers.

JOHN G. PAPAIOANNOU, born in 1915 in Athens. He has been an architect and musician. He was a close personal friend of Skalkottas and has since the latter's death been concerned with the furtherance of his friend's music as well as of contemporary music in general in Greece.

Introduction

THE aim of this book can best be described as mid-century stock-taking: this is not a simple affair for several reasons. We may think that we can now see the wood despite the trees and that we can perceive some of the operative trends in the progress of musical creation and thought in European life. But to write a book describing this in large and in detail seemed to me to call for a devotee with far greater knowledge and aptitude than myself: hence the idea of a symposium emerged, in the hope that some picture of the shape of European music in the first half of the century would be given to those who wished a rough-and-ready introduction, and some impression be given of how the problems endemic in various countries were being tackled by the more adventurous musical spirits in the several centres of musical culture.

The crisis in musical life represents, after all, the greater crisis in political and artistic life. Only ostriches (and some members of the press) can afford to ignore the impact of Darwin, Marx and Freud on the tidy and ordered nineteenth-century concepts which seem to some today so distant and desirable. The beginning of the century saw in all the arts an intense wave of experiment, some of it vital, a lot of it modish, which produced not only the musicians whom we hope to discuss in this book but Picasso and Paul Klee, James Joyce and Rainer Maria Rilke, le Corbusier and Walter Gropius. The clear fact is that as the comfortable bourgeois values of the nineteenth century were, to the majority of creative artists, no longer acceptable or tolerable, and the old disciplines have been shed, the search for new disciplines, or even for the delights of artistic anarchy—expressed perhaps best by the work of the Dadaists in the twenties or the improvised renderings of John Cage on 'prepared' pianos—was pursued intensively and often with violence. In music the signs were also on the horizon before the century ended.

For example, the tides of the German romantic tradition, already showing signs of overflowing in the works of Wagner and Bruckner, found in Mahler a romantic whose innate intelligence and sensitivity made him realise that the banks must burst sooner or later, and the 'Burleske' movement in the Ninth Symphony, although perhaps today the least satisfying in that great work, typifies most clearly the violence of his discontent with the shape of musical tradition that he had found. It was, of course, no coincidence that this acute musician should show personal sympathy with the young Schönberg and his group, for they were to attempt to canalise, albeit subject to a discipline exotic to all that had gone before, the dissipated streams of a no longer homogeneous impulse. Here is not the place to discuss Schönberg's origins or musical parentage, as that will be taken care of by Walter Goehr in the course of this article. But it is a fundamental fact that whether Mahler was in fact one of the last great men in a great tradition or whether he was a prophet of a new age, his music is barometric to the uncertainties of musical climate which were increasingly to prevail during the first thirty years of the twentieth century.

That, partly simultaneously with, and partly resultant on, the Schönbergian exploration of new methods and new worlds, a tendency to explore (or re-explore) the classical world of music should also gather strength is not surprising. The splendour of romanticism had dazzled so many that the history of twentieth-century musical life shows, parallel with its contemporary experiments, a growing interest in music before Beethoven, starting with a rediscovery of Mozart and extending, as the century developed, to names like Schütz, Monteverdi, Vivaldi, the Scarlattis, Telemann, Purcell, Peerson, Gibbons and Machaut: and equally, as the century has progressed, many living composers have shown their interest in earlier and earlier musical antecedents.

The reflection of this absorption in the classical and pre-classical roots of musical culture has, of course, a certain effect on the so-called pre-'neo-classical' tendency which, nearly contemporaneously with the Mahler-Schönberg developments, attempted by quite other means to deodorise the atmosphere of putrescent romanticism. Ferruccio Busoni, an eminent practising musician with a keen analytical brain, tried to remove from the German and Italian romantic traditions the dross which he somehow felt was no longer consonant with the standards of contemporary life. Many other serious and gifted musicians followed in his path: neither did they adhere strictly to his methods nor did they necessarily issue the *rappel à l'ordre* for immediately identical reasons.

INTRODUCTION

In a penetrating broadcast on Hindemith, Iain Hamilton pointed out that the shock impinged on the musical world by the emergence of Arnold Schönberg had results of even wider importance than his direct influence on pupils and devotees: it forced many distinguished musical minds, which reacted sharply away from the implications of Schönberg's example and teaching, to reassess and re-examine their own musical footing. From this revaluation sprang much that is of high and serious value in the European musical picture: the whole twentieth-century panorama would be inexplicable without an understanding of how deeply the appearance of Schönberg shook the entire edifice of musical thinking. Whether a real revolutionary or not, he forced every musician whose face was not turned solely towards the past, to revalue not only the contemporary musical world, but also the musical traditions which had hitherto been blindly, but seldom comprehendingly, accepted.

In France the collapse of the romantic tradition of the nineteenth century led to the impressionist Debussy and the kaleidoscopic Ravel; the mastery of these two composers cannot be denied, but the movement they started has had only a slight independent life and has tended to be integrated into the broader European tendencies. Debussy, for example, had a special influence on Stravinsky—and other examples leap to mind. It is clear that the impressionist solution found an immediate if temporary appeal in many lands, but it is symptomatic of a general discontent with existing standards that, as the twentieth century approached, various paths of development should be explored, in music as in other arts which were of interest: but interest alone does not give life to a movement and in the end it is the vitality of an art which secures its longevity: and many concepts which have genuine intellectual fascination are absorbed in the main and living movements.

The *raison d'être* for this book is that after the eruptions of the twenties, and despite the new tendencies which have their own special problems, one can now perceive traces of a pattern at work in European musical life. By making it a symposium one simultaneously weakens and strengthens the force of argument. It is weakened by the divergence of views necessarily held by contributors of widely differing tenets: strengthened by the fact that each contributor has a reasonably special knowledge of the subject in hand and, obviously, a sympathy with it. We have therefore a series of 'devil's advocates' some of whose pleading may run counter to that of their colleagues. In spite of this a general picture of a shifting world should be perceptible: here and

3

there, inevitably, details will be blurred. Certain names which to us today seem of paramount interest may disappear with the years: having disappeared they may or may not re-emerge when again uncovered. There are always fashions in musical taste and though the whole tendency of this book consists in a real endeavour to avoid what Ernest Newman calls 'tasters', obviously the taste of our day cannot but affect us all. To minimise the effects there has been an attempt to avoid overmuch selection from one group or clique of writers, and axe-grinding of a narrower sort has been, it is hoped, minimised.

Nevertheless a fundamental axe is being ground: the basic right of music as of other arts to continue vital development is the underlying theme of this book. This has meant a serious attempt to make the axe grind on a cosmopolitan line: whereas, if not in the contents at least in the chapter headings, Norman Demuth's ably worked *Musical Trends in the Twentieth Century* tilts slightly for England and France, there is equally no doubt that Karl Heinz Wörner's massive *Moderne Musik in der Entscheidung* has breathed a German air first and foremost and tends to find enormous value in everything that is being done today. The aim of this symposium has been, while affirming the right to progress (sometimes even to regress) along new ways, to adopt a critical and historical attitude towards the musical history of the last fifty years.

But the process of editing the book has been selective: like a panorama from an eminence the book embraces the greater part of the scene but not every detail. To the chagrined composer whose intrepid light still blazes under a bushel, or who has evaded the contributor's notice, apologies are tendered: but although a certain encyclopædic flavour is inevitable, a list of active composers might be useful to the ill-informed critic but hardly more than a bore otherwise. Equally, and here the editorial hand has had to become rather arbitrary, a large number of composers who have been and are still frequently performed have been omitted: these are mostly names of a traditional and conservative mould, who often have works of solid worth behind them, but whose contribution to what seems likely to be the future is probably of less dynamic and immediate urgency: in addition, many of the names thus precluded from full analysis (for example Strauss, Sibelius, Nielsen, Elgar and Vaughan Williams) have had the advantage of a fairly exhaustive literary appreciation: this includes monographs like Frank Howes' on Vaughan Williams and Dr. Robert Simpson's on Carl Nielsen which, critically considered, serve as fully as any one man's

4

work can to cover the field they have chosen. The concept of this book is primarily, therefore, forward-looking: this may not always be tantamount to progressive but it means that the contributors seek to explore the new territories touched during this century.

A constant criticism of all contemporary art is being made: it is that it is discordant (and hence by implication ugly): this criticism has a superficial air of validity. The prospect before any sensitive person today is given: the stresses of sociological conflict, the shadow of more horrifying weapons of war, the sordid poverty still infecting much of the world, these are some of the unpleasantnesses that confront all men of sensibility, and in the first instance the artist today: the Freudian baring of some of our more horrid instincts also deprives us of some of the beguiling detachment possible to composers in earlier times. It can be argued, and justly, that earlier times had their horrors, that Palestrina composed in the shadow of the Inquisition, and Mozart in the wings of the French Revolution. But today the equipment (press, radio, TV, etc.) for propagating the impact of the seamy side of life is so much more efficient and intense that the onslaught on the nerves precludes the carefree and comfortable music from having the validity with which it is too often credited. To compose today consistently in the style of the nineteenth century presupposes the skin of a rhinoceros or the neck of an ostrich. To stress this point may seem otiose, but there are today, frequently in high places, many people who vociferate against any experiment; by corollary the peaceful euphony of the unquestioning traditionalist seems an aim in itself, covering all activity in a stranglehold of inertia. Against these vegetable concepts and their wider implications, the underlying impulse of this book is set.

The situation of modern music today is anomalous and irregular: Nikos Skalkottas has to wait for death before his name makes an impact, yet young composers are frequently commissioned to write large and extravagant works, some of which are perforce limited in the amount of performances they can obtain by the excessive resources they postulate. Young composers are frequently published as an insurance for the future: yet outside the Soviet Union and similarly controlled countries the financial position of the composer lacks stability: his income is based on the performing rights which may accrue, and these are not sufficient to provide a living: hence many composers have perforce to accept some form of regular employment to keep the wolf from the door. It is manifest that a young composer can, therefore, hardly hope to devote himself exclusively to his main task unless he is

5

subsidised by the State: and although patronage can be found flourishing for some composers on a private basis, this patronage is clearly no longer as grandiose nor as widespread as before. The remaining patron can be the State: in Great Britain the Arts Council, heavily pummelled by the bully boys of a section of the press (a section which, Göring-like, reaches for its acidulated ink at the mention of the word 'Culture'), walks a tight rope so delicate and infinitesimal that its effectual labours are of a purely Lady Bountiful variety. A large choral festival in the *embonpoint* nineteenth-century tradition will elicit many more pennies than any experimental propagation of contemporary music. In other countries the situation is more or less the same: the lords of contemporary musical culture are, undeniably, the radio stations: and the operation in these institutes of counterbalances of political and æsthetic intrigue produce a result that is now the only operative factor of real decisiveness in the contemporary scene of organised music. There are other important contributory festivals or summer schools (Donaueschingen and Darmstadt, Dartington and Bilthoven are examples) which serve, or could serve, as weather-vanes in the days of changing climates.

Help could be, but rarely is, forthcoming from the critics: however hotly they proclaim their lip service to the 'Contemporary Cause', should a tug-of-war occur between their attendance at a concert containing a new work or the repetition under Signor X of a programme trite as journalism, one may be sure that Signor X or *Figaro* for the one hundred and seventeenth time will win the day. Help could be, but even more rarely is, forthcoming from the conductors. There are, I suppose, in Western Europe today less than half a dozen conductors who believe it their duty to incorporate contemporary music in their programmes: mostly, if they do incorporate it, the works are very little 'contemporary' in the sense of the word we are trying here to establish and only prove that the conductor in question is not averse to conducting works composed in the twentieth century irrespective of their intrinsic importance. The dangers implicit in the other course are evident: only the 'very latest' music has an interest for some conductors and in some places: a kind of snobocracy for producing the most *outré* noises tends to arise. Nevertheless a snobbism which encourages *any* experiment, good or bad, clearly has advantages over a timorous snobbery that refuses to taste of any new dishes, unless they be yesterday's dict reheated. As propagators of new music tend to glory in experiment for experiment's sake, it is better to encourage them (and at the same time some works of evanescent interest) at the expense of those whose obdurate academicism mainly fetters the spread of interest in contemporary arts. Those who like the works of Mr. X because they sound like Beethoven or Strauss or Mozart are not converted to a keen interest in modern ways of thought: it is arguable, indeed it is practically evident, that Bach, Mozart, Beethoven and Schubert expressed their genius in more valid forms than the kings of contemporary music today. A sane approach to contemporary music requires a real knowledge and comprehension of the great classical masters: Arnold Schönberg was deeply versed in the masters of the past, and Stravinsky (one can also deduce this from his music) has a wide musical education—sometimes idiosyncratic in its selection of models but always spellbinding and vital. But, having once come to terms with the great names, it is not sufficient to waddle in waters of classical stagnation, nor to seek in the work of living composers pale or obese images of classical models, but one must strive to find some elements of the disruptive, even decadent elements in contemporary art and come to terms with them.

It will be seen that here it is hard to make a claim that the word 'contemporary' connotes progress to a higher ethos. Just as in the world of pictorial art Picasso recalls the Byzantines and Giacometti the Etruscans, it is not infrequent that one detects a Brahmsian or Mahlerian mood in Schönberg, or an admiration for Bellini and Tchaikovsky in Stravinsky. All art forms are in the melting-pot, and many forms, such as abstract art and *musique concrète*, which are not precluded from producing moving effects, seem to represent palpable blind alleys—the end of this road is clear. It is probable, particularly in Western art, that a consciousness of the reality of this problem besets many of the best minds, who attach themselves to a system, either of their own evolution or created by the ingenuity of another, in an effort to stave off æsthetic shipwreck. One can neither blame nor praise this development: the fire and quality of the workmanship are decisive, the content and force the only relevant criteria in a world where permanent values swing and the clutched-at straw looks like a rock.

The editing of this book has involved certain difficulties: foreign contributors, when invited, seem loth to answer correspondence, and many delays handicap the production of a cohesive policy. The aim has been, not to present the editor's own views but to establish a factual and critical appreciation of the first fifty years' creative work in this century. The contributors have been picked, not as 'yes-men' to present

7

a clear-cut ideological crusade calculated to shatter the earthworks of reaction, but as men prepared to display their special knowledge of a person's or a country's music. And the editorial policy has, by and large, been directed to that end. Although the bulk of the contributors hail from Great Britain, a serious effort has been made to avert a parochial viewpoint, and this has I think been achieved. Perhaps even Great Britain, as a country which cannot attempt to claim for itself the nineteenth-century position of, say, Germany or Italy, has some advantage as a centre of operations. One cannot imagine, unless one is appointed official critic to a national paper, that British music is the only, or even the best, form of contemporary music. A balanced view may therefore emerge. Some gaps have occurred, inevitable unless the book were to be half a century out of date before it appears. Here, envisaged contributors have failed to respond. The omission of Belgium, Holland, Yugoslavia, Rumania and Bulgaria is attributable to this, but it is to be hoped that the general picture is not too severely damaged through this. The contributions of Walter Goehr and Norman Del Mar are of particular interest because here are two conductors who think about the problems of music and music criticism, and who possess minds iconoclast enough not to accept current shibboleths blindly. The aim of the book, in short, cannot be to produce an encyclopædic analysis of the whole anthill of contemporary composition, but it should provide a handy vade-mecum to the interested students who want to know why and whence appear, say, a Nikos Skalkottas, a Luigi Nono in Italy, a Karl Birger Blomdahl in Sweden, a Pierre Boulez in France or an Erik Bergmann in Finland.

Some of the contributors have been corseted by a necessary limitation on length being imposed:[1] Bo Wallner, in particular, a critic with a rare and discriminating flair, has been compelled to eliminate more extensive consideration of the varying facets of Scandinavian music: and in differing degrees many of the contributors will have felt themselves handicapped. Nevertheless David Drew's exhaustive and valuable review of French music has been included, despite its infraction of the planned proportions of this symposium. This book aims at giving a great deal of information, but an encyclopædia should provide more: it aims at giving an over-all picture of the musical hubbub today, but of course no book can cover all the varying manifestations. It may be observed that, particularly in the articles on the named composers, there

---

[1] Ed. Note. Anthony Milner has generously discussed English music though he himself is a composer of standing.

8

is a certain discrepancy in the approach by the various writers. Walter and Alexander Goehr, for example, have concentrated on a single but comparatively vital aspect of Schönberg's development, whereas Everett Helm's Bartók article examines critically a cross-section of the composer's work and Eric Walter White adduces biographical as well as critical material in his survey of Igor Stravinsky. It was thought on the whole better to allow the individual writers the liberty of tackling their subject after their own predilections rather than here to attempt an arbitrary definition of approach. The concentration, in general, on the so-called 'revolutionary' aspects of music is done with a view to tracing the paths which the various tendencies have trodden in different countries. Bach was mocked in his time as a reactionary, but it does not follow that only the reactionaries are great composers. The pro-verbial saw of the 'test of time' applies to music, not only in the facile crucible of the relegation of all critical judgment to generations to come but also in differentiating the contemporary music, as for example that of Schönberg and Stravinsky which ripens and develops in our consciousness so that we enjoy it the more, as the novelties of technique recede and no longer obscure the intrinsic quality of the composer. Conversely, many works which at first stimulated the imagination have already proved to have less core and substance than had been thought to have been the case at first. For this reason the clarity of the present-day picture becomes less firm in its outlines: yet some pattern can be discerned and, if wrongly construed, at least repre-sents the results of a serious effort in all countries to reach an assess-ment; *musique concrète*, a very natural product of an age of radio, is so far in its infancy: a rounded assessment today would be premature: the bayings of reaction and the ardent pleas of the initiate fill the council room. It is cowardly but also prudent to avoid rushing at a novelty which enjoys the possible strength to demolish the musical structure we know: the development of this movement is of absorbing interest, but it is also a shade too embryonic for critical discussion.

To all such books there should be, however, a deeper underlying im-plication: the lack of interest in contemporary pattern leads some-times to manifestations more aggressive than mere apathy, manifes-tations like the tarring of Epstein monuments or the scandal and hulla-baloo evoked in Paris at the first performance of Stravinsky's *Rite of Spring*. As Sir Herbert Read has pointed out in a recent article, such outbursts of philistinism seem to derive chiefly from the upper middle classes. He further adduced that psychological reasons must play a considerable role in these eruptions. However, the identification of the upper middle classes with this tendency indicates their adherence to an æsthetic as well as an economic *status quo*. Any infraction of a new impulse on values with which they consider their way of living is bound calls forth the sharp reactions indicated by these now historic set-pieces of philistinism; and to those who are interested in the possibility of art finding new ways the varying facets of this book are directed. In a recent broadcast a musician who has been one of the most energetic fighters for contemporary and even Schönbergian music inferred that it was wrong to write in the manner of Webern, whereas it had been right, or at least comprehensible, to write in the manner of Beethoven. This may be correct, but only if Webern's music lacks validity and not *a priori*: otherwise, though we can trace often the influence of Webern on composers of moderate talent, the same applied surely to Beethoven: and, unless aural or other proof is available, determines the non-validity of Webern as a composer.

In the flight from banality, music has moved some way from meeting the current popular taste: this sociological phenomenon has progressively touched all the arts: we are not trying in this compass to find a facile explanation of this trend: it is clearly natural that the palette of music should extend more and more; even now it has reached over the border of known instruments to the sphere of electronics. The contributors to this volume have tried to chart some of the paths followed in European countries, and some of the tendencies which have produced the salient figures. An interim report has, despite its closeness to its subject, certain claims on attention.

The Music of Béla Bartók

EVERETT HELM

B ARTÓK is a composer who is not easily classified and whose style cannot be described either briefly or by means of standard, generally accepted terms or 'isms'. He propounded no systems as did Schönberg and Hindemith, established no clear-cut direction as did Stravinsky (neo-classicism) and founded no 'school'. The direct influence of his music on younger composers, compared to that of the three just mentioned, has been correspondingly small. This may be partly due to his retiring nature and mode of life but even more to the fact that his music is in the last analysis incapable of being codified, hence incapable of being directly imitated. It is witness to the enormous creative imagination of its composer, whose natural musicianship may well exceed that of any other twentieth-century composer. Bartók was more concerned with writing music as he felt it than he was with questions of æsthetics and idiom. His lifelong preoccupation with folksong—a distinctly concrete and vital matter—and its relation to the composer constitute his only theoretical concern. That he was thoroughly capable of the most minute systematisation is apparent from the pains he took in the classification of folk music. In composing, however, he was entirely unsystematic, following only the devices of his own fantasy.

Herein lies, we believe, the key to his greatness. His fantasy was inexhaustible, his musicianship impeccable, and he possessed the technique to translate his ideas into reality. Every composer who achieves greatness, achieves it in his own personal way. And Bartók's way was the opposite, in a sense, from that of his great contemporary Schönberg, who achieved it by means of constantly increasing systematisation and consistent musical thought. While Schönberg struggled with the materials and the organisation of musical composition, achieving in the end his own solution based on a strict discipline, Bartók progressed from one work to another with no visible signs of a similar struggle. The evolution of his style, never so radical as Schönberg's, was accomplished without apparent effort and with no revolutionary 'breaks' such as we find in the works of Stravinsky and Schönberg.

This is not to say that Bartók did not work consciously towards the solution of this or that problem nor that he was less concerned with perfecting the material and language of his works. But his attention would appear to have been concentrated at any given moment on the specific work in hand rather than on evolving an æsthetic, a concept or a system of music. Thus his stylistic evolution was not 'consistent'—that is to say, it did not proceed in a straight stylistic line. A 'radical' work was often followed by a less radical one, and even within a given work there are so-called stylistic 'inconsistencies' in which traditional and advanced idioms rub elbows—inconsistencies that would seem to be the result of Bartók's conception of music as primarily a form of expression, for the achievement of which all means are justified so long as they are genuinely felt. Bartók himself stated: 'I do not wish to subscribe to any of the accepted musical tendencies. My ideal is a measured balance of these elements.'

In achieving this measured balance Bartók stressed now one, now another tendency of contemporary music, with the result that his work displays constant variety of style and idiom. Consequently the division of his work into periods is a ticklish business at best, and the tracing of a straight line of development is as good as ephemeral. Halsey Stevens, in his excellent book *The Life and Music of Béla Bartók*, states: 'Now that Bartók's work may be perceived in its entirety, its evolutionary line becomes its most striking aspect. In no other recent composer is there to be observed such an undeviating adherence to the same basic principles throughout an entire career.' Unfortunately Stevens does not specify what these basic principles were. On the contrary, only a few lines farther on he writes: 'With Bartók there are frequent additions to his creative equipment, but seldom subtractions, "influences" were quickly assimilated, and no matter from what source, they became so personally a part of his style or his technique that their gravitation lost its pull and he continued undeviatingly in his own orbit.' Perhaps Stevens means by 'evolutionary line' that kind of stylistic consistency that is the personal signature of a great musician and that imparts a kind of unity to the most diverse works. In this sense, indeed, Bartók's work is in its entirety thoroughly consistent, the consistency being one of musical personality, not one arising from a straight-ahead evolution that gives the appearance, in retrospect, of being systematic or even, for that matter, logical. When Stevens states that 'there were frequent additions to Bartók's creative equipment but seldom subtractions', he is simply saying that a good composer learns something from every new work and what he learns is never forgotten. But this is not to say that what he has learned is applied *methodically* to all subsequent works.

The idiom of the later works of Bartók gives the impression, indeed, of a certain retrogression and 'unlearning', in so far as they are couched in less radical terms than most works of his 'middle' period. This phenomenon has led some writers to divide Bartók's works into three periods, corresponding roughly to the early, middle and late categories that can be applied to the music of practically any composer—even of such shortlived ones as Mozart. There is some justification for this division, at least on the surface. Bartók's musical point of departure is the late romantic style. In his 'middle' period (roughly 1926–37, including the Piano Sonata, Third and Fourth Quartets, Music for String Instruments and Sonata for Two Pianos and Percussion) he adopts a more radical idiom. And in his late works (Violin Concerto, Third Piano Concerto, Sixth Quartet, Concerto for Orchestra) there is a distinct return to more traditional forms of expression, especially as regards the harmonic procedures. The second period or 'phase' has been referred to as the period of experimentation, the third as that of synthesis, in which all the streams of development of Bartók's life are united.

One author, Colin Mason, declares the eight months between 1927 and July 1928 to be the most important phase of Bartók's entire development—the months intervening between the Third and Fourth Quartets; in his opinion these two works are as far apart as the First and Second, which were separated by a period of ten years. For him the Third Quartet was an experimental work, displaying elements of doubt and struggle, while the Fourth demonstrates that Bartók had now become master of his technical media. Whereas it is true that the Fourth makes even more consistent use of certain practices already strongly in evidence in the Third Quartet, the 'progress' suggested here is not striking. The works are different only as one major work of Bartók differs from every other—namely in the individual solution of a separate problem. Stylistically the two quartets belong together.

David Hall, in dividing Bartók's work into three periods, finds the years 1903–16 to be 'the period during which the musical language was gradually assuming its definite shape' and 1916–39 a period of 'striving for the utmost concentration and perfection of his idiomatic style'. It is true and natural that Bartók in his earlier years went through a period of stylistic formation, as does almost every composer. The year 1916, however, seems to be an arbitrary date for the termination of this 'formative' period. The *Allegro barbaro*, to the style of which Bartók makes frequent references in later works, dates from 1911; the Dance Suite (1923) recalls practices of the 'formative' period, as does the first Rhapsody for Violin and Piano (1928). The fact of the matter is that Bartók's work is so rich and so varied that it admits of many interpretations, no one of which is entirely right or entirely wrong, each being to a great extent a personal point of view.

For Bartók's 'methods' of composition were strictly non-methodical. To a much greater extent than is the case with other contemporary composers, each work posed for him a separate problem that found an individual solution.

In arriving at the individual solutions to the individual works, Bartók availed himself of the entire repertoire of contemporary techniques and practices as they served his purposes. He was, as Stevens so aptly puts it, 'the highest musical synthesis of the era'. Nor did he hesitate to employ the methods and techniques of preceding eras, converting them through the power of his own musical personality into contemporary values. He 'borrowed', so to speak, from Bach, from Beethoven, from Brahms and the late romantics or from Debussy without being a neoclassicist, a neo-romanticist or a neo-impressionist. His own immense fantasy enabled him to transmute whatever he borrowed into his own language—a language that is unmistakably Bartók and at the same time employs the most extensive vocabulary of any composer of the twentieth century.

In exploring this language we shall give close consideration to several of Bartók's key works, from which the characteristics of his style will become clear.

THE STRING QUARTETS

Bartók's quartets present the key to his musical thinking and have for analytical purposes the advantage of extending over his entire career. In them we can note most clearly the changes in his style, idiom and approach to the problems of musical composition. They cannot be said to be entirely representative of Bartók's music, for they make comparatively little use of one element that is of major importance in certain other works—namely, Balkan folk music. The absence of this otherwise so important factor, however, contributes to the loftiness of their conception. As 'pure' music, in which the folk element appears in sublimated form, they represent the culmination of Bartók's creative genius and constitute what is generally considered to be the most important contribution to chamber music of the twentieth century. They have often been compared to the quartets of Beethoven, but nowhere more succinctly than in the short introduction to Mátyás Seiber's small volume *The String Quartets of Béla Bartók*, in which he writes: 'In more than one respect we are reminded of Beethoven: Bartók, too, seems to express his most essential thoughts through the medium of the string quartet. Bartók's style in his quartets, just like Beethoven's, is particularly concentrated and intense, his ideas are most convincing and expressed with the utmost clarity and economy. I believe that for generations to come the string quartets of Bartók will be looked upon as the most outstanding and significant works of our time.'

The First Quartet (1908) might well have been subtitled 'Hommage à Beethoven', for it is clearly inspired by the late Beethoven quartets. The first movement begins with a slow fugal section (cf. the opening of Beethoven's Opus 131) employing many suspensions and appogiaturas; it is based on a chromatic harmonic style that has its prototype in the music of Wagner, Brahms, Bruckner and other late romanticists. Although definite tonalities are suggested, they quickly give way to new ones, so that it is often difficult to determine the tonal centre. A middle section with distinctly 'Ravelian' harmonies is followed by a return of the materials of the fugue, in which the interval of a falling sixth is prominent, trailing off into a short 'bridge' to the second movement, which follows without pause.

The first theme-group of the second movement contains various elements, all seemingly related to the material of the first movement. A rhythmic figure on a low repeated note in the cello reminds one strongly again of Beethoven, as do the procedures of the development section in which the elements of the exposition are worked out and combined in ways typical of the classical period.

An improvisatory passage, in which the free melodic line is most untypical of Beethoven, introduces the third movement, a spirited *Allegro vivace*, full of vigour but somewhat uneven in inspiration. There are passages which would not have satisfied the Bartók of the succeeding quartets, including a further 'reference' to Ravelian style. The *Allegro* is interrupted by an *adagio* passage with highly romantic harmonies, following which the main theme is presented in a new form as the subject for a graceful fugue. This subject is partially given out and then broken off several times before it is allowed to continue, recalling a similar procedure in the *Grosse Fuge* of Beethoven. The romantic *adagio* passage returns again before an extended *accelerando* brings the work to a close.

This First Quartet, unlike other compositions of the same period, displays certain typically Bartókian traits that reappear throughout his later work. First of all there is the remarkable economy in utilising the thematic material. It is not possible to say *post facto* to what extent the similarities of the themes are conscious or unconscious, nor is it important. The fact remains that it is possible, although by no means indispensable, to consider the material of the whole quartet as being derived from that of the first movement. The derivations are often entirely clear; at other times they are more obscure. Nevertheless we can observe a guiding principle of Bartók's formal construction—that of the constant development and variation of thematic material to produce new material. As to the other, external, kind of form—that which relates to the sectional arrangement of a movement—Bartók is here, as in much of his music, relatively traditional, accepting in principle, though never slavishly following, the forms of the classical period.

Counterpoint plays a leading role in this first quartet, and it will remain the basis of much of his subsequent writing—seldom again, however, in the comparatively obvious form of the fugue. The rhythmic vitality of the work is great, although the rhythms are less subtly organised and less original than they will be in the later works. The harmonic idiom is typical of the period in which the quartet was composed, being essentially romantic and derivative, despite certain surprising passages. Yet the work sounds fresh and full of vitality even today, largely because of Bartók's power of melodic invention and finding new expression for what are essentially inherited and traditional material and techniques. The last movement, with its dance-like rhythms and rhapsodic passages, is the only one that betrays a possible influence of Hungarian folk music. The references to folk music, however, are of a superficial nature, more or less in the Liszt tradition, and differ from the integrated use of folk elements at a later period, when Bartók has absorbed and assimilated the true peasant music of his country.

The stylistic gap between the First and Second Quartets is great. In the Second Quartet (1917) Bartók has freed himself from the numerous reminiscences of romantic style and practice that were apparent in the First. In idiom and formal construction it contains the germs for practically all his later practices. Although Bartók employed more radical styles in some later works, the Second Quartet could have been written at any time during his subsequent career.

The opening movement is relatively slow (*moderato*) moving in leisurely 9/8 meter and maintaining a lyrical mood that only occasionally becomes impassioned. It has the outward aspect of sonata form: exposition, development and recapitulation; but it differs from the classical sonata form in that the 'second' and 'closing' themes appear to derive from, or be implicit in, the melody with which the movement opens. This melody contains several elements that are isolated and developed later as separate entities, but that in their first appearance form an integrated part of the 'theme'. (It is perhaps misleading to use the word 'theme'; 'thematic motives' or 'thematic ideas' comes closer to the truth.) At the very outset we are in a different harmonic world from that of the First Quartet. The harmonies, while retaining a certain characteristic Bartókian chromaticism, no longer 'slither' from one apparent tonality to another in the post-romantic vein, and there are few reminiscences of Brahms or Wagner. (If anything, this movement has a certain 'French' flavour, recalling distantly Ravel or Roussel.) It is often difficult to determine in what tonality the music may be at a given moment, for the traditional harmonic concepts no longer apply. But frequently one 'feels' a tonal centre (created partly by pedal points), and at other times the apparent absence of tonal centre relieves the listener of the necessity for making constant mental 'modulations', leaving him free to concentrate on the linear aspect of the music, which is of primary importance. Imitation, not of long lines as in fugal writing, but of short motives that are tossed from one voice to another, is an all-important element, alternating with passages of pure melodic inspiration. The structure is compact, the economy of means remarkable; but the constant variation of the texture as well as the 'thematic' material and its presentation preclude any impression of thickness.

The second movement (*Allegro molto capriccioso*) is a vigorous rondo, the prototype of which is found in the earlier *Allegro barbaro* for piano (1911). It consists of a series of dance-like sections, constantly varied upon their return, interrupted by short episodes of a whimsical nature in slower tempo. The Hungarian element is strongly felt throughout. The tempo changes constantly, the meter seldom. The rhythmic drive is intense. Two intervals are in constant evidence: the tritone and the minor third (alternating with the major third). The movement is clearly conceived in the general tonality of D.

The final movement is marked *lento* and breathes an air of resignation, even of despair, as if the vigour of the preceding movement had been exhausted. It is music of extreme concentration and emotional intensity; the many tritones and minor seconds create an atmosphere of suffering that only occasionally rises above the dynamic of *piano*. It is a truly extraordinary movement, constructed of successive sections related by means of thematic ideas that have certain elements in common either with each other or with material heard in the previous movements.

A minute analysis of the Second Quartet would bring to light a host of thematic relationships that have been no more than intimated here. We do not wish to labour the point. It is of the utmost importance to point out, however, that these complicated structural details interfere in no way, shape or manner with the expressive quality or the emotional content, which is the primary factor.

The ten years separating the Second from the Third Quartet witness the further progression of Bartók away from traditional harmonic and tonal practice. The Third Quartet has been referred to as being in a more 'objective' style, it has also been called an 'experimental' work. Its harmonic language is, to be sure, more uncompromising than that of its predecessor, but the language, after all, is of relative unimportance. The audacities that surprised or upset listeners at the time of its première (1927) have long since been superseded by much greater audacities. The most important quality of the Third Quartet remains its expressive quality. True, the expression is here less directly personal than in other works and is felt more exclusively in terms of the music itself, as is often, indeed, the case in the late Beethoven quartets. It is, in short, highly expressive music, although it may be difficult to define what is being expressed. But it is in no sense 'experimental'. If ever a work were written with a sure hand and a certainty of conviction, both as to form and techniques, this work is.

The Third Quartet is the quintessence of compression, being in one continuous movement, condensed into sections marked *Prima parte*, *Seconda parte*, *Ricapitulazione della prima parte* and *Coda*. The material of the entire work can be traced to a small number (two or three) of germ-motives that are varied, expanded and developed to produce new material. Each of the resulting motives begins with an upward melodic progression, rises in the middle and subsequently falls either to the note of origin or to a lower one. Needless to say, this melodic contour is to be found in the music of all periods and styles, yet the consistency of its appearance here leads one to believe that it is more than sheer coincidence, particularly as the initial rise is in each instance diatonic.

The form of this quartet is interesting not only in itself but as setting the pattern for certain later works. The two main 'movements' (*Prima parte* and *Seconda parte*) are first 'exposed', but even in the expositions the material of each is developed constantly. The first movement is slow, the second fast. Thereupon the two movements are 'recapitulated' but in entirely new aspects and both greatly abbreviated, producing an over-all A-B-A^1-B^1 form.

The work abounds in strong contrasts of tempo, dynamic, texture, idiom and technique. Contrapuntal procedures, including canons (some of which are heard, some not), give way to vigorous chordal passages that sometimes take the form of violent interjections. Cantabile writing alternates with jagged lines and running figures. 'Impersonal' melodic ideas contrast with 'Hungarian-type' tunes. Traditional tonal passages are mixed with acrid dissonant passages. The coloristic possibilities of the instruments are thoroughly exploited (*pizzicato, ponticello,* multiple stops, *tremolos, col legno, glissandos* in individual instruments and in groups) to achieve strange and remarkable sounds.

The Fourth Quartet resembles closely the Third in its relatively uncompromising idiom, being if anything even farther removed from conventional tonal practices and revelling in dissonance. It is the closest Bartók ever comes, in the quartets, to consistent atonality—and it is still far from being atonal. A paper analysis of the work might lead one to conclude that it is essentially atonal, but a harmonic analysis in the traditional sense would be a futile undertaking. One would conclude, at best, that the idiom is polytonal. But the ear, in this case, is mightier than the pen. The contrapuntal nature of this music, in which the voices move independently and the harmony is often the 'casual' result of their movement, is patent. But to the ear not all melodic lines, even when heard simultaneously, are of equal importance. On the contrary, the ear hears one line as more important than the others and takes its orientation from this *Hauptstimme*, which imparts a sense of tonality.

A single six-note motive in various permutations (inversion, extension, inverted extension, with expanded intervals, etc.) furnishes the material of the entire first movement. The second movement is based on two motives that could conceivably be related to the germ-motive of the first movement, although this may be pushing matters too far and is not, after all, of great importance. The third movement employs independent material arranged in A-B-A form; a rhapsodic, recitative-like melody in the cello encloses an impressionistic passage in which the violin 'chirps' a repeated-note motive. From the 'B' section of this movement, the formal structure regresses, so to speak, to its point of origin. The fourth movement is, like the second, a *scherzo* and employs the same material with the simple change of chromatic to diatonic intervals. The final movement is based on material derived from the first. Thus the work is cast in the form of an arch, the keystone being the third movement. Even the key relationships bear out this symmetry: the opening and closing movement have C as the tonal centre, the second E (a major third higher) and the fourth A-flat (a major third lower).

It is even less possible here than in the Third Quartet to speak of 'themes'. There are only motives that are being subjected to constant modification and development, and these motives are spun out and combined to form logical and highly expressive melodies. Except for the outspokenly percussive passages, indeed, this is a highly melodious work—in its own way. It is also a work which flows and moves with complete assurance, continuity and ease. It can be listened to and enjoyed without reference to the complicated relationships that doubtless contribute to its coherence. This is, indeed, the miracle of the 'constructivist' Bartók: the devices never interfere with the music. What might in other hands have been a purely intellectual musical design is transformed by Bartók's genius into a living work of art.

Even more than in the Third Quartet, Bartók exploits the technical possibilities of the instruments to conjure up new sounds: percussive *pizzicatos*, in which the string is lifted and caused to rebound on the fingerboard, *pizzicato sul ponticello, pizzicato glissando, col legno* and the like. The technical demands made on the players are very great—not to mention the demands on their musicianship.

Written six years later, the Fifth Quartet displays the same symmetrical 'arch' form as the Fourth. The first and fifth movements share common thematic material, as do the second and fourth; the third has more or less independent material, although it would be possible to trace relationships even here (e.g. between the main theme of movement III and the second theme of movement II). The tempo relationships are here the reverse of those of the Fourth Quartet, being fast—slow—*scherzo*—slow—fast. Symmetrical design is carried still farther in this quartet. The recapitulations of the first and fifth movements take place in reverse order: third theme, second theme, first theme. The second and fourth movements correspond closely, and the middle movement is in A-B-A form with the return varied. Seiber states: 'The stress has been shifted from *expression* in the earlier works to *architecture* and *construction*.' As his remark appears to apply to the Fifth Quartet specifically, we are inclined to agree.

There is little new in the Fifth Quartet as compared with the Fourth, except for a curious interruption of the vigorous and dissonant finale by a short tonic-dominant episode in barrel-organ style and the introduction of 'Bulgarian' rhythms in the *scherzo*: the division of a bar of $\frac{9}{8}$ into asymmetrical groups of $4+2+3$ and a bar of $\frac{10}{8}$ into groups of $2+3+2+3$ or $2+3+3+2$. Bartók shows great fondness for such rhythms in his later works, and he handles them with such mastery that they sound entirely natural (as indeed they are), even to non-Balkan ears.

Within the individual movements there is considerably more variety of thematic material than in the Fourth Quartet. The first and fifth movements have three distinct theme-groups, which, being cast in sonata form, make the listener's task of grasping the formal construction relatively simple. These are vigorous movements in which development section, recapitulation and *coda* are clearly recognisable. The second and fourth movements, based on two distinct motives, too tenuous to be called themes, invoke the impressionistic, fantastic mood of the third movement of the Fourth Quartet that Stevens so aptly calls 'night music': 'mysterious trills, tremolos, *pizzicato glissandos*, melodic fragments out of which a short cantabile motive emerges and is developed. The other material of these two 'parallel' movements consists of long-held chords that move in modal progressions, over which the violin (in the second movement) interpolates short comments—one of the most impressive passages of the entire quartet. The 'Bulgarian' *scherzo* is the most accessible, posing no problem for the listener. The work abounds in imitative writing, making extended use of strict canons with inversions and mirror forms. The last movement contains a remarkable section marked *oscuro* in which the dynamic never exceeds *mezzo forte*.

There is always a certain temptation to glorify, or even romanticise, the last works of a great composer—a danger which we recognise and are determined to avoid. For there is no indication that Bartók, despite his sickness at the time, considered the Sixth to be his last quartet.

Nevertheless this work does represent in certain ways the crowning glory of the quartets and an apotheosis of what has gone before. But if it is a synthesis (not a summary!) of the earlier five, as a whole, it is entirely distinct from any one of them. It is a work of complete maturity, in which the language and the technical procedures are of far less importance than the expression. Yet the expression is not primarily a subjective one, and it is neither possible nor desirable to define the emotional content except in the most general terms. More than any other, this last Bartók quartet resembles the late Beethoven quartets, in which the expression is intense but of a universal nature, far removed from and on a higher æsthetic plane than the more 'personal' expression of the earlier works. And, like the late Beethoven quartets, it can mean all things to all men but is best understood in terms only of itself—that is to say, as music. A further point of comparison: the character of the individual movements is drawn with great clarity, and the 'moods' are sharply delineated; yet it is difficult to define the exact nature of these 'moods'.

The fact that the harmonic idiom of the Sixth Quartet is relatively conservative, compared with the preceding three, has led some commentators to attribute to Bartók a 'reversal of policy' and has tempted others to compare the Sixth with the First Quartet. The comparison is valid only on the surface, and even there it is only partially valid. The harmonic idiom of the Sixth is scarcely more 'advanced', to be sure, than that of the First; but it is entirely different, having no relationship whatever with romantic practices. Like the First, moreover, the Sixth is constructed fairly 'freely'. The 'arch' form of the preceding works is no longer retained; thematic interrelations within and among movements are present but not developed so systematically as in the works of the 'constructive' period. The form is, in short, less closed than in the quartets immediately preceding and in this respect more akin to that of the first two.

The aggressive dissonances and rhythms of the 'middle' period are only occasionally in evidence in the Sixth Quartet, with the result that the work is in this respect more accessible to the average listener. When it suits his expressive purposes, however, Bartók employs harsh dissonance as well. He incorporates into this quartet many devices that are found in the preceding quartets: howling *glissandos*, improvisatory passages, imitations, inversions, fragmentation and expansion of thematic motives, dance rhythms, percussive rhythms, Hungarian elements, impressionistic passages—all elements that are easily recognisable in former works but that are given new meanings in the context of the Sixth Quartet. Nowhere is Bartók's complete freedom from 'isms' or his non-systematic approach to composition more in evidence.

The Sixth Quartet opens with a slow, chromatic melody of thirteen measures in the viola alone, a kind of *ritornello* that in varied form precedes each movement and contains as well 'germ' motives that are transformed in various ways in the course of the quartet. This melody, without tonal implications, is one of the most impressive examples of pure musical invention in twentieth-century music. Its beauty, its logic and its expressive power are the work of sheer genius and inspiration. It is inconceivable that any other hand than Bartók's could have written it.

The first movement (*vivace*) is preceded by a short introduction (*pesante*), partly in unison, in which the first theme is foreshadowed and which recalls in spirit and in technique a similar passage in Beethoven's *Grosse Fuge*. The formal structure of the movement is clear and precise, each new section being approached by a 'bridge' passage and accompanied by a change of tempo. The first theme, a running figure, is developed freely and by imitation, while undergoing constant modification. The second subject (bar 81) suggests a derivation from Hungarian folk music, particularly in its rhythmic patterns. It is treated briefly and is followed by the closing theme (bar 99) that appears to be derived from the *ritornello*. The development section proper (bar 158) is announced by another short *pesante* passage, upon which the material of the exposition, already developed from the moment of its presentation onwards, is further developed and combined. Various elements of the 'themes' are at times clearly recognisable, but it is unlikely that any two musicians would be able to agree as to the exact derivation of some of the material—nor is such an exact analysis necessary. Suffice it to say that practically every note of the development can be related to what has preceded it. The similarity of the themes themselves, however, often makes it impossible to state which of two or three possible derivations is 'right'. It is more than likely that Bartók himself did not greatly concern himself with the question. The recapitulation (bar 287) is varied and curtailed and is followed by a *coda* in the subdominant (the tonality is clearly D). The movement is rhythmic in character but never aggressively so. Its flow (in $\frac{6}{8}$ meter) is constantly varied, but never broken by *ritardandis accelerandis* and changes in tempo.

The second movement is preceded by another statement of the *ritornello*. The cello now has the main melody; a countermelody is heard in the first violin and the two other instruments have a third, less important, line in octaves or unison, played *tremolo*. There follows a march employing dotted rhythms that alternate with a motive consisting of repetitions of two sixteenth notes a third apart (bar 25). The march theme is developed briefly and leads to a rhapsodic, macabre sort of trio in which the cello plays in a high register with frequent *glissandos*, while the other instruments have *tremolos* and strummed *pizzicatos*. After a short *cadenza* the march returns in entirely altered form, with some of the material inverted. It is a disconcerting movement, with a grotesque sardonic sort of humour that contrasts strongly with the following 'tragic interlude'; this interlude, noble in expression, introduces the Burletta, in which the sardonic mood of the march is set forth and even intensified. The music is of an intensely emotional nature, but the emotion is kept constantly below the surface. The fundamental sadness is covered by a smile—or, better, the fundamental bitterness by a laughing sneer. Under the guise of a seemingly bumptious humour, Bartók has written here (in 1939) what might be considered his strongest musical protest against a world which had never treated him with noticeable gentleness and which was at that moment riddled with deceit and brutality, about to plunge itself into the mass suicide of the Second World War. We hesitate to relate the music of this lonely, seemingly unworldly man to contemporary events, but the connection in this instance may be justified. His letters indicate that he was in no way unaware of the world tragedy about him.

The final movement of this Sixth Quartet confirms, rather than dissipates the sense of tragedy hinted at in the *marcia* and the *burletta*. Here the *ritornello* furnishes the basis of practically the entire movement, although brief references are made to the material of the first movements. The atmosphere is one of restrained despair, not subjective or personal but on a universal plane. There is no *jammern*, no tears, but a true expression of *Weltschmerz* having somewhat the effect of the *katharsis* of Greek tragedy. The awful truth is not concealed, but it is uttered in a quiet language that combines deep tenderness with high nobility. Analysis of the technical means (a freely moving contrapuntal fabric based on chromatic lines and harmony) is of little consequence here. The movement is one of the most moving commentaries on our century so far, just as the entire Sixth Quartet is one of its most searching expressions.

THE MUSIC OF BÉLA BARTÓK

The string quartets are representative of Bartók's style, and his musical thought, with the exception of one important factor—the element of folk music, which can be felt often in the quartets as an indirect (or even direct) influence but seldom plays a leading role. In many other works, however, Bartók makes primary use of folk materials. A considerable number of piano pieces are based on folk music: the collection of eighty-five pieces entitled *For Children* (1909), the Sonatina (1915) based on Roumanian folk tunes, the *Colinde* (twenty Roumanian Christmas songs for piano) (1915), Fifteen Hungarian Peasant Songs (1917) and many of the pieces in *Mikrokosmos*. There are also several sets of folksong transcriptions for voice and piano: Eight Hungarian Folksongs (1907–17), Twenty Hungarian Folksongs (1929) and others, some of which Bartók arranged for voice and orchestra. He made also a number of choral arrangements of folksongs, such as the Four Slovak Folksongs (1917), Five Slovak Folksongs for Male Chorus (1917) and Four Hungarian Folksongs (1930).

Bartók's folksong settings vary from very simple to complex. In some he does little more than provide the tune itself, unaltered, with an appropriate accompaniment. In others he reorganises the original melodic material, repeating or extending one element or another to suit his purposes (as in the *Cantata Profana*), or provides an accompaniment that is much more than a mere support. In some instances, indeed, the accompaniment assumes considerable proportions and demands a degree of virtuosity that precludes performance by an 'average' pianist—particularly in the set of Twenty Hungarian Folksongs. The accompaniment, particularly in the later works, is often entirely independent of the vocal line, employing unrelated or complementary material, sometimes percussive in nature, at others moving on a horizontal plane of its own, giving rise to sharp vertical clashes with the voice. At first blush many of the accompaniments give the impression of being arbitrary, but they are in fact most convincing, even when their relation to the folk material is a purely psychological rather than a thematic one.

Bartók's folksong arrangements are characterised by the impeccable taste and complete understanding with which he treats the material. There is no hint of the stylistic incongruity that often arises when a composer sets his hand to arranging folk material, with results that may be cheap or pompous or 'arty' or tortured. The combination of naturalness and fantasy in Bartók's arrangements gives them a unique place in this category.

THE MUSIC OF BÉLA BARTÓK

A direct relation to folk music is evident in certain original compositions of Bartók, such as the Twenty-seven Choruses for Treble Voices (1927) or the Dance Suite for Orchestra. There is little trace of folk influence in his original songs, however, all of which date from a relatively early period. The two sets of songs, Opus 15 and Opus 16, that date from the year 1916 are difficult, intensely 'expressionistic' works that make strong demands on the singer but that deserve to be heard more often than they are. The language problem is admittedly a thorny one, for the peculiar stress of Hungarian can scarcely be more than approximated in any other language. Stevens suggests that this fact may have discouraged Bartók from further song-composition, together with the evolution of Bartók's style towards a harsher, more dissonant idiom, less suitable for vocal performance. Certain it is that purely instrumental music offers the composer freer scope for his imagination. In any event, Bartók composed no more original songs after 1916.

He also wrote relatively little for piano solo in his later years. Excepting the last books of the *Mikrokosmos*, Bartók's last important piano piece is the 1926 Sonata, a difficult, uncompromising work in which the piano is treated as a percussion instrument. The Sonata generates an enormous rhythmic drive, employing repeated chords based on seconds, sevenths and ninths and making frequent use of tone clusters. In spirit the Sonata is not far removed from the virtuosic and savage *Allegro barbaro* of 1911, except that the earlier piece, equally percussive, is more obviously related to folk music.

The Studies, Opus 18 (1918), for piano solo are veritable studies (often inordinately difficult in that they exploit certain technical problems arising out of the expanding techniques of composition with which Bartók was at that time concerned: bitonality, atonality, interval expansion, 'octave displacement' (the interval of a ninth instead of a second), etc. Their concern with technical problems by no means detracts from their value as concert works. The Improvisations on Hungarian Peasant Songs (Opus 20), in which the folk material is sometimes used only as a point of departure for an entirely original composition, must also be mentioned as one of Bartók's major works for piano solo.

In the collection of 153 progressive piano pieces, written between 1926 and 1937 and published under the title *Mikrokosmos*, Bartók combines his experience as pianist, teacher, folklorist and composer. The purpose of the work is avowedly pedagogical—a kind of contemporary *Gradus ad Parnassum*. Yet, unlike most works of this nature, the pieces it contains, ranging from very easy to very difficult, are much more than a means to a technical end; they are music first and 'exercises' only secondarily. They provide the piano student with a well-planned introduction to the idioms, practices and techniques of twentieth-century music by one of its foremost composers whose many years of teaching practice gave him an unusually keen grasp of the problems he dealt with. They also provide an insight, in simplified and systematised form, into Bartók's creative procedures, for many of the practices one can observe here in isolated form constitute the bases of his compositions in larger forms. Starting from six unison exercises, the pieces progress in difficulty and in scope. Some are designed to solve technical, pianistic problems; others are concerned more with problems of style; still others combine both functions; and some are 'mood' pieces. The titles indicate these various objectives, as for instance 'Staccato and Legato', 'Theme and Inversion', 'Triplets in the Lydian Mode', 'Pastorale', etc. There are numerous direct references to folk music ('Hungarian Song', 'Bulgarian Rhythm', etc.) and two pieces that are of special interest because of the dedications they bear, Numbers 79 and 80 (Book III) are inscribed to Bach and Schumann respectively—striking testimony to Bartók's prime interest in the *content* of music, as distinguished from questions of style.

The *Mikrokosmos* does not contain Bartók's most important writing, although many of the pieces are suitable for concert performance. But as a work concerned primarily with pedagogical problems, not only of piano technique but of music itself, it is unique in the field of twentieth-century music.

The *Cantata Profana* (1930), for double mixed chorus, tenor and baritone solos and large orchestra, is Bartók's most significant vocal work. The story, built on folksong texts, tells of a father's nine sons who were changed into stags while hunting. As the father comes upon them in the mountains and prepares to fire on them, the largest stag (i.e. the eldest son) warns him not to do so and reveals their identity. The father begs them to return home, but he is told that this is impossible. In this work Bartók achieves a perfect synthesis of folk and art music. The melodic substance is related to peasant music—perhaps even derived from it. But the work never for a moment suggests the kind of 'folkiness' that can be embarrassing. On the contrary, Bartók employs many of the methods and techniques of his purely instrumental style, which was at that period terse and comparatively uncompromising; naturally he makes allowance for the limitations of the human voice. It is amazing at what dissonant combinations of sound the choruses arrive with relative ease through the skilful voice-leading of the individual parts. The work is difficult, to be sure, but entirely singable.

The chorus predominates and relates the story, relieved only in the middle section by baritone solo (the father), tenor solo (the eldest son or stag) and a short duet between them. The choral writing is richly varied from strictly canonic or freely contrapuntal to note-against-note or a kind of choral recitative. The orchestra moves independently throughout, almost never doubling the voices, seldom supporting them harmonically and often clashing with them. The problem of translation is particularly difficult here, as the melodic and rhythmic procedures are extremely closely wedded to the Hungarian text.

Bartók's only opera, *Duke Bluebeard's Castle*, has been criticised as being insufficiently dramatic to be entirely successful as an opera. It seems to us that this criticism is unjust. There is little 'action' to be sure, but the music maintains the dramatic tension throughout. The librettist, Balasz, has turned the Bluebeard story into something of a psychological-symbolistic drama that admits of various interpretations. The entire 'action' consists of Judith's insisting upon opening in his presence the seven doors of Bluebeard's darkened castle. The blood motive is strong. In the first room, the torture chamber, the walls drip blood; in the second, the armoury, the weapons are blood-covered; the third room, the treasury, discloses quantities of blood-bathed jewels; the opening of the fourth reveals a blood-soaked flower garden; the fifth door opens into the vast domains of Bluebeard, over which the clouds are bleeding. The opening of each door has admitted more and more light into the castle. Bluebeard pleads with Judith not to open the two last doors. She insists, however, and the sixth reveals a lake of tears. As the last door is opened, the first three wives of Bluebeard file silently past and disappear again, richly clothed and bedecked with jewels. Bluebeard, deeply moved, sings that he has not forgotten them; the first came to him in the morning, the second at noon, the third at dusk. He crowns Judith, who came at night, and she disappears to join the others. Darkness now becomes total, as Bluebeard says: 'Now it is night, always, for ever.'

Whether this early work (1911) is considered to be an opera, or a scenic oratorio, or whatever else one might choose to call it, it contains many splendid passages. Despite the unmistakable influence of French impressionist style it is clearly the work of Bartók. The fact that it is a one-Act opera militates against frequent performance in European opera houses. On the other hand, the fact that there are only two singing roles (the three former wives are silent) is a practical consideration in its favour. It is not quite clear why *Duke Bluebeard's Castle* is performed so seldom.

Questions of 'morality' have interfered in the past with the performance of Bartók's one-act pantomime, *The Miraculous Mandarin* (1919). On more than one occasion the censors have balked at the fantastic story. A girl entices three men to her room (which in the original version was in a brothel) where three thugs are waiting to beat and rob them. The first two 'visitors' turn out to be penniless and are thrown out. The third is an unlovely mandarin, to whose overtures the girl submits unwillingly, then tries to elude his embraces entirely. The thugs strip the mandarin of his jewels and money, then try to kill him; his wounds, however, refuse to bleed until the girl embraces him of her own volition; now at last his wounds bleed and he dies.

The score, like the story, is a vivid and in a sense typical document of the period immediately following the First World War in Central Europe—a period of disillusionment that found expression in such works as Stravinsky's *Histoire du Soldat* and Weill's *Dreigroschenoper*. There is little trace of folk music in *The Miraculous Mandarin*; it is as close as Bartók ever comes to writing 'urban' and urbane music. It is more than likely that it reflects in the score as well as in the plot the desperate post-war situation of Budapest, where Bartók was living at the time of its composition. One wonders how Bartók's style might have developed if he had followed this direction farther—an idle speculation, to be sure, for his next work was the Eight Improvisations on Hungarian Peasant Songs for piano. The score verges at times on violence but never becomes outspokenly brutal. It maintains a high emotional tension from start to finish. The erotic element is portrayed with an intensity seldom encountered in Bartók's music. Rhythmic elements—repeated dissonant chords and motoric figures—play a leading role and are contrasted with shorter melodic passages of an expressive nature. The two principal scenes (the girl's increasingly sensuous dance before the mandarin and the extended passage in which the mandarin chases the girl) constitute a large part of the score and are built up with great skill from both the symphonic and dramatic sides. They constitute the central points of the orchestral suite Bartók constructed from this remarkable score.

To go into details regarding each of Bartók's major works would far exceed the scope of this chapter. The relatively detailed consideration

of the string quartets is designed to throw light on the stylistic development of his style in general as well as to provide a specific introduction
to his most important body of works in a given form. Since exhaustive
analysis of such important compositions as the piano concertos, the
Violin Concerto, the Concerto for Orchestra and the like is not possible,
it seems better to mention these works briefly and devote the space thus
gained to a rather minute analysis of what is, apart from the quartets,
Bartók's masterpiece—the Music for Strings, Celesta and Percussion.

In connection with the First Piano Concerto (1926) Bartók himself
wrote: 'In my youth my ideal of beauty was not so much the art of
Bach and Mozart as that of Beethoven. Recently it has changed somewhat: in recent years I have considerably occupied myself with music
before Bach, and I believe that traces of this are to be noticed in the
Piano Concerto and the Nine Little Piano Pieces.' The First Piano
Concerto does indeed reflect something of the clarity of such pre-Bach
composers as Couperin and Scarlatti, of whose music Bartók brought
out modern editions. Counterpoint plays a much less important role
here than in many later works. Like the Sonata, composed in the same
year, it is a vigorous work with an immense rhythmic vitality. The
thematic material is of a fragmentary nature, yet the driving force behind this music gives it continuity. The harmonic idiom combines
diatonic, chromatic and polytonal elements freely, making constant use
of dissonant intervals such as sevenths and ninths as well as of tone
clusters. This is by no means an ingratiating concerto, but it is a strong
one.

If the First Piano Concerto is relatable to pre-Bach composers, the
Second (1933) is more akin to the music of Bach himself. The opening
theme in the trumpet has a Bachian flavour, and the running piano
part recalls the concertos of Bach. Counterpoint plays an important
part in the form of free polyphony as well as in imitative and *fugato*
passages. As in the First Concerto the outside movements are motoric;
the middle movement (the slow movement) is more relaxed and here
includes a kind of *scherzo* as well as a preceding and following *adagio*
section. In the last movement, material of the first is reintroduced and
reworked in ingenious ways.

The Third Piano Concerto (1945) differs greatly from the other two.
Coming from Bartók's period of complete maturity, it displays serenity
and lucidity that have sometimes been interpreted as weakness and as a
falling-off in creative vitality. The mood is relatively tranquil throughout—even the last movement (*Allegro vivace*) is devoid of all brutality.

The texture is amazingly clear, despite many devices of counterpoint. The second movement, marked *Adagio religioso*, opens with a simplicity that might be compared to that of a late Beethoven quartet—successive entries of the strings in the tonality of C major. The piano then has a choral-like passage, again tonal and diatonic. The remarkable middle section is impressionistic in nature, abounding in trills, twitterings and actual bird-calls. As the movement closes, the chorale theme returns in the woodwinds against the impressionistic background. The entire work is outspokenly tonal and harmonically 'mild'.

The Violin Concerto (1938) is a *tour de force* of variation technique. As Stevens points out, not only the thematic material but also the architectural form of the first movement is duplicated section for section in the last. And the middle movement is in the form of a theme and variations. Yet despite the structural and thematic 'tightness' of the piece, it seems, to this writer at least, to possess less continuity than many other of Bartók's less closely knit compositions. This point is, to be sure, a debatable one and resolves itself ultimately to a question of personal taste. Yet it is remarkable that the Violin Concerto does not appear to have the same effect on the audience as do most works of Bartók—namely, the effect of gripping and holding the attention. At the risk of seeming 'heretical', we would venture the opinion that Bartók was for once so fascinated and occupied with questions of structure, variation and construction that he mistook the letter for the spirit. The Violin Concerto is a virtuosic piece of immense difficulty; and it also appears to this writer that a portion of the work is too taken up with virtuosity at the expense of the musical content.

It might be noted in passing that Bartók makes use of several twelve-tone series in this work. That is to say, he writes melodies both for the solo violin (first movement, bar 73) and the orchestra (bar 76) in which all twelve notes of the chromatic scale are heard before any single note is repeated. And at that he drops the matter. Neither here nor elsewhere does he employ anything resembling orthodox twelve-tone technique. Why the twelve-tone row? Certainly not to show how 'modern' he could be, such an attitude being entirely contrary to his nature. Perhaps by stating a twelve-tone 'theme' and abandoning it at once he wanted to indicate his disapproval of the system. Or perhaps it was mere whimsy that induced him to include this material in a predominantly tonal work. After all, why shouldn't he? The question is in any event of no great importance.

The Viola Concerto was left unfinished at Bartók's death and 'reconstructed' by Tibor Serly. As he was obliged to do this from un-numbered scraps of music paper (some illegible) there is no guarantee that the reconstruction corresponds in fact to Bartók's intentions.

For the first performance of the Concerto for Orchestra (Boston, 1944) Bartók wrote: 'The general mood of the work represents, apart from the jesting second movement, a gradual transition from the stern-ness of the first movement and the lugubrious death-song of the third, to the life-assertion of the last one. The title of this symphony-like orchestral work is explained by its tendency to treat single orchestral instruments in a concertant or soloistic manner. This is one of Bartók's most accessible and most successful works, yet it in no sense achieves success through the sacrifice of quality or artistic level. The fact that it is tonal in character makes it easier listening than the more dissonant, less tonal works, to be sure. But, as has been remarked before, Bartók's latter-day reversion to tonality was not only honest; it was apparently an integral part of his musical evolution. There is no slackening of power or of technical skill in this and other relatively accessible late works (e.g. the delightful Divertimento for String Orchestra, composed in 1939). On the contrary, the Concerto for Orchestra is a work of great vitality and of great expressiveness. It opens with an impressive introduction that gradually builds in volume and speed to the 'stern' *Allegro vivace,* a movement of great vitality and clarity, bearing the unmistakable signature of Bartók. The second movement is subtitled *Giuoco delle coppie;* in it the wind instruments are treated soloisti-cally, first in pairs, then in various combinations. It is a thoroughly charming movement, reminding one distantly of Haydn. After the poetic *Elegia* comes a brief movement, *Intermezzo interrotto,* having the form A–B–A– Interruption –B–A. The A-motive is a winsome, folk-like melody in which $\frac{2}{4}$ and $\frac{5}{8}$ meters alternate. The B-theme is a broader melody, also folk-like in character, in which $\frac{3}{4}$ and $\frac{5}{8}$ meters predominate. The interruption takes the form of a burlesque on a banal theme from Shostakovitch's Seventh Symphony, introduced and con-cluded with really nasty sounds that serve as commentary and leave no doubt as to Bartók's opinion of the work in question. Bartók is not being 'funny' here; the satire is sardonic. And certainly he, who refused to make any kind of compromise, had more than any other the right to such criticism. The passage may, in fact, constitute the only reason for remembering the Shostakovitch Seventh Symphony in the future. The finale is a spontaneous, dance-inspired kind of *perpetuum mobile,* embodying an astonishing fugue that employs the most intricate contrapuntal devices without ever losing its verve.

One of Bartók's most impressive 'experimental' works is the Sonata for Two Pianos and Percussion (1937), later transcribed (1940) for two pianos and orchestra. The original version is the more effective. It is experimental chiefly in regard to the remarkable sounds produced. The technical and idiomatic aspects are anything but experimental; on the contrary they show the sure hand of the master. In this work Bartók explores thoroughly the possibilities of percussion sound (the piano appears to have been for him primarily a percussion instrument) and creates colours that are quite unique. In the extensive first movement the pianos predominate; in the remaining two the battery is of greater importance. The work is harmonically and contrapuntally complex. In this, in its harmonic idiom and its preoccupation with sound (not for itself alone but integrated into the over-all structure), it has much in common with the *Music for Strings, Percussion and Celesta,* which preceded it by a year. It remains one of the most extraordinary pieces of twentieth-century chamber music.

The *Music for Strings, Percussion and Celesta* (1936) is among Bartók's most important works—perhaps his masterpiece. In this composition, which was commissioned and first performed by Paul Sacher, the most diverse characteristics of Bartók's style are united to produce a thoroughly convincing and logical whole. Here Bartók employs practically all the stylistic and technical means of the time. The chromatic, contrapuntal first movement is closely related to the Schönberg school; the second is both in form and in spirit 'neo-classical'. The third movement is an example of modern impressionism, in which sound as such plays a leading role. The fourth betrays a strong influence of Hungarian folk music, and a certain primitivism in some passages recalls Stravinsky's *Sacre du Printemps* and *Les Noces* as well as Bartók's earlier Dance Suite. A less gifted composer might have produced a stylistic hodge-podge in combining these elements in one composition. In this work, however, they are transmuted and transcended by the power of Bartók's musical personality.

The unity here achieved from such varied elements depends not only on the fact that the entire work appears to be derived from one 'Urmotiv', it is even more—a psychological unity that binds the work together. The manner in which Bartók utilises the material of the opening theme in the other three movements is nevertheless an important cohesive factor and thoroughly typical of his methods of composition. The variations and transformations of this germ theme are carried out so expertly and with such a fine hand that there is never an impression of monotony; on the contrary, the rhythmic and melodic changes that are introduced have the effect of creating entirely new material.

The germ theme, in which the interval of a rising second is followed by that of a rising minor third (or augmented second), and which is built exclusively of thirds and seconds, is announced at the very outset in the violas (*andante tranquillo*). In the second movement (*Allegro*) the rising minor third (here A–C) is heard *pizzicato* no less than five times in the first five bars, and the *arco* figure that follows immediately (bar 5) is also clearly related to the germ theme. Here the minor third precedes rather than follows the minor second. This figure, ending as it does with a falling minor second, might be construed as a variation of the retrograde form of the germ theme's first measure.

The germ theme appears in the third movement (*Adagio*) in various new aspects. The first motive to be heard is that of a falling minor third. In bar 18 (viola) the 'head' of the theme is cited literally but in a more regular rhythmic form. At bar 60 (third violin) still another version is heard and in bar 73 (celesta and piano) a compressed variant of this newly derived version appears. In the main theme of the fourth movement (*Allegro molto*) the contour of the germ theme (rising, then falling motion) is inverted and the chromatic twisting of the germ theme is now 'ironed out' in a vigorous, diatonic melody with a Hungarian flavour, from which the introspective quality of the germ theme has largely disappeared. Even this variant has been prepared in the preceding movement; at bars 85–88 of the third movement the second violin has a relatively unimportant *scherzando* figure consisting almost exclusively of seconds and thirds which seems to forecast the main theme of the fourth movement. Towards the end of the work (fourth movement, bar 196, strings) a short figure appears that is clearly derived from the germ theme; and the *espressivo* melody at bar 204 is easily recognisable as a new version of the germ theme. Here the minor second is expanded to a major second, the minor third to a perfect fourth to produce an essentially diatonic melody, the broader character of which seems to be determined by its position close to the end of the finale.

The inner thematic relationships are by no means confined to the instances cited, but can be found on practically every page of the

Music for String Instruments. It is impossible to say whether such relationships were compounded consciously by Bartók, nor is the question of very great importance. It seems quite likely that this constant development, variation and permutation of basic thematic material was both conscious and unconscious, for friends of Bartók testify to his complete absorption in the musical material with which he was working at any given time. Of much greater interest is the fact that these 'constructive' procedures never in any way detract from the primary musical and expressive quality. The work gives the impression, on first hearing and on repeated hearings, of uninhibited spontaneity; it is sheer music from beginning to end. The cross-relationships of thematic material that bind it so tightly together are in general more seen than heard. Only after a close study of the score does one realise that the entire composition is based on one germ theme or germ idea.

The exactitude with which the score is written is astonishing. Each single note is related to the whole by the most explicit indications of dynamics, bowings, length of notes and rests, indications of which string a given passage is to be played on and how it is to be played (*staccato, martellato,* harmoics, *ponticello, flautato, glissando,* etc.) as well as exact tempo indications, phrasings and, on occasion, the subdivision of a measure by means of dotted lines. This practice of indicating a secondary or cross-rhythm within a general prevailing meter (see the opening bars) is found in many Bartók scores.

The instruments are used and exploited in a masterly way. Although many passages are difficult, the impossible is never demanded, and the nature and limitations of the instruments are respected without exception. In spite of the complex texture and orchestration everything 'sounds' in this score; not a single thought or nuance is lost. Some of the sounds are breath-taking, for instance the combination of the piano with strings *pizzicato,* in which the plucked strings are allowed to slap the fingerboard (second movement, measure 199); or the simple addition of the xylophone 21 measures later, producing a new and surprising orchestral colour. Entirely new sounds are created in the third movement where trills and *glissandos* in the strings are combined with celesta and piano (measures 20–31) and where the combination of harp *glissandos,* piano *glissandos,* fast passages in the celesta and *flautato* tremolos in the strings produces an unearthly effect.

Through the division of the strings into two groups, placed to the left and right of the percussion, Bartók is able to achieve subtleties of sound which he exploits to the full. The two groups play, now together,

35

now pitted against each other, with corresponding differentations of sounds and texture.

Counterpoint plays an important role in this work and is of three varieties: melodic, rhythmic, and that which depends on combinations of various timbres.

The first movement is a prime example of linear counterpoint in the form of a fugue or *ricercare*. The long chromatic theme, contained within the interval of a fifth, as first heard in the violas alone, is then developed by means of successive voice entries into a five-voice texture of considerable thickness. Simultaneously the dynamic level is increased, the pitch becomes higher and the mutes are removed. The musical and emotional intensification finally reaches a climax on the note E-flat, *fortissimo*, and is then quickly reduced. A sort of coda, in which the strings (now muted again) have the theme in inversion brings the movement to a mysterious close, *pianissimo*. In contrast to the first, the material of the second movement consists chiefly of small motives which are passed from one instrument or group of instruments to another. Although this movement is in general the most homophonic, it also contains energetic passages of the most complex rhythmic counterpoint,

for example, between measures 190 and 241. Here, in a prevailing $\frac{2}{4}$ meter two *ostinato* figures appear, each consisting of five eight-notes and effecting in each measure the displacement of the accent by one eight-note beat. Against this *ostinato* another section of the strings plays a most fascinating irregular rhythm and the percussion contributes still further rhythmic variety.

The third movement is in a modern 'impressionistic' style, but it differs from French impressionism in its colouristic counterpoint, produced by the movement of sounds and timbres on various levels. Although colour and sound as such are to a certain extent the principal factor, the orchestral colours are not mixed as they generally are in French impressionistic music, but the more or less sharply differentiated timbres are combined like the colours of a Gothic stained-glass window: the individual colours maintain their own characters while contributing to the whole. As in the first movement an enormous crescendo from *pianissimo* to *fortissimo* is developed, this time however through entirely different means. The beginning of the movement is most remarkable and prophetic of future musical developments; here the highest and lowest registers of the orchestra are used together—namely, a single high tone in the xylophone and *glissandos* in the timpani. By the simple means of trills in the strings Bartók produces (measure 20 ff.) strange and weird combinations of sound, which with four other figures produce a five-voice counterpoint of timbres—i.e. a polyphony based on differing sonorities.

The last movement, with its reminiscences of Hungarian music, is essentially an elaboration of a two-voice structure up to the return of the germ theme (measure 204)—that is to say, the musical basis of the often complex structure can be reduced to two main lines, either in canon or consisting of melodically or rhythmically contrasting material (as in measure 121-135). The effectiveness of this movement depends directly on the structural clarity and the simplicity and directness of the material. Again there is a tremendous crescendo (measures 136–181) in which a short *ostinato* figure plays the principal role and which is combined with a *stringendo*. A new version of the germ theme suddenly interrupts the furious *presto*. The theme itself is transformed through the extension of the intervals of the original theme to produce a diatonic melody. At its first statement (in measure 204) this new version of the germ theme is heard in a unison passage; then it is combined with its inversion monorhythmically (measure 210), after which it is further developed in free imitation. This 'interruption' has the effect of a parenthesis in the movement's structure. The manner in which Bartók now brings about the return from the germ theme to the main theme of the fourth movement is most characteristic of this composer's procedures. The germ theme (in its diatonic form) gradually gives way to the main theme (measure 244 ff.) so that for an instant one is not aware of what is going on: a further proof of the fact that the material of the entire work is in the last analysis relatable to a single underlying idea.

The rhythmic aspects of this composition fall into two fairly clear categories. On the one hand are the passages in which the rhythmic flow is so even, being practically without accents, that it is impossible to tell where the bar lines fall, as in the first movement, the polyphony of which can only be heard vertically. Except at the climax (measure 52 ff.) one hears only long waves of melodic lines in a perfectly continuous texture. The constant changes in meter are not felt as such but contribute in fact to the complete freedom of the rhythmic flow. Much the same is true of the third movement.

Other passages, however, are strongly rhythmic in the sense of regularly recurring accents, as, for example, the beginning of the second movement. This rhythmic regularity, however, is not long maintained; from measure 25 on, strong counter-rhythms are introduced which avoid every danger of rhythmic rigidity. As the movement progresses the feeling of regular meter is entirely dissolved, either through the introduction of syncopation (measure 175 ff.) or of rhythmic groups which weaken the effect of the bar lines (e.g. the groups of five eight-notes in measure 186 ff.), or by means of constant change of meter (measure 262 ff., measure 310 ff.). Even the last movement with its elemental rhythmic drive displays astonishing rhythmic subtleties, for example in the theme itself, in which eight eight-notes are divided into groups of 2–3–3 and in the course of which various meters alternate (see especially measures 190–215).

The question of harmony and tonality in the *Music for String Instruments* is so complicated that it can only be mentioned in passing. The work is conceived in great tonal arches and is stabilized by means of unmistakable tonal pillars. The main tonality is A, in which the first and last movements begin and end. The second movement is in C, the parallel major tonality to the first movement. The tonality of the third movement cannot be unequivocally determined but might be interpreted as being in F-sharp, or in F, or in both together. In this work we are not confronted with tonality in the usual sense of a clear tonic with its dominant, subdominant, etc., but with the single notes A, C, F-sharp and F, which act as tonal poles to which the entire material is more or less closely related. These notes are emphasized only in a few important places such as the A in the last movement (measure 198 ff.). The note E-flat plays a remarkable and curious role in the tonal structure. It is strongly emphasized twice: once in the first movement (measure 56 ff.) and again in the last (measure 63 ff.) where it is preceded by its dominant and followed by its subdominant. It appears also at various other points: in the second movement as a kind of organ point (measure 115 ff.), followed again here by its dominant (measure 124); and further at measures 199 and 239. It is prominent in the third movement as a long pedal in the timpani and double basses (measure 31); and in the last movement at measure 83 and again at measure 103. Finally reference is made to the E-flat (D-sharp) three measures before the end of the work.

The above remarks on the harmonic procedures in Bartók's *Music for String Instruments* are no more than external observations; they tell nothing about the thought processes underlying Bartók's view of tonality and tonal functions. It is worthy of attention, however, that the relationship of the note E-flat to A, which is used as a sort of tonic, is that of the tritone, an interval which plays an important role, both melodically and harmonically in Bartók's music. This very interval of the tritone represents of course the most distant relationship possible between two notes or two keys. By analogy one might say that Bartók's preference for the tritone is symptomatic of his entire approach to tonality in certain mature works. He still maintains tonal relationships but they are attenuated to such a degree as to be relatively obscure.

In the last analysis many of Bartók's harmonic and tonal procedures cannot be explained in reference to traditional practice, and an analysis of the vertical structures often yields no tangible result. The harmonies (i.e. the vertical combinations of sound) often appear to be the combined result of various melodic lines moving more or less independently of one another; and in more homophonic passages, where it might be possible to speak of 'chords', the vertical structures, based frequently on dissonant intervals (seconds, sevenths, ninths, tritones), seem to have been chosen more for the isolated sounds produced than for their harmonic function. The harmonic and tonal relationships seem in fact often to be capricious and wilful, and a strict harmonic analysis could perhaps even 'prove' them to be such. To the ear, however, they sound anything but wilful, and the ear is the final judge.

Stravinsky

ERIC WALTER WHITE

T HE need for discipline imposed by order, and the order resulting from such discipline—this is the key to Stravinsky the man and Stravinsky the musician. Sometimes the results may seem to have been due to a restless and unsatisfied craving for change; but more careful examination reveals his varied production as being rooted in unity—the manifestation of an extraordinary capacity for constant spiritual and mental renewal.

I

Igor Stravinsky was born into a Russian upper-middle class family on 5th June (O.S.), 1882. His father, Feodor, had Polish blood in his veins and came of a family of landed proprietors. One of the most celebrated bass-baritones of the Imperial Opera House, St. Petersburg, he was not only a great singer and actor but a man of wide general culture. The young Igor started at an early age to decipher the opera scores in his father's library, and one of his early musical memories was of his father singing the role of Farlaf at a gala performance of *Ruslan & Ludmilla* at the Maryinsky Theatre in 1892. From his father he inherited a lively interest in music; but, as his parents were not in favour of music as a career, he entered the faculty of law at the University of St. Petersburg as soon as he left school. His spare-time interest in music continued, and shortly before his father's death in 1902 he had the good fortune to meet Rimsky-Korsakov, who advised on the direction of his musical studies. In 1905 he passed his final University examinations and on 11th January (O.S.), 1906, married his first cousin, Catherine Gabrielle. By this time the die was cast, and he was deter-

40

mined to make music his career. Rimsky-Korsakov gave him private lessons during the last few years of his life; and Stravinsky passed the period of his apprenticeship partly in St. Petersburg and partly at Ustilug, at the confluence of the rivers Bug and Lug in Volhynia, where he built himself a house on an estate belonging to his wife and sister-in-law.

The even tenor of this life was interrupted by the success of his first ballets for Diaghilev's Russian Ballet Company. In the four years that elapsed between the first performance of *The Fire Bird* and the outbreak of the First World War, the company played in Western Europe and South America, but never in Russia itself; and Stravinsky accompanied them on visits to Paris, Rome, Berlin, Budapest, Vienna and London. His mother, wife and children joined him occasionally in Western Europe—usually at Clarens in Switzerland; and in the winter of 1914 his wife, who was consumptive, spent some time in a sanatorium at Leysin. It was while the family was staying at Salvan in the Valais that they were caught by the outbreak of the First World War.

At first the interruption seemed temporary. Stravinsky's mother returned to Russia; and for a short time it was still possible for him to draw on his resources in Russia for the maintenance of his family. But he lost his properties and investments in the Revolution of 1917 and found himself exiled in a foreign country and deprived of a regular income. At first (as C. F. Ramuz tells us) he was determined to return —his proper place was 'over there'; but this decision was soon reversed in the light of Communist developments. In 1920 accordingly he left Switzerland and settled down in France, living at Biarritz (1921–24), Nice (1924–31), Voreppe (1931–34) and Paris (1934–39). His mother rejoined him in 1922, sailing on a Soviet boat from Leningrad to Stettin, and bringing with her a pile of his early compositions. On 10th June, 1934, he became a naturalised French citizen and shortly afterwards applied (unsuccessfully) for membership of the Académie Française. But France was acceptable to him as a second home only so long as it could provide security and a congenial atmosphere in which he could work without interruption. By 1939 the political situation made him perplexed and nervous; and when in the course of only a few months his mother, wife and one of his daughters died, he decided to leave Europe as quickly as possible and go to America, where life was still well ordered and reasonably secure.

An immediate excuse for this move was provided by an invitation from the President and Fellows of Harvard to deliver the 1939/40 Charles Eliot-Norton lectures. These six lectures (on the Poetics of

Music) were in fact delivered in French; but as time went on his command of English improved, and the break with France became permanent. On 9th March, 1940, he married Vera Arturovna, the widow of Serge Sudeikin, at Bedford, Mass., and on 28th December, 1945, changed his nationality for the second time, becoming a citizen of the United States. So far the years of his American residence have proved one of the most fertile periods of his life, and his influence on American music of the future seems likely to be just as great as his influence has been in Western Europe.

Speaking in Harvard in 1940, Stravinsky referred in such scathing terms to the Russian Revolution that the French publishers of *Poétique Musicale* not only were unwilling to include that particular lecture (on The Avatars of Russian Music) in the edition they published in 1945, but also suppressed any reference to its omission. It is characteristic of Stravinsky that he said he viewed the Russian Revolution as 'a tragic collision of *two disorders*'—the reactionary disorder of the weak and lax government as opposed to the revolutionary disorder of the Bolshevists—which had plunged Russia into 'a militant atheism and a rudimentary materialism'. In view of the fact that he holds such dogmatic views and expresses them so forcibly, it is hardly surprising that at various times he has been denounced by the Soviet authorities, usually on the grounds of 'formalism' in his music. Such an accusation leaves him quite unperturbed. It is well over forty years since he was last in Russia, and he has no romantic nostalgia for the country or the people. After spending the Christmas of 1947 with him in Hollywood, Nicolas Nabokov wrote: 'For Stravinsky, Russia is a language, which he uses with superb, gourmand-like dexterity; it is a few books; Glinka and Tchaikovsky. The rest either leaves him indifferent or arouses his anger, contempt, and violent dislike.'[1]

While at no point of his career has Stravinsky been prepared to compromise with political or artistic policies of revolution or disorder, he has always accepted the dogma and discipline of the Church with wholehearted subservience. For years he was a member of the Russian Orthodox Church; but some time after his second marriage he transferred his allegiance to the Roman Catholic Church. A sign of this change was the reissue a few years ago of his three *a cappella* settings of the 'Pater Noster' (1926), 'Credo' (1932) and 'Ave Maria' (1934), originally written for use in the Russian Orthodox Service, but now with Latin

[1] *Old Friends and New Music*, Hamish Hamilton, London, 1951.

words substituted for the Russian. The 'Symphony of Psalms' (1930), the 'Mass' (1948) and the *Canticum Sacrum* (1955) are evidence of his deep piety; and from his point of view there has never been anything incongruous in the fact that the score of the first bears an inscription saying 'this symphony composed to the glory of God is dedicated to the Boston Symphony Orchestra on the occasion of its fiftieth anniversary'. In fact, it might be said that all his works have been composed to the glory of God, for in the act of creation he apprehends something of the mystery of the Creator. As he wrote at the end of *Poetics of Music*, 'the consummated work spreads abroad to be communicated and finally flows back towards its source. The cycle, then, is closed. And that is how music comes to reveal itself as a form of communion with our fellow men—and with the Supreme Being'.

II

Stravinsky has always been fortunate in finding powerful sponsors for his music.

At the time of his apprenticeship, he maintained close and friendly relations with Rimsky-Korsakov and his family. Several of his early pieces are dedicated to Rimsky-Korsakov himself and his sons and daughters; and he owed the first performance of his Symphony in E♭ (1907) and his *Faun and Shepherdess* song cycle (1906) to his master's active intervention. He had just completed a short orchestral fantasy, *Fireworks* (1908), which was designed to commemorate the marriage of Nadia Rimsky-Korsakov to Maximilian Steinberg, when news reached him of his master's death, and his grief led him to compose a special *Funeral Dirge* (1908), the score of which subsequently disappeared.

When *Fireworks* was performed at one of the Siloti concerts in St. Petersburg in the winter of 1909 together with the *Scherzo Fantastique* (1908), Serge de Diaghilev happened to be present in the audience and immediately realised that this young composer was just the sort of person whose services he wanted to enlist for the ballet company he was planning to present in Paris that summer. The first commission was a simple one—Stravinsky was asked to orchestrate Grieg's *Kobold* for *Le Festin* and two numbers by Chopin for *Les Sylphides*—but a more serious one soon followed. Could Stravinsky write the music for a new ballet to be produced in Paris in the summer of 1910? His acceptance led to the composition of *The Fire Bird*, and this was the beginning of a long and fruitful collaboration with Diaghilev and his company.

The Russian Ballet was a revelation of the art of dancing when it burst on Western and Central Europe in those five years before the First World War, and it provided a magnificent shop-window for Stravinsky's talent. The importance of his scores for *The Fire Bird*, *Petrushka* (1911) and *The Rite of Spring* (1913) was quickly recognised in France and England, even if the real value of *The Rite* was somewhat obscured by the repercussions that followed the scandal of its first performance at the Théâtre des Champs-Elysées, Paris. Although each of his ballets was the result of close and careful collaboration, he was not always satisfied with the work of his collaborators. In particular, he had reservations about some passages of Fokin's choreography in *Petrushka*; and when he came to work with Nijinsky on *The Rite* he was critical of that dancer's musical knowledge and choreographic ability. But these three ballets were sufficient to show that in the hands of a first-class composer the one-act ballet was capable of becoming an art form in its own right, instead of being (as had so frequently been the case) a kind of dance diversion set to a pastiche musical score.

In those pre-war years Stravinsky was carried to fame in Western and Central Europe (but not his home country) on the crest of the Russian Ballet's wave of success; but the disadvantages of being dependent on a peripatetic ballet company, without any permanent base or security of operation, were painfully obvious as soon as war broke out. The company's activities were at once severely restricted. This meant that Diaghilev was not in a position where he could commission new work from Stravinsky, and he was able to make only very restricted use of the ballets already in his repertory. Stravinsky's performing royalties dried up. The three ballets and the opera of *The Nightingale* which Diaghilev had mounted in the summer of 1914 represented by far the greater part of his production for the last five years and had now become almost completely unremunerative. What was he to do?

He realised he must try to make himself independent of the Russian Ballet and accordingly during the years of his Swiss exile began to compose a number of works capable of being performed by small instrumental ensembles. The burlesque *Reynard* (1917), which had been commissioned by the Princess Edmond de Polignac, was written for thirteen instruments and percussion; *The Soldier's Tale* (1918) for six instruments and percussion; the *Ragtime* (1918) for ten instruments and percussion; and numerous smaller-scale chamber works belong to this period. None of these new works, however, reached public performance during the war, with the exception of *The Soldier's Tale*. This was carefully planned by Stravinsky and Ramuz for production, not necessarily in theatres, but in halls and possibly even in the open air. Economy was the order of the day: so Ramuz wrote a story which was to be read, played and danced—in fact, a kind of mimed narration—while Stravinsky devised incidental music that could, if necessary, be performed as a concert suite independently of the text. Ramuz managed to confine his characters to four: Stravinsky chose a miniature chamber orchestra consisting of the treble and bass representatives of the three different instrumental families, plus percussion. A single performance took place at Lausanne on 28th September, 1918; but subsequent performances had to be cancelled owing to the outbreak of an influenza epidemic. Despite the ingenuity shown by both collaborators in devising a special form of entertainment to suit wartime conditions, Ramuz ultimately had to admit that 'the most practical thing would have been to work within a traditional framework and that to innovate a new type of entertainment, even by the process of simplification, meant complicating everything'.

When Stravinsky and Diaghilev met in Paris after the war, Stravinsky tried to interest him in the success of *The Soldier's Tale*: but Diaghilev seemed to regard the fact that the work had been produced outside the ambit of the Russian Ballet as a breach of faith. This difference of opinion was never really healed. Although the Russian Ballet continued to feature Stravinsky's ballets in its post-war programmes, he composed very little new work for the company. In *Pulcinella* (1920) he adapted a number of fragments of Pergolesi (some of them unpublished) that Diaghilev had collected over a period of years; and the result was a gay and amiable pastiche. *The Song of the Nightingale* was a rehash of the second and third acts of *The Nightingale* in the form of a symphonic poem. *The Wedding*, although not performed until 1923, had really been conceived as long ago as 1914, and its composition completed during the early years of the war. Various experiments had been made in instrumenting the score, and the final version was not finished until 1923. The wartime *Reynard* was given in two different ballet versions in 1922 and 1929. Only *Apollo Musagetes* (1928) was conceived and written as a new original ballet score; and that was originally commissioned, not by Diaghilev, but by Mrs. Elizabeth Sprague Coolidge for a contemporary music festival organised by the Washington Library of Congress. By the time Diaghilev died in 1929 the umbilical cord had been cut; and Stravinsky had become completely independent of the Russian Ballet.

His doubts whether the Russian Ballet was an adequate vehicle for his music had been intensified by some of the shoddy performances given by the company after the war. His early ballet scores called for a large orchestra of over one hundred players if they were to be presented adequately—particularly *The Rite of Spring*—but although standards of orchestral playing were usually reasonably high in places like Paris and London, they quickly deteriorated when the company went on tour. Stravinsky felt that he had better opportunities of obtaining a musically satisfactory performance on the concert platform than from the orchestra pit in a theatre; and his conviction was confirmed by his experience with *The Song of the Nightingale*, its first concert performance with the Orchestre de la Suisse Romande under Ansermet (6th December, 1919) being vastly superior to its first performance as a ballet under the same conductor (2nd February, 1920). His hostility reached a point where in a letter to Diaghilev (1923) he apparently referred to the ballet as 'the anathema of Christ'.

His distrust of the theatre led him to decide to strike out a new line as conductor and executant of his own works.

His first attempt at conducting was at Montreux in April 1914, when Ansermet invited him to take the baton at a rehearsal of his early Symphony in E♭; his first public engagement at a Red Cross performance at the Grand Théâtre, Geneva, in 1915, when he conducted a symphonic suite from *The Fire Bird*. Early in 1924 he accepted a number of conducting engagements in Belgium and Spain, and on 22nd May of that year appeared at a Kussevitzky concert at the Paris Opéra as soloist in the first performance of his Piano Concerto. He gave over forty performances of this work during the next five years in most of the countries of Western and Central Europe and in the United States, the idiom of the solo part being ideally suited to his dry, nervous, percussive pianistic style. When the novelty value of the Piano Concerto had worn off, he produced the *Capriccio* for piano and orchestra (1929) and, later, the Concerto for Two Solo Pianos (1935), which was launched by himself and his second son Soulima.

Early in the 1930s a close friendship with the violinist Samuel Dushkin led to the composition of the Violin Concerto in D (1931). Dushkin and Stravinsky subsequently appeared together in a number of violin and piano recitals, the programmes of which included the *Duo Concertante* (1932) and various transcriptions and arrangements of earlier works (including excerpts from *The Fire Bird*, *Petrushka* and *The Nightingale*).

After his breach with Diaghilev, he never had any difficulty in securing commissions from individuals or organisations for ballet scores, symphonic works or chamber music. He welcomed working to order, and in most cases his clients seemed to be well satisfied with what they got.

He has always been interested in the possibilities of recorded music. In 1917 he wrote for the Aeolian Company a special Study for Pianola, which was later orchestrated under the title *Madrid*; and about the same time a complete performance of *The Fire Bird* played by himself was recorded for pianola. From 1925 onwards, much of his music was recorded for gramophone under his own direction. While many improvements have been made to the technique of recording, his own capacity as a conductor has also matured, and many of his recent discs are extremely good. He has always been anxious to control the interpretation and execution of his works if possible; and in both the *Chronicle* of his life (1935) and *Poetics of Music* he has deplored the fact that certain conductors have continued to misinterpret his music by ignoring his own authentic readings which are easily available for consultation.

III

For Stravinsky, the act of composition is an ordered rite that demands a workroom equipped with the appropriate instruments and tools. Nabokov has described his study in Hollywood as being 'another example of the precision which orders his music and his language. An extraordinary room, perhaps the best planned and organised workroom I have seen in my life. In a space which is not larger than some twenty-five by forty feet stand two pianos (one grand, one upright) and two desks (a small, elegant writing desk and a draughtsman's table). In two cupboards with glass shelves are books, scores, and sheet music, arranged in alphabetical order. Between the two pianos, the cupboards and desks, are scattered a few small tables (one of which is a kind of "smoker's delight": it exhibits all sorts of cigarette boxes, lighters, holders, fluids, flints, and pipe cleaners), five or six comfortable chairs, and the couch Stravinsky uses for his afternoon naps.' [1]

When as a young man Stravinsky asked Rimsky-Korsakov if he was right to compose at the piano, his master replied, 'Some compose at the piano, and some without a piano. As for you, you will compose at

[1] Nicolas Nabokov, *op. cit.*

the piano.' He has in fact always done so and enjoys being in direct contact with the physical element of sound in this way. In his *Chronicle* he wrote: 'Fingers are great inspirers and, in contact with a musical instrument, often give birth to subconscious ideas which might otherwise never come to life.' Some of his compositions bear traces of their keyboard origin. For instance, although he apparently prefers to look on the reiterated stamping chord (scored for strings and eight horns) that opens the 'Auguries of Spring' movement in *The Rite of Spring* as a simple chord of the 13th, it seems likely that it came into existence as a bitonal aggregation of the chords of E major and E flat major with a flattened seventh, since these two chords conveniently fit both hands on the piano keyboard. Sometimes he may even have profited by a pianistic slip. The first Variation in the second movement of the Sonata for Two Solo Pianos (1944) is closely related to Satie's first *Gymnopédie* and has an *ostinato* accompanying figure that remains virtually unchanged throughout the movement with the exception of one chord (in bar 13) where a C sharp is unexpectedly flattened to C natural, rather as if the middle finger of his right hand had slipped from the black note to the white.

His manuscripts have been described by Ramuz in a passage that almost rivals Pope's account of Belinda's toilet in *The Rape of the Lock*. 'Stravinsky's scores are magnificent. He is above all (in all matters and in every sense of the word) a calligrapher . . . His writing desk [at Morges] resembled a surgeon's instrument case. Bottles of different coloured inks in their ordered hierarchy had each a separate part to play in the ordering of his art. Nearby were india-rubbers of various kinds and shapes and all sorts of glittering steel implements: rulers, erasers, pen-knives and a roulette instrument for drawing staves invented by Stravinsky himself. One was reminded of the definition of St. Thomas: beauty is the splendour of order. All the large pages of the score were filled with writing with the help of different coloured inks—blue, green, red, two kinds of black (ordinary and Chinese), each having its purpose, its meaning, its special use: one for the notes, another the text, a third the translation; one for titles, another for the musical directions; meanwhile the bar lines were ruled, and the mistakes carefully erased.' [1]

In view of this passion for order, it is curious that there should have been a period (in the 1920s) when his published music was badly and in-

[1] *Souvenirs sur Igor Strawinsky*, Mermod, Lausanne, 1929.

accurately printed. Careless proof-reading was presumably the reason for most of the mistakes: and a correction slip detailing seventy-nine different errata had to be issued to accompany the score of *The Rite of Spring*. Most but not all of these errors have been corrected in the revised editions of his scores issued during the last ten years or so.

IV

George Antheil, who met Stravinsky in Berlin in 1922, has included in his autobiography [1] an account of the method of composition Stravinsky was supposed to be following at that time (presumably in writing the Octet). 'I write my music now,' Stravinsky is reported to have said, 'on sheets of music paper glued together, so that the staves are continuous and then I paste this continuous sheet around the four walls of my study. I start on the right-hand side of the doorway and keep on composing, going as intensely as I can until I reach the other side, or the left-hand side of the doorway. When this happens, the composition is finished. In this way I am enabled to make my music "continuous", that is to say, into large broad lines instead of tiny breathless chunks as, for instance, Schönberg does.' This story, even if apocryphal, illustrates a profound truth. The length of the music paper represents the time duration the music has to fill, and to Stravinsky, time is all-important. He realises that music consists of the organisation of sound in time. Therefore it is vital he should know how long a work or a movement is intended to last before he starts to compose; and the breaking down of that length of time into the musical equivalent of chapters, paragraphs, sentences, phrases and words is a task that fascinates him.

The lowest common musical denominator is the beat; and the organisation and grouping of the beats determines the meter. The musical texture sometimes coincides with the metrical framework and sometimes moves far away from it. From this tension is derived rhythm. Meter can be reduced to formula: rhythm cannot.

From an early date Stravinsky realised that a healthy musical pulse produced an impression of well-being, vigour and excitement; and in movements like the 'Dance of the Subjects of King Kashchei' in *The Fire Bird* and the Russian Dance in *Petrushka* he adhered to a metronomical beat, which was to be disturbed as little as possible by *tempo rubato*, and to a regular metrical pattern. With *The Rite of Spring*,

[1] *Bad Boy of Music*, Hurst and Blackett, London, 1947.

however, a desire for complexities of syncopation led him to experiment with the displacement of accents. This produced a great variety of compound metres (varying combinations of duple and triple time). The metrical foundation was frequently reinforced by powerful *ostinati* and the irregular strong beats emphasised by every form of percussive accent, while different metres were combined in a tense contrapuntal structure. This teasing preoccupation with metrical variety is still noticeable in the compositions he wrote during his residence in Switzerland, particularly in *The Soldier's Tale* (e.g. the percussion solo coda to the 'Triumphal March of the Devil'), but begins to die away in the 1920s. At the same time he was interested in the problem of relating different speeds to each other in the same work or movement. *The Wedding* and the Symphonies of Wind Instruments (1920) each has a highly organised metronomical system in which various speeds are geared together according to a given differential (often 2 : 3 or 3 : 2). The change from one gear to another has to be carried out without any acceleration or deceleration, and the effect is to give these scores a magnificent machine finish. To listen to a successful performance of *The Wedding* is as satisfying as to drive (or to be driven in) a good Rolls-Royce or Bentley.

From *Fireworks* onwards, many of Stravinsky's movements (especially his *Allegros*) have a kind of fatalistic dynamism that drives them irresistibly forward. This is perhaps strongest in *The Rite of Spring* and in some of the other works of that period; but as he has grown older, it has never completely left his music. It is true that in the 1920s a certain relaxation seems to set in. The experiments in compound metres are not pursued so intensely as before; there is less striving after metronomical exactitude; and this makes it possible for him to aim at subtler and more elastic effects of rhythm. But the old dynamic temper still bursts through on occasions: it is as marked in the Symphony in Three Movements (1945) as in the earlier works, and a movement like the 'Dance of the Bacchantes' in *Orpheus* (1947) is as powerfully disruptive in its savage syncopations as the 'Ritual Dance of the Chosen Victim' from *The Rite of Spring*.

In his musical perorations he occasionally achieves a particularly striking effect by slowing down the musical material. There is a mathematical splendour about these endings by augmentation that lifts works like *The Wedding*, *Apollo Musagetes*, the Symphony in C (1940) and *Scènes de Ballet* to the skies.

V

The early works naturally betray the influence of musicians whose music impressed the young apprentice: for instance, Glazounov in the Symphony in E flat, Debussy in the *Faun and Shepherdess* song cycle and the first act of *The Nightingale*, Scriabin in the first act of *The Nightingale* too, Wagner (*Siegfried*) and Rimsky-Korsakov in *The Fire Bird*. With that ballet Stravinsky came of age: its delightful music made it clear that he had fully graduated in the school of Rimsky-Korsakov and that in chromatic brilliance of harmony and orchestration he had nothing more to learn from his master. But *The Fire Bird* was essentially a derivative work. The first of his compositions to reveal the true originality of his musical talent was *Petrushka*. In this score, a bitonal device already implicit in the score of *The Fire Bird* was successfully extended; but its full-scale development was reserved for the subsequent cantata, *The King of the Stars* (1911), and the ballet, *The Rite of Spring,* where it was pushed to its logical conclusion. In the latter work, the exploitation of dissonance allied to Stravinsky's exhaustive permutations of compound metre exasperated the nerves of the auditors to a point where they felt unable to cope with so powerful an assault on their sensibilities. Small wonder that the first-night audience erupted! Since that historic evening in 1913, audiences in the theatre and the concert-hall have learnt to listen to *The Rite of Spring* with greater self-control, deeper understanding and growing admiration; but the score still remains one of the most dangerous ever written—difficult to perform and profoundly disquieting to experience; perhaps the most remarkable musical phenomenon of the first half of the twentieth century.

The *Three Japanese Lyrics* for soprano, two flutes, two clarinets, piano and string quartet which date from 1912 to 1913 and the second and third acts of *The Nightingale* complete the works of this period of chromatic dissonance. The harmonic scheme of *The Nightingale* bears a close resemblance to that of *The Rite of Spring,* but its effect is exotic rather than primitive, the metrical framework is simpler and the musical texture lighter (particularly in the last act). It is lighter still in the *Three Japanese Lyrics,* of which the idiom of the last one (*Tsaraiuki*) shows an unexpected affinity with that of Schönberg. Stravinsky and Schönberg had met in Berlin in 1912 when Stravinsky heard a performance of *Pierrot Lunaire.* According to Wellesz, it is possible he may have had a copy of Schönberg's Three Pieces for Piano (Op. 11) with him when he started to compose *The Rite of Spring*. By 1914 the two composers had reached a similar point of development after working along different and independent lines; but thereafter their paths diverged, until at the age of seventy Stravinsky became interested in musical serialism and started to use tone rows as the basis of some of his composition. At that point, however, it was Webern rather than Schönberg whose example provided the stimulus.

Stravinsky's reaction from *The Rite of Spring* was severe. He seems to have felt he had given free rein to the Dionysian impulse and it was time to pull up before matters got out of control. The first signs of change were his concentration on small-scale ensembles instead of the big orchestras demanded by the earlier scores. For the time being, his melos still remained recognisably Russian (as in *Reynard* and *The Wedding*); but by 1918 it was becoming more eclectic, and *The Soldier's Tale* includes a Spanish *pasodoble* and a chorale as well as various jazz elements. This change was accelerated by Diaghilev's commission in 1919 to use the Pergolesi fragments as the basis of *Pulcinella,* which marked a turning-point in Stravinsky's career. Thenceforward, his work would be conceived in accordance with Apollonian principles. In his own words (*Poetics of Music*): 'The clear integration of a work of art and its crystallisation demand that all the Dionysian elements, which stimulate a composer and set in motion the rising sap of his imagination, be adequately controlled before we succumb to their fever, and ultimately subordinated to discipline; such is Apollo's command.'

The change was radical. As an inhabitant of St. Petersburg in the years of his youth, his natural inclination had been to look towards Western Europe and its artistic tradition rather than to Moscow and the exotic Orient. Now, from his vantage-point in France, he started to explore some of the highways and byways of the European tradition of music. Sometimes this led to trouble. When in *Pulcinella* he advertised his indebtedness to Pergolesi, the preservationists were shocked at what they considered to be his sacrilegious treatment of eighteenth-century material. Better that the music should remain covered with dust in its original state in a library or museum than be given a 'live' performance in the theatre when tricked out with Stravinsky's mannerisms. Subsequently his use of forms like the symphony, concerto and sonata seemed to confirm a neo-classical outlook; and some critics began to look on him as a kind of time-traveller in music. Nearly each new work could be related superficially to one or more composers of the past. At various times, the names of Bach, Beethoven, Rossini,

Weber, Johann Strauss and Tchaikovsky were mentioned in this connection; and accusations of pastiche were levelled at him. The truth was that he was steadily developing an acute historical perception of the presence of the past, and at the same time successfully extracting the objective content of such historical material as interested him and using it for his own creative purposes.

The Rake's Progress is perhaps the apogee of this particular aspect of Stravinsky's genius. Here form and content are ideally united. The fact that the libretto by W. H. Auden and Chester Kallman is set in an imaginary eighteenth-century London where the action consists of one act written as a comedy of manners, the second as a farce, and the third as a melodrama, and the whole can be understood as a morality, gives Stravinsky a perfect excuse for founding his own idiom on any appropriate cue offered by the music of the eighteenth or early nineteenth centuries, and making the resultant number irrevocably his own.

It should not be thought that his interest in classical music led to his adoption of academic formulas for producing classical forms. His symphonies, concertos and sonatas all have a proper regard for the periodicity of their constituent movements; but since the years of his apprenticeship he has never been able to summon up a real interest in regular sonata form so-called. This is not because of any disbelief in the functions of tonality, which he has always recognised as being of fundamental importance in music, but because of his dislike of the development section. Talking to Antheil in 1922, he is reported to have said of Mozart, whose music he then particularly admired: 'If I had my way, I would cut all the development sections out of Mozart's symphonies. They would be fine then!' And when he came to write his Piano Sonata two years later, he 'gave it that title without, however, giving it the classical form such as is found in Clementi, Haydn and Mozart' (*Chronicle*).

The form of his symphonic works has been affected by his liking for including *concertante* instruments in his orchestra. This is what happened in the case of *Petrushka*. Conceived originally as a *Konzertstück* for piano and orchestra, it subsequently became a ballet score with an important piano part. During the First World War he succumbed to the fascination of the Hungarian cimbalom, which is specially featured in *Reynard* and the *Ragtime*. In the score of *Orpheus*, the hero's lyre is translated into sound in terms of the harp, and this is treated throughout as a *concertante* instrument. The Symphony in Three Movements includes both piano and harp in its orchestra, and each is used in turn as an orchestral instrument and a solo instrument playing with the orchestra on *concertante* lines. In the first movement, the piano is treated first as an instrument of the orchestra and then as a solo instrument; in the second, the harp (which has been silent during the first movement) imitates and elaborates the business of an orchestra reduced by the omission of brass and percussion; in the third, both harp and piano rejoin the orchestral ranks, with the exception of two solo entries that are entrusted to them in a *fugato* passage. It is considerations like these that determine the form of this remarkable symphony, and not the arbitrary adoption of some formula or other.

The Rake's Progress marks a clear break in Stravinsky's production. The subsequent compositions—the Cantata (1952), Septet (1953), the Three Songs from William Shakespeare (1953) and the *Dirge-Canons and Song* 'In Memoriam Dylan Thomas' (1954)—all show a completely new preoccupation with serial technique. As has been said above, he has chosen Webern rather than Schönberg as his model. This means not that he has become a convert to atonality—far from it!—but his interest in counterpoint has led him to wish to exploit a limited series of different notes (eight, for instance, in the gigue of the Septet; five in the Song 'In Memoriam Dylan Thomas') in their basic version, inversion, retrograde version and retrograde inversion. The contrapuntal complexities and felicities of these masterly works are something quite novel in his output and show clearly that in his seventies he is still capable of astonishing powers of renewal. This is particularly evident in the *Canticum Sacrum*, where he successfully reconciles the chromatic implications of serial technique with the tonal implications of diatonicism. It is in this connection that his moving tribute to Webern should be read:— *The 15 of September 1945, the day of Anton Webern's death, should be a day of mourning for any receptive musician. We must hail not only this great composer but also a real hero. Doomed to a total failure in a deaf world of ignorance and indifference he inexorably kept on cutting out his diamonds, his dazzling diamonds, the mines of which he had such a perfect knowledge.*

VI

Rimsky-Korsakov was a virtuoso where instrumentation was concerned. From him Stravinsky learnt how to handle a large orchestra with assured brilliance; but it was primarily an orchestra that had been built up to suit the needs of the romantic composers of the nineteenth century. The various orchestral families had been enlarged to a point where thick doublings were the order of the day, gaps were filled in, and the rich coagulated sound was given a slick surface finish like varnish. The need for a monster orchestra to play *The Rite of Spring* brought a strong reaction in its train; and after Stravinsky had experimented for a few years with various small-scale ensembles he found himself with a congenial orchestral job on hand when he set about converting the last two acts of *The Nightingale* into a symphonic poem (1917). The original orchestration of the opera was considerably lightened, thereby enabling solo instruments and groups of instruments to be treated almost on *concertante* lines; and this suited the new score well, since the song of the nightingale was now entrusted sometimes to a solo flute, and sometimes to a solo violin. A similar work of simplification was carried out in 1919 when he prepared a concert suite from *The Fire Bird* for medium orchestra.

Since then his usual attitude has been to treat a symphony orchestra almost as if it were a chamber orchestra, to avoid the blurring caused by unnecessary doublings, and to free the instruments so that each can speak with a clear individual voice. His use of instruments is economic, his choice of different combinations unusual and original. Some works are so lightly scored and their instrumental phrases so carefully punctuated that the musical line stands out in relief against a surrounding background of silence and the musical texture becomes aerated, almost transparent. This is particularly the case with passages like the second movement of the 'Dumbarton Oaks' Concerto (1938) and parts of *Persephone*. A good example of his flair for choosing the right instrumental combination is to be found in the last movement (Apotheosis) of *Orpheus*. There a harp maintains an undercurrent of slow ascending scales, while a muted trumpet doubled by a solo violin weaves its way through a two-part fugue played by two horns. This fugue is twice interrupted (in Stravinsky's words, 'Cut off with a pair of scissors') by a two-bar harp solo, which is the accompaniment to the dead Orpheus's missing song.

One result of his interest in the instrument as an individual instead of as an ingredient to be used for blending purposes is a new attitude towards the deployment of instruments of accompaniment. Whereas, formerly, instruments were often used to block in accompanying harmonies, now the tendency is for them to develop a linear figuration, and for this linear figuration sometimes to lead to elaboration. The difference can be clearly seen by comparing the different figurations used in the original version of *Petrushka* (for a large orchestra with quadruple

55

woodwind, 1910) and the revised version (for smaller orchestra with triple woodwind, 1947).

As a footnote to this section, the following anecdote may be told. *Scènes de Ballet* (1944) was commissioned by Billy Rose as a ballet score for inclusion in his revue *The Seven Lively Arts,* which had its preview in Philadelphia prior to its Broadway production. After the first night, Stravinsky received a telegram couched as in the following terms: *Great success stop could be sensational if authorise arranger Mr. X revise orchestration stop Mr. X arranges even for Cole Porter stop telegraph agreement.* He did telegraph back; but all he said was *Am content with great success. Igor Stravinsky.*

VII

Stravinsky's published writings consist of the *Chronicle* of his life, written in 1935 and covering his output up to *Persephone* (1934), and *Poetics of Music,* the Charles Eliot Norton lectures delivered at Harvard in 1939/40.

In addition, he has issued a number of brief statements about music at various times. For instances, a little manifesto entitled *Avertissement* [1] warned those who in 1927 were talking glibly about a return to classicism on the part of certain contemporary composers that it was not sufficient to base such a judgment on 'superficial impressions created by the use of certain technical devices which were current in so-called classical music', since classicism was characterised rather by its 'constructive values'. Shortly afterwards, an article in the *Journal de Genève* (14th November, 1928) called *Pourquoi l'on n'aime pas ma musique* showed why he calculated that no more than ten per cent of the musical public in any country was willing to defend him and his music, and less than that percentage in England. Prior to the first performance of *Persephone,* he issued a particularly dogmatic manifesto in *Excelsior,* saying: 'This score, as it is written and as it must remain in the musical archives of our time, forms an indissoluble whole with the tendencies repeatedly asserted in my previous works. It is a sequel to *Oedipus Rex,* the Symphony of Psalms, to a whole progression of works whose musical autonomy is in no way affected by the absence of a stage spectacle. . . . All this is in no way due to caprice on my part. I am on a perfectly sure road. There is nothing to discuss or criticise.

[1] Printed in *The Dominant,* December 1927.

One does not criticise anyone who is functioning. A nose is not manufactured—it just exists. So it is with my art.' If the purpose of this rather aggressive manifesto was to rile the critics, it certainly succeeded.

In writing his *Chronicle*, however, he was much more judicious and less intransigent when referring to his own compositions. As regards *Persephone,* he briefly mentioned the production at the Paris Opéra, adding 'But it is all too recent for me to discuss it with the necessary detachment'. Granted. But, in that case, it might have been thought that *The Rite of Spring* was sufficiently far away from him to be able to view it dispassionately. It is true that he described in some detail the ballet's production and first performance; but he had hardly a word to say about the music. He explained: 'The omission is deliberate. It is impossible, after the lapse of twenty years, to recall what were the feelings that animated me in composing it. . . . Any account which I were to give today of what my feelings were at that time might prove as inexact and arbitrary as if someone else were interpreting them. It would be something like an interview with me unwarrantably signed with my name.'

Both in the *Chronicle* and *Poetics of Music* he allowed himself to deliver a number of personal judgments on the music of other composers—particularly Beethoven, Bellini, Verdi, Wagner and Tchaikovsky. Some of these caused dismay in quarters where academic opinion, having surveyed the past, has created a certain hierarchy of composers which it expects to be universally accepted. Stravinsky himself compares the great composers of the past to beacons, 'by whose light and warmth is developed a sum of tendencies that will be shared by most of their successors.' But what seems not to be generally realised is that the great composers of the past who appear to us in Western Europe in the form of familiar constellations in the musical sky may have a completely different appearance and relationship when viewed by someone born and brought up in Russia. And when reading Stravinsky's writings, one should bear in mind that as the initial thought process was probably in Russian, the English (or German) translation from the French may really be at two removes from the original instead of one, and the exact meaning even more elusive than is usually the case with translations.

VIII

In his seventies, Stravinsky finds it just as necessary to subject his body to the daily ritual of Hungarian callisthenics as to submit his mind to the rigours of musical serialism. He accepts discipline willingly, but has always been ready to exchange one discipline for another. Not for him the adoption of a ready-made formula or the artificial manufacture of copies of his own earlier successes. That is why many of the admirers of *The Fire Bird, Petrushka* and *The Rite of Spring,* which were written before his conscious break with romanticism, have found it hard to accept works like *Persephone,* the Symphony in Three Movements and *Orpheus* as their legitimate successors.

A sign of his ability constantly to renew himself is to be found in the variety of his compositions. Here form and content should be looked on as being inseparable. Since *The Song of the Nightingale,* each of his orchestral works has been written for a different instrumental specification, each chamber music work for a different ensemble; and even when symphonic form has been adopted as a common basis for symphonies, concertos and sonatas, each composition differs from the others in idiom, gravity and shape. His intellectual explorations in the medium of sound have rivalled in their novelty, variety and complexity those of his former collaborator, Picasso, in the visual arts.[1]

Stravinsky's melos has never moved very far away from its Russian origins, despite his sympathetic preoccupation with the works of many composers ranging from Monteverdi to Webern. Personal antipathies have also played some part in directing the conscious course of his aesthetics—for instance, his juvenile interest in Wagner soon changed to strong dislike; his mother's weakness for Scriabin only confirmed his own distaste for this 'musical traveller without a passport' as he called him; and even his personal friendship with Debussy could not reconcile him to musical impressionism as such. But subconscious motivations may have been more important still; and in this connection, three dream sequences may be referred to.

Ansermet tells the story of how some years ago Stravinsky experienced a frightening nightmare, in the course of which he found himself hiding in the grounds of a country house while an armed guard marched up and down the terrace facing the garden. He was trying to take advantage of a moment when the sentry's back would be turned, or his attention distracted, to slip into the house unobserved; and the agony of his position caused him to wake up suddenly, bathed in sweat. If the significance of this nightmare is perhaps not of immediate musical interest, the same can hardly be said of the following. According to

[1] Picasso designed the scenery and costumes for the Russian Ballet production of *Pulcinella* in 1920.

André Schaeffner, Stravinsky dreamt one night that he saw a gipsy woman seated on the steps at the back of a caravan, playing a violin with the full length of the bow at the same time as she suckled her baby. On awakening from this Giorgionesque scene, he was able to salvage the violin tune, which became one of the main motifs of *The Soldier's Tale*. More important still, in his *Chronicle* he describes how, when he was finishing the score of *The Fire Bird* in St. Petersburg, he had a dream in which he saw 'a solemn pagan rite: wise elders seated in a circle, watching a young girl dance herself to death. They were sacrificing her to propitiate the god of spring.' Here was the visual clue that led directly to the composition of *The Rite of Spring*.

In the course of time, other material will become available which may help one to carry out a deeper psychological exploration of his music, and make a more penetrating assessment of its value. Meanwhile, Stravinsky has retained his position in the vanguard of musical progress. He has passed through a world of chaos, revolution and change, and remained true to himself, his standards and beliefs. Those who have experienced the unforgettable impact of the first performances of his major works, who have seen his short birdlike figure jigging on the podium as he conducts his own music with resilience and the utmost economy of gesture, occasionally inflecting one of his fingers or shrugging his shoulders or swaying his hips, are not likely to forget the man or his music; and the corpus of his works undoubtedly represents one of the most courageous feats of musical exploration and discovery in the first half of the twentieth century.

Paul Hindemith

NORMAN DEL MAR

THE gradual emergence of Hindemith as one of the undisputed, and even venerable figureheads of contemporary music is a comparatively recent development in musical history. The cause and effect of the time element in the rise of this indefatigable master is of a significance not always fully realised. Yet it bears directly upon his outlook, stylistic evolution and eventually upon the particular niche which he has carved out for himself in the modern world of music.

Paul Hindemith was born in 1895—that is to say thirteen years after the birth of Stravinsky, fourteen after that of Bartók, and no less than twenty-one after that of Schönberg, to cite the three key figures of his generation whose influence on the course of twentieth-century music have been parallel in importance, if widely divergent in direction. This disparity of age becomes immediately relevant on consideration of the progress of music during the years surrounding the First World War.

For this was the period of extravagant experiment, when the great war-horses were being produced on the largest scale in the spirit of *fin-de-siècle* super-romanticism, and often with the deliberate intention of shaking the foundations of conservative tradition. During these years, each of the younger exponents of advanced techniques followed the example of the already established Strauss in his *Salome* and *Elektra*, and precipitated towards each his *ne plus ultra* in his own particular direction, whether it was *Le Sacre du Printemps*, *Erwartung*, or *The Miraculous Mandarin*. Each in turn then passed through phases of violent reaction which formed part of a general movement in post-war music.

PAUL HINDEMITH

This period of revolutionary excesses and abrupt *volte-faces* was entirely missed by Hindemith. At its eruption no more than a student, he was towards its decline still only beginning to cultivate, simultaneously with his first engagements as executant (later to prove so vital to his artistic stature), his newly acquired technique in contrapuntal ingenuity and other branches of original composition. In this he was at first influenced to a considerable extent by the scholastic tradition still exerted so powerfully on the conservative background of German music by Reger and his admirers.

It was in fact during the passing of this era that the first flood of original work poured from Hindemith's pen, including the three startling one-act operas and the first great spate of chamber music. Several of the works contained in this mass of writings are of particular importance for the way in which they show for the first time so many features of Hindemith's later manner. The splendid Viola Sonata (one of the six sonatas for various instruments bundled together under Op. 11), for instance, already conceals the cynic and the humorist within its still fundamentally romantic nature. Its form, too, is immensely ingenious and accomplished in the way the finale roughly interrupts the Theme and Variations which constitute the middle movement only itself frequently to be interrupted by further and increasingly grotesque variations. In addition, the use of folksong-like material, the freely irregular bar-lengths and the block chord formations are all early instances of devices which remained for a long time important landmarks in his technical equipment, even though his mental outlook was to pass through radical changes.

For, with the universal post-war reaction fully set in, it was hard for the young composer to evade the psychological influences which this had brought in its train, and from which few composers throughout the world escaped altogether. In the utterly disillusioned and unsettled society of the 1920s artists of all kinds, not only in music, found that they had lost the ability to take themselves or their emotions seriously. Introspection and any philosophising tainted with *Weltschmerz* seemed to belong wholly to the past, whilst in its place came indulgence in the ridiculous and in all forms of satire. Nothing is more characteristic of this aspect of the prevailing mood than the texts chosen by composers, such as Milhaud's *Catalogue of Agricultural Implements* set to music complete with prices, or Stravinsky's *Mavra*, with its exploitation of the newly arisen servant shortage. The keynote is a resolution on the part of the composer to avoid at all costs showing his heart even under his shirt—let alone on his sleeve, as had been so predominantly the tendency so very few years earlier.

A second trend characteristic of post-war psychology was towards the equally unemotional neo-classic movement so often attributed exclusively to Stravinsky but to which the other great figures also contributed in their own way. This fell naturally into the young Hindemith's lap since its seeds are already discernible in Reger's outlook despite the lush romanticism of his harmonic language.

In addition, one more practical feature of the music of this period came as a natural outcome of the radically altered economic conditions. In place of the huge trappings of the Mahlerian orchestral and choral forces, many composers took pride in limiting themselves to tiny groups of sometimes oddly miscellaneous performers.

Fascinating, even laudable, as this reversal may have been, it scarcely provided the atmosphere in which a new master could create an international reputation on account of the epoch-making impact of his work. Unperceptive and ill-humoured as it proved, Cecil Gray's description of Hindemith in 1924 as a 'sandbank in the wide ocean of notes in musical Germany' can today raise a smile of understanding. After all, if by comparison with the excesses of his older colleagues Hindemith's *enfant terrible* period seemed tame and of merely ephemeral importance, this mattered not at all to the enthusiastic young composer who poured out music of all kinds in fabulous quantities, the true evaluation of which has only gradually become possible in retrospect. In fact each of these new stylistic trends, and, above all, the increasingly workaday attitude of composers to their craft, happened to fit in admirably with the lively humour and unselfpitying inventive spirit of Hindemith who embraced them all eagerly as ideal vehicles for the development of his natural form of self-expression.

The first of these tendencies, the cynical evasion of romantic or personal emotion and the liberal use of the grotesque, made its first wholly uncompromising appearance in Hindemith's work in such pieces as the Kammermusik No. 1, with its incredible outer movements and its stipulation that all performers be invisible to the public! Professor Tovey, who always had a soft spot for Hindemith, although it is clear that he knew only one side of the composer at the time, wrote amusingly about this work and its creator: 'Hindemith's music, even in his earlier works, will sound strange to many listeners. It is a severely disciplined art and rests upon massive and extensive theoretical foundations. . . .' (Tovey little knew that these were as nothing to what was to follow one day!) '. . . I know what I like, and I know what bores me; and I am at present quite satisfied to know that I like Hindemith and that he does not bore me. As far as I can judge, his music does not bore many people, though it annoys some. He is never very long, he thumps no tubs, and his attitudes are not solemn. He is manifestly humorous, and he makes the best of modern life. . . . Neither with Hindemith nor with Haydn can I undertake to preserve a solemn countenance while I discuss their works, but I hope that none of my irreverent digressions will leave the reader in any doubt as to the importance of the subject. . . .' (The reference to Haydn with its implied comparison is of quite special significance.) '. . . The listener must not expect too much help from an analysis. The most experienced score-reader would be little the wiser if I gave quotations from the opening movement, *sehr schnell und wild*. It is a short movement alternating between a shrill bickering motive in a treble region around F sharp, and deeper pentatonic objurgations around and about C on the fourth string of the violins. It ends with a universal *glissando* and bump.'

The Finale centres round a Foxtrot by Wilm Wilm which Hindemith mischievously accompanies by scale passages simultaneously on all twelve degrees of the octave. The movement is entitled '1921' and like a similarly dated piano piece of the same period reflects the Pagliacci-like 'laugh for very misery' philosophy so prevalent in Germany at that time.

As for the one-Act operas already referred to above, their attitude to life is apparent in the very titles: *Murder, Hope of Women* and *Das Nusch-Nuschi*. The latter is a superb piece of riotous tom-foolery intended for performance by Burmese marionettes. There is scarcely a serious moment from first note to last. The quotation of the 'King Mark' music from *Tristan,* as the Emperor discovers that his favourite general has seduced all four of his wives, merely provides the *coup d'état* for a score bristling with satirical effects of every kind, from a chorus by a couple of dressed-up monkeys to an extremely high falsetto part for the chief Eunuch. The *Nusch-Nuschi* itself turns out to be half gigantic rat and half alligator. This charming apparition supports the smiling figure of Kamadewa, the god of desire, who sings a short duet with a cor anglais before vanishing into thin air to the accompaniment of a trombone solo.

But this form of artistic mockery is perhaps epitomised in the three-act opera of 1929, *Neues vom Tage.* Here all the traditional operatic 'numbers' are reversed. In place of a Love Duet there is a Hate Duet with husband and wife throwing the breakfast things at each other. Instead of a Wedding March we have a Divorce Ensemble, and the big conventional Scena of every Act 2 consists here of the notorious scene with the heroine (in the revised version the hero) sitting naked in her bath surrounded by, amongst others, the co-respondent, the hotel manager and his entire gesticulating staff. The music to this magnificent burlesque is set for an utterly unconventional semi-chamber orchestra the use of which contains one happy idea after another. It is apparent on every page that Hindemith is enjoying himself hugely.

It is, however, the neo-classic movement which ultimately had the more important impact on Hindemith and became increasingly in evidence in the easy fluency of his style. The purely formal pieces naturally reflect most clearly this aspect of his early work, although the ruthlessness of his counterpoints and their aggressive cumulative effect gave him at one time the reputation of a confirmed atonalist, this view being supported by even so wise a scholar as Professor Scholes. Though this was actually incorrect, the illusion was certainly given at times by the way in which Hindemith threw himself into the general rejection of Romantic euphony, despite his persistent mannerism of weighing anchors of block tonality at intervals during the stretches of harmonically starved part-writing.

But although he later admitted, in an extended Preface to be discussed in due course, that the counterpoint of this time 'left the satisfactory logical sound of the whole in the care of Heaven', this was by no means always true. This apparently atonal style was only one of the many devices in which Hindemith experimented in his ardent interest in every form of technical skill. Polytonality, composition based on unconventional intervals such as fourths and sevenths instead of thirds and sixths, use of unexploited modes and scales in whole or part, everything was grist to his mill. The works of this period frequently have no signatures of time or key, his assumption of tonal and rhythmic elasticity being complete and undemonstrative. The ingenuity of his derivatives or elaborations of all the classical forms fills one with delight, while his inspiration is usually at hand to prevent his skill from deteriorating into mere note-spinning.

Nor was his preoccupation with technical resources confined to those of composition. The possibilities of tonal colour and executive agility intrigued him equally and seems at times to have provided him with the main stimulus to compose. In this he was, of course, splendidly provided for by the current interest, born of economic necessity, in small and varied groups of performers. This last of the post-war trends discussed above Hindemith pursued to its bitter end. The variations of the ensembles required for even his larger works of this period are innumerable, with only one exception: the standard symphony orchestra appears scarcely at all for purposes of accompaniment and not once on its own until the Concerto for Orchestra, Op. 38! Even this is an isolated work, seven years passing before the next of its kind appeared, the Philharmonic Concerto of 1932. As can well be imagined, the results of this fascination with medium as such are sheer joy to perform. Indeed this emphasis on music-making is crucial to the understanding of this first main period of Hindemith's development. The well-known *ben trovato* of Paul Bekker, 'er componiert nicht, er musiziert', stands equally as a compliment to his musical sincerity and as an indictment of the ultimate worth of his output. Certainly the *musizieren* has always been above all the most genuine part of his artistry. Apart from his international status as viola-player, in which capacity he gave the first performance of Walton's Concerto, it is said that he writes nothing for any instrument throughout the orchestra that he cannot play himself. Although, in the face of the fiendish difficulty of many passages, instrumentalists tend to regard this statement as a justifiable exaggeration, it gives a valuable insight into the mental approach to the music of this formative period, of which so much seems to have been drawn from the same spiritual fount. Cecil Gray expressed this very clearly in a later essay, this time with greater justification: 'His style in all his music is remarkably consistent and homogeneous, and his numerous works are apt to give the impression of being lengths of the same material cut off according to the requirements of the moment.'

From here to *Gebrauchsmusik* is obviously the closest possible step. Today Hindemith rejects the label (literally, 'Utility'-music, if one can overlook the misleading wartime connotation of the word) with impatience. But the provision of *Spielmusik*—that is, music written to be piayed or sung in the home by the music-lover as opposed to its specific creation as an art-form—had logical precedence in musical history. Hindemith wrote quantities of this kind of music ranging from 'Five Easy Finger Pieces for Piano' and 'Educational Work for Violin Ensembles in First Position (four grades)' to the more advanced type of 'Music to Play for Strings, Flutes and Oboes' and the 'Cantata for Children's Choir, Solo, Speaker, Strings, Wind and Percussion' which latter forms part of a *Plöner Musiktag*.

Unfortunately, symptomatic as the movement was of the constant concern on the part of the present-day composer at the broad schism between his work and the great general public, it was based on a misconception of the causes and nature of the decline in amateur music-making in a mechanical world. As a result it never caught on to any extent and faded away having achieved little more than yet another outlet for the apparently inexhaustible flow of Hindemith's music-making.

Yet a composer often learns equally from failure as from success, and there was something stimulating and maturing for the thoughtful artist in the *débâcle* of even such a phenomenon of *Gebrauchsmusik* as the *Lehrstück*, written for literally any combination of instrumentalists (high, middle, and low), two male voices, narrator, chorus, dancer, clowns, and crowd! The storm of indignation evoked by this extraordinary affair was entirely out of proportion to its artistic importance and was no doubt occasioned by its overpowering philosophy of mass-humility and abnegation of all human achievement. In this depressive campaign the audience were expected to contribute the part of the *Menge* (crowd), their music being projected by means of a magic lantern!

This, however, proved a final fling in the era of disillusionment. As the twenties gave way to the thirties a desire for important artistic utterance once more arose, and Hindemith readily fell in with the new spirit, none the worse for having marked time during an experimental phase.

It would, however, be entirely false to imply that up to this time Hindemith had produced nothing of more than academic or curiosity value. The fine Third Quartet, with its magical, haunting slow movement, and the profoundly inspired song-cycle *Das Marienleben*, of which more will be said later, both date from as early as 1922. One need only remind oneself of such masterpieces as these to realise that behind the façade of humorous cynicism and the refuge-like role of carpenter-musician, as it were, lay a true and serious artist who was maturing fast and was constantly, if quietly, proving that so far from a local 'sandbank' he was soon to be an international figure to be reckoned with.

Hindemith had in 1929 suddenly abandoned the classification of his works by opus numbers after the attainment of his half-century (though many works of similar nature are grouped together under a single opus number, thus making the true score rather higher!). This might suggest that the relative merits of worth and quantity had begun to weigh more and more heavily upon the prolific composer until in self-conscious awareness of his already mountainous output he determined to set aside so convenient yet implicating a yardstick.

This maturing period culminated in a number of works similar in conception and execution to those of earlier years, but now more consistently serious in the thought that lay behind the easy, if still dry and acrid contrapuntal style. The Second String Trio of 1933 contains something akin to the spirituality of the posthumous Beethoven Quartets. The high-minded intention of the Oratorio *Das Unaufhörliche* ('The Perpetual') is self-evident and most impressive, though the layout of the work is unexpectedly conventional. Even the still numerous examples of the typical genre of the first period, now described as *Konzertmusik* for assorted combinations, are all on an increasingly high level of integrity. When the social structure of internal Germany was rocked to its foundations by the Nazis, the mature musician was ripe for an artistic comment that the world could not ignore.

The Opera, *Mathis der Maler*, remains even today the outstanding landmark in Hindemith's entire career. The libretto was the composer's own and shows a depth of philosophic thought wholly unprecedented in his previous work. It expounds in historical guise the ever-living problem of the function of the artist at times of national stress. Should the artist remain aloof from the turmoil raging around him, perhaps at most expressing through the agony of his search for unattainable truth and beauty the troubles and torments of his miserably unsettled age? Or should he, from pity and humanitarianism, enter blindly into a conflict the implications of which he cannot fully understand, the course of which he cannot hope to alter? As Hindemith, in the guise of Mathis, his mediaeval painter hero (a figure, incidentally, taken from life), asks himself: 'Have you fulfilled what God required of you? Is what you create and portray enough? Are you not only of use to yourself?' Set at the time of the Peasants' Revolt, in scenes of bitter violence, the action plunges the wretched painter into perplexing mazes of power politics in which he wallows hopelessly. His heart-searchings are brilliantly transformed in the Sixth Tableau into a symbolic struggle of the Temptation of St. Antony as depicted in one of the actual paintings of the real Matthias Grünewald. The device is clearly born of Wagner's use of the writings of the real Hans Sachs, yet it never fails to impress, not only by its scholarship but by its aptness and sincerity. The overriding problem remains at last an inevitable enigma, Mathis returning tired and discouraged to his beloved work, having caused more harm than good by his interference in a problem many times too big for him. Nevertheless the opera leaves one convinced that the author by no means absolves the artist from a share in the common responsibility.

The implicit reference to current events was obvious enough for Hindemith to incur the disfavour of his country's new rulers, though in their philistine detestation of any *avant garde* artistic movement they had already labelled him a 'cultural bolshevik'. As a result the work was banned, thus indirectly serving Hindemith's purpose better than a blind eye would have done.

Yet even Furtwängler's famous act of defiance to the Nazis with respect to *Mathis,* and the consequent notoriety of composer and opera, would not have had such a far-reaching artistic effect had not the music itself also shown a generosity of spirit and accessibility of style far in advance of even the greatest of the earlier pieces. At one stroke Hindemith attained full international status as one of the outstanding composers of the century.

The Symphony which Hindemith built out of extracts from *Mathis* quickly became a standard work in the concert repertoire and it might well have been hoped that the newly acknowledged master would now concentrate on cementing the link which he held at last with the wider music-loving public. But this prospect was interfered with by yet another of Hindemith's activities.

Already in 1927 the erstwhile *enfant terrible* had assumed the role of *maître,* and this teaching connection had ever since continued to grow in importance alongside the unceasing creative work. With *Mathis* behind him, Hindemith turned his attention to crystallising into formulas the principles and technique which had hitherto unconsciously stood him in such good stead. In 1937 he published the first volume of the great textbook, *Unterweisung im Tonsatz* (rather too freely rendered by *The Craft of Musical Composition* in the American edition, although the translator apologises for this in a footnote). A later volume and other text-books have since followed at regular intervals up to the present day. In these Hindemith exposes in unique detail his workshop both of composition and musical instruction, analysing everything down to the smallest tool. *Unterweisung im Tonsatz* is a truly astonishing work which has been justly compared in importance with the theoretical writings of Rameau. For, in the first chapters, Hindemith goes right back to the fundamentals of music, suggesting logical revisions in the tuning of the tempered scale. From this beginning he evolves by radically slow degrees a system of musical construction and analysis based entirely on acoustical principles. His researches delve into the mathematical origin of tonal colour and the scientific relationships of each note of the chromatic scale derived from combination tones. Here he was palpably working in direct opposition to what he regarded as the unnatural tonal anarchy of the Schönberg school, even though in the conclusion to the first volume he subjects one of Schönberg's later piano pieces to analysis according to his, Hindemith's, own constructional concepts. A valuable précis on Hindemith's methods and intentions is given by Mosco Carner in his *Study of 20th Century Harmony*. Moreover, as he quite rightly says, 'modern composers are given a means by which to control and plan in a very deliberate manner the choice of chords and the harmonic disposition of a work'. As a vehicle for teaching, and as a vade-mecum for the apprentice composer, it is clear that such a volume of scientifically evolved dogma is beyond price. But it is somewhat doubtful whether the cold-water influence of the master-professor upon the white-hot inspiration of the master-composer in the person of the same man could ever be beneficial. For creative style needs to retain a generous if not undisciplined degree of fluidity to meet the often wayward requirements of genius. It is not hard to assess the reputations as composers of the great theorists of the world through the centuries, beginning perhaps with Fux himself, who is listed as the author of over four hundred compositions! Indeed, in the case of at least two modern masters taken at random, Dukas and Dohnanyi, their assumption of professorships led to the total drying up of their creative originality and effort, at one time so striking in both cases.

The effect on Hindemith was indeed perceptible, though it is largely a matter of contention as to how damaging it has been. For throughout this extended period of technical consolidation Hindemith continued to produce works amongst which were isolated but regular masterpieces, such as the *Symphonische Tänze* and the Ballet *Nobilissima Visione*, the whimsy and spontaneity of which were unimpaired by the rigidity of his avowed system. The ballet music in particular has, in keeping with its title, a degree of nobility quite unique in Hindemith's work, and it is very well that he brought it within the range of the concert programme by selecting from it a well-balanced and soberly contrasted suite of movements. The action centres round the life of St. Francis of Assisi, and Hindemith's music describes the meditative fervour and asceticism with consummate understanding. The cadence figure in the second section of the first movement, describing the mystical wedding of the Saint with Poverty, is extraordinarily affecting in its simplicity. But it is the wonderful closing *Passacaglia,* headed in the original with the Latin words: *Incipiunt laudes creaturarum,* that represents the culminating point of Hindemith's classical style.

Nevertheless the tendency towards dryness and uniformity of colour in his fundamentally unemotional style did become accentuated at this time. If the personal idiom of the later works is more cultivated, the unfailing variety of invention in the course of a work is no longer so intriguing. His concentration on the colour of melodic and chordal progressions turned him away from his earlier enthusiasm for dabbling in the broader colours of exotic instrumental combinations. Above all, in his teaching he discouraged his students from experimenting with instrumental colour, an incredible dictum from the composer of the *Kammermusik* and *Konzertmusik* series! It was only the quality of the musical line that mattered, just as Brahms used to circulate the opinion that he cared little on what instrument his music should be performed, although anyone who has heard Brahms' wind-instrument chamber music played entirely on strings cannot fail to doubt that composer's sincerity in this matter!

Hindemith's sonatas, dashed off easily for in turn every instrument of the orchestra, typify this period which reached its climax with the famous *Ludus Tonalis* for Piano Solo, written in 1942. This vast undertaking represents Hindemith's *ne plus ultra* along his newly chosen scholastic path and corresponds roughly with Schönberg's Suite, Op. 29, for Piano, Clarinets and Strings, as being the most uncompromising embodiment of his theoretical principles. The fact that despite its severity it immediately reached an unusually wide audience can no doubt be attributed in part to its high level of artistry throughout. But history shows that this does not always follow, as no doubt it should, and at least half the credit for its ready universal acceptance must go to the circumstance that it was in perfect accordance with the contemporary spirit of wide classical sympathies which were an odd characteristic of artistic taste during the Second World War.

Hindemith subtitled the work, *Studies in Counterpoint, Tonal Organisation and Piano Playing.* As far as the last category goes, this is no more applicable in *Ludus* than in any other of Hindemith's piano works and in any case the difficulties in his pianistic style have always been less on technical than musical grounds. These are, of course, quite another matter, and from this point of view the work deserves the closest attention.

It consists of a set of twelve fugues interspersed by Interludes and enclosed within a Prelude and Postlude. The fugues, all in three parts without exception, are arranged in order of key, corresponding with Hindemith's basic scheme of tonal relationships as laid out in *Unterweisung im Tonsatz*. The Interludes serve both to modulate from one fugue to another, and to provide opportunities for as many varieties of style, mood and form as possible within the over-all scheme of the work. As regards the Prelude and Postlude, they have attracted more attention than any other section owing to the brilliantly successful device that the latter is the exact mirror inversion of the former. All in all, it is clear that, as Matyas Seiber says, the work is planned as a kind of latter-day '48'-cum-'*Kunst der Fuge*', a dangerous and courageous undertaking, for it courts inevitable comparisons—not work for work, that would be naïve; the question arises rather over the validity of any possible view of Hindemith as occupying an equivalent position in the present century to that occupied by Bach in his. In this it would be important to bear in mind not merely the ultimate value of the works, but the functional circumstances in which they were created. The parallel is by no means exact; the claim happily not made. But the haunting analogy cannot wholly be forgotten by the critical mind in its approach to an otherwise masterly product of scholarship.

Despite the success of *Ludus Tonalis*, the professional view of Hindemith's position which it naturally enhanced scarcely improved the universality of his prestige, which had always inclined towards esteem rather than popularity. With the abandonment of his earlier policy of avoiding the use of normal forces, the standard popular orchestral forms were now open to him and in fact the last few years had seen the appearance of such, once unthinkably conventional, pieces as a true Violin Concerto, Cello Concerto, Symphony, and Theme and Variations for Piano and Strings. This policy he now continued with the Symphonic Metamorphosis of Themes by Weber, an Overture, *Cupid and Psyche*, and a Piano Concerto. The first of these (an undeniably attractive work despite the provoking liberty taken with the *Turandot* theme!) has had considerable success in recent years; nevertheless, in view of the now firmly set medium of expression which he had during this period resolved upon, with its predominantly dry harmonic flavour, thickness of texture and uniformity of orchestral colour, this attempt at deliberately feeding the standard concert repertoire was only moderately successful.

In 1946 Hindemith celebrated the end of the Second World War with a Requiem which showed an entirely new depth and spirituality. Entitled 'For those we love', it is a setting of the poem by Walt Whitman, 'When lilacs last in the door-yard bloom'd'. Hindemith had been constantly in America since 1940, but it is impossible to detect any American influence in his general style or outlook. His discovery of the work of this great American poet seemed, however, at this awesome moment in the world's history to open wide momentarily the sympathetic reaction of Hindemith's genius. The sad intensity of the instrumental prelude, built throughout on an organ-point; the great central fugue; the poignant hymn 'For those we love' set as a duet for the two solo singers, followed by the choral 'Death carol'; the magnificent stately introduction and March with its use of Parade Drum and Army Bugle so beloved of Whitman; and the heartrending Finale; all are the work of a deeply inspired tone-poet and architect.

Once again, however, this proved an isolated work of its kind, Hindemith's restless spirit moving off at a tangent. His next important production was an entirely revised version of his early song-cycle *Das Marienleben*, settings of the fabulously beautiful poems of Rainer Maria Rilke based on the life of the Virgin. These songs, originally composed in 1922, had understandably always been close to the composer's heart, and already in 1939 he had returned to them and recast four for voice and orchestra, settings of exquisite taste and sensitivity. The newly revised version of the whole cycle had been announced as 'in preparation' ever since 1941, but the work had proceeded gradually and with immense care. When it finally emerged in 1948 it proved to carry with it a lengthy manifesto describing in detail its *raison d'être* and comparing the relative merits of the two versions with the composer's customary thoroughness. This manifesto is, of course, extremely revealing of Hindemith's changed attitude to the stylistic trends of the 1920s. But many of the hot-headed and hence less carefully practical results were inseparable from so violently reactionary a period, and much as one may agree in principle with an older and wiser composer's indictments, a feeling of concern that he may spoil something of the initial spark is aroused when it becomes clear that he intends to revise on a large scale the work of his youth.

The new version of *Das Marienleben* is indeed radical, some of the songs being not merely revised but entirely rewritten, while only a single song remains wholly untouched. For example in the 'Introductory Remarks' he says of the third song, 'The Annunciation of Mary': 'The old version judged by the severest standards could in no way stand up to serious examination. It is accordingly replaced by quite a new setting. This attempts a peaceful sonority in direct contrast with the disturbing harmonic and tonal restlessness of the old song. . . . In place of the intensely penetrating repetition of individual motifs separated by rests, we now have long-drawn-out lines of melody.' This quest for continuity, for smoothness of sonority and line, is one of the main features of Hindemith's changed attitude to his art. Yet in the maintaining of variety and interest, the dramatic impact of the central recitative-like middle section of this song was not without its effect. Moreover, the use of terse figures built up through repetition, which now evokes such severe censure, was a welcome change of *modus operandi* after the habitually even-flowing style of also the young Hindemith.

Nevertheless, most of the revisions are unquestionably beneficial. The raising of the tessitura, if once again at the expense of variation of colour, removes from the vocal line the strain of unfair competition with the intricate piano part and other unpractical effects born of inexperience. This elimination of the necessity of forcing the lower voice also has the desirable result of placing the cycle within the range of a far greater number of sopranos. Again, Hindemith says with noteworthy humility: 'Should the composer notice that the singer continues to stumble at the same places even after zealous and thorough application, then he must ask himself whether his work is really worth such fruitless strain.'

Practical considerations of balance are also in strong evidence in the redrafting of some of the songs. In deciding to retain the Fugato which formed the basis of the ninth song 'Of the Marriage at Cana', Hindemith realised that its violence and busyness obscured the clarity of the all-important vocal line. He accordingly gave the Fugato its head in a tremendous piano introduction, using it thereafter only with the greatest discretion as an accompaniment. This had the effect of doubling the length of the song, and this new stature, together with the immensely impressive introduction, makes of the piece 'the dynamic climax of the complete plan', as Hindemith puts it. Here we reach a further crucial guiding principle constantly before the composer during his work of revision. This is nothing less than a double graph of dynamic and expressive intensity as drawn by the succession of songs in their new form. 'The old version,' he writes, 'was essentially a row of songs held together by the text and by the continuity of its action, but beyond that following no general plan of over-all composition. . . .

Wise distribution of power, calculated placing of the points of greatest and least intensity—all this was unknown to the composer of the old version. Like all else of which he knew no better, he left it to his musical instinct.'

Despite the justice in all this, perhaps the professor in correcting the results of his own impetuosity like that of any of his pupils underrates the value of instinct. The proverb 'First thoughts are best' often has real validity in artistic matters, and in many places the burning virility and direct sincerity of the original work has faded to a comfortable glow of accomplished writing.

Hindemith now embarked on a series of works featuring wind instruments, beginning with a Clarinet Concerto, a Wind Septet, a Symphony for Full Military Band and a Sonata for Four Unaccompanied Horns. To this burst of specialised activity belongs also the Concerto for Horn and Small Orchestra with its utterly unorthodox last movement. This consists itself of a series of smaller movements arranged palindromically one within the other, the outer ones being the slowest so that the entire Concerto ends in effect with the dying notes of its slow movement. The centre of the palindrome is in two parts, the first a short rapid movement, while the second is an extended recitative above which stands a short poem marked *declamation*. This proves upon examination to fit to the notes of the solo horn's recitative line which it comments upon in poetical analogies.

Such a conception gives rise to uncertainty as to the correct procedure in performance, but clearly springs from a return to Hindemith's youthful delight in playing with colouristic and formal devices. This seems, moreover, to have revived yet again the freshness of his invention, for in the midst of these works there appeared in 1950 a Sinfonietta which can only be described as 'vintage'. In addition, he seems at this time to have been drawn to other works of his first period, making in his nostalgia revised versions of several of them. Even his 'occasional' pieces are amusingly reminiscent of earlier days such as the 'Canticle to hope' written for the UNESCO convention of 1953, the material for which contains parts for two orchestras of indeterminate size, and song sheets for the audience!

At the time of writing (1955) Hindemith's last work of importance suggests that he may have reached one more turning-point in his output. The Symphony *Harmonie der Welt* is an enormous work of great complexity derived from a new opera which has yet to make its appearance. The subject-matter may well be the most elaborate Hindemith has yet tackled. It concerns the life of one Johann Kepler, a seventeenth-century astronomer and philosopher who overstepped the boundaries of true scientific calculation and attempted to co-relate the mathematical laws of the universe with the modes of music. The concept of the *Music of the Spheres* is one of the oldest in the history of philosophy, and Hindemith derived the titles to the movements of his Symphony from a sixth-century Roman author who is believed to have been himself propounding Ancient Greek theories. These titles, 'Musica Instrumentalis', 'Musica Humana', 'Musica Mundana' are of course highly evocative to a musician of Hindemith's inventive capacity and the results are full of startling flights of imaginative fancy, while the virtuosity required from all departments of the orchestra is of a wholly new order in Hindemith's work.

The relationship of this Symphony to its parent opera naturally recalls that of *Mathis*, and it may well prove that Hindemith has reached a climax in his work comparable with that earlier pinnacle. Bearing in mind that he is still no more than sixty years of age, that his fertility appears to be as inexhaustible as ever, while his indomitable spirit is once again ready to dare new and formidable problems of style and texture, one may reasonably look forward to a new period of creative activity which will link up and pursue the more enduring elements in each of the remarkable phases of his exceptionally full career. Above all does one await with eagerness the appearance of further enduring masterworks with that inevitable quality yet varying character which prove that the fine artist has the stature and personality of a great man. Whatever may transpire, however, his position and influence as classicist, theorist and master, with that so endearing love of his subject, is assured for all time.

Arnold Schönberg's Development towards the Twelve-Note System

WALTER AND ALEXANDER GOEHR

A<small>LTHOUGH</small> the conditions and problems facing a creative artist vary in different times, an ethnic culture imposes a certain common tradition and leads to a fundamental similarity of outlook. An understanding of the roots and historical development of a culture is essential for an assessment of any individual artist. Assuming this fact, the opportunity is given of seeing the comparative value, the parallels and divergences of individual composers, seemingly unrelated, in a logical and responsible manner. For example, Brahms and Wagner were for decades believed to be antipodes, while we today, in comparative detachment, are able to see the affinities in the common national character of their work.

The German school of music at the threshold of the twentieth century based its teaching upon the study of German music from J. S. Bach to the romantic masters, virtually neglecting earlier music or that of other nationalities. The melodic and rhythmic idiosyncrasies, the harmonic subtleties and the freedom of expression attained by these composers were measured by comparison with arbitrary prototypes of so-called normality (or regularity) created by the theorists. Mastery over technical material was obtained by a study of traditional harmony and academic counterpoint, based upon Fux rather than upon Palestrina and his Italian and Flemish predecessors. Although the music of France, Russia and other nations was studied, a fundamental schism had developed between the outlook of German musicians and those of other national schools. Heinrich Schenker, in his illuminating article 'Rameau or Beethoven' (*Das Meisterwerk in der Musik III*, München, 1930), heads his article with a quotation from a letter of C. P. E. Bach: 'You may loudly proclaim that the fundamentals of the art of my father and myself are anti-Rameau.' This divergence of attitude continued and grew, and even when German composers were influenced by the works of other national schools, their attitude remained (and remains) sharply differentiated. The very nature of the German tradition and method is a dialectical one and its development is one whereby each successive composer builds upon the technical achievements of his precedessors. There was little place for eclecticism. French composers, eclectic by nature, were much more open to newly discovered technical possibilities and to influence from hitherto unknown types of music. The German remained comparatively little affected by the new experiences made possible by a rapidly improving system of communication and the consequent opportunities for cultural exchange with remote regions of the earth. The teachings of Vincent d'Indy and Paul Dukas illustrate the eclectic and experimental tendency. The influence upon Debussy of Eastern music at the Paris World Exhibition is well known. The differences in method between the two traditions is clearly seen at times when Debussy and Schönberg work with similar musical material, but with utterly different approaches and results. The German attitude of mind, one that can hardly be found in any other cultural sphere of the West, results in a cumulative style steadily and logically progressing to great subtlety and complexity.

One must remember that the German musical language was already in a state of advanced development at the time when Schönberg entered the field. Brahms and Wagner, the former with a subtle juxtaposition of new asymmetries of form and rhythm beneath a surface of the traditional, the latter with his liquidation of the old formal divisions and functions into a dramatically coherent whole, founded the style which composers like Wolf, Mahler, Reger and Strauss developed towards a flowering in the art of music completely original in its plasticity and powers of free and largely asymmetric construction. The developments of Wolf and Mahler in the elaboration of the melodic line (continuing what Wagner had begun) and the widespread adoption of Brahms' great developments in the variation of harmony, brought the musical language to a point at which Schönberg's principles of 'varied repetition' and 'musical prose' can be considered a realistic assessment of the musical style of the time. It is our purpose to demonstrate the processes by which Arnold Schönberg, in the period of his creative

77

life until 1923, was to bring this musical language towards its logical conclusion and subsequent, seemingly revolutionary, development.

Development of artistic style stipulates a dual process: on the one hand, an accumulation of increasingly varied elements, an extension of the means of relating previously unrelated material and consequently, a persistent replacement of comparative regularity and symmetry by asymmetry and irregularity. On the other hand, it stipulates (and this must be particularly emphasised) restriction, reduction and simplification, seemingly retrogressive habits, and the deliberate neglect or sublimation of traditional elements arising from new æsthetic considerations. There results a positive process of addition and accumulation in the creative mind and imagination and a quasi-negative restriction determined by choice and individual preference. When we consider the various facets of the progress of Schönberg's music, we see that the balance between these two contrasting elements of development more than anything else distinguish him from his contemporaries and mark him as a great composer. The farther his style progressed (seemingly away from the German past), the more he concerned himself with analysis and thought upon the fundamental problems inherent in classical and romantic German music. His particular path as an innovator was largely achieved by his more than usual powers of perception to understand and analyse the problems which had faced Mozart, Beethoven, Brahms and many others. Although his musical language was from the beginning one of great originality, the technical means which he used were, to a great extent, derived from the processes of his predecessors in German music. Aware of the continuous striving towards a new musical language, Schönberg wrote in a letter at the time of the completion of *Das Buch der hängenden Gärten*, Op. 15: 'I have succeeded for the first time in approaching an ideal of expression and form that had hovered before me for some years. . . . I may confess to having broken off the bonds of a bygone æsthetic...' (quoted by Dika Newlin in *Bruckner, Mahler, Schönberg*, New York, 1947). Seemingly contradictory is the famous sentence in his article 'Brahms the Progressive' in *Style and Idea* (London, 1951): 'Analysts of my music will have to realise how much I personally owe to Mozart. People who looked unbelievingly at me, thinking that I made a poor joke, will now understand why I called myself a pupil of Mozart, must now understand my reasons.' These two quotations (and many similar ones can be found in Schönberg's writings and sayings) are characteristic of the duality of his purpose and his development.

DEVELOPMENT TOWARDS TWELVE-NOTE SYSTEM

In attempting to trace the continuity of musical thought employed in Schönberg's compositions from the *Gurrelieder* (1901) to the Serenade, Op. 24 (1923), we shall deal separately with the different aspects of construction: first, with his treatment and subsequent dissolution of the functions of tonal harmony; then with the significance of his return to the use of counterpoint; and finally, with the character of his rhythm and with other elements which contribute to his conception of form and the novelty of his expression.

Throughout his life, Schönberg occupied his mind with the problems of tonal harmonic structure (*Harmonielehre*, Vienna, 1911, *Structural Functions of Harmony*, pub. posthumously 1954). His system of describing structural harmonic processes may be said to be based on the progressive theories of Simon Sechter, who was Bruckner's teacher and the master with whom Franz Schubert had decided to study counterpoint a few weeks before Schubert's death. In his *Die richtige Folge der Grundharmonien* (Leipzig, 1853), Sechter greatly extended the harmonic vocabulary by acknowledging, describing and analysing chords and harmonic progressions which, although used for a long time by individual composers (even as early as J. S. Bach) for certain purposes of expression, had not previously been granted a theoretically clarified inclusion in the system of tonal harmony.

Schönberg (as others before him and with him) developed the theory of harmony, following Sechter's pattern of incorporating into the system of functional harmony increasingly complex harmonic phenomena which appeared in the works of contemporary composers, sometimes for reasons of freer part-writing and sometimes with the aim of achieving ever more subtle expression. At the beginning of the century, composers like Reger, Mahler and Strauss wrote in an idiom which went very far in the elaboration of harmony and, while adhering to the basically diatonic construction of tonal harmony, included in their vocabulary more and more chords of a chromatic character or chordal combinations of intervals not primarily connected with diatonic harmony (intervals of the whole-tone scale, chords built on fourths, combination of tritone with other intervals, etc.). Some of the harmonies used (especially passing chords in vast prolongations) are of a nature only loosely connected with the idea of diatonic harmony. Schönberg, feeling that here the limits of tonal harmonic analysis were reached, started calling certain types of chords 'roving harmonies'. He saw in these novel chordal phenomena, quite rightly, the source of astonishing new developments and, at the same time, the danger of over-development and of obscuring the basic cadential structure. Wagner had already seen this danger and after *Tristan and Isolde* largely withdrew from the advanced position he had established. Some of these new harmonic happenings in the works of Reger, Strauss (in *Elektra* and *Salome*) and Mahler (particularly in the Seventh and Ninth Symphonies) met with very severe censure from the more conservative contemporary critics and some novel management of chords which Schönberg used in his early works was strongly criticised, e.g. the inversion of the chord of the ninth in *Verklärte Nacht* and the use of the *Quartenharmonien* (chords built on fourths) in the first Chamber Symphony, Op. 9.

Schönberg's use of the whole-tone scale can be compared to good advantage with the practice of Debussy. We find in Debussy's works passages which are almost entirely built, harmonically and melodically, on elements of the whole-tone scale. His predominantly vertical approach to harmony, which takes the actual character of the sound as a basis for the unity of the harmonic structure, has led to very impressive innovations and has influenced many of Debussy's contemporaries (and even composers up to the present time). Schönberg uses the whole-tone scale in a completely different way. In the Chamber Symphony, Op. 9, written in 1906, the fundamental structure is considerably influenced throughout the work by the partially whole-tone character of the first subject, but nevertheless all appearances and developments of these whole-tone elements are strictly subordinated to the functional plan of harmony which binds together the whole work. Furthermore, Schönberg uses many other methods of harmonic form-building (*Quartenharmonien*, varied sequences etc.) which, although apparently complete innovations, are also fitted into the plan of the whole harmonic layout in the manner of the German tradition of composition, and his ability to connect seemingly heterogeneous elements into one logical whole shows him clearly as a follower of Brahms and particularly of the later Beethoven. No such over-all construction can be detected in composers of different traditions, as for example—Debussy.

The Chamber Symphony, Op. 9, is of the greatest significance when showing Schönberg's progress in the harmonic sphere. We cannot, within the scope of this article, describe in detail the complete freedom and mastery Schönberg achieved in this idiom, using all kinds of means in expanded tonality, creating a structure unparalleled by previous music in its variety and subtlety of harmonic form-building, but we want to mention his use of free and more varied relationship of consonance and dissonance. Through his use of the widely leaping and internally varied melodic lines which were his heritage from Wagner and Wolf, he created a new and striking independence between horizontal melody and vertical chord. The result appears to approach in certain places some form of polytonality. Schönberg in subsequent works made considerable use of this and even applied, instead of polyphony in single lines, a technique of passing chord anticipations and suspensions to whole complexes of chord movement. It may be defined, to use the term of Joseph Schillinger, as 'Strata Harmony'. If we compare movement to a succession of vertical straight lines, we see in the application of this technique that these lines become distended and, as it were, distorted. This led to a weakening in the effect of the functional harmonic structure. Thus the technique, grown from humble beginnings where composers ornamented and contrapuntally prolonged their cadences, now brought music to the point where these cadences had been decorated and disguised to such an extent that in many cases they completely disappeared from view, or rather from hearing. Schönberg's use of roving harmonies, his contrapuntal prolongations and the all-important obscuring of the cadences, led him imperceptibly to a position where he had to withdraw key signatures, which became obsolete and gave a false impression of the harmonic structure (starting with the last movement of the Second String Quartet). This was a step towards that 'mythical' atonality which was attributed to Schönberg, yet it was the logical dialectical development of his technique.

It is, of course, an error to see the so-called 'atonal' works as representing some entirely new concept which fell from heaven. Schönberg had stretched the harmonic structure to a point at which the fundamental harmonies and cadence points no longer had full functional significance either aurally or intellectually. For a time he was still prepared to use the technique of harmonic composition which became completely free, and relied more and more on his individual powers of imagination. It is indeed true to say that in works such as the Five Orchestral Pieces, Op. 16, or *Erwartung*, Op. 17, although the over-all harmonies might still be analysed according to the principles of tonal structure, the overlapping and frequent use of the neighbour-note technique, combined with the propensity of octave displacement, although completely coherent, make the works practically free of a felt tonality. Even as early as the Three Piano Pieces, Op. 11, we see, as it were in embryo, the kind of technique which he later brings to fruition. In the second half of the first piece, the subject is varied by a replacement of its smaller intervals, the ninth replaces the second, the eleventh the third, etc. In observing this octave displacement, one can understand better the characteristic sound of this music. Whereas in music from Bach to Brahms, the octave had played a most important part in the harmonic and melodic structure, the development of chromatic elaboration and the whole system of extended harmony show us these new intervallic progressions as well as many fourths and a great insistence on the old bogey, the tritone, taking a preponderance of emphasis in the melody and harmony. The traditional functions of a harmonic structure could no longer be said to apply to Schönberg's music. Sooner or later the composer had to face the problem of finding other form-giving elements to substitute for the lessened harmonic functions. From this time onwards, the analysis of his music in terms of fundamental harmony, which had generally been the satisfactory method up to this time, must of necessity be insufficient, artificial and contrived. One need only examine Hindemith's attempt to analyse the third piano piece from Op. 11 to see how little it helps towards an understanding of the musical structure.

It will now be necessary to occupy ourselves with the analysis of those elements which Schönberg found satisfactory to introduce into his work as substitutes for functional harmonic structure, and all subjects which will be discussed in the further part of our enquiry must be understood as such. The development of his counterpoint, his rhythmic practice and other new elements which he saw fit to introduce into his music, will be assessed primarily according to the purpose with which they were introduced, namely, the substitution of form-giving elements for the faded ones of tonal harmony. Schönberg's progress from *Pelleas and Melisande*, Op. 5 (1902–3), to the Serenade, Op. 24 (1923), the point at which he introduced the twelve-note technique, can now be seen as the gradual introduction of such new elements, in their elaboration breaking more and more into the domain of the functional harmonic structure. Certainly the most significant among these elements is Schönberg's reintroduction into his music, at the most fundamental level, of the principles of counterpoint.

During the nineteenth century the German composer's approach to counterpoint underwent a considerable change. Although Beethoven, especially towards the end of his life, and later, to a lesser degree, Reger and Mahler, made considerable use of counterpoint and concerned themselves with the problem of integrating it with their basically homophonic styles, the romantic followers of Beethoven (Weber, Mendelssohn, Schumann and also Brahms) tended to give up the procedures of real counterpoint and to replace them with a harmonically inspired polyphony. With Wagner, who most clearly represented the spirit of the nineteenth century, the polyphonic texture developed still farther away from the original contrapuntal methods, even remembering that the point of departure was not a strict modal style of counterpoint but the well-developed harmonic style of the seventeenth- and eighteenth-century German contrapuntalists. Strict counterpoint was the product of a musical age which thought not in the major-minor tonic system but in a system of authentic and transposed modes, the fundamental difference being that the modal form had a wider degree of possibilities for cadencing. Schönberg realised that with the disappearance of a valid tonal centre, the possibilities for introducing a freer approach to the cadence again existed, in fact his adoption of the twelve-note technique placed him under the obligation of regarding all twelve chromatic notes as equally valid for cadencing, i.e. a dodecatonic system. But at the period in his work before the twelve-note system had crystallised, we see him introducing the elements of a strict contrapuntal practice into the gradually dissolving tonal framework.

In treating the development of music of this period, T. Wiesengrund-Adorno observes that in harmonies composed of an unusual combination of intervals, the single note becomes less integrated in the unity of the chord. In a series of such chords, these comparatively loose notes lend themselves more easily to polyphonic treatment than they would do in more simple diatonic progressions. Chord progressions of relatively constant and similar tensions (according to Schönberg's theory, dissonances are equal to heightened consonances) demand new means of counteracting the greyness and uniformity of harmonic texture. Schönberg felt the need to reintroduce elements of strict counterpoint into his music. There are many examples of this in such works as the Five Orchestral Pieces, the opera, *Die glückliche Hand* and *Pierrot Lunaire*. For example, in the first movement of the Five Orchestral Pieces at Fig. 10, the trumpet plays a *cantus firmus*-like motif of ten bars in minims. This motif enters simultaneously in crotchets in the trombone part while at the same time the violins and violas play the motif as a canon at the octave in quavers. Eight bars later the strings bring a four-part canon of the motif at only a quaver's distance. Such adaptation of the principles of imitation to form the musical basis of the texture is one of the more simple examples of Schönberg's contrapuntal practices. He took the devices known to contrapuntalists farther than did even Bach in his most strict contrapuntal compositions. Besides making continous use of prolongation and contraction, canon, *fugato, passacaglia* and other contrapuntal forms, he introduced inversion, *cancrizans* and quite a number of even more obscure contrapuntal practices which had not been in use since works such as the *Musikalisches Opfer* and the *Hammerklavier* Sonata. In the times of Bach and Beethoven, the strict contrapuntal devices had been modified according to the principles of tonality. While this was essential for the expressiveness and perfection of the harmonic style, the musical form-giving significance of real counterpoint was weakened. For example, in Beethoven's Op. 135 Quartet, the interversions of the three-note motif are only of limited significance, the musical structure being achieved by other means. For Schönberg, such procedure had far more importance in that he treated the contrapuntal devices as form-giving elements in themselves. In doing this, he certainly made a major formal innovation within the principles of musical structure of his time, as such contrapuntal methods had hardly been used for three hundred years. Even now, only a few specialists know in any satisfactory detail the methods and procedures of the composers of early contrapuntal schools.

Schönberg went very far in the emphasis on counterpoint. His music was impelled more and more by purely contrapuntal means, rather than by a fusion of harmony with counterpoint, so that in certain passages he factually endangered the primarily harmonic validity apparent in the post-Wagnerian musical language. In this, he went farther than Mahler, who had also been working in this direction. Thus, comparing the *Adagio* of the Tenth Symphony, sketches of which were published after Mahler's death, with the first or last movements of his Ninth Symphony, which in its finished state it would no doubt have resembled, we see that Mahler still conceived his work in the first instance vertically and later dissolved it into polyphonic texture. But even in a work as early as Schönberg's Chamber Symphony, Op. 9, although it is still to a great extent conditioned by functional harmonic construction, many passages are no longer harmonically conceived, to such an extent are they primarily contrapuntal. The introduction of this rigid contrapuntal practice not only realised vertical combinations which were to become Schönberg's normal in later times, but also tended towards the even further liquidation and invalidity of other traditional formal principles. In the final works of this period the whole texture becomes so detailed, so attenuated and fragmentary, that harmonic development as it had been understood ever since the time of Bach virtually disappeared.

DEVELOPMENT TOWARDS TWELVE-NOTE SYSTEM

Among the younger generation, there is frequent criticism of Schön-berg's seeming lack of method in rhythmic construction. This criticism, made especially by non-German musicians, is based on a completely erroneous comparison between the characteristics of Schönberg's German cultural tradition and those of other national schools. We do not wish to minimise the validity of Stravinsky's rhythmic methods or the other forms of rhythmic construction resulting from stricter attention to the combination of numerical values. On the contrary, one may sympathise and find a development of this long-neglected aspect of musical composition desirable. But it is valueless to criticise a com-poser from a viewpoint he did not share and consequently could not consider. The thinking which led Messiaen and his school to their adop-tion of rhythmic composition and eventually to serial forms of rhythmic construction, could only have been alien to Schönberg even if known to him. It is important to remember that German music had always been rather simple in its rhythms—Luther's hymns had been a typically Protestant simplification of the subtle style of Gregorian chant. One need only look at the simple metres of German poetry of the Middle Ages, which always had a far more limited range of rhythmical interests than did that of other nations. The essence of German music can be found in rhythms of more or less regular patterns within binary and ternary forms. It was these, and not the more varied rhythms of the South or of the Slavs, which were in use in Germany throughout most of its musical history. The Germans wholeheartedly accepted the simple peasant dances of their own and neighbouring countries, and the March and *Ländler* form the main source of rhythmical inspiration in German music. (The other characteristic ingredient of German music, the sen-timental song, is to be found at a very early date in the *Locheimer Liederbuch;* its simple and primitive rhythm and its free layout became the main source of the characteristic singing melodies of the German slow movement.)

In the late eighteenth and early nineteenth centuries, the German composers developed a refined and subtle manner of using the few rhythmic elements which were known to them. The most astonishing examples are Haydn and above all Mozart, who brought to perfection a technique of composing with varied bar- and phrase-lengths. In doing this, they accorded with modern concepts concerning the nature of rhythm. Matila C. Ghyka, in his *Essai sur le Rythme* (Paris, 1938), quotes several remarkable definitions of rhythm, among them: 'Rhythm is in time what symmetry is in the Platonic sense, viz. the proportional arrangements of elements in space' (E. d'Eichtal). Again, Professor Sonnenschein (*What is Rhythm?* Oxford, 1925): 'Rhythm is that property of a sequence of events in time, which produces on the mind of the observer the impression of a proportion between the durations of the several events or groups of events of which the sequence is composed.' If we agree with these definitions or with the definition of James Joyce that rhythm is the relation of the parts to the whole, we find that in the music of the time of Mozart and Haydn, many elements contributed to the expression of the rhythmic structure. In a deceptively simple manner, Mozart manages to create a form which is built of asymmetric quantities. We find examples of the contractions and prolongations expressed not only in the juxtaposition of rhythmic elements, but also in the closely calculated interchanges of different types of musical texture (diatonic scales, chromatic scales, *arpeggios*, etc). Alban Berg in his article 'Why is the music of Schönberg so hard to understand?' draws attention to this characteristic of Mozart's music. He quotes the nineteenth-century German theorist, Büssler: 'The greatest masters of form cherish free and bold constructions and rebel against being squeezed into confines of even-numbered bar groups.' This method was further developed in the nineteenth century. The English writer C. F. Abdy Williams (*The Rhythm of Modern Music*, London, 1909) devotes a great deal of space to the analysis of the music of Brahms and others from this viewpoint. Wagner with the free declamatory style in his *Musikdrama* also contributed greatly to the freeing of the musical construction from the 'prison' of the regular bar groups.

Schönberg was particularly interested in these rhythmic methods and created forms in which the music became almost totally free of metre. In this way he composed *Pierrot Lunaire, Erwartung*, Four Orchestral Songs, Op. 22, and *Die glückliche Hand*, among other works. Later, with his adoption of twelve-note technique, it is a matter of great interest that he tended to abandon this style of 'musical prose' and in such works as the Piano Suite and the last two String Quartets, wrote phrases of varied lengths within a simple, almost static, rhythmical form. Here he is most closely allied to the eighteenth century. Whether this was a satisfactory development of the early twelve-note technique could be disputed, and it is certainly a proof of the clearsightedness and the genius of Schönberg that during the last years of his life he returned to the richer rhythmical structure of the works which he had written just before the adoption of the twelve-note system.

These rhythmic developments went hand in hand with Schönberg's development of the free-moving melody. Schubert, Schumann and Wagner had contributed towards a melody of great subjective expression. Schönberg, after Wagner and Hugo Wolf, introduced the wide spans of series of compound intervals into his melodies. Although chromatic elements, variations of character and creation of interval-contrasts are already well developed by Wagner in the singing line of the parts of *Brünnhilde* and *Isolde*, Schönberg's freeing of the octave led to a melos in which intervals appear as a result of melodic, as opposed to harmonic, elaborations and octave displacements. The abundance of passing notes and rhythmic decoration, in relation to the structural movement of harmony, which was a well-known characteristic of post-Wagnerian style, led Schönberg to a form of melody which, for the sake of tension and variety, carefully avoids the notes sounding in the supporting harmony and gets more and more shy of repeating notes.

Schönberg continued the endeavours of composers of the nineteenth century to expand and extend the existing forms of music. He went farther than Mahler, who had considerably developed traditional forms. At the turn of the century, the discovery by Freud of the existence of free associations and the consequent feeling for less logically and more subjectively connected associations in art had the greatest significance for the development of Expressionism. They led Schönberg to a greater degree of formal detail, an increasing amount of variation and a tendency to compress the single ideas of a piece into shorter spaces of time. In the first Chamber Symphony, although he is still working within a traditional form derived from the one-movement symphonic structure probably invented by Liszt, he liquidates many elements of this form and resorts frequently to a method which can be considered an equivalent to free association (Schönberg liked to call these passages, which one can already find in Mahler, *Inselbildung*). Gradually, his habit of rarely repeating any subject, even in a varied form, led to the difficulty of understanding Schönberg's music. This is certainly the underlying reason why the works of Schönberg are, and probably will continue to be, more difficult for the ordinary listener to appreciate than the music of Webern, Berg and other contemporary composers. Schönberg himself seemed conscious of, and disturbed by, this fact, and he adopted many methods, some successful, some less so, in his efforts to overcome these difficulties. Many of the innovations he introduced, culminating in that of the twelve-note technique, were designed to clarify and illuminate the highly individual development of his musical thinking. He dispenses with colour for its own sake and in his instrumentation uses the orchestra to bring the important lines of his musical argument into greater relief. At the same time he invented a new type of the application of orchestral colour, the *Klangfarbenmelodie* or melody of 'timbres', first to be found in a systematic application in the third of his Five Orchestral Pieces, *Farben*. The musical argument of this piece is carried by changes of emphasis in instrumental groups, creating an entirely new kind of expression. In the fifth piece, *Das obligate Rezitativ*, the instrumentation is used to give the melody a constantly changing colour. (This technique is obviously an extension of the Wagnerian *ewige Melodie*.) The result of this experiment is that the natural connections and logical developments in his music can sometimes be more easily understood by the ear than by the eye.

As we have shown with the development of his harmony and counterpoint, when Schönberg's works were no longer effectively bound by traditional structural forms, he was faced with the problem of finding suitable new forms. In his Six Little Piano Pieces, Op. 19, he attempted to restrict himself to the exposition and variation of one single idea. The best example is the last piece, allegedly inspired by Mahler's funeral, in which the alternation of chords and fragments of motifs, probably derived from the memory of bells, constitute the piece. In these pieces, Schönberg attempts something fundamentally different from the short pieces of Berg and Webern. Whereas Berg in his Clarinet Pieces tended to contract what had been large forms and Webern in many of his short pieces used traditional formal principles, which found here the utmost concentration imaginable, Schönberg made his ideas suitable to the limitations of a completely integrated short form. Later, when he attempted larger forms again, we find a seemingly chaotic juxtaposition of such short forms, and it is in these works that the most daring and far-developed examples of Schönberg's personal, essentially expressionistic, art are to be found. Yet they remain valid as a perfect development of the characteristic integration of form and content.

In order to conclude this part of the discussion, we shall examine a work which may be regarded as typical of the most advanced and most individual Schönberg ever reached: the monodrama in one act *Erwartung*. Unfortunately it is not possible here to go into sufficient detail to clarify all our opinions, but it is hoped that it will be sufficient to justify our argument.

The first reaction upon hearing *Erwartung* is the very antithesis of the experience when listening to the perfection and apparent Apollonian symmetry of the eighteenth-century classicists. That particular effect upon the listener of classical music at its zenith was obtained by a skilful balance of asymmetries and variants which was so well realised that it resulted in the illusion of perfect symmetry. The style of Schönberg's music tended to cover the well-calculated proportions in its texture which has, as has that of Wagner, an appearance of almost continuous unbroken movement. In *Erwartung* we experience a sense of being overwhelmed and lost in a maze of variation and juxtaposition of elements which are hardly memorable and result in a seeming structural incoherence. But as we know the composition better, we find that all these variants and 'free associations' are well moulded into an overall shape and can be understood in a similar way to the works in the style of the preceding post-Wagnerian era. Though the chordal structure is complex and the individual parts are heavily doubled in augmented fourths, sevenths, etc. (which in this case tend to loosen the vertical coherence), an arc is circumscribed and the basic tonal principle of movement away from and towards a point or centre is retained. The technique of the work does not in itself seem to be a new departure. The basic idea for such immensely long and involved tonal structures had already been developed by Wagner, Mahler and Strauss. The novelty of the aural harmony results from the development described above. One feels that Schönberg here already starts 'composing with notes'; that is, that he tended to replace triads as the functional agents with the identity of individual tones.

The music of *Erwartung* falls into two parts. The over-all 'top line' (Schenker might have called it *Urlinie*), whether expressed by the voice or by the instruments, is clearly delineated, although it cannot everywhere be found in the apparent main themes and motifs of the music. The first section commences with a progression from G sharp via B natural to C sharp at the beginning of the composition and closes at bar 270 at the words 'Nun küss ich mich an dir zum Tode'. The climax is reached at bar 194, at the cry 'Hilfe', an accent and leap down directly from the highest note of the voice part (B natural) to C sharp above middle C, a fall of well nigh two octaves. The second part proceeds from bar 270 to the end. The general division is a dramatic one; the first half consisting of the Search and Discovery of the lover's body and the subsequent dementia; the second part of a kind of *Liebestod* sung by the women in a fervid state of anguish and jealousy of the other 'She' (Death, who has taken her lover).

The orchestral introduction of four bars makes a clear movement from G sharp through B natural to C sharp (quasi-dominant/tonic). It is repeated in a contracted form, this time moving to the leading note C natural–B sharp); the soprano enters for the first time on C sharp. The first scene, as it were in closed form, is clearly founded on a structure in which the notes C sharp and G sharp are predominant. To add to the illusion of a closed form, many of the chords are retained literally and appear throughout the scene. Practically all important structural notes, the notes which begin and end all phrases, are C sharp and its neighbour notes. There is a movement towards an emphasis on the semitone below at bar 29 *et seq.*, but a clear return to the quasi-tonic of C sharp in the *codetta* of the scene, bar 35 *et seq.* In the following scenes there is a gradual heightening of tension. Twice high B flats in bars 153 and 179 lead to the cry 'Hilfe' in bar 190 on the high B natural which falls back to C sharp. This is the over-all climax and highest point of the melodic line. From here the melody falls, often in long leaps, back to the C sharp in bar 270. (It is interesting to observe the parallel of the falling minor sixth (A–C sharp) in bars 194 and 270, obviously characteristic as a cadential movement as well as a psychological weakening, a premonition of death.).

The second half commences from G sharp (the first note of bar 273 and 274) and moves up to the B flat of bar 313, cadencing back to G sharp at bar 317, just before the extraordinary bars where the voice sings the words 'Oh, der Mond schwankt. . . .' From here, the music falls again with greatly augmenting note values, to the dramatic point in bar 350 'für mich ist kein Platz da. . . .' The final section, which seems to act as a kind of spiritual resolution, lowers the tension by the introduction of chords of whole tone triads, which move in regular manner and, turning, reach again a section in which a C sharp seems to take its important position, introduced as a pedal in bar 416 and remaining a key note of the voice part, especially at the cadencing on 'dir entgegen . . .' in bars 422-3. The C sharp disappears completely in bar 424, allowing the bass to make a determined step towards B natural. The final solution comes in the contra bassoon's C sharp in the middle of bar 425, introduced most characteristically by the last melodic phrase of the opera. The voice, which had again taken the G sharp (quasi-dominant) at bar 424, continues in bar 425 to the last utterance and reaches by a tritonus step the G sharp, slightly later than the C sharp bass has been established by the bassoon. The oblique vertical resolution of the harmony is characteristic of Schönberg's methods. It is also not without importance that three trombones have the triad A, C sharp, F natural at the point where the contra bassoon reaches the C sharp in the higher octave.

It might seem that an analysis which is made in the ways briefly indicated above would have but limited validity in this type of music. Yet we feel that the replacing of a harmonically valid form by an overall melodic one, though it could not have the significance of the old forms, nevertheless enabled the composer to differentiate between sections which return to their starting-point and those which move away from it. This is of the greatest importance towards an understanding of the subsequent revolution in the manner of composing music. The position may be compared to that reached by Joyce in *Finnegan's Wake*. In this work, the author could hold the thread through the maze of images, diversions, etc., only by continuous and relatively unvaried repetition of the so-called story (the death and rebirth). The conclusion reached is that the method of free association could no longer in itself prove to be a satisfactory manner of creation. The artists concerned seem to have realised that to create wider and more variegated forms they needed some valid structural principle, which would enable them to give more finite form to the perpetual variants their expression demanded.

After the astonishing realisation of the last works described, it became apparent to Schönberg that to continue his musical creation he had now constantly and intellectually to develop the composition with twelve notes. He saw clearly that for a time he would have to apply this entirely new method to forms much less elaborate than those he had used before. He made concessions in using older and simpler forms which he had discarded for quite a time. Even the regular sonata form and the form of the classical variations were used again and again, but filled with the completely new content resulting from his now strict use of the twelve-note system. Although the last period of Schönberg's musical creation (which does not come within the scope of this article) must be considered quite as important as the earlier periods, and he achieved works which can in every way stand comparison with his earlier achievements, perhaps even in some cases surpassing them, the line of development in this last period is not as clearly definable as it had been earlier. While endeavouring to give older forms new content, Schönberg creates intermittently works which might at first sight appear to continue directly the style of the great expressionist compositions like *Pierrot Lunaire, Die glückliche Hand* and *Erwartung*—for example, *Ode to Napoleon, A Survivor from Warsaw* and especially parts of his opera, *Moses and Aaron*. But when observed and analysed in more detail, these works, although in effect and texture frequently reminiscent of works of an earlier period, speak in a completely new musical language and the use of the twelve-note system is here, quite naturally and logically, freer and less strict than in those works based on older forms (which, for want of a better word, may be described as 'neo-classicist'). Schönberg also, in some of the masterpieces of the last period (e.g. Orchestral Variations, Op. 31, and particularly *Moses and Aaron*), combines new forms, which he went on creating in direct continuation of his expressionist period, with more stylised classical sections. The introduction and the extraordinary finale of the Orchestral Variations, Op. 31, are much nearer to this free expression than the variations themselves, which are kept to a large extent within the classical frame. And in the opera, *Moses and Aaron,* for dramatic and other reasons—some of the material had been sketched many years earlier, during Schönberg's expressionist period—free forms, with all the manifold applications of *Inselbildungen* and purely linear-based formulations (as explained in our analysis of *Erwartung*) alternate with the more consolidated and simplified forms of the dance movements. Schönberg's treatment of harmony and counterpoint certainly went into a period of great simplification as soon as he had decided to compose in the strict twelve-note system. Harmonically, this system gave him security in its definite application, and in counterpoint he was no longer hampered by the unclear position in which the polyphonic style had been ever since the introduction of tonal and later functional harmony. In fact, only then did counterpoint regain the freedom and expression which it had had at the time of the early Flemish and Italian schools.

Schönberg's rhythm (except in those few compositions in which he kept very close to traditional dance or *Lied* forms) and basic adherence to musical prose was not developed much farther in his last period. Here and there a simplification may be observed, but seldom a further refinement. The tonal works of the last period need not be discussed here, as they were written partly for teaching purposes or as commissions for certain American institutions. And Schönberg has told us that several of these compositions, especially the very beautiful second Chamber Symphony, were based on material invented in his youth.

Schönberg was a master of German music. Even the fact that he spent the later part of his life in America in no way changed his determination to follow to the end logically and methodically what he felt was the right way (although living in America had considerably changed the style and attitude of many composers, e.g. Hindemith and Bartók). We should like to see in Schönberg's last achievement, the opera, *Moses and Aaron*, on which he worked practically all his life, the climax of his musical creation. Unfortunately he did not live to finish this work. The short experience we have of the opera (it has been performed only once so far, in 1954) gives us the impression that this is a work of supreme inspiration, perhaps Schönberg's greatest. Quite new experiences in sound, harmony and rhythm take us by surprise in the famous dances from the opera. The rhythm especially, as never before in Schönberg's works, moves in an orbit not far from Stravinsky's, and the whole expression is far more striking than in any of Schönberg's works after *Erwartung*.

We are not here concerned with the fact that Schönberg's work will always be much more difficult for the listener and the student than the works of his pupils and other contemporary composers. We do not think that this fact has anything to do with the greatness of his inspiration and fulfilment. It will always be amazing to observe the particular intellectual quality of Schönberg's compositions, their fast-moving sequence of thought and invention, their most imaginative colours of orchestration and the sometimes harsh and insistent reiteration of strong sounds and expressions. Just as we must recognise that Wagner's work, although prepared by many major innovators, was the culmination of nineteenth-century German music, we must without doubt recognise that Schönberg's achievements—his compositions, his teachings, his writings—as well as his personal seriousness and belief in his mission, make him surely the greatest and most important musician of the first half of the twentieth-century.

Alban Berg and Anton Webern

IAIN HAMILTON

ONE of the greatest stands ever taken by a creative artist was that taken by Schönberg. The results of his great faith in his ordering of the twelve notes of the scale and of his slowly evolved method of strict serial composition have, as yet, been only faintly discerned after thirty years. The potentialities of this system are greater than most musicians imagine. Two immediate facets of his work have been developed and thoroughly explored by Berg and Webern, and their work, particularly. that of Webern, has in turn led to some of the most advanced and challenging musical thinking of the present time. These two composers were not only pupils but ardent disciples of Schönberg. Working in close contact with him they not only adopted his new methods but contributed independently to the order which Schönberg, amongst several others, sought to impose on the chaos into which music was plunged at the end of the nineteenth century with the fall of the old diatonic régime.

The system of chords built in superimposed thirds had finally reached an impasse owing to the extreme chromaticism which had developed during the latter half of the century and which had shaken the foundations of the old major-minor tonal system. A similar impasse was reached in 1600 with the rejection of the old system of the church modes and in roughly 1750 with the move away from fugal and linear forms to those which culminate in the perfection of Sonata form.

In 1900 and long after, many composers still clung to the old system, and such composers as Richard Strauss, Sibelius and Rachmaninov were still able to use it in an alive and creative manner, but they stand at the very end of a long tradition as their dogged imitators were to discover. Other composers of this period of experiment gave themselves to the bizarre and new fashions at all costs and, as that has nothing to do with true creative work or artistic expression, they have passed into oblivion. Still other composers sought to combine what was undoubtedly the sincere attitude of the former group with new means of expression. They saw unlimited fields open to them when once the system of building chords in thirds had been opened up to include those derived from the other intervals.

Those whose new methods were founded on the sincerest and most serious basis have eventually had by far the greatest influence. Though the path for them may have been harder, the result has been infinitely richer. Stravinsky won early fame and has been an indefatigable explorer and creator. Bartók and Hindemith found acceptance of their methods and work harder, but none found their path so hard as Schönberg and his school, and, with the exception of Berg, they were to be almost continually hounded during their lifetime. Misunderstanding of their work and aims has been greatly aided by their numerous adherents who have so often confused the means with the end. Young composers who have avidly seized the method to cover their poverty of true inventiveness have helped in the general campaign towards misunderstanding and it has been left to surprisingly few to show how beautiful can be the results of working in this system when the system is entirely in the composer's control and not he controlled by it. Let us mention but one person here who is of these few, Luigi Dallapiccola.

If one approaches the work of Berg and Webern without former knowledge of it and with an open mind, and whether one enjoys the music or not, one finds at once in Berg an effusiveness that is not to be found in the economic texture of Webern. Strict twelve-note music is a highly chromatic music with no tonal centre, yet strict serial music can be of other kinds, and Stravinsky's recent use of serial techniques has revealed a serial diatonicism, music which is essentially tonal. The handling of the row itself is the interesting thing with these composers and particularly with Berg and Webern.

Fundamentally the school of Schönberg is romantic, with expressionism, highly charged textures with their infinite detail of dynamics, continually changing tempi and underlying introspection and eroticism all playing a part. Their literary taste bears witness to the emotions and sentiments which they are most keen to express. There is little here of the direct expression of lofty, noble or heroic motives, the assured faith of a Bach or a Beethoven in the purest and highest ideals

95

is not to find expression in the music of these composers. A certain classicism, a feeling of restrained emotions, is indeed to be found in Webern, but it is here to be found in almost microscopic form and the spaciousness required for the sentiments expressed in Beethoven, for instance, is therefore not to be found in the highly organised, almost intimate art of Webern.

The twelve-note school of composers has not yet produced a master of the completeness of those of the great classical tradition. It has succeeded as probably never before in the expression of the most intense emotion, introspection and sordidity, and in their choice of texts the composers have stressed their predilection for such emotions almost without exception. It has been an unfortunate trend of so much of the creative work of this century to regard this form of expression as the only true one, but an artist who *confines* himself to it is unable to manifest himself as a complete artist expressing a wide range of human emotion as did the great masters in all the arts in past time.

One must assess these two composers on what they have done, however, and not on what they have not done. They are both masterly figures and this mastery asserts itself in each one in an entirely different way. Berg does much to bridge the gap that is so often felt to exist between composers of this method of composition and those of the past. Webern, on the other hand, points directly to the future, and his treatment of the system is the gateway to so much of the most advanced and compelling musical exploration of today.

Alban Berg was born in Vienna on 9th February, 1885, of a family of comfortable means, and his life shows many signs of a happy background. His thorough training under Schönberg and their resultant deep friendship, his happy marriage contracted in 1911, together with the international success accorded to his work during his lifetime—these are not features of the lives of many composers, certainly not of those whose methods are extreme.

Before the age of fifteen he had written some seventy songs and duets without any musical training. This concentration on vocal music is interesting, for whereas most of the twentieth century composers, particularly the leading figures, Stravinsky, Bartók and Hindemith, have tried to divorce music from the various literary, philosophical and mystical associations which it acquired during the nineteenth-century, the Schönberg school is in this respect more allied to the immediate past. With regard to literary influence they are ultra-romantic and expressionist. Also for reasons of form in their early experiments with the new technique they found the basis of a poem essential as a means of architectural unity, something which at once stresses the music's need of something other than music itself even in such fundamental matter as form. This romanticism is, of course, not that of the heroic and grandiose flights of Strauss or Wagner, it is a mystical, dark, morbid, unearthly thing more akin to a certain side of Schumann. Religious influence is felt heavily in the work of Schönberg and to a lesser extent in that of Webern, but hardly at all in Berg, yet his use of the choral 'Es ist genug' which is closely woven into the final pages of the haunting Violin Concerto like a priceless gold thread is as moving in a devotional sense as anything in the work of his two confederates.

In the autumn of 1904 Berg met Schönberg, and this meeting was decisive as Berg became his pupil for the next six years. One has only the deepest admiration for Schönberg's rigorous methods of training. His *Theory of Harmony* and the much more recent *Structural Functions of Harmony* show his infinite understanding of every manifestation of the traditional system of harmony, its function in the works of various classical masters and its final disintegration into total chromaticism. Let this great musician's severe system of training and his logic and understanding as set down in these two books be contrasted with the aimless, pointless misguidance offered to most students by harmony teachers who can only think of harmony as a set of dull symbols in an eight-bar exercise and not in relation to its function in the great masterpieces themselves. Let it also stand as a model to ill-advised young people who 'adopt' twelve-tone methods before they have even a fresh idea to bring to the setting of a chorale or a folksong. Schönberg himself would never give instruction in serial composition and had no use for those who sought to employ it before they had worked through a long and complete training to the rank of true professional quality.

Thus were Berg and Webern trained and thus we find them as complete masters of their material and of its manner of presentation. The high professional standards of the Viennese school of 1800 had not declined by 1900. Between the master and his two pupils developed a lifelong and devoted friendship as well as between the two pupils themselves. The qualities of loyalty, respect and admiration which they felt for each other and put into practice are matters to be reflected on with pleasure.

While a pupil Berg began his short but magnificent list of works. That of Webern is longer, but each work in itself is infinitely shorter. Berg's list is shorter, his individual works longer. *Wozzeck* and the

Chamber Concerto are as unthinkable in the oeuvre of Webern as are the Bagatelles for String Quartet, Op. 9, in that of Berg. The Seven Early Songs (not orchestrated until 1930), the Piano Sonata and the String Quartet date from this period of study. Several lasting influences and characteristics already appear in these works. Berg's later intense treatment of the vocal line is seen in the songs to arise directly from the *lieder* style of the nineteenth century, particularly from that of Brahms. These songs offer us more direct stylistic influences than anything which is to follow. Brahms, Strauss and Debussy lie behind much of this music.

The first three songs of Op. 2 for soprano and piano, as well as the Seven Early Songs, employ key signatures and are decidedly tonal; the last song of Op. 2 and the Piano Sonata are without key signatures but are almost equally tonal. In the Quartet, Op. 3, however, there is a definite move away to a less clearly defined tonality which points to the following group of works and eventually to *Wozzeck*.

In the Sonata and in the Quartet one finds a fine sense of form. Accepted forms are used in a new way, giving the music a shape which the listener can grasp; this strong element of form in Berg's work has done much to win a wider acceptance of his music. In the Quartet come the first examples of his building of enormous emotional climaxes. These are evolved with a logic of part-writing, a rhythmic tautness and an intensity of feeling which, in the later works, make one shudder. The sureness of touch and complete certainty of what he wishes to say give Berg's music an elemental power of the most shattering nature for all its complexity of texture. In these early works there is also a dramatic factor which is an element of that romanticism which goes back by way of Mahler to *Tristan*. This dramatic power is later to make *Wozzeck* into something achieved by so few contemporary operas, a piece which comes off completely in the theatre and moves even those who would find Berg's music itself hard to grasp in the concert hall.

As a colourist Berg is unique. His treatment is highly virtuosic, as is his treatment of every medium in which he works. His colourful harmonic and melodic palette, allied to this and his fantastic imagination, produce dazzling colours and textures.

In a group of works written between 1912 and 1914 Berg developed still farther along these same lines. This group consists of the Five Orchestral Songs, Op. 4, the Four Pieces for Clarinet and Piano, Op. 5, and the Three Pieces for Orchestra, Op. 6. Here for the first time Berg is using the orchestra, an immense one, as was the fashion of the time, including quadruple woodwind, six horns, four each of trumpets and trombones, two harps and an enormous percussion section. The complexity of this work is very great, but every page reveals the same clarity of conception and execution which one finds in a large impressionistic score of Debussy or in such a web of sound as Stravinsky's *Fire Bird*—two works with which it is interesting to compare this score. Another interesting comparison may be made with the early Four Orchestral Pieces, Op. 12, of Bartók written at about the same time. Here, as in the clarinet pieces, the move away from tonality is very great, but there is typically always a glimpse of it to be found and the second of the clarinet pieces centres firmly round D. In these pieces wonderful sonorities are used, and the use of the piano is masterly in its complete understanding of what the instrument can do and where its beauties lie. So much later serial music is to find no very happy medium in the piano, an instrument which becomes it far less well than, for example, the medium of the String Quartet.

Berg's great ability to create a highly evocative atmosphere is very evident in these three works and this together with the other elements of his style already mentioned leave him in a position of great mastery. These various features coalesce in his next work, the opera, *Wozzeck*.

From 1915 to 1917 Berg worked on the text of his opera, which he himself compiled from the fragments of George Büchner's drama. He finally evolved a libretto which is a model of conciseness and direct simplicity. It is divided into fifteen scenes which are grouped into three Acts. These are in themselves quite short, and deal mostly one by one with a single aspect of the unfolding tragedy or of part of its development, very often between only two characters at a time. There are few large-scale concerted dramatic scenes—the influence is Wagner, for instance, far more than Verdi.

This was one of many ways taken by Berg to solve the problem facing him now that he had evolved a style in which he could no longer avail himself of the vital element of all earlier music—that of key-relationship and tonality as the foundation of all form. Up till this time, and for some time to come, his music is not of course twelve-tone in the serial sense. Not until the Lyric Suite of 1925–26 will Berg finally adopt this system of organisation and thereafter retain it as a basic part of his style no matter how freely and personally employed. Tonality is, however, in *Wozzeck* almost non-existent. There are admittedly places where it is strongly felt, as in the D minor entr'acte before the final scene and in the choruses in the tavern scene, and there are countless examples of bitonality throughout the whole work, but these are only short passages in the whole. The problem is still greater when one takes into account the fact that the entire work is based on instrumental forms of the past which are wholly reliant on tonality and the contrast of key-centres which it affords. These forms in his work naturally lose a considerable amount of their logic and strength, but he felt the need for them, and his use of them is remarkable in a position which is in part one of compromise. By many ardent followers of Webern, particularly by many who cling to him for what they do not understand, such a trend in the music of Berg is held to be something at which to shake one's head, but one wonders what these critics would have had Berg do. He found this manner of allying elements of past forms to elements in his own personal style a means of giving it shape and a sense of direction. Webern's ways were far less compromising. Both produced works of complete sincerity and, no matter how long is spent on judging a work by the means whereby the end is attained, a process which any masterpiece can well withstand, the end alone is of consequence.

The problem, then, of giving unity and variety to a work in the large form of opera is solved by Berg by employing smaller instrumental forms in the fifteen individual scenes which make up the whole. The first Act uses suite form and contains a rhapsody, a military march, a lullaby, a *passacaglia* and a *rondo*. In Act Two symphonic form is employed with movements in the form of fantasia and fugue, Largo, *scherzo* and *rondo*. In Act Three inventions are the basis.

These forms were considered as purely functional by the composer, and he had no desire that the audience should prepossess itself with such purely musical features of the work, but that they should listen to it as a dramatic work in the theatre. Berg himself never allows his attention to the handling of the musical forms themselves to overcome his handling of the dramatic situations, and that is why the piece is so very successful as an opera quite apart from its musical merits. The piano score was finished in 1920; the work orchestrated in 1921. In 1922 the piano score went the rounds of the German opera houses but without success, and Hermann Scherchen suggested to the composer that he extract a suite from the opera to be played in concert halls. This was duly done and given with great success under Scherchen in 1924. This finally made Berg's name and the performance of the complete opera in Berlin under Kleiber in 1925 placed him amongst the most controversial and esteemed figures of the time. One hundred and sixty-six performances took place in Europe and in America before his death in 1935.

Wozzeck remains for all time one of the most evocative of operas. It is the most ultra-expressionistic work which defines almost to break-ing-point the neurotic surgings which Wagner had first stated in *Tristan.* The disintegration of *Wozzeck* could never before have found such a parallel in music as it did in Berg's style. The symbolism of the setting sun, of the watery death, the unbridled lust and the diseased minds of the characters, the emphasis on ferment, decay and death before the final and so utterly romantic, transfiguration—all these find complete and masterly expression in this unique and tragic opera. Tragedy is here revealed in the lowest grades of humanity; that, how-ever, makes it no less poignant, for the suffering and death of the humblest, most wretched man will ever remain a tragedy.

The return of Berg to composition in the purely instrumental forms in the Chamber Concerto and in the Lyric Suite after the opera is understandable. The opera had set many problems and the composer had handled these with great assurance and care, but the problem of unity and shape in this highly chromatic style was not yet solved as he wished it. The Chamber Concerto composed between 1923 and 1925 is for solo violin and piano with a chamber orchestra of thirteen wind instruments. The first movement is for piano and orchestra, the second, a slow one, for violin and orchestra, and the last for all combined. In the first movement, a set of variations, the piano, as is too often the case with composers of this school, indulges in full heavy writing which least well suits this very chromatic style. Webern is to show a fuller sense of the piano's subleties in his work and Berg had done so already in the earlier works, but here the jagged writing is apt to pall, after a while, and seem colourless.

The slow movement, on the other hand, is, although very long, a beautiful piece of writing. The orchestra here as throughout the work is expertly handled and achieves the most wonderful textures and sounds against which the solo violin soars and arabesques with the greatest eloquence: Even this work does not pass without its dramatic moments. The most effective is the solo violin's entry, which is most arresting, and the climaxes are there as always in Berg in the most exciting manner.

With the Lyric Suite for String Quartet of 1925-26, Berg was to achieve one of his greatest successes. This work is remarkable in its resourceful and imaginative employment of the medium of the string quartet, for although verging on the extremes of what a quartet can do, it never passes into the realm of orchestral textures but realises fully the utmost to be got out of every member of the ensemble. Bartók and Schönberg realised this factor no less, and Webern does so in an entirely different way, using the minimum of notes invested with every conceivable effect and nuance.

The technique used bears many resemblances with that of the early String Quartet, particularly as regards handling the fullest possible textures in every grade of dynamics. The style now is much more defined and the form clear and logical throughout the entire work. The over-all form shows the first, third and fifth movements each written at a faster tempo, while the second, fourth and sixth are each at a slower tempo. The final movement includes the opening phrase of the prelude to *Tristan* in the form of *Klangfarbenmelodie*, that is the melodic line being run through the various instrumental colours, each playing possibly only one or two notes of the theme at a time and passing it note by note from one instrument to the other as it proceeds. This is one of the features of Schönberg's serial technique and is to become an integral part of the highly economic art of Webern.

Berg and Webern were immediate followers of Schönberg in his final synthesis of the principles of serial composition which he reached in 1923. Berg's first work which shows him using the system in his highly individual way is the Lyric Suite. The first and sixth movements are written wholly in this system as are also the main part of the third and the middle section of the fifth. Each successive movement also utilises material from that preceding it. From this time onwards Berg is to work exclusively within this system of compositional organisation. This, however, in Berg's case does not mean that we shall never again meet recognisable chords, even if these are used mostly in a bitonal way, or that we shall never see anything resembling a scale in his music—the basic row of the concert aria 'Der Wein' is largely a rising harmonic minor scale of D. To almost all listeners, in fact, the difference will not be in any way noticeable and that is precisely how it should be, for we must listen to what the works try to express as music, not as examples of a system. The incorporation of the *Tristan* excerpt and of the folksong and the chorale 'Es ist genug' in the Violin Concerto are proof of how complete is the composer's control of the means he employs. These interpolations do not obtrude, but merge naturally with the texture. The tonal elements still asserting themselves in Berg and in Schönberg are interesting, for they suggest an allegiance to and a natural derivation from the late nineteenth century which is almost wholly absent from the work of Webern. His tradition is much more that of the fifteenth and sixteenth centuries certainly as regards his contrapuntal usage, which is a highly organised and rigid one, as was that of the Netherlands school. The counterpoint of Schönberg and Berg, on the other hand, derives from Wagner by way of Mahler, whose shade lies heavily over much of the music of this school and who was one of their strongest protagonists although, of course, long before the serial methods had been finally evolved. It is interesting to find *Wozzeck* dedicated to Mahler's widow.

The unfinished opera *Lulu* occupied Berg until the end of his life in 1935. During this period he composed two other works, amongst the finest he ever wrote, the concert aria 'Der Wein' and the Violin Concerto. 'Der Wein', to a text by Baudelaire, has been described as a study for *Lulu*. More so than the Lyric Suite, it is a fine example of the tonal side in Berg's later work after his adoption of the serial method of composition. The row of this aria and that of the Violin Concerto are remarkable for their tonal structure and this pervades the whole of each work as a result. The fact that the first seven notes of the row of 'Der Wein' are the rising harmonic minor scale of D does not, of course, mean that we shall encounter a feeling of D minor, such as we should expect to find in Mahler or Strauss; but it means that many of the melodic lines in the work will move by interval relationship based on the original row, or some form of its inversion; and this recognisable scale-like movement will forge a link between this style and certain elements in music of the past. But the vertical relationship will, however, be entirely different, for in Berg there will be very little connection with harmonies built in superimposed thirds. Instead we shall have a harmonic texture of greater complexity, and bitonal elements will be the nearest we shall really ever have to anything harmonically resembling the components of the older system.

This work shows a very important feature of all creative twelve-note composition, the row is not a mere functional series of notes and intervals, but a melodic idea from which the whole work springs. Schönberg always stressed this point and Berg here gives one of the finest examples of its application. It is stated in the lower regions of the orchestral introduction and then used as the first theme, of what is really a sonata form movement, given to the solo voice on its entry. A subject in tango rhythm follows and finally a third idea in rising minor thirds. The development section is a whirling *scherzo* and in the recapitulation there is a reversal of the themes of the exposition, the third changing places with the first, which on its entry is combined with the orchestral introduction. This is the larger symmetry somewhat akin to that practised by Honegger who advocated the return of the second subject always before that of the first. There is apt to be confusion here between the symmetry in time and symmetry in space, but only the barest elements of real sonata form exist in Berg and a readjustment such as this is apt to tauten the form rather than loosen it. One always has to remember that these forms have lost their full meaning in any case with the abandonment of tonality.

The orchestration of this aria is lucid in an almost uncanny manner. The texture is immensely complex and full yet never thick. It must be the clearest complexity ever achieved since the overthrow of the older methods. One is nevertheless very often reminded of the taut, almost breakable, texture of so much of Mahler's music. This is the nearest parallel there is in traditional music. The language, on the other hand, and often the lie of the vocal line, is Wagnerian and in this work one sees vividly Berg's two immediate descendants. Many of Berg's personal traits in scoring are highly in evidence here, the love of endless passages for muted trumpets, the delicate texture of the string writing and the economic and effective use of solo piano and the saxophone. This texture even at its wildest never becomes harsh or jagged. Here is the complete opposite of Stravinsky and Bartók, with their pungent rhythms hurled at us in blazing and stabbing orchestration. Besides this, Berg is of an almost unbearable refinement and sensitivity; over the whole lies a sheen of something almost unreal—unearthly.

It is in the opera, *Lulu*, based on the tragedies, *Erdgeist* and *Pandora's Box* of Wedekind, that one discerns some of the most amazing developments in the composer's work, and we wonder what new things he might have done had he not died at the age of fifty. There is here a simplicity at times and a form of directness which is not to be found in his earlier work to the same extent. The forms are not only instrumental as in *Wozzeck*, such as sonata, canon and *ostinato*, but vocal such as *Canzonetta*, *cavatina*, hymn, *arioso* and chorale as well as many passages marked *recitativo*, a full sextet and many duets. In the scene with jazz band there is a ragtime and an English waltz.

The stylistic developments are to be found in the clearer harmonic texture, considerable use of the whole-tone scale and an immense use of bitonality which at times remind one of the methods of Honegger and Milhaud. Considerable use of plain choral passages culminates in that built of chords without thirds in Act Two beginning on a chord A and converging. Later there is an equally definite anchorage on a chord of B flat. Triads are used in thousands in this work, but it is as if they had attained outer space; for they are unrelated to a bass which in classical harmony acts as the force of gravity, and they seem now to be related to each other horizontally and much less seldom vertically. Their use in streams and particularly the use of streams of more clustered chords are interesting in relation to the work of Olivier Messiaen. The triad bitonal accompaniment to the quartet in Act Two is astonishingly conceived within the twelve-tone methods. This work, more than the Violin Concerto, reveals the infinite resource and imagination of Berg, as well as numerous points in the score, adequate assessment of which would require a volume.

Lulu he finished in piano score but not completely in full score as regards the third Act. A suite was drawn from it as with *Wozzeck* and was performed under Kleiber in Berlin in 1934. This was the last work of his own compositions that the composer was to hear, for he was stricken by a long and painful illness from which he died in the following year. In these last two works Berg used greatly the principle of taking, for example, every third or fifth note of the original row and thus, by going through the row again and again, he was able to derive new rows from the original. In the Violin Concerto his use of this means applied to a row built largely in thirds and whole tones produces a luminous texture of the most entrancing sounds.

On hearing of the death of Manon Gropius, the daughter of Mahler's widow, at the early age of seventeen, Berg was so intensely moved that the concerto on which he was working became a memorial to this beautiful young girl and was composed in a remarkably short time. The opening of the concerto is one of the most haunting pages in all music. The work is cast in two movements, each of them in two parts. In the final section the old choral 'Es ist genug' is woven into the texture and completes in a moving manner a most beautiful and elegiac work.

But Alan Berg was to die before he heard either this concerto or *Lulu*. When we remember, however, the rigours and strife that greeted the performances of the works of his devoted friends and fellow-artists, Schönberg and Webern, on so many occasions, it is with pleasure and relief that we recall the many successes his works won him during his life. Only in Vienna did he find success difficult to achieve, as did Webern even after considerable recognition abroad. But how cruel Vienna has been in the history of its high days to so many of its great composers. Mozart, Beethoven, Schubert, Schönberg, Webern, Berg—

all of them shamefully ignored when their fame was spread far afield. Yet with the exception of Schönberg they remained there all their lives, refusing fine offers to settle elsewhere. But when the new Vienna opera opened its doors in 1955 it was with *Fidelio* and with *Don Giovanni* that the consecration was made and not with a piece by one of those who delighted the Viennese when a little more of their attention or discernment might have eased the lives of two of the greatest artists of all time. And then only a few days after these two works came *Wozzeck* and who would not say that the wheel had turned full circle on Vienna?

As compared with the art of Berg, that of Anton Webern is one of infinite economy, condensation and cohesion. There is in his mature work nothing extraneous and the utmost sensitivity of ear and imagination endow isolated notes with an importance and expressiveness never conceived before in the history of music. Three elements are of outstanding importance in his work—an oeuvre of remarkable consistency and economy. Firstly the employment of canonic devices in combination with serial techniques; secondly his own development of *Klangfarbenmelodie* and thirdly the perfection of the smaller symmetry.

The use of canon is an outcome of his immersion in mediaeval music during his period of study in the University of Vienna for his Ph.D. in musicology under Guido Adler. This element features early in his output in his Op. 2, though not here allied to serial methods with which he will eventually combine it and reach the full maturity of his style from Op. 21 onwards. The perfection of the smaller symmetry is the logical outcome of these canonic principles, being used by a composer working in minute forms which are sometimes only ten bars long. A difference between this small form and that of, say, the small forms of the past must be stressed at once. The previous small forms had been largely song forms or their equivalent in which any form of development was out of place—they were essentially lyric pieces. No matter how fine these pieces may be they cannot attain to the stature or complexity of the larger forms; indeed the composers never intended that they should be regarded in this manner.

Entirely different from this is Webern's smaller symmetry. Here is a highly developed structure and form of expression in microcosm: each cell a perfect whole and related in the subtlest and most logical manner to the whole. In the Symphony, the Concerto, Op. 24, the Piano Variations, Op. 27, and the Quartet, Op. 28, we shall find the mirror canon in particular a highly vital part of this close-knit formal unity.

The *Klangfarbenmelodie* is employed at its subtlest in Webern and in the Symphony, Op. 21, the lines are cross-sectioned through the orchestra in a remarkable way. The apparent isolated notes here and there, first on one instrument and then on another, which one meets in every mature work of Webern, are nothing less than successive notes of the melodic lines which are traced and retraced through the various parts of the orchestra. This is a new form of colour but used in the finest sense as a natural outcome of the musical substance itself. This is very far removed from the highly complex textures of Berg and Schönberg.

The result of these very radical and economic trends is one of infinite wealth of expression in a field hitherto almost wholly unexplored. Those who look for the form of expression one finds in the spaciousness of the works of Beethoven will certainly approach Webern in entirely the wrong way. Proportionately everything is here and the logic and imagination are in no way hindered by what is to him a natural and congenial field in which to work. The most approachable examples are the second and fourth movements of the Five Pieces for String Quartet, Op. 5. These are more moving and profound in their wealth of expression than many a ten-minute movement and yet are only fourteen and thirteen bars long respectively. Through these and one or two other earlier works one is able to come to the later works of his mature period with an approach which is logical in that it is not anticipating what it could not possibly find.

Webern at one stage in his life took part in much of the intellectual life of Vienna, although later he retired from these circles and, living at Mödling, devoted himself to composition and teaching. He had his portrait done by Kokoschka and had contact with the eminent writer Robert Musil. There seems to be more in common between Berg and the creator of the extraordinary Moosbrugger, however, than between the latter and Webern. Oddly enough, because of its period one expects Musil's *Man without Qualities* to be heavy and, because of its length, verbose. It is really neither and has a curiously heady unearthliness about it which is decidedly Bergian.

It is impossible to think of so much of the work of Webern without immediately calling to mind the work of Paul Klee. The minute, sensitive purity of vision and its realisation through a remarkable technique, are uncannily paralleled in Webern's purity of sound and his translation of this into his works by a technique no less superb than that of Klee. Klee's masterly and ethical essay on painting is in so many ways applicable to the aims and ideals of Webern, at least in so far as we are able to divine them from his oeuvre itself. Both remain as two of the sincerest and most radical figures of the century. In relation to this it is interesting to note certain elements in the later works of Debussy and in particular the Cello Sonata. These cannot have affected Webern, of course, as the Debussy Sonata dates from 1915, while many of the Webern works in question were composed as early as 1909. The affinity lies in the refinement in texture and the emphasis given to the individual note in a manner hardly touched on before; or is there already somewhere a zealous soul analysing and relating those amazingly used isolated notes in the woodwind and brass in the development section of the overture to *A Midsummer Night's Dream*? This would be as pointless as the craze for turning Beethoven and Mozart into users of serial techniques, a craze which is keeping so many people very busy just now. The affinity with certain things in Debussy is much sounder; it is as if something of this kind were in the air at that time. And, after all, Debussy was one of the greatest contributors to the emancipation of harmony away from the hidebound rules of the past and a great freeing influence on the bonds of tonality—the total whole-toneness of the prelude *Voiles* allows it to be virtually in no key at all.

A man of great intellect and breadth of culture, Webern therefore began his career equipped with logic and balance in his mind; to this he brought a natural imagination and an ear of the highest sensitivity. There has been, as there is inevitably bound to be about such a great and controversial figure, far too much nonsense talked and written. Isolated events and personal idiosyncrasies have been blown up and forced before us in a manner quite out of proportion to his real greatness and worth. These details may interest us; they should not, as they may tend to, render farcical what are elements of great musicianship and finessé in a highly creative mind.

Anton Webern was born in Vienna in 1883. He did a research degree in musicology under Guido Adler, taking his Ph.D. in 1906. He was then for some time a theatre conductor in Germany and in Prague, that city which recognised so much in such composers as Mozart, Beethoven and Mahler that Vienna was to discover only much later. Webern's recognition in his native town was never great, but in 1918 when Schönberg organised his Society for Private Performances, Webern supervised many of these concerts. He was also the conductor of the Vienna Workers' Symphony Concerts and he founded the Kunstelle choir. He also conducted on the Vienna radio and a great deal abroad. In 1918 he moved to Mödling where he composed and taught. His life was uneventful save for the storms often occasioned over performances of his works and save for his tragic death.

His creative life is of remarkable consistency and purpose for that of a twentieth-century composer. His Op. 1, a *passacaglia* for Orchestra, is the only work with marked traditional influences and these are often quite Brahmsian. The very D minor feel of much of the music and the large texture and scale are features hardly ever touched on again in his work. Yet side by side are many elements of his later style. There is the translucent scoring, at times like impressionism and Brahms at once; there is the contrapuntal feel of most of the music; the use of triplets, something which is to become such an important factor in his later rhythmic texture; there is the importance vested in the single note and the copious use of rests, mutes and wide-leaping parts.

Webern became Schönberg's first pupil and studied for four years with him. He was his keenest disciple. The first product of this is Op. 2, an unaccompanied choral work 'Entflieht auf Leichten Kähnen' of 1908. Here at once he establishes so much of his later highly personal idiom: the use of strict canon throughout almost every bar of the piece, the brevity (it lasts only two and a half minutes), the much freer use of tonality employing many bitonal combinations and the use of different metronome markings for almost every bar. These various features are even more clearly defined in the five songs of Stefan George of Op. 3 for Soprano and Piano. The bitonality is here again, they are tonally freer and each piece is shorter.

The five movements for String Quartet, Op. 5, of 1909, are still freer and the principles of the smaller symmetry are already being explored with the use of small imitative figures which are developed at once, whereupon the method of immediate development is applied to another cell. This is what Webern himself said of Schönberg's Op. 11 piano pieces: 'No motive is developed (here Webern infers development in the classical sense which is not that of immediate development except for instances in Schubert): at most a brief progression is immediately repeated. Once stated, the theme expresses all it has to say: it must be followed by something fresh.' The texture in these five pieces is fascinating, and every device of string technique is employed but in an entirely different way from Berg, Stravinsky or Bartók—all highly resourceful in their employment of string instruments. Webern's favourite intervals of the major seventh and the minor ninth are often to be heard in this work.

The intense but economic beauty of the second, fourth and fifth movements is comparable to that of the evocative scene in the first Act of *Wozzeck* in which Wozzeck and Andres are cutting sticks at sunset. This mood has never been caught so well as by these two composers. Already the individual note is being given its full effect; an odd cello *pizzicato* quaver or a few *pizzicatos* on the viola in the middle of the fourth movement. The first and third movements are less fine than this. They are faster and the third in particular is over all too quickly in relation to its neighbours. The tonality in these pieces is almost non-existent.

In the Six Pieces for Orchestra, Op. 6, Webern applies his newly evolved concise style to a mammoth orchestra of quadruple woodwind, six each of trumpets, horns and trombones, etc. The climaxes are enormous, especially in such short pieces, for the whole work lasts only six and a half minutes. In the third the celli have only one note to play. In the fourth there is a very poignant funeral march. Fantastic sonorities are achieved, but the architecture, especially for Webern, largely disappears in favour of colour and sonorities—in fact it is a kind of impressionism.

The Op. 7 pieces for violin and piano are minute. The crescendi are now used within the bar and here we have the first examples of the composer in his smallest dominion. The texture, however, is still large harmonically and the lyrical element of Op. 5 is missing. The two Rilke songs, Op. 8, show for the first time Webern's cruelly wide-leaping vocal style. This must always remain a problem for singers; the adjustment from one register has to be made in a flash and then the readjustment back to the original register has to be made almost at once. These songs are accompanied by nine instruments: clarinet and bass clarinet, horn, trumpet, celesta, harp, and string trio. These unusual chamber groupings are to be a feature of Webern's work and this combination is highly novel for 1910. The large and regular forces have now been renounced by him in line with the evolution of his form of expression, which is of a concentrated intensity hardly ever met before. The use of the larger forces, larger textures or larger symmetries are as alien to him as they are congenial to Schönberg and Berg.

It is in the Six Bagatelles for String Quartet, Op. 9, of 1913, that Webern states his ultimate point in the minute forms. The number of bars in the movements are respectively: 10.8.9.8.13.9. This is also the first real statement of his use of *Klangfarbenmelodie* as an integral part of the structure. Sensitive playing will show a line between these apparently unrelated notes. A melodic line is traced through the texture, and unless this is understood and realised in performance, no convincing account of the work could be given. The quartet of players is here unified to the function of one player. Each quaver has its own dynamic marking and intensity. So much of the work of Pierre Boulez and Karl Heinz Stockhausen and the work in electronic music is a logical development of this vital feature which is to become purified and mastered in Webern's later works.

The Five Orchestral Pieces, Op. 10, are for twenty-two players and include guitar, mandoline and harmonium, bells and xylophone amongst a chamber group of instruments. They are equally terse, the fourth is only six bars long and its dynamic range *pp* to *ppp*. Only one of the pieces exceeds fourteen bars in length. The disintegration of music as it was conceived previously is here complete. These pieces caused a sensation when performed at the Zürich festival in 1926. The Four Songs of Op. 12 are again in this small idiom, but the scale is slightly larger. The piano part is more chordal than is usual in Webern, but the texture is lucid in the extreme. The Four Songs with Chamber Orchestra, Op. 13, enlarges the scale still further and the first and last items each last five minutes. The *Klangfarbenmelodie* is here beautifully applied to the chamber group, the economic use of celesta and harp is interesting and damping is used in the extreme; in Webern the brass is almost always damped.

The Six Songs of Op. 14 are highly complex and are accompanied by clarinet alternating with bass clarinet, violin and cello. The integration is here arrested, for these are highly organised and coherent pieces. The tendency to individualise each note dynamically is further developed as is the use of triplets in combination. The vocal writing here is often of ferocious difficulty and this also applies to the Five Songs of Op. 15. These are slightly less complex, but the double canon by contrary motion in the fifth song is a landmark in the composer's work and leads straight to the Five Canons for Voice and Three Clarinets of Op. 16 (1924) and thence to so much in his full maturity. These songs of Op. 16 are the strictest canons in various combinations and have a vocal line of unbelievable difficulty. The final bars are quite startling.

That this work should precede the first work in which Webern makes use of serial technique, the Three Songs, Op. 17, of 1924, is of great interest as the serial and canonic elements are now to combine and dominate everything in the maturing of his style, especially in his use of mirror canon. Without these two factors the mirror symmetries would be impossible and Webern as the master of the smaller symmetries unthinkable.

After these developments one comes upon the String Trio, Op. 20, of 1927, with something of a surprise, for outwardly here are the larger forms of *rondo* and sonata even to the extent of using double bar and repeat. But when one examines the actual evolution of the material it is at variance with the principles of the classical methods of development. The immediate development of scraps of material is used continually within the larger framework. The row also is used in a concentrated and close style, as is always the case with Webern, and this is something incompatible with the whole idea and aim of classical form. The work makes far greater sense in the line of the composer's evolution if one considers it as an attempt to align his very original and personal idiom with the larger forms. This is the one occasion on which he attempted to do this and it does not wholly succeed as it seems too much of a compromise in comparison with such a work as the Symphony, Op. 21, which follows it. The texture of the trio is very complex and interpolated harmonics and grace-notes give its texture an even greater degree of fantasy. The finale is of the greatest difficulty from every point of view.

The Symphony is exactly the opposite. Here is the surest mastery and maturity, so far hinted at often but never sustained throughout the length of a whole work. This work is the outcome of the Op. 16 and 17. Here also is a classical poise and clarity of mind. Every note is of consequence and the use of mirror canons has the direct simplicity that only a great mind and experience could conceive. The first has the over-all shape of sonata form but is entirely evolved from close canonic devices and the *Klangfarbenmelodie* is now perfected, the line being shot with the most delicate colours and tracing through the orchestra, thus uniting material, texture and scoring as logically as in Bach or Beethoven although in an entirely different manner. The work is scored for clarinet and bass clarinet, two horns, and string quartet. Its duration is only ten minutes.

The canons of the first movement are surpassed by the mirror canon variations of the second and last movement. In this each variation is a perfectly symmetrical mirror canon. The coda's mirror hinges on a bar of silence and even each half of the coda contains in itself a bar of silence. The scoring and texture are as near to the individualised note style as he has yet attained and it is imperative that one thinks of each of these notes in relation to others and not as isolated notes without context. This, one feels, is the result of Webern's incredibly sensitive ear; it has nothing to do with mere graphic notation as has been the case with so many of his followers. A note on the harp, one on the horn, a *pizzicato* in the cello, two notes on the clarinet—all meaningless unless considered as a line—each element as part of the whole. A conductor who was not aware of this line would give as vague and unconvincing a reading of the whole work as he would in a traditional work if he went merely from tune to tune without regard to the growth and shape and logic behind the beauty of the material itself. So many episodic performances of the classics result from this unawareness in performers who play the notes with great proficiency and often beauty but who have no knowledge of the underlying unity of the work, without which no music can be of stature, no matter how powerful its expression and how fine its content may be.

In this matter of symmetries one can criticise from the point of view that the visual may tend to outweigh the aural element, but this is only applicable to Webern's imitators. His use of retrogrades is so simple and direct that an immediate aural symmetry is felt. This is the essence of the smaller symmetry and it gives it the unity that so small a form must have. In this and in Op. 27, the Piano Variations, Webern seldom overlays the clear use of canons and they shine out in a crystalline beauty of their own. He limits his chords, such as they are, to two notes, although at times four notes sound at once. But the linear element is so novel as to defy the use of the word chord except where the harp or strings actually play two notes per player.

The Quartet, Op. 22, of 1930, and the Concerto, Op. 24, of 1934, are further manifestations of Op. 21. The former, which is for violin, clarinet, tenor-saxophone and piano, contains in the middle of the second movement some of the sparest writing in his whole output and in this work the chord as a musical entity no longer has any function. In the Concerto scored for flute, oboe, clarinet, horn, trumpet, trombone, violin, viola and piano, the chord has a new function; for here it is used as a contrapuntal element in the texture rather than as an outcome of the vertical. These piano chords are perfect examples of chords functioning horizontally without relation to a root. The row in this concerto is divided into four members of three notes each and these are presented in every form of inversion although often the actual order of the four main groups remains the same. The series as in Op. 21 and 22 is exposed every two bars and in the last bar of the first movement the whole series is stated in three chords, two of three notes and one of six. The last two movements carry economy to the extreme.

In the Cantata, Op. 26, *Das Augenlicht*, to words by Hildegarde Jone, there is a full texture and a greater use of real chords in the choral parts although the orchestral texture is as in Op. 24 fundamentally linear and jagged—the intervals are mostly of a major seventh or greater; the vocal lines are much smoother than in earlier Webern. The work is for mixed chorus with a remarkably assorted chamber orchestra and lasts only four and a half minutes.

The Piano Variations, Op. 27, of 1936, stem directly from Op. 21 and combine the delicacy of the opening with the stark grandeur of the third movement. The mirror canons of the first movement are exposed in chords, but in the last two movements he returns to the much more usual linear style. In the String Quartet, Op. 28, the stark writing of the last movement of the piano variations is further developed. How very different is this quartet from the Op. 5 or from the Trio, Op. 20! The Op. 9 Bagatelles are its real progenitor, except that in Op. 28 we have a development and evolution of the musical ideas not to be found in Op. 9 which had not the advantage of Webern's perfection of serial and canonic techniques to give it strength and unity. This quartet is quite long for Webern and is also one of his most extreme works. The individualisation of notes is here carried to its limit and the enormous intervals and spare style make it one of his most provoking works, yet one which has probably been more responsible for the most advanced and extremist tendencies felt in musical thought since 1950 than any other work by him or anyone else.

The Cantata No. 1, Op. 29, of 1939, is at once different and yet derives from the previous works. The intervals are almost all of much smaller size—the fascination for thirds and sixths is amazing. The initial presentation of the row is in three remarkably constructed chords which mirror each other from every angle. The second movement is for solo soprano and instrumental accompaniment and is akin in style to the first movement of the Op. 27 Variations. The texture is very complex and the building of chords here in fourths is interesting when compared with Hindemith's handling of similarly constructed chords. The middle of the third movement reaches momentary but great contrapuntal complexity. The chorus in this work is used less chordally than Op. 26 and more often in separate strands. The orchestra is here composed of similar instruments to that of Op. 26. Webern is particularly fond of including such instruments as mandoline, harp and celesta in his chamber group. His predilection for the clarinet must have been noticed; it appears, or at least one of the family appears, in nineteen of his thirty-one works. The brevity of these later works is also interesting. Op. 24 lasts six minutes, Op. 26 lasts four and a half minutes, Op. 28 lasts under eight minutes, Op. 29 under seven minutes.

With the Orchestral Variations, Op. 30, and the Cantata No. 2, Op. 31, we come to the last stages in the development of the work of this extraordinary man. One element is common to both—an increased interest in the use of almost constantly changing tempi per bar. This is a great difference from the Symphony, where the tempo does not change during the course of the movements and where *ritardandi* and *accelerandi* are few. The exploration of symmetries is now far less direct and in the Variations the series is mostly used in four-note groups either vertically or horizontally. This conditions much of the phrasing and the chordal textures, although two- and three-note groups are to be found in the later stages of the work. The orchestra for this piece comprises flute, oboe, clarinet, bass clarinet, horn, trumpet, trombone, tuba, celesta, harp and string quartet and the duration is six and a half minutes.

The Op. 31 is concerned with more various groupings of the series. In the first movement groupings of three and six predominate, but the second employs groups of two and five. Later those of five and six are constantly used and both melodic phrases and chords are composed of only those numbers of notes for considerable periods. In such passages it is impossible to find Webern using other groupings at the same time. This prepossession with consistent divisions of the series is a marked feature of the later works, as for example in the Concerto, Op. 24, but in this last Cantata it is carried to extremes and in fact verges on the purely constructional. Webern's imitators have made us fully aware of the dangers of this technique.

Economy is now carried to extremes and creates great difficulties for the performer. The music seems, at times, to be only there and no more, so evanescent and sparse is the texture. One cannot conceive what would have followed the final movement of the Op. 31 with its minims and semibreves set in constantly changing and irregular time-values, with every vocal line doubled by an instrument. Here are all the astonishing vocal leaps and subtleties of every kind carried to extremes, yet in this last movement there is not one *ritardando* or *accelerando* and in this sense it is as strict as anything that he ever wrote. Whatever may be the final influence of this music, one feels that it will be of a very positive nature either for good or bad, as the logic and clarity of vision are of the utmost compulsion. The Cantata was composed in 1943 and is his longest work since Op. 1; it lasts ten and a half minutes. No further record of his creative activity is known before his tragic death on 15th September, 1945, when he was mistakenly shot outside his home by a sentry of the occupying forces.

The work of Berg and Webern can be seen therefore even from these very brief sketches of their individual works and methods to develop along almost entirely separate lines. They are both pupils of Schönberg and worked closely with him, adopting his principles of serial technique at the same period. They are both influenced with the expressionism of the early twentieth century and have worked in antithesis to the attempts of Stravinsky and Hindemith in their fight to establish a new function of tonality. However, for all these similar trends in their careers and within this unity of their aims is apparent the very great diversity of two highly individual creative artists accepting willingly rules of order and logic which serve only to fertilise and enrich a true creator's mind and not to hinder it in any way. He who creates without a conscious or unconscious logic in his work, creates in chaos. At times of great change in music—in 1600, 1750 and 1900—we see various chaotic attempts and equally sincere and successful ones —to re-establish some method and order into the new style, which has found the old order to be no longer fertile or able to yield anything other than a pale copy of what has been already so well done. Bach, Mozart and Beethoven came at a time when this initial ordering had been done —they developed and enriched what they accepted. Theirs was largely an unconscious use of the strong and magnificent logic on which their great works are built and without which their finest inspiration and imagination would have produced only episodic, uncorrelated work. The latter half of the nineteenth century is so much encumbered by this discrepancy between form and content; the content often so fine and alive—the form so dead or merely functional.

The greatest musical minds of the twentieth century sought to re-establish a logic and order into what had become a chromatic chaos. The overthrow of a system had taken place, a system which was outworn and paradoxical in the light of every attempt being made to abolish the fundamental feature of that system—tonality. It is essential to recapitulate these facts to see the proper significance and necessity of the work of the Schönberg school and, of course, no less that of Stravinsky, Bartók and Hindemith.

It is little wonder that many ask of this century's music: 'Why is there such prepossession with technical means which have too often meant only a new harmonic or rhythmic system?' This is, of course, a sane and wise question, for what is any experiment or exploration worth for itself alone? If these works do not continue the force of true expression indigenous in man since he first felt the urge to express himself, then they must certainly fail. If they appeal for ever to only the few and do not lead to the establishment of something as universal as the great artistic movements of past time—if they cannot become a medium for the expression of the human comedy and tragedy—then indeed they cannot fulfil what they set out to do, to fertilise, clarify and order what had become confused so that the sublime intangible force vested in man may create anew and eternally.

It is fashionable, and therefore of no importance save to the dilettante and sterile extremists, to deprecate the popularity of music. That there is too much music too badly performed is clear for anyone to see. But this attitude can become vicious if creative artists feel they are the better for being scorned by the greater number of people. It is but a short step from this to the mind which looks with disdain on any composer who has reached a wider public—a wider field of expression. This is only touched on to place in perspective the work and efforts of great men such as Berg and Webern who sought to give new life and forms to music and indicate new paths for others to follow. He who scorns these and treads the already too-well-trodden paths is as illogical, stale-minded and lacking in vitality as he who may have composed masses and motets in the system of the church modes in 1640 or as he who may have based his works on the fugal system in the year 1800. For him we feel as Burns did in contemplating the future before the little field mouse—we may hope; but we may also fear.

Modern Music in Scandinavia

BO WALLNER

O<small>N</small> a general view, the music of the Scandinavian countries forms a unity. Their folk music is, with few exceptions, closely interrelated; and the same is true of the development of classical music. However, on closer examination, the special characteristics of each stand out more clearly. This applies not least to modern music.

Denmark

Denmark was the first country to assimilate and adapt for her own use the advances made by modern music. This was partly a result of her advantageous geographical position in relation to the Continent; the remoteness of the other Scandinavian countries, and also their great internal distances, have always been a serious obstacle to cultural development. But the Danish lead was also largely due to the outstanding personality of Carl Nielsen, one of the leading symphonic composers and boldest innovators in Scandinavian music hitherto. His work provided an invaluable stimulus—even though it also had a certain limiting influence at times: the same may be said of Grieg's role in Norwegian music and of Sibelius' in Finnish.

The foremost representatives of the first generation of Danish composers to adopt modern ideals are: Jørgen Bentzon (1897–1951), Knud-Aage Riisager (b. 1897) and Finn Høffding (b. 1899). Already in their work one of the central questions of the new music comes to the fore—the problem of contact. Bentzon's development is typical. The greater part of his earlier production consisted of exclusive chamber music. He employed, among other methods, a movement-construction

118

technique known as 'character polyphony'. He has described this as follows, in connection with his *Intermezzo espressivo*:

'Its form, and whole musical structure, is from first to last determined by the instruments' individual life. The instrument is thus not just an orchestral "colour", but a being in its own right, characterised by a special thematic value and a special expressiveness. To tone contrast and sound colour contrast corresponds the contrast of expression, which for the composer is the necessary inner complement to the free tonal (not atonal) play of the instrumental voices. Hence the term "espressivo".'

But the public showed little understanding of works written in this manner. And the composer, for his part, accepted the situation as a break in his own creativity; the social role of music was an axiom. In this crisis, his contact with Fritz Jode and the *Jugendbewegung* (Youth Movement) was of the greatest importance. His aim was to popularise his music; to work, through music schools for amateurs, for a spreading of interest in serious, and especially in contemporary music. The tragedy in Bentzon's development was that this popularising mood also brought about a flagging, a watering-down of his creative powers; his first symphony (1939-40) and the rather later opera *Saturnalia* scarcely bear comparison with the chamber music written by the individualist of the 1920s. But the second symphony of 1946-47, one of the composer's last works, is of artistic importance: the title—*Framdrift, Växt, Konstruktion* ('Energy, Growth, Construction')—reflects the strong interest in musical architectonics which, together with lyrically expressive moods, is so characteristic of Bentzon's tone language.

Constructive, organic growth is also the focus of Finn Høffding's music. He has been director of the Copenhagen conservatoire, and a leading figure in the educational field. Just as in Bentzon's case, this 'social' orientation has set its mark on Høffding's work, which includes school operas, light choral and instrumental compositions, text-books, etc. In a couple of minor works for wind instruments—often with a humorous, serenading note—Høffding carries on a characteristic Danish chamber-music tradition which has its roots in Carl Nielsen. In his symphonic works he sometimes employs a technique reminiscent of Bentzon's 'character polyphony'.

The most prolific composer of this generation, and the best known outside Denmark, is Bentzon's contemporary Knud-Aage Riisager, who has leanings towards neo-classicism. Both his refined movement construction and the nature of his work—among the most important are a series of ballets—betray the powerful influence of French tonal art of the 1920s; he is a pupil of Albert Roussel among others. With Riisager the architectonic aim is overshadowed by a more episodic and additive form construction; the refinement of the ideas plays a greater role than linear development. As we might expect, the broad symphonic form has had few temptations for him. Among Riisager's work, special mention should be made of his melodious and charming little string overture composed in 1934; and of his ballet, *Qantsiluni*, based on a Greenland cult, with its rhythmically suggestive wizard's sun-dance.

Other composers of this generation include the sly humorist, Fleming Weis (b. 1898), and Ebbe Hamerik (1898-1951), an experimentalist who was chiefly concerned with operas and symphonies.

The next generation is well represented by composers with widely differing artistic aims. Svend Tarp (b. 1908), Svend S. Schultz (b. 1913), and Jørgen Jersild (b. 1913), with their light, serenading style, closely resemble their Swedish contemporaries, Lars-Erik Larsson, Dag Wirén and Erland von Koch. Vagn Holmboe (b. 1909) and Herman D. Koppel (b. 1908) have felt their way ever deeper, over the years, towards a personal, serious style.

Tarp carries on, to a certain extent, the line followed by Riisager. His work is often chequered in style like the latter's, and the influence of modern French music is obvious. Among works of this kind are a series of frequently played piano sonatinas, and two elegant and playful short solo concertos and serenades. In recent years Tarp has shown a striving towards greater breadth and depth, as witness a symphony, written in 1949, and a Te Deum. The music of Svend S. Schultz has much in common with Tarp's, both in style and genre. But Schultz has found with the years a field of his own which he has successfully cultivated; opera, or more precisely, 'chamber opera', in which he has followed a popular rather than an exclusive line, with a strictly limited number of characters and of instruments, a light and supple dialogue, and solo and ensemble numbers arranged in numerical order. Among those operas may be mentioned *Solbadet* ('The Sunbathe'), *Høst* ('Autumn'), and *Bryllupsrejsen* ('The Honeymoon'). The last-mentioned scored for only three singers, piano and the simplest possible stage props, has been put on with great success in the Danish provinces. Jørgen Jersild is mainly occupied with teaching and composes very little. Like Riisager and Tarp, he has French leanings. He has had special success with a serenade for wind instruments, 'At spille i skoven'

('Playing in the Woods') and three piano pieces in a style clearly influenced by Couperin and Rameau.

Denmark's leading symphonic composer at the moment is Vagn Holmboe. In the spring of 1955 he completed his *Tia*. Most of what he writes is pervaded by a deeply serious note; despite its power and monumentality it often tends towards the ethereal. Linear development is what matters; musical effect is pushed into the background. Holmboe has been strongly influenced by Nielsen—naturally enough—but also by Bartók. Like the latter, he studied south-east European folk music for a short time, and the effects are sometimes noticeable in his thematic material. Among Holmboe's most important works are a number of short solo concertos for various instruments—including the oboe and the bassoon—and his four string quartets, in which his pure and noble manner of writing, and his very personal combination of severity and joy in melody can most clearly be studied. Finally, he has written a piano work of considerable stature, *Suono di bardo*. Whereas Holmboe's development is centred consistently round certain vital problems—for example, the question of a modern symphonic form—Herman D. Koppel's road appears at first sight much more adventurous. This is doubtless connected with his passionate early interest in jazz. Hence also the prominence of rhythm in Koppel's music, especially in his earlier work, e.g. in the first of his three piano concertos. In later years, however, lyrical expression has come to play a greater role. In such works as his cello concerto and his three Psalms of David for choir and orchestra, the hard-boiled jazz-fiend has developed into a poetically expressive composer.

Niels Viggo Bentzon (b. 1919), Denmark's other leading contemporary composer with Holmboe, is probably the most prolific in the whole of Scandinavian musical history. At thirty-seven, he has written more than a hundred works.

Bentzon's most important work is for the piano; he is himself an outstanding pianist. Out of the inheritance of Brahms, Nielsen and Hindemith he has developed a personal synthesis which often takes on monumental, expansive forms, as in the Partita of 1945, which brought him success. Apart from piano music, Bentzon has composed a number of symphonies, solo concertos and chamber music for various ensembles. Against much of this, however, it can be objected that Bentzon tends to think always in terms of the piano; and also that, quite naturally, his tremendous output does not always go with an adequate sifting of the material. But for Bentzon it seems natural to create quality out of quantity. His composition style has developed from linearity to ever greater musical effect: in his latest piano work there is even a noticeable tendency towards expressionism and atonality. One of the most interesting examples of this in *Kalejdoskop* ('Kaleidoscope'); another important work is his String Quartet, Opus 72.

Other young Danish composers who deserve mention are, in the first place, the church musicians, Leif Thybo (b. 1922) and Bernard Lewkovitch (b. 1928). The former, who is organist in a Protestant church, has made his greatest contribution in the sphere of organ music (in particular, he has written imaginative and accomplished choral preludes); the latter is a Roman Catholic composer of sonorous choral works in a somewhat late-romantic style. He has also written a number of piano sonatas. Leif Kayser (b. 1919) made a sensational début just before the Second World War as a symphonic composer, but has since made only sporadic ventures into creative music. The most important of these consist of organ music and choral works, with a note of sacred purity and pastoral gaiety. Kayser was formerly a Roman Catholic priest.

Finland

For the outside observer, the figure of Sibelius wholly dominates the field of Finnish music. However, the internal tradition also counts other composers of importance, chief among them Leevi Madetoja, Toivo Kuula and Selim Palmgren.

Modern Finnish music is of rather later date; the above-mentioned belong almost entirely to the late romantic period. As in the other Scandinavian lands, it was launched by a number of composers born in the 1890s. The oldest of them was Väinö Raitio (1891-1945). He made his debut with works in the late romantic spirit, but after he had studied in France and Moscow his style became freer and more radical. An expansive sonority plays a vital part in Raitio's music, and his orchestration is colourful and effective. His best-known work is the orchestral poem *Svanarna* ('The Swans'); and he has also written a *Fantasia estatica* and a *Fantasia poetica*. His last years were devoted to composing operas. But the real innovator in Finnish music is Aarre Merikanto (b. 1893), formerly professor of composition at the Sibelius Academy. In contrast to Raitio he has a remarkably polyphonic style— he was a pupil of Reger, among others—and is distinctly more radical. He won international success with one of his earlier works, the Concerto for Nine Instruments. Other important works include his second symphony, the cantata celebrating the four-hundredth anniversary of the city of Helsinki, and the choral work *Ukri*. Yrjö Kilpinen (b. 1892) an odd character, is the leading song-writer of modern Finnish music, and closer to the late romantic tradition. His work comprises about six hundred songs, with words in Finnish, Swedish and German. He has also written a certain amount of chamber music.

Uuno Klami (b. 1900) is the leading man in the next generation. His French training shows itself in, for example, his artistic, melodious piano concerto. But there is also a patriotic note in his work, especially in the Carelian Rhapsody, written in 1928, which was regarded at the time as an important advance for Finnish music. The musical researcher and conductor Toivo Haapanen puts the matter thus: 'The composer here appears wholly free from the romantic approach to folk tunes, and in particular from the usual stressing of their sorrowful and gloomy tone: on the contrary, he accentuates their naïve, instinctive beauty, their unison with nature.' The composer has continued along these lines, in particular with his Kalevala Suite, written in the mid-1930s. Other important works are his violin concerto, and the fresh, humorous overture to *Kivis Sochenskomakarna*.

In his 'international' production Klami is influenced to a certain extent by neo-classicism, and the same is true of Sulho Ranta, his junior by one year. Ranta is a prolific composer within the field of absolute musical forms, and a well-known teacher and writer on music. He has also produced a great number of vocal compositions.

A number of rather younger composers have won noteworthy positions in the musical life of their country, without awakening much interest beyond its boundaries. Among them are the church musician, Taneli Kuusisto (b. 1905), who has chiefly composed songs and chamber music; Nils-Erik Ringbom (b. 1907), the scientist and writer on music, who has composed symphonies, vocal works and chamber music, in particular a sextet for wind instruments; and the chief conductor of the Finnish Radio, Nils-Erik Fougstedt (b. 1910), who has even used the twelve-tone technique in his latest work. Generally speaking, one can discern a split in modern Finnish music; the Swedish-speaking composers usually adopt a more positive attitude towards radical currents than their Finnish-speaking colleagues, for whom the national romantic tradition is still a reality.

This split is especially noticeable in the youngest rank of Finnish composers. Erik Bergman (b. 1911) follows in his piano music, chamber music and romances a more radical line than, for example, Tauno

Pylkkänen (b. 1918), the leading dramatic composer of the new generation. In 1950 the latter won a remarkable international success with his radio opera *Vargbruden* ('The Wolf Bride'), which was one of the prizewinners in the Italian radio's composer competition. Pylkkänen's style has been described as a 'Finnish realism'. Ahti Sonninen (b. 1914) is a temperamental composer of works in a kind of late romantic style flavoured with modernism. He is much prized for his choral songs, but he has also composed works in the larger forms, notably a piano concerto. Finally Einar Englund (b. 1916), a Swedish-speaking Finn, turns in his symphonies and tone poems to more radical paths. There is no doubt that Finland's political division is reflected in the differing aims of the two groups of composers.

Norway

In Norwegian music, Grieg was for long the overshadowing figure who determined the style of all the others. Just as he was inspired by folk music, so also were the majority of his successors. This tradition continues unbroken today: the boundary between late romanticism and modernism is far harder to refine in Norway than in her Scandinavian neighbours.

During the 1920s, when the new stylistic ideals were making steady, if not sensational progress, in both Denmark and Sweden, Norway was experiencing a revival of national romanticism. In the vanguard was David Monrad Johansen (b. 1888), well known not only as the composer of a number of inspired romances and colourful orchestral and choral works, but also as the author of the first important biography of Grieg in Norwegian. Also in the national romantic tradition is Arne Eggen (b. 1881), who made his greatest contribution in a field which has hitherto received little attention in Norway: namely, opera. His *Olaf Liljekrans*, with its mediaeval theme and its music pervaded by folk tunes, was first performed in 1940, and eight years later came his interpretation of Shakespeare's *Cymbeline*.

A group of rather younger composers, of more convincing personality and freer and more modern outlook, have used the material of folk music in their work. Among them are Ludvig Irgens Jensen (b. 1894), who has made his greatest contribution in orchestral music. His *Passacaglia*, his Theme with Variations, Symphony in D minor and the suite *Drifte-karlen* ('The Grazier') all show an architectonic gift which is not altogether common in Norwegian music. Another important name is Eivind Groven (b. 1901). He began his musical career as a fiddler, and music for the fiddle has always been his great source of inspiration. Groven is a self-taught composer who has developed a personal style uninfluenced by the traditions of classical music. While Groven cannot be called one of his country's ablest composers, he is undoubtedly one of the most original. He has won much popularity in his own field, especially with his symphony of 1946 and his piano concerto of 1950. Sparre Olsen (b. 1903) awoke great interest in 1948 with his *Music for Orchestra*, an inspired and interestingly formed work, which gave many people a new outlook on a composer otherwise chiefly known for his gay and sentimental melodies. Yet even his earlier works include a number of important compositions for both choir and orchestra.

Another group of composers have made a more radical approach to folk music, combining the national element with the influence of the new Continental movements. Bjarne Brustad (b. 1895) is a characteristic example. He has been influenced by both Hindemith and Bartók, whose pioneering work and styles of composition have formed his model, in his larger works, including his two symphonies. In this way Brustad has helped to blaze new trails for the national tradition, from the romantic and idyllic towards a more modern and bolder style and a greater and broader aspiration. But the two really important names in this circle are Harald Saeverud (b. 1897) and Klaus Egge (1906).

Saeverud has scored his greatest success to date with his music for *Peer Gynt*, composed for a new production of Ibsen's play at the National Theatre in Oslo in 1948. Here we can study his special characteristics and his composition technique. It is obvious that he also draws his inspiration from folk music; but not in any mild spirit of national romanticism. Its influence is seen rather in the bold, richly decorative vitality, the rhythmic power and the refinement of his music. Saeverud generally builds up his effect through sharply expressive repetitive phrases, a kind of monumental monotony, as in the popular orchestra piece *Kjempviseslåtten*. Saeverud had a rich orchestral imagination, as can be seen in his symphonies, of which three are specially worthy of note: No. 5, *Quasi una fantasia*, No. 6, *Sinfonia dolorosa* and No. 7, *Salmesymfonin*, all of which were written during the Occupation. Other well-known works of Saeverud include two sets of orchestral variations on Norwegian folk tunes, and a piano concerto.

Klaus Egge works in a more polyphonic style. His *Fantasi i halling*, for piano, is a characteristic example. He takes as his motto, his thematic starting-point, the rhythmic structure of one of the commonest Norwegian folk dance tunes, and from it he spins a richly intertwined contrapuntal movement. In his second piano concerto he has taken an ancient ballad as the starting-point for a long set of variations with a closing fugue; in his second symphony, on the other hand, we find a more international inspiration (especially from Bartók and Stravinsky). Egge has also composed chamber music—an unusual genre in Norwegian music—a violin concerto, and choral and other works.

Other well-known names in Norwegian music are Erling Kjellby (b. 1901) who has written mainly string quartets, organ music and choral works; Knut Nystedt (b. 1915), a pupil of Copland, known for his *Divertimento* for Three Trumpets and Strings, and a symphonic poem, *Spenning ens land*; Edvard Fliflet Braein (b. 1924), who has composed a concert overture which aroused much interest, and two symphonies; and Finn Mortensen (b. 1922) with his Quintet for Wind Instruments and piano music in moderately modernistic style.

The biggest name in modern Norwegian music has not yet been discussed. Fartein Valen (1887–1952) was a solitary figure who went his own way, far from the beaten tracks of folk music. His style can almost be called atonal, although it has little relation to the Schönberg school. Valen reached his aim along other lines of development; in particular, he learnt more from Reger than from Wagner. He has no consistent twelve-tone technique. His style may be described as an attempted synthesis of old-fashioned polyphony, traditional Viennese classical forms (he has nothing to do with neo-classicism), high romantic orchestral technique (though never aiming at mass effect) and his own characteristically melodic and sonorous mode of expression. There is often a gay pastoral and lyrical mood in his work, pervaded by an inner religious feeling. Valen was for long ignored, both in his own land and abroad. Only towards the end of the 1940s did he reach the position he deserves in contemporary Scandinavian music. Valen, whose work is published through a special Valen company, has composed symphonies, two solo concertos—for violin and piano respectively—a number of lesser orchestral works, chamber music, piano works and songs.

Whether Valen will find followers among the younger Norwegian composers remains to be seen. But it would seem that the national tradition still has the strongest hold on the new generation's talent.

Sweden

The central figure in modern Swedish music is Hilding Rosenberg (b. 1892). By his side stand his two contemporaries, Gösta Nystroem (b. 1890) and Moses Pergament (b. 1893). The 1920s saw their early struggles, in particular against a national romantic tradition which had already passed its zenith, and whose champions saw dangerous signs of decadence both in the universalising and radical development of the tone language and in the ever-growing interest in larger and more complicated instrumental forms. With the coming of the new music, the idyll was ended.

Rosenberg is an especially prolific composer, even though he cannot be compared in this respect with Niels Viggo Bentzon. His work ranges from romances, piano pieces and chamber music on the one hand—his string quartets belong to the most vital part of his development, and the seventh in particular has aroused great interest—to oratorios and dramatic musical works on the other. Although Rosenberg was at first regarded as an extreme radical, today he may be looked upon rather as an artist in a vital relationship both with the late romantic tradition and with more radical currents. Lyricism and melody are important for him; not in the intimate song-like form which was for so long typical of Swedish music, but rather in relation to an architectonic, formal aim. He has here learnt much both from Sibelius and Nielsen. Rosenberg has written a number of solo concertos for various instruments, three orchestral concertos—the first, for strings only, is one of his most frequently played works—symphonies, theatre music and ballets (among them *Orpheus i stan*). His oratorios are important and deeply personal works; in *Johannes uppenbarelse* ('The Revelation of St. John') and *Ortagårdsmastaren* ('The Gardener'), written early in the 1940s, he has tried to form a synthesis between the symphony and the oratorio; while his main work of the mid-1940s, the great song-cycle based on Thomas Mann's *Joseph and his Brethren* is an attempted synthesis between oratorio and opera. Rosenberg's role is given further importance by his considerable activity as teacher; among his pupils are Karl-Birger Blomdahl, Sven-Erik Bäck and Ingvar Lidholm. Rosenberg may be called the artistic conscience of modern Swedish music, since the 1920s.

Gösta Nystroem's work consists mainly of symphonies and romances. He has been strongly influenced by French music, that is, by both the Impressionists and 'Les Six', Honegger in particular. His compositions sometimes also show neo-baroque tendencies. Nystroem's work is otherwise marked by an expressiveness very much his own, often with a tragic undertone, as in his three most important orchestral works: *Sinfonia espressiva* (mid-1930s), *Sinfonia del Mare* (1948) and the Concerto No. 2 for String Orchestra (1955). His solo concertos—

for cello and viola—have a more idyllic, melodious note. Foremost among his vocal works comes the cycle *Sånger vid Havet* ('Songs by the Sea') for mezzo-soprano and orchestra (piano). The tension in Nystroem's music between naïve, song-like simplicity, and dramatic outbursts of feeling is sometimes reminiscent of Pär Lagerkvist, one of the outstanding figures of modern Swedish literature; and, in fact, the two have worked together in an inspiring manner. Moses Pergament made his name in the first place as an original and combative writer on music, but in recent years his activity as composer has aroused steadily growing interest. Most important are his great choral work *Den judiska sången* ('The song of the Jews') (1941), the ballet *Krelantems och Eldeling* (1920s), and, in recent years, a string quartet, a double concerto for two violins, choral movements, and a chamber opera based on Lagerkvist's early expressionistic play *Himlens Hemlighet*. ('Heaven's Secret').

The early 1930s saw the débuts of a number of young Swedish composers whose style and artistic approach were closely related. The oldest of them is the French-trained Dag Wirén (b. 1905), whose chief interest is in instrumental music. His works include symphonies, solo concertos, string quartets, suites and overtures: his vocal works are very few and of no great interest. A light, serenading style is common to all his music; his popular Serenade for Strings (1937) is a good example of this. His tendency towards neo-classicism is especially clearly marked. Wirén frequently works with small, sharply-defined motifs which he builds up according to often original formal ideas; as, for example, in his third symphony, in which the first movement corresponds to the major group of themes, the second to the minor group, and the third—a sonata movement—to the development. In later years Wirén has turned his gaze more and more towards the Scandinavian tradition; Nielsen, and above all Sibelius, have given him valuable stimulus.

Lars-Erik Larsson (b. 1908), formerly professor of composition at the College of Music, showed at first many common traits with Wirén. His reaction to modernistic tendencies also took the form of neo-classicism: thus he composed, during the 1930s, elegant, smooth-flowing, humorous serenade music, a *divertimento,* a melodious little saxophone concerto, and so on. But at the close of the decade came a marked change of style in favour of Scandinavian romanticism; the most important works from this phase are the choral cycle, *Förklädd Gud* ('God in Disguise'), and the popular Pastoral Suite. Finally, in the mid-1940s,

Larsson went over to a more radical style, somewhat influenced by Hindemith; his *Music for Orchestra* is a particularly important example of this. In his recent work, romanticism and radicalism have undergone an effective synthesis, illustrated in a violin concerto, a *Missa brevis* and a string quartet. Gunnar de Frumerie (b. 1908), the third composer of real importance in the generation of the thirties, is French-trained like Nystroem and Wirén; but he has been influenced by Brahms as well as by the impressionists and 'Les Six'. De Frumerie is one of the few Swedish composers after Nystroem to carry on what used to be the most vigorous of all Swedish musical traditions, the romance; his exquisitely poetic *Songs of Lagerkvist* have become especially popular. Piano music holds a leading place for him, both as solo pieces in chamber music—noteworthy in this respect are a piano quartet and a piano trio—and in solo concertos. He has also composed an opera, *Singoalla,* a ballet, *Johannisnatten* ('Midsummer Night'), and choral works.

To the same generation of composers belong Hilding Hallnäs (b. 1903) whose work comprises symphonies, songs and church music, including a mass—and Erland von Koch (b. 1910), an especially prolific composer who began in a virile neo-classical spirit, but later, under the influence of Swedish folk tunes, turned to a more expressive and emotionally richer tone language.

The outstanding figures among the next generation of composers, Karl-Birger Blomdahl (b. 1916), Sven-Erik Bäck (b. 1919) and Ingvar Lidholm (b. 1921), are all pupils of Rosenberg. They have again brought the most radical currents in modern music to the fore, partly in opposition to the restorative tendencies of the composers of the thirties. Hindemith's *Unterweisung im Tonsatz,* Bartók's quartets and more important piano works, Stravinsky's music of the thirties and forties, Schönberg's and Krenek's theoretical work, and even, in the last few years Webern's works and the 'point music' theories, have all been studied and discussed. Their styles have also at times been influenced by Renaissance and baroque tonal art.

Blomdahl, the leader of the group, has for some years been the internationally best-known and most-discussed of Swedish composers, apart from Rosenberg. His early work was influenced by composers such as Nielsen, Rosenberg and Hindemith, but also shows a marked personal element in its rhythmic vitality and invariable tendency towards architectonic forms. Examples of this are his String Trio of 1946, the rather earlier First Symphony, the Bach-style Violin Concerto of 1947 and the *Concerto Grosso* of 1944. Towards the end of the 1940s he developed a more radical tone language, and at the same time came a marked broadening of his mode of interpretation, in the spirit of expressionism. In 1950 he completed his third symphony, the magnificent set of variations known as *Facetter* ('Facets'); in immediate succession came the choral cycle *I speglarnas sal* ('In the Hall of Mirrors), composed for the most important work in modern Swedish poetry, *Mannen utan väg* ('The Man without a Path'). Other works which have aroused international interest are the Chamber Concerto for Piano, Woodwind and Percussion Instruments, and the choreographic suite, *Sisyfos*. His most recent work includes a Trio for Clarinet, Cello and Piano. A common element in most of these works is the strong emphasis on the principle of cumulative effect; the architectonic form has here reached full bloom.

Church music has an important place in Sven-Erik Bäck's work; he has composed, among other things, a motet, cantatas, and a *Sinfonia Sacra*. The earlier works are dominated by a cool, almost archaic mood; later a romantic-subjective note breaks in, and is combined with influences from Renaissance and baroque music—Bäck is an outstanding interpreter of early music. In a final phase, he has been decisively influenced by the twelve-tone technique; and also, in an internationally known chamber symphony from 1955, by the 'point music' style. Bäck's music chiefly comprises works for various chamber ensembles, ranging from a solo sonata for the flute to chamber symphonies for the lower strings, wind and percussion. He has also composed music for a large number of plays, including Christopher Fry's *The Boy with the Cart,* and Goethe's *Faust*.

Ingvar Lidholm's development is reminiscent of Bäck's. He began in a modernistic, national romantic style, exemplified by his *Toccata e Canto,* which brought him success. In his choral work *Laudi* he has been decisively influenced by Palestrina, Stravinsky and others; in his later music, especially by Bartók and Alan Berg, e.g. in a string quartet and a violin concerto. In a final phase—after studies under Mátyás Seiber —he has followed Webern and Dallapiccola, producing a concertino for chamber ensemble, a song cycle, a cello suite, and above all the dynamic orchestral work *Ritornell*. In the latter, as in Bäck's chamber symphony, certain 'point music' methods are introduced. In recent years, yet another interesting composer has made his appearance: Allan Petterson (b. 1911), a pupil of Blomdahl and Leibowitz, who has written two highly expressionistic symphonies and a series of sonatas for two violins.

The youngest generation of Swedish composers may be divided into two groups, of which one has turned towards neo-classicism, taking Prokoviev and Shoshtakovitch as models, while the other is following up the twelve-tone technique and is eagerly engaged on 'point music' problems. The former group includes Hans Eklund (b. 1927), and Maurice Karkoff (b. 1927); the latter, Bengt Hambraeus (b. 1928), who has also engaged in electronic music at the studios of the Westdeutsche Rundfunk at Cologne. Gunnar Bucht (b. 1927), a pupil of Blomdahl, has taken up an intermediate position: his symphonies and chamber music are strongly influenced by Nielsen and Bartók.

English Contemporary Music

ANTHONY MILNER

I

IF England in the nineteenth century was known to many Europeans as 'the land without music', there was much in the state of the national music to justify this appellation. The brilliance of the Tudor and Stuart periods had been followed by a decline which continued for nearly a hundred and fifty years. Italian fashions dominated English music in the eighteenth century; German in the nineteenth. While something of the national talent for vocal composition was maintained in choral music (even if distinguished works were few), the style displayed throughout the Victorian age was unashamedly Teutonic. Matters were not noticeably improved by the impact of Elgar's genius at the century's end; there were too many composers who preserved an academic competence without having much, if anything, new to say. Wilfrid Mellers wrote in 1945: 'That if one reflects on the situation in English music at the turn of the century it seems astonishing that the creative spark should have been rekindled at all!; the scope and variety of creative musical activity in this country today is certainly greater than any impartial, intelligent observer would have bargained for thirty or even twenty years ago.' [1]

This variety of musical style exhibited by the works of living English composers makes any assessment of their relative significance difficult to achieve and extremely tentative in its conclusions. It is very largely due to the coincidence of the English musical 'renaissance' with the series of 'revolutions' in the European music of the twentieth century.

[1] Wilfrid Mellers: *Music and Society*, p. 105. Dennis Dobson.

132

ENGLISH CONTEMPORARY MUSIC

From the vantage-point of mid-century it is possible to distinguish three main trends in the course of this renaissance which may be described as the abandonment of the German classical and romantic schools as models for imitation, the revaluation of the elements of the musical language in the light of the rediscovery of the national musical past, and the assimilation of contemporary developments in Europe. The first two were very largely the result of the work and influence of Gustav Holst and Vaughan Williams. Comment on the compositions of these two men lies outside the scope of this article. It must suffice to say that all English composers born in this century are greatly indebted to their pioneer work and to their insistence on the study of the English music of the sixteenth and seventeenth centuries. By directing their attention to folksong, the madrigalists and Purcell, and by their efforts to recreate an English vocal line which should avoid awkward word-setting, Holst and Vaughan Williams produced works that were both genuinely English and novel in style. On the basis of a tradition thus purified and reaffirmed, the composers born in the first decade of the twentieth century were able to commence the task of reintegrating the national music with the main stream of European development. The influence of Continental innovation was seen at first more obviously in instrumental music. Vocal, especially choral, music, the stronghold of traditions good and bad, was slower to show it. It must be admitted, however, that not all contemporary English composers seem to have felt the need for this integration. In their support such composers can point to the confused welter of styles that is European music today, contending that the national tradition offers greater security for the unfolding of a composer's talent than the chase after the meteoric fashions of the *avant-garde*.

II

Edmund Rubbra (b. 1901) reveals the effect of the influence of Vaughan Williams and Holst (he studied with the latter) more obviously than any other composer now living. The style of all but his earliest works is basically polyphonic, being built on melodies which derive much of their strength from his study of Tudor and Jacobean composers. His forms for the most part rely for their development on the free polyphonic expansion of their themes and thus are essentially melodic in impulse. This technique, which can be related to the forms of sixteenth-century motifs, appears on a small scale in the Masses, motets, and two sets of madrigals. Rubbra has applied it to the construction of

133

large instrumental movements in his six symphonies. (Here it is possible to notice a connection with Sibelius' attitude to symphonic form.) Thus he avoids the dramatic contrasts of sonata-form, substituting for them flowery melodic lines from which all subsequent thematic material unfolds by means of polyphonic elaboration and variation. The first two symphonies apply this formal principle with merciless logic; the third and fourth relax the polyphonic to incorporate homophonic passages. In the fifth and sixth symphonies Rubbra achieves a symphonic texture of balanced contrast utilising both polyphonic and homophonic elements. The chief interest of his music is to be found in his solutions of the problems of polyphonic texture, for his melodies are not often distinctive nor are his rhythms arresting. He avoids harmonic innovation. One of the more obvious features of his harmony, blocks of chords in parallel movement, derives from Holst. This he sometimes uses for long sketches without a break, as in the *Credo* of the *Missa in honorem Sancti Dominici* (1949), where it produces a somewhat mechanical effect. Although it has been asserted that his harmony is the result of his counterpoint, this is true only intermittently; the 'free' contrapuntal lines are often conditioned by semitone movement determined on purely vertical grounds. His mood is habitually elevated and often noble in its expression, particularly in slow movements. The instrumentation of the symphonies is, though sensible, conservative; in a big contrapuntal *tutti* he tends (as does Vaughan Williams) to score heavily and thickly.

While rooted in native traditions the music of Alan Bush (b. 1900) reveals its composer's wide awareness of contemporary trends and of all Western music from mediaeval times onwards. In many of his later works Bush employs a technique that he calls the 'thematic' method of composition, in which every note is thematically significant. The material is constructed from series of notes which are quite frequently derived from common chords. Thus, although the method bears a superficial resemblance to the twelve-tone technique, Bush does not use it atonally. He produces excellent results with it in contrapuntal style, but when he applies it to a rhapsodic movement such as the *andante* of the Violin Concerto (1948) the result seems less satisfactory. His forms are melodic in impulse, like Rubbra's, but more compact, since they are not only more logically ordered but also more tense in their rhythmic organisations. Rubbra's music is characteristically meditative; Bush's is essentially epic and dramatic. His vigorous rhythms and alert wide-leaping melodies make his contrapuntal textures clear and vivid.

Although the harmonies they produce are sometimes extremely dissonant, they are always truly the result of the movement of the melodic lines; every note is necessary and every note tells. The 'Dialectic' for String Quartet (1929) is a work outstanding for its contrapuntal brilliance.

Despite its power and originality Bush's music is undeservedly neglected in comparison with that of other composers. This neglect is perhaps partly due to his display of Marxist beliefs in the texts of his vocal works and in the 'programmes' attached to his vocal compositions. The propaganda contained, for example, in *The Winter Journey* (1946) where the divine element is removed from the story of the Nativity in such a way as almost to convert it into a Marxist tract, seems faintly ridiculous to the non-Marxist. Bush's use of chorus occurs mainly in works of this sort; he writes simply, avoiding much contrapuntal texture so that the words may be heard by an audience with minimum difficulty. A typical example of his Marxist choral style occurs in the final movement of the Piano Concerto (1937) in which a male chorus sings either in two parts homophonically or in unison lines of which the following are typical:

> *These are they who propagate subtle falsehoods*
> *Daily, like poisonous gas, to corrupt opinion.*
> RANDALL SWINGLER.

The choruses in *Wat Tyler* unite the direct simplicity of such passages with an eventful handling of large ensembles in crowd scenes which (as far as can be judged from perusing the vocal score, since the opera has not yet been performed in England[1]) may prove to be the most stirring in any English opera yet written; they seem to have a sweeping dramatic urgency by which they transcend even the magnificent choruses of Britten's *Peter Grimes*.

William Walton (b. 1902) seems a more typically English figure than either Bush or Rubbra. He continues the Elgarian tradition by his orchestral brilliance and a flair for occasional music of a ceremonial nature. Although in his youth he was classed as a revolutionary, today many regard him as the musical embodiment of the national genius for compromise. He is truly neither rebel nor conservative but an example of that type of artist whose position is the most difficult of all to estimate: a man of original mind, sensitive not only to his native traditions but also to contemporary trends, who in assimilating both pursues a

[1] Editor's Note: Written prior to the BBC performances.

strictly personal path in which innovation is incidental rather than fundamental. Walton has always been slow-working and severely self-critical and if his fame rests on a small number of compositions these nevertheless have not been equalled by any other English composer of his generation. The Viola Concerto (1929), *Belshazzar's Feast* (1931) and the Symphony (1934) are major works. All three are characterised by incisive scoring, tense rhythms and a melodic line both lyrical and forceful built into closely organised forms. Compared with these the later works, from the Violin Concerto (1939) to *Troilus and Cressida* (1954), are less compelling. There is in Walton's earlier works a strongly romantic impulse in the melody which in those written after 1937 seems to dominate the music to the detriment of its impact and conciseness. The manner is brilliant but the form has relaxed. *Troilus* suffers somewhat from this. It has everything a good opera requires: a love-story plot, ending in tragedy and death, a competent libretto and an excellent sense of the stage, yet something seems to be lacking, perhaps an elevation of mood. For example, the love duet in the second Act inevitably invites comparison with those of other operas and by the light of such comparison it is found inadequate.

Lennox Berkeley (b. 1903) received his final musical education in France from Nadia Boulanger, and his music therefore shows less of the influence of the national tradition than does that of the three composers discussed previously. Two of its more noticeable characteristics, lightness of texture and delicate instrumentation, probably owe much to his French training. Berkeley is essentially a miniaturist. His form does not rely so much on a logically developed thematic structure as on sectional contrast and alternation. His counterpoint of diatonic lines combined in a mildly dissonant harmony tends to suffer from this thematic and formal looseness: there is often no apparent thematic or harmonic reason for the occurrence of a dissonant note. Perhaps his best, and certainly his most deeply felt, works are to be found in his vocal compositions. Those to English texts are rather unenterprising in the vital matter of verbal setting; the speech rhythm is seldom the model for the musical. His religious works to Latin texts, especially the *Stabat Mater* (1940) and the recent *a-cappella Crux Fidelis* are more sensitive to the patterns of the verbal inflexions. Of his two ventures into opera, *The Dinner Engagement* is by far the more successful; the medium of a comic chamber opera is innately suited to a miniaturistic and delicate style. *Nelson* suffers from its composer's inability to sustain a long dramatic action in musical form. The libretto and the awkwardly constructed scenario are partly to blame for the work's episodic character, but they cannot receive the blame for the lack of musical impetus and unity.

Berkeley's instrumental works reveal his feeling for instrumental sonorities and colour. They possess, as do all his works, a melodic charm which, delightful as it is in itself, is all the more valuable in that it appears so seldom in contemporary music. But this charm has its drawbacks; it is too often merely superficial, and does not arise from melodic strength but from the instrumentation. Accompaniment figures in both the vocal and instrumental works frequently depend for their material on harmonic figuration of a somewhat facile sort. This weakness is most marked in his otherwise effective writing for the pianoforte.

It could be argued that at the commencement of the century English composers wrote far too little instrumental music and that what they did write was generally mediocre. Alan Rawsthorne (b. 1905) marks the commencement in our music of a tendency to avoid the vocal media hallowed by tradition; except for a small choral cantata and a few songs his output is entirely instrumental. His first works to receive public performance were heard at the international festivals of the I.S.C.M. where they won equal praise from foreigners and Englishmen. Rawsthorne is thus one of the first composers since the early seventeenth century to gain an international respect in this field. It is due to him, to Walton, and to a few younger men, that English instrumental music is now considered to be on an equal standing with its choral and vocal music. Like Walton, his works are few, but are all of a high standard of technical achievement. Harmonically, he is the most consistent composer of his generation. In an era of stylistic transition harmonic figuration presents a composer with very difficult problems to solve, yet Rawsthorne has made it an integral and wholly successful feature of his style. Based on a shifting chromaticism derived from the constant use of false relations, it nevertheless permits a frequent use of common chords and simple two-part counterpoint. Much of his melody, contrapuntal or otherwise, is figurative; he thinks in patterns of notes, and it is possible to detect basic patterns in all his works. Counterpoint, melody and harmony are only units of a remarkably homogeneous and attractive style. He pays the price of this consistency in a restricted range of emotion: he reaches neither the heights nor the depths, but is always urbane and polished, a Horace rather than a Catullus.

As might be expected from his harmonic traits, he has a special feeling for the piano. The *Bagatelles* (1938) and the extraordinarily original and deft duet-suite, *The Creel* (1940), present in miniature the technique he so brilliantly exploits in the concertos (1943 and 1951), two of the most popular instrumental works by any living English composer. His forms are concise, even terse, because his figurative style demands a quasi-baroque treatment of the thematic material. A fine example of this is to be found in the Chacoune of the first piano concerto in which the traditional scheme is transformed into a form at once new and convincing. The *Symphonic Studies* (1938) for orchestra are another demonstration of Rawsthorne's gift for revaluing the old in terms of the new: the *baroque* formal organisation lightens and clarifies the orchestral texture so that while the music remains truly symphonic the sonata-form dualism is replaced by a process of thematic elaboration. The Symphony (1950) is not quite so successful as the earlier work, probably because there are traces of a return to the older and more conventional methods of presenting symphonic material.

III

Though vitally different, Michael Tippett (b. 1905) and Benjamin Britten (b. 1913) have certain traits in common. They share an instinctive understanding of the English music of the sixteenth and seventeenth centuries that has ripened with experience to a profound sympathy but which excludes any influence from either Handelian grandiosity or the Three Choirs Festival style of the nineteenth century. In both may be perceived a renewal of all that is best and freshest in English melody, a melody which, when not actually vocal, derives its impulse from vocal connotation and association. Both have experienced fruitfully the impact of the music of the great European composers of the age. They have won as much success with Continental as with native audiences.

Tippett has developed slowly and at first hesitantly (he has withdrawn everything written before 1935), more because of the rich complexity of his style than through infertility. The most obvious feature of this complexity (and one frequently overstressed by critics) is a remarkably individual approach to rhythmic problems. His rhythm is perhaps coloured a little by the influence of Stravinsky and Bartók, but owes far more to his study of the cross-rhythms of the madrigalists, the dance and the delicate word-setting of Purcell. As with all true rhythm (i.e. rhythm that is a truly vital element in the musical organisation and not a series of metrical patterns imposed from without) it is highly expressive because it always serves a deeply felt melodic line of which it is the organising vehicle. The contrapuntal combination of such lines is intensely forceful. Although the listener may sometimes think at a first hearing that too much is going on, he is always aware that the excess is one of passion, not of ingenuity. Tone polyrhythm is rare in Tippett's work (the best examples occur in the fugues of the third string quartet, 1946); additive rhythms with pulses of varying lengths are more frequent (the *Presto* of the second quartet is built entirely on these); but generally he uses a combination of transferred accents, syncopations and cross-rhythms in a closely knit contrapuntal texture.

The melodies of his earlier works, when not strictly polyphonic, are often reminiscent of folksong, as, for example, those of the second movements of the Piano Sonata (1938) and the Double Concerto (1934). In the later instrumental works there is an increasingly apparent tendency to over-ornamentalise the melodic lines. It weakens the otherwise effective *Fantasia Concertante* for strings (1953) and some of the orchestral writing of *The Midsummer Marriage* (1952). Its origins may be traced to his pianoforte writing. The last movement of the early piano sonata (1938) and the Fantasia for piano and orchestra (1941) derive most of their ornamentation from harmonic figuration. Tippett's harmonic sense seems his weakest asset; whenever he has to think in predominantly harmonic terms, as in the piano accompaniments to his songs, he tends to stress the importance of the manner over that of the matter. The extremely difficult ornamental writing of the accompaniments in the song-cycle *The Heart's Assurance* is not fully justified by the rather unoriginal patterns of the figuration; too many of the notes seem to be there merely to ensure a rapid flow of sound by maintaining a basic harmony, yet there is sufficient quasi-melodic writing to disturb this impression. Thus this ornamental style is ambiguous; it partakes both of harmony and melody and fails to be either. This conclusion would seem to be proved by the fact that Tippett's use of vocal melisma (where he is using ornamentation in a purely melodic manner) is almost always convincing. (A comparison of the vocal and pianoforte parts of the second song of *The Heart's Assurance* is very revealing on this point.) It is an integral and very lovely constituent of his vocal style, whether he uses it chorally, as in the astonishing mirror canon 'Where lies the jewel' from *The Child of our Time*, or soloistically in the triumphant leaps and trills of *Boyhood's End* (1943).

Music rich in melody, especially when polyphonic, can bear a good deal of repetition. Hence Tippett's forms are usually simple. He often repeats sections without any alterations other than transposition to a new key, and his recapitulations (especially those in the second quartet and Double Concerto) are unusually exact for contemporary works. The driving power of his rhythms gives to all his music a strong feeling of line; his forms are the necessary results of his thematic material. He is equally successful in choral and instrumental music, and maintains a similar style in both media. This unified idiom is rare today; many contemporary composers seem to give the impression that writing for choir imposes ungrateful restrictions.

The plot and libretto of the opera raise problems which cannot be discussed adequately here. Even if the composer's mythological approach is dramatically unconvincing and occasionally absurd, the music reveals Tippett at the height of his powers. His polyphonic conception of orchestration, revealed convincingly for the first time in the Symphony (1945) dominates the work, sustaining the vast, almost Wagnerian form with unabating intensity. Much of the ornamentation, however, tends to lose its effect in the theatre; the *Ritual Dances*, for example, can be heard adequately only in the concert hall. The melismata of the solo voices are more elaborate than any Tippett has yet done (with the possible exception of those in the short choral pieces *The Source* and *The Windhover*, two of Tippett's rare failures) and are so difficult as to pose sharply the question whether this kind of song is suitable for contemporary opera. Yet when considered purely as music, it is impossible to deny their splendour; vocal lines of such magnificence and emotional range are so lamentably infrequent today that one hesitates to cavil, even in a small way, at what Tippett has given us.

Britten's gifts show themselves most directly in his feeling for verbal setting. Since Purcell we have had no other composer to whom Playford's words may be more fitly reapplied: 'He was particularly admired for his Vocal Music, having a Peculiar Genius to express the Energy of English Words, whereby he mov'd the Passions as well as caused Admiration in all his Auditors.' His early works, such as the settings of Auden's poems in *Our Hunting Fathers* and *On this Island*, play genially with texts of involved, even nonsensical, meaning without going deeper than superficial brilliance. *Les Illuminations* (1939) and the *Michelangelo Sonnets* (1940) reveal a more emotional approach to the poetry which subdues mere cleverness to its properly subordinate task of assisting the musical expression. After these Britten returned to English texts in the masterly and wonderfully beautiful *Serenade* (1943) and *The Holy Sonnets of John Donne* (1945) in which he displays the most delicate, expressive, and varied songwriting to be found anywhere today. The same high standard is revealed in the choral works from the unaccompanied *Hymn to St. Cecilia* (1942) to the *Spring Symphony* (1949), in which occasional polyphony is never allowed to obscure the poetry and whose melodies are always truly vocal.

Allied to his gift for melody is Britten's characteristic lightness of texture, which gives his music a clarity and zest that has been almost entirely absent from our music since the seventeenth century. Unlike Tippett he is not a great contrapuntist. His transparent texture is obtained only partially by polyphonic means. Instead he employs a highly personal technique of harmonic figuration realised in an intensely melodic manner. It is never safe to ignore a figurative pattern in his works; however unassuming it may sound when first heard it will nevertheless probably prove to be vitally important for textural development. One of the most highly organised examples of this method occurs in the finale of the *Spring Symphony* which, though so immediately attractive and easy to listen to, presents a rich manipulation of apparently inconspicuous thematic elements that repays the closest study. His harmony is basically diatonic since it derives from vocal techniques and styles, but can include the harshest dissonances. Mannerisms from the music of Ravel, Mahler, Bartók, Stravinsky and Berg may be noticed, but all are thoroughly digested constituents of his highly consistent harmony. Here he invites comparison with Rawsthorne: the older man has achieved a unified harmonic technique at the expense of melodic variety, Britten, because his inspiration is fundamentally vocal, maintains his harmonic style by reason of his melody.

He seems to prefer miniature or sectionalised forms such as the song cycle and the variation. Even in his larger works this attitude is maintained. The so-called *Spring Symphony* is truly a cantata of twelve sections, while *The Turn of the Screw* is built ingeniously on a series of variations. His most successful instrumental works follow the same pattern: one has only to think of the brilliant variations on themes of Frank Bridge and Purcell. The quartets and concertos suffer from a failure to invent themes and methods of treating them that will sustain a large movement. Very noticeable in this connection are his longer contrapuntal forms; the Chacony of the second quartet has neither the thematic nor contrapuntal impulse to maintain the movement as long as he wants it, so cadenzas are used to break up the structure, thus concealing its essential deficiency as much as possible. In the 'Prelude and Fugue for Eighteen-part String Orchestra' he frankly evades the contrapuntal problems posed by his chosen medium. His remarkable feeling for instrumental colour and amazing flair for chamber orchestration make considerable amends for his inability to construct large forms, but in large orchestral works, such as the *Sinfonia da Requiem* (1940) these are not a sufficient compensation.

It is difficult to overestimate Britten's importance in the field of contemporary national opera. Operas had been written before by Englishmen, but Britten is unique in that with his second opera (his first, *Paul Bunyan*, was withdrawn) he succeeded not only in convincing his own countrymen but the rest of the world. Which is as much as to say that at one step he not only revived the national operatic tradition so wretchedly dormant after Purcell, but proved the validity of that tradition to international audiences. *Peter Grimes* was, and still can be, regarded as the symbol of England's successful musical renaissance. Considered in the light of his later operas it stands as one of Britten's very best works. From all points of view it is his only opera that can be truly classed as a 'grand opera'. *Billy Budd* (1951), by reason of its all-male cast, and *Gloriana* (1953), by reason of its episodic scenario and curiously chamber-styled orchestration, lie outside this category. The chamber-operas, especially *The Rape of Lucretia* (1946) and *The Turn of the Screw* (1954) contain some of Britten's most attractive and ingenious music. It is remarkable that none of the plots (save for the arguable exception of *Gloriana*) is essentially concerned with love between the sexes 'without somewhat of which Passion', Dryden averred, 'no opera can possibly subsist'. Britten's heroes are largely innocent and suffer unjustly; their stories are not so much tragic as pathetic. Plots of this kind, even when assisted by brilliant musical invention, fail 'to purge us by pity and terror' (Aristotle's definition) we feel merely rather sorry for the unfortunate characters involved in such difficulties. Therein lies their fundamental weakness: their dramatic independence is curtailed by the substitution of sentimental sympathy for tragic fear, and therefore the music is hampered so that, like the libretti it serves, it lacks moral strength. Britten's latest opera offers no hope of any change in his fundamental attitude to plots. *The Turn of the Screw* presents the problem of the suffering innocent in a most aggravated and exaggerated form, providing no solution, dramatic or otherwise.

IV

The music of three women composers born in the first decade of the century affords a sharp contrast to the gracious, melodious styles of Tippett and Britten. Extreme economy of thematic material characterises the works of Elizabeth Maconchy (b. 1907) and Priaulx Rainier (b. 1903); Elisabeth Lutyens (b. 1906), while not so restrictive, is the pioneer of English dodecaphony.

Maconchy's attitude to composition is revealed in her own statement that 'writing music, like all creative art, is the impassioned pursuit of an idea. . . . The great thing is for the composer to keep his head and allow nothing to distract him. The temptations to stop by the way and to be side-tracked by felicities of sound and colour are ever present, but in my view everything extraneous to the pursuit of this central idea must be rigorously excluded—scrapped.'[1] The logical working-out of this conception of her art entails a style and forms that are severely contrapuntal. Her range of themes is limited: very many are built entirely from small intervals in an almost obsessional repetition. Perhaps the best example of her intensive use of a theme of this sort occurs in her fourth quartet (1943) whose basic motif is a series of major and minor seconds, EFEFG♭ E♭ F G♭. The relentless mastery by which this pattern is made to provide all the music of a four-movement work creates a terrifyingly insistent unity which is hardly attractive but whose manipulative ingenuity commands respect. Yet it is difficult to avoid the judgment that this style is the result of a fundamental melodic costiveness. In itself the material is neither ingratiating nor compelling: what power it has derives from the treatment it receives. In so far as her harmony can be considered apart from the counterpoint, it is often strikingly reminiscent of Bartók's in its predilection for what have been called 'secundal' dissonances which emphasise the individuality of the melodic lines. Maconchy's most successful and representative music is to be found in her chamber works, particularly the string quartets. Her works in concerto form, which have been very favourably received at several international festivals, show some relaxation of her monothematic attitude. A more lyrical style makes a welcome appearance in some of her recent works, as, for example, in the finale of the Symphony for double string orchestra (1953). Her vocal works are far fewer and of

[1] Quoted in 'Elizabeth Maconchy' by Anne MacNaghten, *Mus. Times*, June 1955.

less importance than the instrumental; most of them are still unpublished.

Rainier's melodies are as limited in their basic patterns and motivic construction as Maconchy's, but expand more freely in their generation of new material. The early *Greek Epigrams* (1937) exhibit typical features of her melodic style; the first song's vocal line is built from descending thirds, the seconds from scale figures. (The shape of this second melody is almost instrumental, having a rather more than superficial resemblance to that in the *andante* of the first quartet.) Her preoccupation with the details of thematic derivation seems to hinder her from producing a truly song-like melody, while she frequently ignores the niceties of musical word-setting: too often a syllable such as 'kills' or 'breeze' is either held for a long note or put to a melisma. The recent *Cycle for Declamation*, three songs for unaccompanied tenor to prose texts of John Donne, compensates for this insensitive treatment by using long lines with freer rhythm, but the motivic construction still entails a repetitive and restrictive use of selected intervals which ultimately palls.

Of Rainier's instrumental music, the most interesting part of her output, Colin Mason goes so far as to say that 'the melodic interest is subordinate'.[1] Her harmony very seldom draws attention to itself: with rare exceptions (to be found far more in the earlier than the later works) anything like a chord is sedulously avoided. The peculiarly individual quality of her instrumental writing results from a predominating concentration on textural problems. There is nothing reminiscent about it after the first String Quartet (1939); the nearest correspondence is probably to be found in the analogically abstract approach of Barbara Hepworth's sculpture. (It is significant in this connection that Rainier composed music for a film about Hepworth.) The *Barbaric Dance Suite* for piano (1949) and the *Sinfonia da Camera* for string orchestra (1947) reveal a sensitive and original handling of stringed instruments employed to build wiry formal structures out of tiny rhythmic patterns, reiterated notes, and occasional percussive note-clusters. The rhythmic organisation of these works is remarkably vital, even though the musical development proceeds very little by contrapuntal means, for the texture is always lucid and therefore convincing.

Elisabeth Lutyens' adoption of dodecaphonic technique was the consequence of a largely independent development of chromatic styles. She has employed it in all her works written in and after 1940, but with personal modifications so that her music seldom reveals the direct in-

[1] In his article on Rainier in *Grove's Dictionary*, 5th ed.

fluence of Schönberg. The contrast presented by the early second quartet (1938) and the later dodecaphonic third quartet is instructive in that it shows clearly the effects of her technical change. While the first movement of No. 2 is obviously tonal (being centred on F), the second and third, having no fixed tonal centre, may therefore be classed as atonal. The chief theme of the *allegretto scherzando* is built from triadic elements, but the first subject of the *poco adagio* uses a motif whose intervallic order resembles that of Maconchy's fourth quartet mentioned previously. Despite the somewhat apparent lack of stylistic unity in the melodies, the work's turbulent and occasionally syncopated rhythms, its passionate ornamentation and especially its terse and concise, yet flowing, form are very impressive. Quartet No. 3, written ten years later,[1] is noticeably less urgent in impulse, though melodically consistent: the rhythms move easily and there is even a dance-like trio to the second movement whose relaxed homophony seems strangely unconvincing in a dodecaphonic work. The texture of both quartets depends little on contrapuntal organisation; that of the third quartet is almost too simple to sustain interest.

Lutyens' mature instrumental music includes a good many works for unusual chamber combinations which exhibit a delicate sense of the colouristic properties of combinations of instrumental timbres. Her works for full orchestra are few, but include *Three Symphonic Preludes* (1942), perhaps her most important work so far. The Viola Concerto (1947), her solitary essay in this form, is typical of all her best work; its themes are clearly presented, the texture is widely spaced, and the form simple and direct. Though its more linear passages for the viola are expressive, the use of harmonic figuration in bravura sections is, as so often happens in dodecaphonic music, rather mechanical in its effect and poor in inspiration. Most of her vocal music is of early date, but an *a cappella Motet*, a setting of selected aphorisms of Wittgenstein, appeared in 1954. It is obviously influenced by the example of Schönberg's *a cappella* pieces, Op. 27, and, like them, is extremely awkward to sing. Months of practice may possibly secure an accurate performance, but its vocal lines, with their large leaps and absence of tonal security, can never be felt to be truly choral in style by the singers. This application of dodecaphony runs counter to the strongest native traditions and will therefore hardly be encouraged by those anxious to preserve high standards of singing.

Grove gives its date as 1949, but the printed score is marked 'November 1948'.

145

V

These women were among the first English composers to come to terms with the more extreme developments of European music during this century. The influx of musicians and composers from Central Europe in the years immediately preceding the Second World War has greatly assisted the change of tastes and attitudes of which their music was the harbinger. To mention but a few of the Continental refugees whose presence has been so valuable, England is honoured to shelter Egon Wellesz (b. 1885), a pupil of Schönberg and the last surviving representative of the older Viennese tradition; Roberto Gerhard (b. 1896), a Spanish dodecaphonist; and Matyas Seiber (b. 1905), who by his teaching and compositions has profoundly influenced many of the younger composers now rising to fame. Today there is in England a greater interest in the newest Continental fashions than for a long time previously, and Europe in its turn is learning more of English music.

Of the rapidly growing group of English dodecaphonists Humphrey Searle (b. 1915) is the most important representative. His style owes much to his study of Liszt and Schönberg, and to the teaching he received from Webern. The works he composed before adopting dodecaphonic technique are unashamedly romantic and lushly harmonic. In the D minor piano concerto (1944) this is coupled to a quasi-Lisztian *bravura* style for the solo part, which, though effective, depends rather too much on a conventional use of harmonic figuration and not enough on melodic organisation. The ground bass theme of the second movement is weakened by its persistent chromatic descent. His first twelve-note work, *Intermezzo*, for eleven instruments (1946), shows the influence of Webern's works in its logically ordered melodic lines and leaps of large intervals. *Put away the Flutes* (1947), for tenor, flute, oboe and string quartet, is perhaps the first of his works to reveal a truly personal style: the voice has a grateful part to sing that skilfully follows the delicately balanced rhymes and assonances of W. R. Rodgers' verse. The *Poem* for twenty-two stringed instruments (1950) recaptures the romanticism of his earlier works in a most sensitive and beautiful handling of contrapuntal texture which makes it the most successful work by any English dodecaphonist to date. In the three works for speakers and orchestra (plus male chorus in the first and third) Searle has investigated novel problems of sound. *Gold Coast Customs* (1949) is perhaps a little too long to sustain an unbroken interest in its musical development; *The Shadow of Cain* (1952) is more concise and much more tense in its rhythms and orchestration. The middle work of the three, *The River-run* (1951) is perhaps the most outstanding of the set: the combination of spoken word and orchestral timbres is especially suitable for the later prose of Joyce. Stimulating and evocative though these works may be, it is debatable whether their medium will prove valuable in the future development of musical art; its use suggests an evasion of that most central and fundamental problem, the treatment of the singing voice. Searle's Symphony (1953) is his largest instrumental work to date, revealing a successful and individual solution of the formal problems of an atonal symphonic style.

Peter Racine Fricker (b. 1920), Malcolm Arnold (b. 1921) and Iain Hamilton (b. 1922) are the most gifted of the new composers who came to the fore at the conclusion of the Second World War. All three possess wide technical resource and ample fertility of invention which (though each has written a few vocal works) they prefer to exhibit in symphonies, concertos and chamber music. They thus continue the trend commenced by several of their older contemporaries.

Fricker has already won a considerable reputation both at home and abroad and may well prove to be the most important composer of his generation. His complete command of twentieth-century harmonic and contrapuntal idioms is revealed in a homogeneous, varied and very forceful style organised by a logical yet individual form. The most obvious characteristics of his music are its strength and assurance, coloured by a rather grim earnestness which some have miscalled austerity. The first string quartet (1949) in one movement reveals Fricker's tensely unified formal methods: the alternation and development of its sections, the inevitable but not over-obtrusive motivic connections and derivations, and the urgent sweep of its rhythms produce a work of great power. In some of his later works, as, for example, the Second Symphony (1951), he broadens his form without relaxing its intensity by a remarkable and wholly original use of *rondo* structure. It would be meaningless to attempt a separate discussion of his harmonic and contrapuntal methods, for Fricker's synthesis of the two is complete. Consequently when he employs figurative patterns they never seem less interesting or compelling than his other melodic devices. His instrumentation derives much of its clarity from his part-writing and careful consideration of texture.

The purely melodic aspect of his style is the least impressive. When he writes a sustained melody, e.g. the *Elegy* of the *Prelude, Elegy and Finale for strings* (1949), its rhythms frequently suggest those of other

147

melodic styles but which his notes belie. Speaking personally, I find that all too often the shape of one of his melodies leads me to expect something extremely beautiful and moving of which I feel myse'f deprived at its conclusion. The clue to this (if, indeed, it is anything more than a personal reaction) is perhaps to be sought in his rare vocal works. The *Sonnets of Cecco Angiolieri* for tenor and a largely woodwind ensemble (1947) have a harsh, even disjointed vocal line: it may seem to be vocally conceived, but its frequent resemblances to his instrumental writing dispute this. In his recent anthem *Blessed be the God* for unaccompanied choir (1954) he has achieved truly vocal melody only by sacrificing his individuality.

Arnold's music is cheerful and immediately attractive, providing a welcome relief from the gloomier styles so fashionable at this time. It recalls Wilfrid Mellers' recent warning that we 'should beware of assuming that the art most relevant to our time is that which makes the overt reference to the distress among which we live'.[1] Arnold writes quickly and therefore sometimes unevenly, but the general level of his published works is very high. He has a gift for diatonic melody which, coupled to his flair for orchestration, ensures the immediate success of whatever he writes. His texture is always lucid and simple, whether it be experienced in the charming chamber music for wind ensembles or the more ample symphonies and concertos. He relishes impish touches of rhythm, occasional bizarre combinations of timbre, and, having been an orchestral player, knows what to write not only to sound effective but also to give pleasure to the performers.

His formal structures are occasionally inconsequential, but are nearly always easier to follow than those of his contemporaries on account of their diatonic material. Up to now he has not produced anything profound; even when setting a religious text (e.g. the *Laudate Dominum* for chorus and organ, 1950) cheerfulness keeps on breaking in. At the present time his main weakness appears to lie in his very frequent employment of scale and *arpeggio* figurations of a somewhat facile type: the Clarinet Concerto (1952) suffers considerably from this fault. When he organises his music more strictly, more concisely, as in the lovely opening movement of the *Sinfonietta*, no one among his contemporaries can surpass him in delicate charm.

Hamilton resembles Fricker in his wide awareness of contemporary trends, but has not yet shared Fricker's good fortune in securing fre-

[1] 'Recent trends in British Music', Wilfrid Mellers: *The Musical Quarterly*, April 1952.

quent performances of his works. His melodies are deeply expressive in their sustained flow: indeed, he has a greater gift for extended, soaring lines than anyone since Tippett. This is already apparent in his Op. 1, *Variations for Strings* (1948), whose theme is a typical example of Hamilton's lyrical feeling. It is revealed at its best in instrumental works, but his recent *Songs of Summer*, for soprano, clarinet, cello and piano (Op. 27), exhibit it with equal effectiveness. In his unaccompanied choral pieces, particularly the settings of Border poems, it seems a little restricted by purely harmonic considerations.

This melodic style is the source of Hamilton's contrapuntal strength, as the Quartet (1949) and the Second Symphony (1951) amply demonstrate. Much of his music, however, relies mainly on harmonic techniques which may avoid contrapuntal textures entirely. He uses figuration and percussive chordal reiteration in a manner which, while it may at the beginning have owed something to a study of Bartók, is now exceptionally underivative. The Piano Sonata (1951) contains many examples of his individual techniques of this sort which in the Viola Sonata (1954) give rise to an impassioned intensity which is not only profoundly moving but is sustained throughout one of the most successful works for a difficult medium. Another striking characteristic of his style is his fondness for widely spaced instrumental textures, especially in slow movements and quiet passages, used with equally fine effect in orchestral works (e.g. the Second Symphony) and chamber music (e.g. the recent Clarinet Sonata). A reading of the scores of the still unperformed Violin Concerto, Op. 12, and the *Sinfonia Concertante*, for violin and viola with chamber orchestra, Op. 8, is enough to prove that they are worthy of the composer's other large works.

VI

This survey of the composers who may be said to form the main stream of contemporary development in the national music has neglected so far some of the more marginal figures who, though in a more solitary way, yet testify to the breadth of variety of our present renaissance. Stanley Bate (b. 1913) and Arnold Cooke (b. 1906) are probably the only English composers to exhibit the direct influence of Hindemith, with whom both have studied. Cooke's style is the more deeply indebted to his master, particularly in its open contrapuntal texture; Bate's style reveals several contending influences of which those of Vaughan Williams and Hindemith seem the strongest. Bate's third symphony (1940) shows this lack of stylistic integration very strongly, despite its obvious power, but in the later Second Quartet there are signs that he has now achieved a consistent personal manner. William Wordsworth (b. 1908) is superficially conservative in his use of harmony, especially when he writes for piano. His chamber music is often severely contrapuntal in its manipulation of romantically melodic lines. The symphonies suffer from his rather undistinguished rhythms, failing to ensure a true inevitability of form. Richard Arnell (b. 1917) is completely eclectic in an efficient but (as far as his present development goes) undistinguished style which is to be heard at its best in his orchestral works; his vocal writing frequently lapses into banality.

There are many composers working in the older choral and vocal tradition who, because they rarely write orchestral music, tend to be overlooked in any general estimate of English music. Gerald Finzi (b. 1901) is typical, in his disregard of all contemporary development other than that to be observed in Vaughan Williams' music, of this group. He has written much fine and beautiful music which nevertheless seems to belong to a past age. Therefore it fails to convince many of the younger generation; nostalgia, however finely displayed, always contains a hint of weakness. The more positive side of the purely choral tradition is represented by Bernard Naylor (b. 1907) who explores the application of a modern harmonic and contrapuntal techniques to choral writing in a manner at once individual and compelling. His three Latin Motets (1949) are not only fine music, but completely unlike any other choral music written in England today.

Among the youngest composers beginning to appear in concert programmes the number of those who employ dodecaphonic technique is increasing. Here English music mirrors a fashionable trend of the rest of the world. Others reveal the influence of the harsher and more mechanical German composers, such as Orff and Blacher, which is perhaps to be deplored. It would be strangely ironic if the movement of English music away from the Teutonicism of the nineteenth century were to finish in the adoption of later and less distinguished styles from the same quarter. The more aberrant fashions, such as electronic music and *musique concrète*, have also claimed English adherents, but mercifully few so far.

The chief strength of English music has hitherto resided in its vocal and choral traditions. Britten and Tippett have shown in their music and in their attitude to contemporary styles that it can still so reside, and yet be the source of strength in the development of native instrumental music. But the prevailing tendency today is for the instrumental and vocal styles to become so separated that there is no longer any fruitful interaction. Worse, inconsiderate (because quasi-instrumental) writing for voices seems to be on the increase. If English music can avoid the further development of this tendency by remaining true to her native traditions, it is possible that it might ultimately commence a return to a more healthy state of music in the rest of the world. Slavish pursuit of foreign fashions will help nobody in the long run.

Swiss Contemporary Music

IAIN HAMILTON

A REMARKABLE feature of Swiss music is its lack of insularity. This is interesting in the music of such an independent and proudly individual people. The country's linguistic division into three may in part be responsible for the influence exerted by the trends of French and German music in this century but Italy has, on the other hand, had very little influence. Nationalism of any kind it is almost impossible to trace.

Is this a lack of strength and individuality in a country's music, or a sign of open-mindedness in its artists? The question of nationalism in art is always a problem, and such elements of it which may have helped to enliven one country's music may have most successfully deadened that of another.

Hungary is immensely the richer for Bartók's national influences. His individuality was great enough to transcend the weakening powers which national traits can have on an artist. Would Nielsen be worse or better for national trends in his work? Is it not just the subtle imprint of Italian lucidity and a superb national sense of vocal writing which raises Dallapiccola's cosmopolitan style far above that of others? Is Valen better for the lack of any Norwegian elements? It is so often this very national flavour which keeps Grieg and Dvořák alive today. A certain Russian element hardly ever leaves the most classically moulded works of Stravinsky—it is indigenous to his style. Whereas in the highly conscious political-nationalism of Shostakovich it is so sadly lacking. And what of the deadening 'Englishry' which lies so heavily on our music as compared with Britten's subtle assimilation of the finest and most enduring of English national traits? These are fascinating and paradoxical questions.

The two outstanding Swiss composers, because of their maturity and mastery of their personal idiom in numerous works, are Arthur Honegger and Frank Martin. Both have achieved international reputation. Although they are both of the same generation, success came to Honegger almost twenty years earlier than to Martin, whose works began to reach a widespread public only in the early 1940s, when the composer was over fifty. This reputation is maintained almost entirely by works composed from that time onwards.

The difference between these two composers is a very definite one as regards style. This is all the more interesting as they have concentrated generally on works for the same medium. Large-scale choral works feature largely in their output and, no less, purely orchestral works so often concerned with handling of new timbres and textures. Honegger has written for the stage, Martin has recently produced an opera on Shakespeare's *The Tempest*. Neither have, however, been very attracted to the piano, used alone, to song-writing or to chamber music to the same extent as other contemporary composers, although both have written works for these media.

Both are remarkable for the clarity and logic with which they handle musical textures, Martin with his delight in employing such diverse layers as piano, harp, harpsichord and strings within one work; Honegger with his dark luminous colours which flash like dark crystal. To his early influence from the French school with its emphasis on clarity and precision, he has brought a rugged, dark and ironically humorous quality as well as a contrapuntal vigour. So many of Martin's finest works are almost self-imposed problems of handling textures. These he solves with true mastery. In the Concerto for seven wind instruments, percussion and string orchestra, his achievement in this field reaches its highest point, but hardly less so in the *Petite Symphonie Concertante*, the Harpsichord Concerto and in the Violin Concerto. The various layers of contrasting instrumental sound which he employs blend perfectly, never becoming turgid or heavy as could happen all too easily with the instruments which he chooses. Martin's music is so often a quest in the realms of light as is the case, pursued by entirely different methods, with Britten.

Arthur Honnegger was born in Le Havre, of Swiss parents, in 1892. He studied at the Zürich and Paris Conservatoires and became a member of the group known as 'Les Six'. His earliest works date from about 1916 and show a fascination for an essentially Gallic sensitivity and fine sense of shading. This is evident in the *Pastorale d'Été*. In *Horace*

Victorieux, a symphonic work, however, a panache worthy of Strauss is achieved. This element is seldom to occur in his later work, but in the oratorio, *Le Roi David*, of 1926, Honegger wrote one of the first large musical frescoes in his output—a form which was to engage him so often later.

In *Le Roi David* he achieves an economy of expression and simplicity of style which, no matter how large his conception may be, remain as essential features of his work as a whole. His definite liking for a contrapuntal texture never oversteps the bounds of symphonic style to clog and confuse the fabric. The use of bitonality and polytonality is also always well calculated and telling in its effect. A recent and particularly fine example of this occurs at the beginning of the fifth symphony where the bitonal harmonies are so spaced and so simply manoeuvred in contrary motion that a feeling of great dignity and grandeur is achieved.

In 1930 Honegger wrote his first symphony. This is a much more turgid and thick work than one associates with him and is hardly prophetic of the many splendid pages in the four later symphonies. The second, for string orchestra with trumpet *ad libitum* in the finale, was composed in 1941 and is one of his finest works. He regarded it as a poignant expression of his feelings towards the beleaguered state of Europe at that time and the inclusion of the trumpet in the finale is to kindle a feeling of hope and belief in final deliverance. In this work we have copious examples of his predilection for dark colours; these continue for long stretches and are contrasted with powerful muscular rhythms, ironical grotesque humour and moments of tranquillity. The work is superbly conceived for the medium and has that ring which always proves the successful use of a body of strings.

In the third symphony, the *Liturgique*, the opening movement, 'Dies Irae', is wild and rugged and employs a considerable amount of virtuosity as in the finale of the fifth. The second and third movements, 'De Profundis Clamavi' and 'Dona Nobis Pacem', are set extensively, in the dark regions of the orchestra, especially the latter, which only rises at the climax and then remains high in register for the serene and ethereal close.

The fourth symphony is scored for chamber orchestra and is an interesting example of Honegger applying himself to this reduced combination and still obtaining so often a dark-hued palette. But this is in no way a dark or tragic utterance as the sub-title would suggest—*Deliciae Basiliensis*. It is very diatonic in style and employs extensively

154

one of the composer's favourite rhythms, the dotted rhythm which is associated with the opening of the old French Overture. Woodwind decoration is employed in a refreshing manner, something which is to form an important element in the first movement of the fifth symphony. The piano is used as an orchestral instrument to vary the texture and not at any time as a soloist. This work, written in 1946, is, together with the *Concerto da camera* for Flute, Cor Anglais and Strings, amongst Honegger's most diverting and delightful works. It reveals the finest of Gallic influence and is a miracle of scoring. This work, together with so many others by the most eminent contemporary composers, was written for Paul Sacher, the distinguished Swiss conductor, who has always shown himself a true patron of the finest in the century's music.

The fifth symphony was commissioned by the Koussevitzky Music Foundation for the Boston Symphony Orchestra in 1951. One cannot help but think that Honegger had this fine body of players very much in mind when he conceived the work, for the finale is one of the biggest *tours de force* he has written since the early *Mouvements Symphoniques*. The achievement of this in the finale of this symphony cannot be denied—the result in a fine performance is staggering indeed. However, this is obtained at the expense of the symphony as a whole, coming as it does at the end of a work which is anything but frivolous in its other two movements. The first has a glow and dignity about it which is somewhat lacking in the third symphony and, one feels, not aimed at in the second and fourth.

Into these symphonies one feels Honegger has put his purest musical thought and concentration. In the delightful *Concerto da camera* he has matched the lucidity and grace of the fourth, but there is in addition here an element of virtuosity which is called for and most certainly achieved. None of these works, however, reflect the one element which is inherent in almost all composers who have come under the influence of the French, that is the literary element. Honegger has said often that he is no slave to texts or words as regards the form of the works themselves, and this is largely true, but the very number of times he has employed voices and narrator in his output shows his fascination for forms in which literature plays a leading part.

His large frescoes, *Le Roi David*, *Judith*, *Antigone*, *Jeanne d'Arc au Bûcher* and *Le Danse des Morts* reveal a fine sense of panache. Here there is an opening of the texture and a relaxing of the purely musical concentration to accommodate the added element of words and to suit the dramatic medium of the theatre.

Le Roi David, *Jeanne d'Arc* and *Le Danse des Morts* are, however, quite as satisfactory in concert performance and this Honegger himself is said to prefer. This is largely because the action is very slight and such a passage as the Dauphin's entry into Rheims in *Jeanne d'Arc*, which employs the use of the cinema, is an incongruity which is a welcome loss in concert performance.

If a producer of genius and certain particularly gifted performers could be secured to deal with the static roles, an amazing effect could be achieved as this last work in particular has a fervour about it which could be realised in such a performance. These three works are, however, better classed as oratorios.

Antigone, said to be Honegger's favourite amongst his own works, is quite another matter, for here the setting of a Greek subject in an adaptation by Jean Cocteau demands an essentially statuesque grandeur in stage presentation and this Honegger achieves superbly. This, together with *Persephone* and *Oedipus Rex* of Stravinsky, must stand as the finest result of the century's prepossession with the Greek theme in the lyric theatre.

In this work Honegger uses a highly contrapuntal style and seems to achieve an essence which he dilutes in varying degrees in his other works. The inevitability of the tragic theme is ideally contained in the score and the relentless rhythms and the clear driving use of them has a terrifying effect.

As compared with this, *Jeanne d'Arc*, for which Paul Claudel supplied the text, is a much more loosely constructed work and at times there is only the minimum of musical interest going on. The speaking parts no doubt invite this less tense musical treatment, as the increased rate of words uttered in speech as opposed to singing at once creates for a composer a hard problem. If an equally interesting accompanying part is played while the narrator is speaking, the listener is apt to become confused and concentrate on one element only. This concentration on words during singing is easier to balance with our concentration on the music, no matter how complex, as the meaning of the words and their utterance is spread over a greater space of time. Various ways of solving this have been attempted by different composers; Honegger's is one of the most direct, the only danger being the tendency to make the musical fabric very tenuous at times—certainly in a work where the central figures do not sing at all. The end of this piece is, however, very moving and achieves a tension and then, no less successfully, a relaxation which is admirably suited to the tragic incident.

These large-scale choral works, although falling between two stools as regards musical form, and in a sense, as far as presentation is concerned, have nonetheless brought Honegger before a large public and have acquainted them with what is a large and significant part of his output.

In common with many other composers who began their creative life after the First World War, Honegger showed interest in jazz and lighter forms of music. He has never at any time made great use of his interest as for instance did Milhaud or Stravinsky. In *Le Roi Pausole* he created what is almost a revue and this has recently been revived in Hamburg with great success. In such a small but effective movement as the finale of the Sonatine for Clarinet and Piano he shows himself to be more than able to adapt the jazz idiom to his own style without losing too much in the process.

In the three *Mouvements Symphoniques,* which include *Pacific 231* and *Rugby,* he has attempted to create music of an entirely exteriorised kind and has achieved this by writing works in the nature of a *tour de force.* This was first seen in his *Horace Victorieux* and has appeared again as recently as 1951 in the fifth symphony, in the finale of that work.

In chamber music, song and piano music, Honegger has created several works of great charm and finesse, qualities so sadly lacking in a great many of his contemporaries, but has seldom put his most intense and powerful thoughts into these media. A composer who has proven himself so at home in and so inclined towards the larger forms and particularly to large fresco-like creations, is apt to find the intimate realms of chamber music less satisfactory for his sweeping gestures if, however, perfectly suited to his less intense expression. Many works in the twenties prove his delight in the smaller combinations for less weighty purposes.

His enormous output shows a lively interest in all manner of musical styles and trends but, as with any great artist, he is able to assimilate them into his own personality and withstand their turning him into a mere eclectic. The concentrated grandeur of *Antigone,* the *virtuoso finale* of the fifth symphony, the chamber-like delicacy of the fourth symphony, the jazz elements in the clarinet sonatine, the copious examples of the grotesque humour side by side with the dark luminous tragedy that pervade so many pages of his *oeuvre*—all these are elements of a many-sided and mature creative artist. Here one does not see only a polyglot assembly and a frantic desire to change style for its own sake.

Like Stravinsky, Honegger has been fascinated by all musical developments and both have drawn from these various movements something
to enrich their several palettes. Neither has for a moment considered
the use of any of these elements without the greatest sincerity. But then
they are both masters and in the arts masters alone are sincere.

Frank Martin was born in Geneva in 1890. He has had an astonishing
rise to international fame since the end of the Second World War and
this fame rests almost entirely on works composed since 1942, the date
of *Le Vin Herbé*, when he was already fifty-two years old.

His first appearance as a composer dates from about 1911, when he
is influenced by Fauré and Ravel, the latter influence dying hard during
many evolutions in his style at a later date. His early interest in Jacques
Dalcroze's Eurhythmics is not to be overlooked with regard to his
experiments in rhythmic patterns. These are often felt to be an influence
of Stravinsky, but this seems a considerable misinterpretation of
Martin's purpose.

In 1926 a work *Rhythms* appeared which testifies to his preoccupation with this element at that time. In 1928 he was appointed a professor
at the Dalcrose Institute in Geneva.

By 1930 the twelve-note serial technique of Schönberg had become
of great interest to Martin. Although an admirer of the technique,
however, he never allowed it to become part of his real aesthetic and
he employs only such elements of it as he finds essential to the enrich-
ment of his style. He never uses it in a serial sense as in the manner
of Schönberg and cannot even vaguely be termed a twelve-note composer. His use of the row employed as a harmonic basis at times is
enough to show his independent attitude. This is a negation of what
Schönberg intended. The method of welding an element of twelve-
note technique to the ordinary tonal system is interesting but hardly
novel as it is virtually a return to the attitude of transition through
which Schönberg passed to arrive at his mastery of pure twelve-note
composition. Martin is in no sense atonal. An interesting parallel is
Bartók's employment (consciously or unconsciously) of a series of
twelve notes as one of the subjects of the first and third movements of
his Violin Concerto. A series is not used here, as, in the first movement,
four rows are employed one after the other and this is no facet of
twelve-note composition. What really happens is that Bartók uses the
twelve notes unrepeated in various versions as his subject and that in
itself has nothing to do with serial composition. No atonal feeling is
even felt as he is careful to begin each 'row' on either an A or à D and

this, with a considerable amount of D and A in the accompanying parts, anchors the passage soundly in D.

This is very much the attitude of Martin in his employment of rows and he makes beautiful and consistent use of it as part of his style. The opening movements of the *Petite Symphonie Concertante* and of the Harpsichord Concerto furnish fine examples of this.

From 1934 to 1938 there appeared a Piano Concerto, a Symphony and Ballades for Piano, Flute and Trombone; in each case accompanied by orchestra or, as an alternative, piano in the case of the last two. Although these Ballades are sometimes heard, it is not through any of these works that we know him. In 1942 there appeared *Le Vin Herbé*. In this reflective version of the Tristan and Isolda legend for solo voices, small chorus and strings and piano, Martin at last seems to have achieved his personal idiom as never before. This made him known far and wide and was followed by the *Sonnets of Cornet Rilke,* for low voice and chamber orchestra, and the *Six Monologues from 'Jedermann',* again for low voice but with medium-sized orchestra. Both include parts for harp and piano, two instruments which are seldom absent from Martin's scores. These three works, together with *Golgotha* of 1945-48 form a vital part of his output and are works of deep feeling and expression, the voice being used throughout in a serious manner and never being employed for extrovert dramatic effect or in any way sensationally. This is to remain an indigenous part of the composer even when employing the concerto form, virtuosity does not seem to appeal to him and showy passages are seldom to be found in his works, no matter how much true virtuosity he himself may exhibit as a composer in his employment of novel textures for so many of his works. The often spare and homophonic accompaniments to these vocal works invest them with a dignity and restraint which is so entirely in keeping with the subject in each case.

Another very important element in Martin's style also becomes evident in these works.

In the Rilke Sonnets major and minor triads and their inversions are used continually in a free and unrelated manner, while in the Jedermann Monologues the predilection for the minor triad, one of the real fingerprints of his style, is very marked. This is to reach its apotheosis in the Preludes for Piano of 1948 and in the Harpsichord Concerto of 1952. This insistent use of triads adds greatly to the peculiarly Ravelian flavour of so much of Martin's music.

In 1945 Paul Sacher conducted the first performance of what was to become not only one of Martin's most popular works but also one of the most-played of contemporary pieces; the *Petite Symphonie Concertante* for String Orchestra, Piano, Harp, and Harpsichord. In this we encounter a feature which has continued to fascinate the composer, the almost self-imposed problem of handling textures usually of three or more layers, each really self-sufficient, but fused together in a masterly and inevitable manner. This problem Martin solves each time most satisfyingly to the ear; the glow and clear brilliance of the texture of the *Petite Symphonie* is delightful.

The form of this work is, however, less convincing than that of the wind instrument Concerto or of the Harpsichord Concerto. The metamorphosis of the subject of the slow movement with its dropping semitone, into the quicker march section of the same movement, is something as disappointing as is this procedure when employed by Liszt. In this work it is ill-assorted with the music which has preceded it.

The virtuosic solution of this problem of texture is, in the Concerto for seven wind instruments, timpani, percussion and strings, quite amazing. Here what is virtually a chamber orchestra with percussion is handled so as to justify the title of the work exactly and a concerto in the classical sense emerges. This work dates from 1950. The Violin Concerto of 1951 again poses the problem of textures, this time by using an orchestra composed of two each of flute, oboe, clarinet, bassoon, horn and trumpet, one trombone, harp, piano and strings. Much of the accompanying texture moves in streams of thirds, fourths and fifths, and the pairs of instruments employed create a homogeneity of colour which is an important feature of the whole work.

The Harpsichord Concerto of 1952 is yet another example of this problem. This time in addition to the soloist there is an orchestra of two flutes, one oboe, one clarinet and one bassoon, two horns, one trumpet and strings. The style is again linear in his own clear fashion and the minor triad is apparent as a part of his harmonic thinking throughout. The solo part is virtuosic and often dazzling in its brilliance, but this arises always directly out of the musical logic itself and is not a mere laying-on of flashy decoration. The flavour of Ravel is often felt, due, not only to the use of triadic movement, but to the extreme finesse of texture and scoring. The work has achieved what one must term popularity in the case of a concerto for an instrument such as the harpsichord.

In the eight preludes for piano and the Five Ariel Songs these stylistic features are shown in other media. The choral pieces are interesting, as Martin here uses his choir almost, one might say, in 'layers' and we hear each moving in its own orbit and yet always combining within the whole. The composer has recently completed an opera, based on Shakespeare's *Tempest*, which has had its première in Vienna. This should be of great interest as, so far, his attitude to setting words has been essentially a musical-dramatic one, this being admirably suited to his choral works. In opera, however, a wholly dramatic setting is required, for, no matter how good the musical quality of an opera may be, a great part of its eventual success lies in the forthright dramatic and theatrical presentation of the subject. In choral music this is not a vital element, highly effective as it may be.

As with Honegger, there are in Martin's *oeuvre* two principal sections, that of the large choral but essentially non-theatrical works, and that of the instrumental, largely orchestral works. Both have written chamber music, but have not found in it their most vital medium of expression. This is notable in a period when the field of chamber music has been enriched by some of the finest of the work of contemporary composers. One has only to consider the importance of the music of Bartók, Schönberg, Berg and Hindemith to be found in their composition for string quartet, and the employment of the piano in their works and those of Stravinsky, to realise by comparison how unimportant these media have so far been to Honegger and Martin.

The element of experiment in its more novel forms is definitely more readily to be found in Honegger. A movement such as the finale of his fifth symphony is outside Martin's scope and equally far, one feels, from his ideals. His reticence as compared with Honegger in this is no doubt in part due to his work having matured at a much later stage in his creative life than that of Honegger, as well, of course—and this is all that really matters in a sincere artist—to his true individuality which, whether one likes its flavour or not, is something positive.

Conrad Beck (b. 1901) is a composer of quite another kind. He has pursued paths very different from those so far mentioned. Any prepossession with musical textures in the sense of those used by Martin and Honegger is foreign to the very linear and much more severe style of much of Beck's music, particularly that of his earlier period. From 1923 to 1932 he settled in Paris and was a member of a circle which included Honegger and Roussel. In no direct way is he influenced by either except possibly in the sense that both these are so much more contrapuntal and linear than the majority of French composers at that time. Beck can therefore be said to be influenced up to a point by these composers in his especially contrapuntal approach even to the symphony, the form least at ease in assimilating large and continuous contrapuntal textures.

Beck won early recognition in the United States while still under thirty. Koussevitzky had performed his third symphony in Boston and shortly afterwards he won a Coolidge prize with a Concerto for String Quartet and Orchestra, this being performed under Stokowski. In 1934 he completed a large-scale choral work based on the sayings of Angelus Silesius and this is considered, together with his recently completed work for the same medium, *Der Tod zu Basel,* to be amongst his most impressive and moving works.

His output includes six symphonies, four string quartets and concertos for piano, cello and viola. In such works as the fourth, fifth and sixth Symphonies, the forthright movement of the whole and the strong linear nature of the music are immediately felt. There is nothing here in the way of effect indulged in for its own sake and, as is the case with so many highly contrapuntal composers, little use is made of orchestral colour. The orchestra is here used as a medium for the expression of the musical ideas and the resultant sound is the direct outcome of the musical texture itself with hardly any assistance or heightening of colour from the orchestra.

An immediate comparison here may be made with the works of Hindemith, where a similar method of scoring what is so often a contrapuntal texture is employed. Accompaniment figures, figuration, timbres are seldom to be found, the music moving with a logic that seems to disdain any helping hand or relief which might be sought from the medium of performance which is used.

The fourth symphony (Concerto for Orchestra) offers many examples of delicate scoring in this contrapuntal manner, and its use of various and interesting groupings conveys Beck's meaning of the word concerto —an earlier meaning than that which suggests the *pièce de résistance.* The virtuoso element is absent from such a composer's outlook, and even the gay active finale has no showmanship about it and has hardly a trace of colour or effects. The middle movement, a set of variations, is beautifully conceived and the variations are always recognisably related to the theme. Conciseness is a guiding feature here; nothing is extraneous or *al fresco.*

The fifth symphony goes much farther in the use of contrapuntal methods and the opening movement is built around several cells which occur over and over again, not in a dramatic-symphonic sense but in a way conceived by a mind at home in contrapuntal thinking, and working in this way with ease and certainty. The alto saxophone is used throughout the work. Although Beck's style is highly linear and discards many outwardly attractive elements of compositional techniques, he is anything but severe or unapproachable, and certainly not gloomy. No movement proves this more than the finale of this symphony which is a wild tarantella with many a wink at Rossini. Here, however, Beck never abandons his own style, and the orchestra, though handled brilliantly, never indulges in effects which would be more than excusable in such a gay piece.

More recently Beck has eased his highly-taut fabric, as is very apparent in the recent *Der Tod zu Basel*. At once one comes upon a style which achieves a dignity in a personal manner, but by much simpler and more direct means. Also the tonality now is much clearer. His work has always been basically tonal, however free the juxtaposition of unrelated lines may have been, and each movement centres round a tonal pole which is never lost.

In *Der Tod zu Basel* the earnest nature of the subject has drawn a distilled clarity from the composer and even the great *tutti* are remarkably free from any highly active polyphony; yet they have sufficient substance to give them a musical value far higher than that of so many loud empty *tutti* in this century's music—so often a lot of sound and colour and little musical content beneath.

Beck's texture is now much barer and the solo soprano and baritone are often accompanied by only a single line. The sense of growth is nevertheless always there and this barely wrought passage expands into something fuller and compels us to feel the necessity for the momentary spare texture. The strings form the basis of the orchestra and play mostly in quite a simple and unobtrusive manner. The other instruments are employed with the most telling effect, but there is seldom full scoring except at the climaxes and here a stark grandeur is aimed at and achieved in a manner wholly at one with the austere and serious subject. Beck certainly impresses by his sincerity and his unwillingness to charm by splashes of known or unknown colour.

To turn to the music of Heinrich Sutermeister (b. 1910) after that of Beck is to meet an exact opposite in almost every way. Sutermeister enjoys a success with his opera *Romeo and Juliet* which has hardly been equalled in European opera houses since that accorded to *Der Rosenkavalier*. It has held the stage for over fifteen years and has always made immediate contact with the public, facts which not only cannot but must not be ignored in an era in which so much in music is written for and heard only by the few. In the opera house, what does not instantly and dramatically convey its meaning to the audience is bad opera in any age. This is no suggestion that only popular or easily assimilable *musical* styles will do. Any musical style, provided that it is wedded to dramatic force and a sense of theatre, will have its effect even if not always at first hearing. *Wozzeck* is a fine example of this—a work as telling in the theatre as any work of Verdi. Both Berg and Verdi, however, are masters of theatre sense.

In *Romeo and Juliet* Sutermeister has shown himself a master of this theatre sense but has chosen a musical style which is certainly no problem to anyone. Here effects are the thing, and often there is hardly any content when the colour and orchestration are accounted for. When any content *is* apparent it is very slender and unabashedly tonal and diatonic. That is no fault and is the very strength of some of the finest music of the present day; in such an idiom, however, the material has to be of the strongest, and too often in this opera the melodic style is lacking in distinction.

When one casts aside so many of the useful twentieth-century devices for covering up the potential musical weaknesses of so many composers and chooses to write in A major, then one is indeed on trial, and few ever take this step—how wise they are, for so many works of apparently wonderful complexity and deep searching would emerge instead as terribly boring and prosaic academic attempts! The new academicism of confused musical thinking does not cover the paucity of true invention, imagination and true and easy application of technique, any more than did that of any other academicism to a sincere and experienced judge. Stravinsky, Hindemith, Britten and Orff can work wonders in C major, but largely because of an ability to raise it above mere 'C major all-over-again' or 'C major with wrong notes'. Their new conception of tonality and diatonicism is *really* new and distinguished. With Sutermeister, highly effective though it often is in the theatre, too much is basically of the older diatonicism with a leaning to newer methods, particularly the use of parallel moving streams of unrelated harmony.

The two piano concertos further illustrate these tendencies. They are highly effective and engaging, the second in particular, and must be regarded primarily as show pieces. Texture is used in these works for its own sake without particular regard at times for the actual quality of the material. The opening march of the second concerto is highly extrovert, flashy, full of passage-work and a good deal of effective panache. The slow movement opens with a well-conceived passage for all the strings in *pizzicato* and then employs almost Beethovenian methods of solo line piano writing. This is a grilling test. The effect of the whole work is rhetorical and after a time such music can pall unless touched with the sublime.

It would, however, be grudging and impossible to deny the charm and other merits of much of Sutermeister's work. It is well planned and clearly thought out and if not of great profundity or originality it at least reveals a composer who is sincere enough to say just what he wants to say and who has succeeded, in the opera house, in entertaining and engaging the interest of thousands, a task nowadays too often left to the theatre, cinema or the world of sport.

Also born in 1910 was Rolf Liebermann. His affinity as a composer with Sutermeister is in his interest in the theatre and in that only, as Liebermann is a twelve-tone composer; the only prominent Swiss composer in fact to have employed the technique to any great extent. This does not exclude his utilising other techniques, and one is often taken aback by the variety of styles encountered in one work. In one of his most recent pieces, for instance, the opera *Penelope,* one meets twelve-tone technique in a rather free style, a Hindemithian form of diatonicism, bitonal chordal streams, use of the whole-tone scale and some very effective boogie-woogie. In the Concerto for Jazz Band and Orchestra of 1954 twelve-tone technique is used serially in a strict sense. A row is chosen which admits of much diatonic writing—a wise step in a work so much of the interest of which lies in the jazz ensemble.

The Symphony of 1949 already shows many of these traits. The expression is forceful and intense. The *Streitlied zwischen Leben und Tod* of 1950 employs more clearly diatonic methods, while the opera *Leonora '40-'45* is full of harmonic writing based on bitonal triads. The multiplicity of styles in this work is almost parodied in Act One, scene one, where, in a scene during which a piano recital takes place, first a contemporary piano sonata is heard and shortly afterwards the third *Liebestraum* of Liszt. The sonata is in fact Liebermann's own, published as a separate work, and the two works share much of the material, the opera in several places using themes from the sonata.

Dotted rhythms are used copiously in Liebermann's work as they are in that of Honegger. The texture varies from extremely contrapuntal writing to certain passages in the operas where the music becomes a mere background and negates any effect from the orchestra almost entirely. The style is also often very showy, but in quite a different way from that of Sutermeister. With Liebermann it is much more wild and hectic—an almost unfettered element.

Both the operas deal with the subjects of war and the constancy of women as wives. Both revive in different ways more than twice-told tales. For some time now we seldom see a year pass without either its Antigone, Helen, Joan of Arc, Ondine, etc. Amphitryon now has many rivals. Liebermann chooses for reincarnation Penelope and Leonora. He and his librettist, Heinrich Strobel, twist the latter's environs to Paris during the Occupation. Penelope finds herself in post-war Rome. Each work ends with a peroration on the subject common to both and in the case of *Penelope* this draws from the composer some of the finest music in the score.

The effect of both is swift moving. The scenes are short and generally deal with only one point or situation. One is rushed through the years with abandon and thus a widely spread tale in time is compressed into a work lasting in each case about two hours. This is a great feature of a good libretto, and although in these works one feels sometimes jostled overmuch in the fourth dimension, the skill of welding the original situation to the present is very admirable in an age of abysmal libretti. In *Penelope* we even move in both planes of time simultaneously, Ancient Greece and today, with only Penelope herself appearing in both. This is effected so closely as to require the use of a telescoped setting.

These two composers have adopted in their work as a whole several diverse elements and methods of composition which have not yet always managed to fuse into a very personal style as with Martin and Honegger. This is not to condemn their work as eclectic, but to stress a certain lack of homogeneity which one finds in an individual form of expression.

Liebermann's new Concerto for Jazz Band and Orchestra is a case in point. In the preface to this work the composer says his intention is to '. . . bring the current dance forms of today into "art" music'. He then writes the work in the strictest twelve-tone technique. An extreme, but not new, means of composition is therefore allied to such extremes in the other direction as a jump, blues, boogie-woogie and a mambo. Stylistically unity will be gained by the strict use of twelve-tone technique—his essay into the field of allying the two sides of musical activity is, in this work, the contradictory but fascinating element.

A composer enjoying a position of esteem equal to that of Martin,

Honegger and Beck in his own country is Willi Burkhard who was born in 1900 and died in 1955. He was a pupil of Karg-Elert in Leipzig in the early 1920s and a certain amount of the tradition of his training has remained in his work; although having composed in all forms, his choral works have done most to establish his reputation. His output is enormous, extending to Opus 100.

His style is highly linear and contrapuntal in an almost baroque manner. The work most representative of this highly-taut style is the large-scale oratorio *Des Gesicht Jesajas*, written between 1933 and 1935. Again there is a strong inclination to bitonality, especially in the use of unrelated triads vertically.

In the cantata, *Herbst*, of 1933 the linear writing is again combined with this use of bitonality; for example in the third item, *Der Wiesenbach*, and again in the sixth, *Blätterfall*. Later there are more examples of this to be found in the cantata, *Das Ewige Brausen* of 1937. The lines in this work have become much more colouristic and often less rigidly contrapuntal. The effect is of greater variety given to the texture as a whole, and relieves what can so easily become dull in a continuously contrapuntal texture. The last page of this work is important from this point of view. The four *ostinato* lines of the accompaniment give the effect of a moving background of colour rather than of four independent lines of equal importance.

The Oratorio *Das Jahr* of 1942 is another matter. Here the influence of Nature has drawn from the composer a less relentless and more sensual—even colouristic style. Polyphony gives way to more definitely harmonic methods, and a more open texture suits the nature of the work which is in fact on the subject of the Seasons. There is a greater use made of actual accompaniment figuration. This is interesting as contrapuntally-minded composers are often slow to make such a form of writing part of their style. Hindemith and Beck may be cited here. In this work the tonal element, always a strong feature of Burkhard's style, is further strengthened by a lessening of the use of bitonality. The opening of *Der Sommer* still touches on this, but in a less consistent' way, and later the use of a murmuring semi-tonal figure is purely colouristic. There follows on this a rugged contrapuntal fugue. The various features of his style are therefore well applied in this powerful work. In Burkhard one senses only the German influence as in a sense one does also in Beck; their use of counterpoint is of an entirely different kind from that used by Honegger.

Othmar Schoeck, born in 1898, is a pupil of Reger and in every sense a late romantic. He has a great reputation in his native country as a composer of *lieder*. His output in this field is enormous, and the German tradition is to be found in him more completely than in any other Swiss composer. His other works include five operas and much music for voices. There are, however, three concertos in his *oeuvre*, one each for cello, violin and horn. The last of these was written in 1951 and performed at the Edinburgh Festival of 1954.

Another composer influenced by Reger, although not actually one of his pupils, is Albert Moeschinger, born in 1897. An austere style changes to something more impressionistic about 1940. His output again is large and includes three piano concertos, three symphonies, a set of variations on a theme of Purcell for strings and percussion, as well as chamber and choral works.

The work of these composers viewed as a whole is stimulating, then, from the attitude of nationalism. There is hardly a thing in their combined work which can vaguely be termed nationalistic. It has been cited on occasion that Beck and Burkhard, in the severe and often rugged style of their work, reflect the strong independence of the Swiss people. Such remarks seem pointless and meaningless; austerity of style and texture is not by any means confined to the independent Swiss but can also, for instance, appear in contemporary Italian music—and the Italians may be independent, but they are, one feels, hardly austere. With more point one might say that the remarkable concentration on oratorio and choral works reflected something of a people so strongly Protestant, and the austerity of the subjects of certain of these might further strengthen this; but still nothing is shown of national musical style and this alone is really of importance. We do not even come upon a hearty *Ranz des Vaches* such as Beethoven and Liszt allowed us by way of change of locale.

In spite of this we have a picture of a country with several composers of considerable stature, though only one at present assumes masterly proportions. There is about Honegger, indeed, something of that complete and all-round nature which is to be found in almost all masters. There is a variety in his expression, yet a consistency which defines a true style. The oft-mentioned gloomy art of Honegger produces anything but a boring grey world, for flashes of light and splendour illumine his generally dark fabric with infinite imagination and variety. He has the quality of panache, but he also has it within his control, something not always the case with Sutermeister and not, maybe, quite evident enough in Martin. Martin has, however, this masterly ability to handle his textures and weave a web of sound of a novel kind, and the occasional flavours of Ravel, Stravinsky and the freest use of twelve tones blend into a personal idiom of great charm and refinement.

The work of Beck and Burkhard is of much greater sobriety but has features of great worth and a dignity which is entirely in keeping with the subjects of many of their works. The work of Liebermann and Sutermeister, on the other hand, presents exactly the opposite situation; here sobriety is hardly ever met with and many styles conflict in the case of the former, while the latter adheres to the simplest language. At times one feels here the shade of Orff.

This makes a fascinating contribution to the European musical scene and the ample performances of these works testify to the interest they arouse and hold both here and in America.

Italian Contemporary Music

REGINALD SMITH BRINDLE

R<small>ATHER</small> than bewilder the reader by plunging him straight into the ramifications of Italian post-war dodecaphony, neo-classicism and the host of today's other 'isms', I think it important to help him associate the contemporary world with the Italian past he knows well. Two world wars and the fascist period have not helped our acquaintance with Italian contemporary music, and readers cannot be blamed for assuming it to be something like the theatre of Puccini or the tone-poems of Respighi. In actual fact, Italian music has moved a tremendous distance since Puccini's heyday, much farther than has British music since the time of his contemporary, Elgar.

Let us look for a moment at Italian music around the time of the appearance of *La Bohème* in 1896. Opera filled the whole musical field, and opera meant *verismo*—the display of super-emotional sentiments dramatised in a crude 'melodramatic' form. It was a supremely popular art and completely obscured the great Italian instrumental past; if instrumental music was heard at all, it was imported from Germany. At least three pioneers—Martucci, Sgambati and Sinigaglia—realised the one-sidedness of Italian culture, and dedicated themselves exclusively to instrumental composition and initiating concerts, but being ignorant of the wealth of the Italian past, they succeeded only in imitating Germanic (particularly Brahmsian) models. Germanic symphonism is a speciality of the Germans, anyhow, and eventually their efforts foundered against the breakwaters of disinterest erected by opera lovers. It was left to the next generation, that born between 1880 and 1890, to change the whole climate of Italian music from the then existing parochial operatic atmosphere, and guide it towards today's almost cosmopolitan spirit. This generation included Casella, G. F. Malipiero, Pizzetti, Respighi and Ghedini. Casella was the prime mover, some were to follow his lead all the way; others (Pizzetti and Respighi) were destined to break away towards other ideals and even (in 1932) to condemn Casella's efforts. This generation's task was no easy one; violent campaigns of opposition met the 'new music', and their goal, even to themselves, was uncertain. But in choosing to construct from the base of pre-romantic Italian music (especially instrumental) their work had a foundation which Martucci, Sgambati and Sinigaglia overlooked.

This 'musical renaissance' was championed by the poet d'Annunzio who, instituting the National Music Collection to rediscover Gesualdo, Vivaldi, Monteverdi, etc., provided models of the Italian 'classic' spirit and style which served as starting-points for the new music.

To sum up the objectives of Casella and his associates—they desired to break away from the parochial atmosphere in which they were born, that of the *melodrama,* and join the anti-romantic European movement then rising from the ruins of impressionism.[1] This aspiration towards a new order, this so-called *neo-classicism,* had as its main principle the return to the Golden Age of Italian instrumental music. In reality it signified renouncing the un-Italian rigid Beethovenian form of construction, the easy seduction of the symphonic poem, and the inconsistency of impressionism, substituting instead the discipline of polyphonic instrumentalism—discipline not for its own sake but as a means of finding in modern terms the old classical flow of Italian music.

Casella's role between the two World Wars is so important, and sums up in itself so many developments, that I consider it indispensable to make a brief summary of his work. That he lived abroad from the age of thirteen to thirty-two is the immediate clue to his later impact on Italian music. A cosmopolitan upbringing, contact in France, Russia and Germany with Europe's greatest musicians, made him see Italian music for what it really was, originating his passion for a national musical renaissance, but not providing the answer as to what form it should take. This problem was to cause him many anguished years. Born in 1883, he studied in Paris from 1896, co-student with Ravel and

---

[1] In Casella's own words: 'We are in the presence of a total reaction against immediate and superficial sentiments, in place of which we are trying to substitute the return to the contemplated feelings of the greater classicism. Therefore not "neo-classicism" improperly called by certain critics, but a true and right return to the pure classicism of our ancestors.'

Koechlin under Fauré. From 1906 he travelled Europe for three years as harpsichordist in the *Societé des Instruments Anciens,* meeting Balakirev, Rimsky-Korsakov, Mahler and the young Stravinsky. Not unnaturally his two early symphonies (1906 and 1908) show strong Russo-German influences, though strangely little influence of French impressionism, in spite of the strong Debussian atmosphere which must have constantly assailed him.

In 1909 he resolved to dedicate himself to the re-creation of the Italian musical language, but the path to take eluded him. Searching for a style, he tried using ancient dance forms (e.g. the *bourrée* of the Suite in C); then in the rhapsody *Italia* he tried folk material as an easy path to achieving 'nationalism'—a temptation he yielded to later, even when realising that this artifice is not valid in music which pretends to high aesthetic value. Until his return to Italy in 1915, this search continued, exploring Franco-Russian paths (e.g. *Il Convento Veneziano,* 1912) and demonstrating an increasingly unsatiable harmonic curiosity and experiment with dissonance. Returning to Italy, a long crisis followed —Casella was under the spell of Schönberg's atonalism. Absolute chromaticism was his goal (e.g. Piano Sonata, 1916, *Elegia Eroica,* Op 29, for orchestra, and *A Notte Alta* for piano and orchestra) and the Italian public, unprepared for this music, opposed it violently. Critics named him an anti-patriot and a peril to Italian culture—accusations which were to continue for many years. This perilous interlude, ending in 1920, was followed by three unproductive years; we find him, therefore, at the age of forty, with more than half his opus numbers completed, tasting the bitterness of defeat. A lesser man would have ceased the struggle. Only in 1923, during a journey in Tuscany, did he achieve interior liberation; he wrote: 'Tuscany . . . impressed me enormously, not only with its Art but, above all, for its wonderful Nature; I understood that an Italian can never be an impressionist, and that the transparent clarity of that landscape is that of our own Art.' An imprecise basis for composition, but a very valid aesthetic creed. Casella, matured by this experience, recommended composition on the lines of clarity in tonality, and classic lucidity in form and content. In the ballet *La Giara* he succumbed again to using folk material; only in 1925, with the *Partita* for piano and orchestra, did he consolidate a technique based on the old instrumental forms (*passacaglia, gagliarda, giga* etc.) with a light, agile contrapuntal movement excelling in lucidity and freshness— the so-called 'neo-classic' style. With the *Concerto Romano* (1926), inspired by the monumentality of Roman baroque architecture, he drew near Bach and Vivaldi in big contrapuntal episodes of pure construction—a baroque style in which all trace of impressionism and late romanticism were eliminated, and which formed the solid basis of his later music.

Casella therefore restored instrumentalism and counterpoint to the Italians, freed them from the provincialism of *verismo*, and formed in its place an austere, lucid and vital style which for the next twenty years was the mainstay of Italian music.

It would be unfair to give the impression that Casella's contemporaries played no part in these developments, but as at this point we are more concerned with music's progress than with individuals, I think it sufficient to summarise their chief characteristics and then pass on to the next generation.

G. F. Malipiero (b. 1882) was Casella's greatest companion-in-arms during the years of battle. As early as 1902 the revelation of Monteverdi's *Incoronazione di Poppea* set him on the colossal task of rediscovering and editing all Monteverdi's works and Vivaldi's concertos. His special gift is a symphonism which denies all German principles of thematic development and recapitulation; like early Italian models, his themes are open linear designs, achieving that continuous discourse typical of the true Italianate style.

G. F. Ghedini (b. 1892) identified himself closely with the new instrumentalism, specialising in the revival of the Vivaldian *concerto-grosso* manner, using severe contrapuntal lines tinged with a radical and aggressive modernity.

Pizzetti (b. 1880) took little part in the instrumental revival, opera reform has been his chief contribution to the 'musical renaissance'. His principles demand a subjugation of the music to every dramatic need; lyricism for its own sake is ostracised, and instead he creates a new lyricism with dramatic functions, flexibly changing from dramatic speech rhythm to an open *arioso* as the words and drama demand. Music as pure sound does not exist for Pizzetti; his symphonic music is born from an inner drama rather than by the logic of real symphonism.

Respighi (1879-1936) had little affinity with Casella's music and was hostile to the anti-romantic movement. His orchestral works, sumptuous, impressionistic Straussian tone-poems, are in the teutonic romantic manner (he studied under Max Bruch) and by their popularity have certainly had influence in Italy, and abroad seemed to represent Italian music. He has had a considerable following among younger composers, but as no vital personality has emerged to keep this style alive, it may be considered as now decadent and without influence.

During this period, even until today, the traditions of the Puccinian theatre have been kept alive by innumerable composers—the names of Alfano and Zandonai are perhaps most prominent—but as this tradition has lost its artistic validity I consider it not worthy of investigation.

Summarising events until the thirties, we have followed the growth of an anti-romantic, 'neo-classic' movement acting in the name of true Italian art and borrowing from the seventeenth- and eighteenth-century instrumental styles as a means of rediscovering the true 'classic' spirit. But I think it right at this point to question the validity of translating into modern terms the language of Bach and Vivaldi and ignore the spiritual motives which inspired their constructions. Is this true 'classicism'? In order to destroy *verismo*, was it revolutionary and 'classic' to make music out of bygone formulas, or was it merely reactionary and formalistic? In other words, was neo-classicism only a makeshift? Later events in Italy will help us solve these problems; we will therefore examine the work of two of the next generation, Petrassi and Dallapiccola, who represent the two main channels which Italian music has followed until today.

Goffredo Petrassi, born in 1904, was trained as a chorister in Rome and later studied at the S. Cecilia Conservatoire under Bustini. His works up to 1932, naturally influenced by Casella and Hindemith, belong to the neo-classic school (a title which Petrassi repudiates) and he quickly affirmed his personality with the extraordinarily mature *Partita* (1932) which won him immediate renown in Rome and at the Amsterdam I.S.C.M. festival. This work, in three dance movements (*gagliarda, ciaccona, giga*), has bold, vigorous thematic material and resolute contrapuntal lines urged forward by an inexorable rhythmic drive typical of all his early work. The harmonic and melodic idiom is diatonic, weaker semitonal formations are discarded, and he creates harmonic stress through bold diatonic clashes or brief linear excursions out of the established tonality (a frequent neo-classic cliché). This style is common to the Introduction and Allegro for Violin and Eleven Instruments, a piano *Toccata* and the Concerto for Orchestra which followed. This music has an extrovert boldness at odds with Petrassi's real nature, and we find that, later, especially with his three major religious works, this extrovert quality gradually diminishes; there is an increasing tendency to withdraw into introspection, towards a greater humanity, in spite of the increasingly cold and uncompromising idiom.

Psalm IX (1936), his first big choral work, is a masterpiece in the fusion of the strident rhythmic and tonal conflicts of the orchestra with a vast choral fresco which with its *organum* and Palestrinian polyphony reveals Petrassi's upbringing as a chorister. This choral polyphony, however, loses the Palestrinian contemplative atmosphere; in its orchestral setting it has the opulence of Roman baroque.

The *Coro di Morti* (1940-41), Petrassi's second large choral work, has nothing of the baroque. It shows an astonishing advance since *Psalm IX* into a world of absolutely modern sensibility. This 'dramatic madrigal', charged with a sense of supernatural irreality, has a cold, impersonal idiom which seems to aim at eliminating all emotion, but with its singular orchestral sonority (based on three pianos, brass, percussion and double-basses) illustrates superbly the sinister hallucinatory atmosphere of the Leopardian text. The choral part departs very little from a modal language, the brass is confined to tonal and polytonal worlds, while the pianos freely move into the atonal sphere, but these disparate elements are welded into stylistic coherence by a rigorous and logical construction. There is a certain affinity with Stravinsky's *Les Noces* and the *Symphony of Psalms*, but there is no question of imitation; Petrassi has merely availed himself of what has become common European musical language.

The *Coro di Morti*, with its increased interiorisation, hard skeleton form, and problematical disparate elements, is the turning-point in Petrassi's career; but his next compositions avoid the issues arising from this work, and during the war years he concentrated on stage works, temporising with his old idiom in two ballets, *La Follia di Orlando* (1943) and *Ritratto di Don Chisciotte* (1945), and the opera *Il Cordovano*. But the *Coro di Morti* marks the point where Petrassi had to choose whether to retain the forms and formulas of the past and continue the illogical fusion of modal, tonal, polytonal and atonal elements, or whether he should break with this idiom and embrace the greater means of expression offered by organised pantonality. It is only ten years later, with the cantata, *Noche Oscura* (1951), that the stylistic and intellectual development promised in *Coro di Morti* is fulfilled, and he definitely breaks with his old idiom. This cantata has no trace of the sumptuous baroque religion of *Psalm IX*, nor the inflexible texture of the introspective *Coro di Morti*; instead of the diatonic foundation and aggressive rhythmic impulse of his earlier music, he here explores the total-chromatic space with oscillating, fluctuating melodic lines and harmonic planes emanating from semitonal material (the formula BACH) which is the very antithesis of his early diatonicism. This thematic formula, forming the whole melodic and harmonic structure, is handled with a new technique—that of Schönberg's tone-row composition. His language is strengthened and more flexible, the whole idiom is unified, and is no longer a fusion of disparate elements. This technique is handled freely and Petrassi maintains his characteristic thematic definition; serial construction is used according to his own expressive necessities, absorbing it into his own style without accepting the aesthetics of expressionism from which dodecaphony sprang. Two other works written about this time, the opera *Morte dell'Aria* and the Second Concerto for Orchestra, show no suggestion of this development, but in the later *Récréation Concertante* (1952-53) for orchestra, he again uses serial technique absorbed into his own characteristic orchestral style.

We leave Petrassi therefore at this period of development between the diverging currents of diatonicism and total chromaticism. His has been the strange fate of beginning his career brilliantly with a virile and apparently mature style, only to find himself at fifty years of age faced with the alternative of making temporary compromises with dodecaphony or accepting its technique and aesthetics in full. This problem, we will see later, is common to numerous Italian composers, but certainly Petrassi has shown resources and genius sufficient to find a solution of integrity and high aesthetic value. At this point we will trace the entry of dodecaphony into Italian music in the person of Luigi Dallapiccola.

Three major influences have determined the course of Luigi Dallapiccola's work, each sufficient in itself to distinguish his production from that of his Italian contemporaries. Born in 1904 at Pisino, Istria (then within the Austro-Hungarian Empire), he witnessed, during his most impressionable years, the humiliation and suffering of his family's deportation to Graz during the First World War. Later, the fascist 'race manifesto' of 1938 and the German occupation of Florence in the Second World War cast the shadow of fear over his family, and enchainment of the spirit, if not the flesh, became a reality. This destiny of man so common in our European 'civilisation', this loss of freedom, inspired Dallapiccola with the theme of 'Liberty'—liberty not only of the body, but of the spirit—and his three major works are all dedicated to this theme.

The second important factor in his development is his great literary culture and sensibility, which, inspiring him to expression through vocal

rather than instrumental means, has not only destined his major production to be vocal works, but guided it away from the neo-classic
instrumentalism of his contemporaries.

The third big influence on Dallapiccola was the revelation of the
atonal world he received on hearing Schönberg's *Pierrot Lunaire* in   •
1924. The realisation of this world for himself, in isolation from the
Viennese school, was only achieved after twenty years of slow, patient
struggle. Information on Schönberg's twelve-note technique was very
scanty; in fascist Italy atonal music was regarded as a product of anti-
fascist 'internationalism' (therefore communism!) so that performances
were discouraged. There was no way, therefore, of taking up the dodecaphonic technique without a long process of trial and error, and
Dallapiccola affirms that literary sources, especially the methods of
construction of Joyce and Proust, helped him greatly to master the
secrets of the new dialectic.[1]

The genesis of Dallapiccola's music is very different from that of
Schönberg; his journey towards pantonality received its impulse not
from a crisis in tonality and the aesthetics of *expressionism*, but has been
the realisation of a vision perceived, not as an aesthetic or a technique,
but as a musical truth as great as any previously experienced in the
world of sound. The very foundations of Dallapiccola's music seem to
have been the antitheses of those of Schönberg. There seems to be
no semitonal heritage, but rather that of modality, or even, from evidence we shall note later, a more primitive source still may be divined
—the pentatonic scale, in which the semitone is completely excluded.

Dallapiccola's first definitive composition, the orchestral *Partita*
(1930-32), betrays no atonal tendencies, and would ally itself to the
'neo-classic' but for two things which show that even then he did not
belong to this movement—the recourse to a vocal form for his finale,
and his fastidious use of orchestral colour to convey emotion. The
Three Studies (1932) and the *Rapsodia* (1933), both for voice and
chamber orchestra, foreshadow his later predilection for this medium,
but only in the *Divertimento* (1934) for voice and five instruments,
does he take the first tentative step along the 'twelve-note road'. In the
first three movements the vocal melody is designed in melismatic
modal curves, but for his finale he resorts to a theme of very different
shape, an angular chromatic form ranging over nine of the twelve
available semitones—not a particularly important fact but for the pre-

[1] 'On the Twelve-Note Road', by Luigi Dallapiccola. See *Music Survey*,
October 1951.

sence of a four-note nucleus (comprising two rising minor thirds sur-mounted by a fourth) which is later to play an important role horizon-tally and vertically in his serial compositions. This note-nucleus, some-times slightly altered, later assumes almost a quality of symbolism; even more so is the case of Dallapiccola's increasing use of quintuplets (symbolising the five syllables of his name) from about 1940 onwards.

The next step towards pantonality is in the third series of the *Sei Cori di Michelangelo Buonarroti il Giovane* (1936) for chorus and orchestra, when a formation of rising fourths (alternately perfect and augmented) as a structural design penetrates through the C minor tonality until the total chromatic is exhausted. The intention here is a mere creation of atmosphere, as also at the conclusion when the piano plays a tentative series of eleven notes over a sustained C major chord.

The *Tre Laudi* (1936–37), written as studies for the opera, *Volo di Notte*, are much more adventurous, testing the possibilities of melodic construction with a series in original and retrograde forms, and of serial construction in close canon. The opera *Volo di Notte* (1937–39) de-velops the same music considerably, especially the canonic structure, which now takes considerable responsibility in the development of the musical discourse. The harmonic construction, however, is constantly tonal, but so devised as to explore the total chromatic to a considerable extent. This opera has a particularly original subject—night-flying over the Andes—and develops the theme of today's dispassionate sacrifice of the individual in the cause of progress: 'Only that which is before us, the future, is important.'

The *Piccolo Concerto per Muriel Couvreux* (1939–41), for piano and chamber orchestra, plays little part in the composer's progress towards atonality; rather is it a retrograde step, recuperating what must have been an early device—the pentatonic scale, treated in canon with con-siderable skill, but in its modality it turns its back, as it were, on panton-ality. These returns towards modality or tonality are not infrequent in Dallapiccola's progress, they signify a weighing in the balance of tonal and atonal values, so that his 'twelve-note road' is not straight, but fre-quently turns back on itself. This concerto is remarkable for a strange finale, with Slav-like melody and rhythms, foreign to Dallapiccola's style.

The *Canti di Prigionia* (1938–41) are the composer's protest against the 'race-manifesto' of 1938. This music is not only a prayer for free-dom but a cry of defiance against the oppressors, affirming that even if the flesh be imprisoned, the spirit can rise to a still greater freedom.

With texts from Mary Stuart, Boezio and Savonarola, the composer uses a mixed chorus and the very unusual accompaniment of two pianos, two harps, tympani, xylophone, vibraphone, bells and a large percussion section. This singular sonority seems not only logical, but absolutely fitting to the subject, creating an atmosphere of fear and captivity to an overpowering degree. The three parts of the work use the same basic material—liturgical chant (*Dies irae, Dies illa*), and a series formed of transpositions of the four-note nucleus noted in the *Divertimento* (here comprising two minor thirds surmounted by a minor sixth). These two disparate elements, modal and chromatic, are kept in equilibrium by perfect stylistic fusion, and as the work progresses the composer penetrates even farther into atonal territory until, in sections of the second and third parts, complete pantonality is achieved.

The ballet, *Marsia* (1942–43), Dallapiccola's only orchestral work which excludes the voice or a solo instrument, is a singularly unsymphonic work, yet a masterly example of that ideally balanced union of music and choreography essential in 'total' ballet. Music and movement depend entirely on each other for their significance to be realised and fulfilled. Here the composer was obviously beset by other problems than progress in the direction of atonalism, so that in this respect *Marsia* belongs rather to his past than his future.

After revising his attitude towards tonality in the *Sonatina Canonica* (1942) for piano on *Capricci* by Paganini, Dallapiccola embarked on the task of achieving a completely dodecaphonic discourse in the three sets of Greek Lyrics for voice and chamber orchestra. The *Cinque Frammenti di Saffo* (1942) are made from constantly varying material, different series appear in each song, usually integrated in a freely tonal accompaniment. In *Sex Carmina Alcaei* (1943) a tremendous advance is made, the whole discourse is formed from one series only, presented in various canonic forms—perpetual canon, canon cancrizans, double canon by contrary motion, etc. The rigidity of this texture is relaxed in *Due Liriche di Anacreonte* (1946), the serial writing is now flexible and every residue of diatonism is absorbed in a completely pantonal discourse. These *Greek Lyrics*, as also the *Three Poems* (1949) for voice and instruments, are intensely poetic in spite of their logical construction, and in their contemplative lyrical expansion and delicacy reveal Dallapiccola's complete dissimilarity to the Viennese school both in aesthetics and dialectic.

After attaining mastery, in the *Greek Lyrics*, of a freely dodecaphonic discourse, he began his greatest work—the opera *Il Prigioniero*

(1944-48). Imprisonment is again his subject, but here he deals particularly with torture of a special kind—torture of the spirit. The prisoner is continually fed on hope by a gaoler who eventually allows him to escape, but when he seems to have achieved freedom, the gaoler, now revealed as the Grand Inquisitor himself, awaits him and leads him to the gallows. The incredibly poignant atmosphere and expressive beauty of this work, together with its great humaneness seem to me the greatest proofs we possess that atonal music can serve mankind in the future as effectively as tonal music has in the past. The accessibility of this work to persons unversed in dodecaphonic music, apart from the humane interest of the libretto, is partly due to a number of 'concessions' Dallapiccola's twelve-note technique then made towards conventionality, and as his later developments eliminate these 'liberties' it will be well to dwell on them for a moment. First, *Il Prigioniero* is based on diverse series, each obviously shaped so as to have distinct thematic possibilities; thematic cells are also designed with the special purpose of symbolism and characterisation. This is therefore music which has definite thematic shape, and adds a further element to help comprehensibility—a subtle version of the *leitmotiv* technique. A number of classic forms are used (at least in name) as an integral part of the dramatic development (e.g. *ballata, aria, ricercari,* etc.) and there is even a considerable quotation from a previous work—the *Canti di Prigiona*. Choral writing is on a fairly simple tonal basis, obviously for practical reasons; some beautiful string passages are based on polytonality by doubling each voice with common chords, and even in atonal passages there is an obvious attempt to maintain a certain standard of euphony. These practices, as well as the frequent use of octaves (both 'real' and 'hidden'), have gradually been eliminated in his more recent works.

The *sacra rappresentazione, Job* (1950), is constructed entirely from one series, choral writing is noticeably less 'tonal', and the orchestral part is less thematic, tending towards an abstract Viennese style. Comprehension is again facilitated, as considerable parts are spoken and solo singing is largely thematic in character.

In 1951, the composer made his last contact with tonality in *Tartiniana,* for violin and orchestra, in which he again examines his tonal conscience, using several of Tartini's themes—material highly resistant to polyphonic organisation—treated in canonic structures in the manner of tone-row composition. After this final contact with tonality, the composer's aim was to reach the goal of 'pure' serial technique. Easier contact with works of the Viennese school developed his artistic sensibility and revealed elements which his own development had by-passed, especially the possibility of evolution in rhythmic articulation.

In the *Quaderno Musicale di Annalibera* for piano (1952) we therefore find him observing rigorously for the first time the principles of 'pure' dodecaphony, and evolving a greater serial and rhythmic subtlety. Cerebral canonic structures alternate with pieces designed by pure fantasy, but it is typical of Dallapiccola's artistry that the canon *Cancrizans*, the most 'constructed' piece, is also the most beautiful.

The *Goethe-Lieder* (1953), for voice and three clarinets, carries this process a step farther: rhythmic articulation is particularly complex and flexible. The work is completely polyphonic, and though canonic structures are occasionally used (one piece is in mirror canon), the work exhibits chiefly the polyphony of pure dodecaphony, where each voice evolves the series in a rhythmic aspect diverse from that used by any other voice, i.e. there is no thematic imitation.

Dallapiccola's third great work, again on the theme of 'liberty', is the *Canti di Liberazione* for chorus and orchestra. This work is only just being completed, so I consider it premature to anticipate a view of the developments it is sure to bring.

Unfortunately I have had to dwell on the technical aspect of Dallapiccola's works rather than on their artistic value, which may give an erroneous impression that he is obsessed with constructivism. On the contrary, though his works show an increasing evolution in construction, they also reveal an ever-increasing standard of artistic value, confirming that music's cerebral aspect is to him always secondary to the aesthetic result.

Before studying the work of other composers, let us look briefly at the situation created by the musical tendencies so far considered—we have noted a 'neo-classic' movement based on a 'return to the past' which, by its anti-romantic attitude, was compelled to abandon the melodic (vocal) expansion natural to the Italians, and substitute contained, emotionless melody—a state of affairs which could never last. This movement, influenced from without by atonality, had to abandon its diatonicism and form a harmonic language more contemporary in idiom; this was accomplished by various clichés which are at best contrivances and not true developments of the musical language. On the other hand, we have seen that the twelve-note technique can restore expanding lyricism to the Italians (e.g. Dallapiccola's *Greek Lyrics*), that it can explore the whole tonal and pantonal space, that it lends itself to a completely contrapuntal discourse, and furthermore is a genuine expansion of the musical world and not a mere expedient. Also, this technique can be used independently from the aesthetics of expressionism from which it sprang and freely adapted to an individual composer's ideals. We shall therefore see later that a number of composers began as 'neo-classics' but changed to the twelve-tone technique to avail themselves of its greater means of expression. Some even destroyed or negated all they had written previous to this conversion. We will now consider some contemporary musicians who use the twelve-note technique:

Riccardo Nielsen (b. Bologna, 1908) is now director of Ferrara Music Lyceum—the first dodecaphonist (at least in Italy) to be head of a music school. Until 1942 he followed the neo-classic style with considerable success, and was the only Italian represented at the 1938 I.S.C.M. festival in London. Yet he regards all his productions previous to his change to dodecaphony as being purely formative. First attempting tone-row composition in 1927, but failing through lack of technical preparation, it was only after fifteen years that he again turned to this technique, aware that neo-classicism could not fully express his personality, and that only tone-row composition could enrich his language sufficiently to satisfy his expressive needs. In taking up dodecaphony in 1942, when it seemed to have no future, and to be only of a polemic nature, Nielsen's act was all the more remarkable in that his greatest artistic ideal is to re-establish contact between contemporary music and a wide public. His music therefore shows no polemic nature but aims at a simplicity, comprehensibility and absence of harsh dissonance unusual in twelve-note music. However, he does not stoop to a cheap, popular style; his music has the austerity and nobility we associate with early Italian models. He has revised a large amount of seventeenth- and eighteenth-century Italian music, and it would seem that his present works associate themselves above all with the clarity and felicity of that epoch. His principal works include: the operas L'Incubo and Il Giudice; the radio drama, La Via di Colombo (Italia Prize, 1953); two choral rhapsodies; two piano sonatinas; music for strings.

Mario Peragallo (b. Rome, 1910) studied composition with Donato and Casella but repeatedly failed to gain a composition diploma. Until 1942 he wrote exclusively for the theatre; the two operas, Ginevra degli Almieri (1937) and Lo Stendardo di San Giorgio (1941), influenced by verismo and particularly the style of Zandonai, had successes which seemed to lead to an easy future. But after five years' inactivity during the war, he returned to composition with higher ideals, resolved to avoid sensational music lacking in substance and refinement. Beginning with the dramatic madrigal, *La Collina* (1947), his work undergoes a radical change, showing determination to acquire a more evolved technique. Written in a concentrated contrapuntal style which seems to weigh heavily on his inspiration, this work adopts an anti-romantic attitude very different from his previous work; the style, freely tonal, owes much to the heavy baroque of neo-classicism. After this experience, Peragallo adopted the twelve-note technique, and not unnaturally his works for some time reveal a struggle to master a new dialectic. The Concerto for Piano and Orchestra (1950) shows many pages of genuine inspiration alongside others which are merely academic. His work gradually turned to rendering the dodecaphonic language more humane and accessible, and in 1954, with the opera, *La Gita in Campagna* and the Violin Concerto, he reaches a point where musical inspiration has complete dominion over the medium. The opera failed completely because of a libretto quite unsuited to the stage, but the Violin Concerto thoroughly merited the prize awarded by the Rome International Convention of Contemporary Music. This concerto has none of the stress and anguish common to modern music, rather an unusual benignity, warmth and optimism. Though written entirely serially, Peragallo has concentrated on themes which have a precise physiognomy, on rhythmic vitality, and on eliminating the obscure and pedantic. The serial technique is treated so freely, the style lacks so many characteristics of 'pure' dodecaphony, that we could justly say this concerto is not dodecaphonic at all; but what really matters is that Peragallo has created an inspired work of art which effectively bridges atonal and tonal worlds. His other recent compositions are: Double String Quartet (1948): Fantasias for Piano, and for Orchestra (1951): *De Profundis* for *a cappella* chorus (1952).

Roman Vlad, born in Rumania in 1919, has lived in Rome since 1939, and in 1951 obtained Italian nationality. He has richly developed his creative, intellectual and critical faculties, and occupies a unique position in Italian musical life as not only a prolific composer, but as an equally capable lecturer and critic. After completing his studies with Casella, his non-dodecaphonic works show a distinct tendency to disrupt tonality; for instance, in the ballet, *La Strada del Caffè* (1944), this amounts almost to a fixation—the tonality of the main idea is always refuted by one completely at odds in the accompaniment. This procedure is carried into his freely dodecaphonic works, especially in his big output of film music; for example, a normal diatonic melody may be surrounded by an accompaniment of scales and *arpeggios* which include the whole total chromatic. But these are conveniences resorted to through sheer haste; his more meditated works are distinguished by a successful fusion and unity of tonal and atonal material, clear rhythmic definition, and an admirable spontaneity of expression. He adopts a polemic attitude towards dodecaphonic 'super-constructivism', and if some of his works are distinctly complex (e.g. the cantata, *Le Ciel est Vide*) this is a *result* of expressive necessity and not, as in 'constructivism', predetermined. Other important compositions include *Sinfonietta* (1942), Enesco Prize; *De Profundis* (1942–46); ballet, *La Dama delle Camelie* (1945); Symphony (1947–48), *Divertimento* for eleven instruments (1948); opera, *La Storia di una mamma* (1950).

Riccardo Malipiero (b. Milan, 1914) gradually approached tone-row composition since 1940, and takes up a central position amongst Italian twelve-tone composers, midway between the extreme liberty and anti-constructivism of Peragallo, Nielsen and Vlad, and the rigorous radicalism of younger composers mentioned later. Structurally his music has a clear, traditional architecture which avoids the complex, and a rhythmic definition which makes for easy comprehension; on the other hand, his serial writing has no spirit of compromise, so that a certain hardness of texture results, somewhat at odds with the simple structure. His principal works include: the opera, *Minnie La Candida* (1942), Piccolo Concerto for Piano and Orchestra (1945), *Cantata Sacra* (1947), Symphony (1949), Violin Concerto (1952), *Studi per orchestra* (1953).

A small but important group of dodecaphonic 'extremists'—Maderna, Togni and Nono—is geographically confined to the north-east Veneto area. Their work—received with little sympathy in Italy but valued abroad, especially in Germany—is a logical continuation of the rational principles of Schönberg and Webern, in that the tone-row itself, previously responsible only for the ordering of sounds, is now also made responsible for the conception of the music's rhythmic configuration, i.e. the series predetermines the whole of the music, except for grades of volume, expression, instrumentation and silences.

Camillo Togni, born near Brescia in 1922, studied under Margola and Casella, but as early as 1942 he adopted the twelve-note system. His efforts have been largely directed towards finding a principle for determining rhythmic structure analogous to the manner in which serial technique governs the ordering of sounds. His first efforts sought to base compositions entirely on preconceived rhythms, on the principle that each rhythm can exist in six forms (i.e. the original and its retrograde, and augmentations or diminutions of these). We therefore find, in the *Coro di T. S. Eliot*, Op. 33 (1951), for chorus and orchestra, that the rhythmic structure of the whole work is potentially contained in the first three bars. In Op. 34, the *Cantata di T. S. Eliot* for a *cappella* choir, this system is applied with even more logic. In the introduction, each voice in turn propounds a different rhythm; the first part of the cantata is then based on rhythm A, the second on A and B, the third on A, B and C, and the fourth on A, B, C and D. The coda is then a retrograde version of the introduction.

So far, Togni had sought to impose a rhythmic construction on serial technique from *without*, but with *Ricerca*, Op. 36 (for baritone and five instruments), he followed the more logical path of finding a rhythmic principle derived from the series itself. This work comprises six studies, the first based on a series of semitones (the chromatic scale), the second on tones alternating with semitones, the third on minor thirds interspersed alternately with tones and semitones, and so on, until the sixth includes the largest possible interval, the diminished fifth, in its six possible transpositions, interspersed with the five smaller intervals. On this basic material, Togni then applies the principle that the duration of each note is in direct proportion to the interval it initiates; the semitone, the minimum basic value, is given in turn the duration of demisemiquaver, semiquaver, quaver or crotchet, so that each study is in four-part form, and the character of each part is governed by the basic value given to the semitone. Therefore the architectural form, rhythmic configuration and sonoric structure all generate from one basic principle—the twelve-note series.

The reader may well ask how music can result from such a mechanical procedure, but reserving freedom in three factors—organisation of silences, formation of chordal groups, and note repetitions, Togni has succeeded in producing a work of high fantasy and undoubted originality. Of his large production, other important works include: Variations for Piano and Orchestra, Op. 27; *Psalm 127*, Op. 30; Three Studies for *Morts sans sépulture* of J. P. Sartre, Op. 31, for soprano and piano, *Omaggio a Bach*, Op. 32, for two pianos.

Bruno Maderna (b. Venice, 1920) attained early fame as a boy conductor, and though he later studied composition under Bustini and G. F. Malipiero, his formation was influenced most by the conductor Hermann Scherchen, who in 1948 directed his interests towards the dodecaphonic technique. Maderna's affable, man-of-the-world exterior belies his high intellectual qualities, capable of applying a mental discipline and rationalism to composition which has been rarely equalled since Schönberg's discoveries.

Maderna's technique is largely based on mathematical principles; by using a large number of permutations (variants, not transpositions) of the series, he establishes the note-order for a whole musical structure. Then, from this note-order, by mathematical devices far too abstruse to analyse here, the whole rhythmic edifice (including silences) is constructed in such a way as to ensure alternations of tension and relaxation, coupled with greater or lesser degrees of intensity. From this basic material is then constructed the actual composition in its final form, the composer choosing his own instrumentation, arranging the height or depth of sounds (the series does not determine this) and suitably adding indications of volume and expression.

Naturally, in this music, there is no harmony, polyphony, melody or accompaniment in the conventional sense, one can only perceive a *total* effect. Notes no longer have individual value except by their height, depth or intensity, and by how much they contribute towards the tension or relaxation which is communicated to us by means of harmonic and rhythmic stress or enervation.

This music, of course, is largely experimental, but it is of value apart from its aesthetic quality (which is difficult to judge) through the remarkable possibilities in rhythmic configuration which it reveals, developments which could hardly have come about without recourse to cerebral methods. Maderna wisely keeps in touch with 'free' composition, as in his two Improvisations for Orchestra, in which he applies in free form the musical patterns which have resulted from previous calculation. There is naturally a great danger, in this super-constructivism, in that one piece of music sounds very much like another, yet Maderna has undoubtedly a high degree of fantasy which stamps his personality unmistakably on all he writes. His other works include: three *Composizioni* for orchestra; *Serenata* for two instruments; the cantata, *Kranichsteiner Kammerkantate '4 Briefe'*; Two-dimensional music for flute and electronic tape montage; String Quartet (1955).

Luigi Nono (b. Venice, 1924) studied law at Padua University and has had no conventional academic musical training. His teachers have been Hermann Scherchen and Maderna, and fundamentally his compositions follow the principles applied by the latter. Nono's work is almost unknown in Italy; for some reason there seems to be considerable opposition to his music on the part of those responsible for music promotion, but in Germany he is held in high regard. From the small amount of his music I have heard, I have been impressed by his originality and ingeniousness, but left doubtful of the strength of his musical personality. His works include the ballet *Der Rote Mantel*; the choral-orchestral works—*Epitaffio per Garcia Lorca* (three parts), *La Victoire de Guernica, Liebeslied* and *Il Canto Sospeso*; and for orchestra— *Composizione, Variazioni Canoniche, Due Espressioni, Polifonica-Monodia-Ritmica*, and *Incontri*.

After this investigation of the most 'advanced' school in Italian music, we will turn back and examine briefly a few followers, like Petrassi, of the Casellian 'neo-classicism'.

Antonio Veretti (b. Verona, 1900) studied composition at Bologna under Alfano, his early style reflecting that of his master and Pizzetti. Taking up later the forms and ideals of neo-classicism, he reveals himself above all as a constructor, subjecting his works to a vigorous formal discipline which finds its ideal expression in the *Sinfonia Sacra* (1946). The influence of Stravinsky's *Symphony of Psalms* and Bartókian percussive technique is evident, but he captures ideally the violence and crudity of the biblical text in a work which makes no compromises in its stark severity. Veretti has turned to twelve-note technique during the last few years; his first work, *Quattro Poesie di Giorgio Vigolo* (1950), revealed him still a prisoner of the serial language, but the later *Ouverture della Campana* (1951) and the Violin Sonata (1952) show a return to the thematic coherence and rhythmic intensity characteristic of his previous work. Other compositions include the *Sinfonia Italiana* (1929), *Sinfonia Epica* (1939), and the oratorio, *Il Figluol Prodigo*, (1942).

Vittorio Rieti, born at Alexandria, Egypt, in 1898, of Italian parents, studied under Frugetta and Respighi. Rejecting the romantic style of his masters, he embraced the neo-classic cause, and remained faithful to it consistently. His activity is now mostly confined to the U.S.A.

Bruno Bettinelli (b. Milan, 1913) has specialised mostly in orchestral works, and has written four symphonies, two concertos for orchestra, and several *Ricercari, Divertimenti*, etc. His style is essentially linear, dominated by a strong dynamic pulse; his latest *Sinfonia Breve* tends to form its melody and harmony from atonal sources, though retaining its neo-classic rhythmic and contrapuntal construction.

Though we have noted considerable influence from without on Italian music by the Viennese school, Stravinsky and Hindemith, little has been said so far of Bartók's influence—not the Bartók of the Magyar

Folk Music, naturally, but Bartók the thinker as revealed in his intro-spective later quartets. He has influenced two composers, Guido Turchi and Franco Donatoni, acting rather as a spiritual guide and fertilising process in their development than as a mere technical example to be slavishly copied.

Guido Turchi (b. Rome, 1916) studied under Ferdinandi, Bustini and Pizzetti, but his early compositions reflect the influence of Petrassi and Hindemith. He is a slow worker, a complex personality, self-critical and introspective, and such works as the Trio (1945), for flute, clarinet and viola, reveal him as seduced by intellectualism and the idea of pure form, designing geometric sound patterns which have no vital musical existence. In the *Invettiva* for choir and two pianos (1946) the cold mono-timbric construction again seems to lack the breath of life. It was at this juncture that Bartók's influence came to bear as a spiritual fertiliser which helped Turchi slacken the bonds of a too-severe formal discipline, warming his productive and imaginative faculties and guid-ing him towards a more spontaneous expression. The *Homage to Béla Bartók*, a concerto for strings (1947–48), is by normal standards a work of severe formal discipline, but compared with his earlier works it breathes a warmth which foreshadows a new epoch. This relaxation of formal discipline and tendency to warmer expression is much more evident in the *Piccolo Concerto Notturno* (1950), which, inspired by Bartók's neo-impressionistic 'night music', is a luminous, delicate noc-turnal contemplation of great beauty. At this juncture, Turchi evidently felt the need to liberate himself from Bartók's manner. Faced with the problem of a new style, it would seem logical, in view of his early work, for him to choose the twelve-note technique. But the only work we can judge, the orchestral *Cinque Commenti alle Baccanti di Euripide* (1951) goes right back to Pizzetti's 'Greek Theatre' style. Ad-mittedly, this work was written for the Syracuse Greek Theatre, but these outmoded dramatic clichés can hardly be regarded as a true development in Turchi's style.

Franco Donatoni, born at Verona in 1927, studied at Milan and Bologna, and later with Pizzetti. At the critical moment of his rapid de-velopment he was influenced by Bartók's work, not merely from the technical aspect but through an inner affinity with the world of sadness and suffering which Bartók expresses with such humanity. But while assimilating certain Bartókian constructive and harmonic procedures, he realised the necessity for re-creating this sound world with a language distinctly his own, and such is Donatoni's strength of musical character that his works quickly assumed a completely personal physiognomy. Donatoni's work reveals an increasing interest in logical construction; he rationalised Bartókian dialectic by extracting all melodic and harmonic matter from the highly chromatic symmetrical scale $\underbrace{CDE\flat}$: $\underbrace{E\natural F\sharp G}$: $\underbrace{G\sharp A\sharp B}$, and its three transpositions. Combinations of the minor triads in each three-note group form a harmonic basis, while successions of small intervals interspersed with large leaps are characteristic of his melody. Two contrasting aspects of Donatoni's work, intensely rhapsodic melody and constructive canonic designs, are combined with a refined felicity, avoiding the ponderous and excelling in a light rhythmic vitality. In his *Divertimento* for Violin and Orchestra (1954), a new development took place in his work—the tendency to establish a design (in this case the four-note nucleus noted as characteristic of Dallapiccola), and from this construct the whole melodic, harmonic and contrapuntal texture. This nucleus, with its transpositions, is already almost a series, and it is therefore not surprising to find Donatoni taking the short and logical step to dodecaphonic usage in his Five Pieces for Two Pianos. His recent *Musica per Orchestra da Camera* (1955) reveals a quick assimilation of tone-row technique, and his future development would seem, given his tendency for logical construction, to be in the direction of twelve-note formalism. As he is also geographically in the midst of the dodecaphonic 'extremists'' territory, it will be interesting to see whether he resists or succumbs to their influence. His other works include a String Quartet (1951); Viola Sonata, Concerto for Bassoon and Strings, Concertino for Tympani, Strings and Brass (1952); Symphony for Strings and Orchestral Overture (1953).

It would give quite a false picture of the Italian scene if some composers were not mentioned who have avoided Central-European influences and adhered to a more 'traditional' Italian style.

Vieri Tossati (b. Rome, 1920) adopts a polemic attitude to Viennese and Germanic influences, and by parody and satire holds up the more *outré* elements of modern music to ridicule. But this modern 'Erik Satie' wields a two-edged weapon, for satire is not communicable in music; when he pokes fun at modern 'isms' by using the 'wrong-note' technique, the joke is on him, because the public needs an explanation to understand such banter, and a joke explained is a joke no longer. He works chiefly in the operatic field; his *Partita di Pugni* (1952) is an ingenious representation of a boxing match, *Il Sistema della Dolcezza*

(1950) has its scene in a lunatic asylum, but though his works reveal an engagingly droll personality, they are musically insignificant.

Another composer, Mario Zafred (b. Trieste, 1922), condemns equally the 'return to the past' and atonal 'formalism', but for political reasons. A communist, his music follows the artistic dictates of the Soviet régime in the ideal of immediate communicability, and the research for a language which is 'healthy and robustly popular (not vulgar), and not too distant from the national *melos*'. He is a profuse writer of considerable technical skill, and after experimenting with dodecaphony (in the Concerto for Two Pianos (1945) and Trio (1946)) and with other contemporary influences, he has settled down to a production which compromises communist ideals and the technical means available today. His large production includes five symphonies, numerous concertos and chamber music.

Valentino Bucchi (b. Florence, 1916) is the unique case of a composer who defies classification. In a musical world all too prone to the formation of cliques and obligations to pursue one style and one only, he maintains absolute independence, using whatever technical means we have inherited freely and as the occasion demands. Far from resulting in an agglomeration or *pastiche* of diverse styles, his work has a distinct character and unity through his determination to avoid the obscure and problematical. Above all, he aims at lucidity, lightness of texture and easy comprehensibility, and such works as the opera *Il Contrabbasso* (1953-54) and *Cori della Pietà Morta* (1950), for chorus and orchestra, are admirable examples of high aesthetic worth achieved through this luminous clarity and simplicity. Two works based on mediaeval music—the opera, *Li Gieus de Robin et de Marian* (from Adam de la Halle), and the *Laudes Evangelii*, based on thirteenth-century Umbrian texts, are very successful examples of this composer's speciality for re-creating mediaeval music in a form suitable to modern stage needs. Bucchi's other works include the opera, *Il Giuoco del Barone* (1937), the cantata, *La Dolce Pena* (1946) and the *Ballata del Silenzio* for orchestra (1951).

Little mention has been made of folksong in this chapter—there has been no introduction of folksong elements as a solid basis for symphonic music as in England, this is excluded by the Italian's aesthetics, but some use of modality (e.g. Pizzetti) has emerged through the influence of Gregorian chant, which is still the basis of church music. However, popular folk music has been used to give local colour (e.g. Respighi's *Feste Romane*) and especially Gianandrea Gavazzeni (b. Bergamo,

1909) has a whole symphonic repertoire inspired by his native Lombardian folklore. Ennio Porrino (b. Cagliari, 1910) has also made use of Sardinian folk music in such works as the symphonic poem, *Sardinia*, but such usage is pictorial rather than truly stylistic.

Summing up briefly the Italian scene at this mid-century—we have seen the birth of an instrumental revival as a reaction against *verismo*, forming a 'neo-classic' style which in turn has reached an *impasse* through its impact with dodecaphony. We have seen at least one composer, Dallapiccola, turn the twelve-note system to a thoroughly Italian form of expression, while others have developed two opposite tendencies, the one conventionalising dodecaphony, the other carrying it to the utmost limits of constructivism. At the same time, a haphazard Italian 'traditionalism' has pursued its way, but seems either too weak and inconsistent to combat dodecaphony, or lacks the presence of a composer of sufficient stature in its cause.

German Contemporary Music

HOWARD HARTOG

T HE fact that modern Germany acts as a microcosm for the whole variegated conflatus of contemporary trends in European music makes the more interesting the actual trends which operate inside the framework of Germany; that is to say we must ask how far the keen and competitive attitude adopted by radios, critics and the whole considerable paraphernalia which contemporary—and particularly experimental—music has enlisted has found a response in the creative products of our time.

Although German music throughout the ages has had certain clear directions and even individual characteristics, the historical emergence of Germany from the Austrian Empire, as well as the closeness of cultural and linguistic ties, implies that inevitably a certain confusion of line between German and Austrian musical thought must exist, for the borders are at no time since the eighteenth century well defined. This is not to say that 'Viennese' characteristics are absent from Hadyn or Schubert, Mahler or Berg, Brückner or Schönberg. It is, however, equally possible to sense their adumbration in Beethoven or Brahms, to take two names of prominence, even if the German approach tends to assimilate these colours into a more highly organised and classical mould. It is perhaps for this reason that Brahms, in many ways a composer consistent with the romantic era, should have employed a far more classical mould than Schubert or Mahler. Nevertheless, the generally parallel developments in Germany and Austria eminently justify Walter Goehr's brief historical analysis of the German musical tradition in his article on Schönberg: not only retrospectively is he justified but also today the catalyst of Schönberg's thought operates very fully in Germany not least upon those who affect to deny the importance of Schönberg and to refute the validity of his ethics.

For the reason then that most of the matters relevant to the historical approach to German music have been explored by Walter Goehr, such preamble as may occur before we arrive *in medias res* must be sketchy if it is not to be repetitive. All the same, the present apparently chaotic picture must be explained slightly from a historical viewpoint to avoid muddling the picture. It is fair to say that in contrast to Slav music, German music has always manifested a tendency towards the 'ideal' conception of art rather than a realist one. It is, in fact, rather curious that some critics jeer at 'socialist realism' in music, while frequently admiring its realist origins in, for example, Smetana and Mussorgsky. But just as in Smetana some works bear distinct traces of the contrary influence exercised by the strongly idealised romantic impulse of nine-teenth-century German music so, of course, 'realist' and folky manifes-tations have made their appearance, however coyly, inside the framework of the German tradition. All the same, it is fair to generalise to the effect that German music concentrates on the manner rather than the matter, that is to say that the German composer today, as in the past, is not so much concerned with what he has to say as how he is to say it. Hence it is easy to see the historical reasons for the accusations of 'formalism' levelled at composers such as Hindemith and Schönberg. Careful scrutiny compels the rider that, fundamentally at least, Wagner and Brahms as well as Bach and Handel cannot escape tar from the same brush.

The disrepute into which German romanticism in its traditional form fell at the end of the nineteenth century gave rise to a situation among German composers which neither the experimental maelstrom of the twenties nor the strangulatory interregnum enforced by the Nazi régime contrived to resolve. Despite the apparent moribundity of this roman-ticism, manifest in Wagner and Mahler, Richard Strauss by his enor-mous orchestral technique has, in Germany at least, become a recognised classic of the popular order. This phenomenon has been made possible for a variety of reasons which must be alluded to if what may be called 'the revolt of the intellectuals' and the post-war move-ment centripetal to, if not solely deriving from, the summer school at Darmstadt are to be understood. First, there are Strauss's own un-doubted gifts; as an example of a composer mastering the technique he requires he is a model. This is by no means to say that he should be a model for rising composers, either in texture or harmonic variety. He did not aim, as so many young composers do now, to explore farther the orchestral palette or to take to extremes the sounds of the instruments at his disposition. (The fact that he added on occasion exotic instruments to his orchestra does not disprove this, for these instruments, and his use of them, were relatively simple extensions of the traditional orchestra.) Nevertheless, as an heir to a tradition he developed his own gifts, within the shards of this very tradition, with exemplary mastery. In addition his operas for all their seeming traditionalism touched on the borders of the Freudian discoveries which have impinged on the general intelligent public even more inevitably than the contemporaneous discoveries of Schönberg. It is also necessary for each country to discover one contemporary figure which links with the past, not only to refute the alleged dangers of the innovators but also, in an almost tangible manner, to connect the whole past of music in an easily comprehensible way with what the listener considers to be the living present. Richard Strauss availed himself copiously of these opportunities. Indeed without entering into his own political loyalties it is possible to aver that the moratorium of the Nazi decade prolonged and exaggerated Strauss's importance. Today we tend to forget that Strauss can be otiose and empty, and that his adroit and metallic technique sometimes conceals a poverty of melodic invention, curiously endemic in German composition, and that his episodic method of writing, while offering an equipment for the stage, hardly convinces in his lengthier orchestral compositions. The result has been that, for all his personal success, neither his great rival and contemporary, Hans Pfitzner, nor his successors, men like Graener and Trunk, have made more than a local impact. Pfitzner's *Palestrina* is an example of a respected opera, full of lovely music, which has seldom been given outside Germany or Austria.

Richard Strauss is a fascinating red herring in the German scene. But if twentieth-century composers were to find masters to show them the way, whither should they look? Two paths lay open and these two paths have, by and large, remained those along which the major talents in Germany have marched. Ferruccio Busoni's *rappel à l'ordre* took the form of a neo-classicism which claimed—though obviously in widely differing ways—such eminent figures as Stravinsky and Hindemith as advocates, apart from direct Busoni pupils of widely various aims, such as Philipp Jarnach, Kurt Weill and Vladimir Vogel; though Vogel was later to find his footsteps straying more towards Alban Berg than his Italian mentor. But obviously the work of the neo-classicists alone, important as it was, could not have induced the radical examination of methods of composition which has so exercised the minds of the German composers. In the twentieth century, with few considerable exceptions, it is in the shadow of his far-reaching iconoclasm that their decisions were achieved.

The historical past of Germany, in which the cultural snobbery of petty principalities led to a rivalry in the patronising of the arts, has even today left Germany in a strong position for the presentation of music. The regional radios hand out with imperial partiality munificent commissions to their favourites of the moment. It is as common to find the impecunious composer, Herr X, in the ante-chamber of Dr. Y, the official empowered to distribute the largesse, much in the same way as eighteenth-century princes were courted by the needy composers of their time. Also every town of importance has a tradition of opera-going, so that, even despite the bomb damage caused in the last war, a continuous tradition is present, a tradition which, with few but flagrant exceptions, regards it as right and incumbent to salt the salad of their repertoire with contemporary works. Therefore, purely from a monetary point of view, writing for the theatre has become attractive, and in Germany, at least, the prospect of another Brahms, Mahler or Bruckner emerging has become slimmer. (In the nineteenth century the composers could court publishers with the prospect of piano-duet versions of symphonies selling handsomely.)

In view of this situation it is not surprising that one of the best-known figures in German theatrical life is the Bavarian composer, Carl Orff. He is a thoughtful and vital composer who has extended the so frequently misunderstood Hindemithian concept of *Gebrauchsmusik* to include—in his own case as a primary sphere of interest—the writing of music for the stage. He has stripped his music of all the accoutrements of Wagnerian language and deliberately conscribed his harmonic orbit. By use of *ostinato* and simple rhythmic devices he contrives to underline the drama taking place on the stage. Allying his rhythmic gifts to a fresh stream of melody and the bucolic bounce of the Bavarian *Oktoberfest*, he has written a triptych of pagan, not unaphrodisiac scenic cantatas which have during the last twenty years won wide acceptance, and are now beginning to become 'popular' in a sense in which no composer has become popular since Rachmaninov. The first of these cantatas, *Carmina Burana*, has won the widest acceptance, and is in many ways the most spontaneous composition of Orff in this vein, though his fable, *Die Kluge*, has a unity and enchantment which makes for a really 'theatrical' entertainment. The sequels are: *Catulli Carmina*—perhaps the most frankly erotic of his works—and *Trionfi di Afrodite*. Orff is, as will be clear from these terms of reference, absorbedly interested in percussion; he has a fine collection of Oriental percussion instruments. *Catulli Carmina* is written for two singers, chorus, ballet, four pianos and percussion. Perhaps his most ambitious work is his opera, *Antigone*, a work in far more serious style and aiming at less ebullient or magical targets than most of his previous works. His orchestra contains a huge number of percussion instruments and the work runs uninterrupted for just over two hours. It has all the concentration and drama needed for the august theme. It may be debatable how far the setting of Greek mythology is justifiable today, but there can be no doubt that Orff has seldom shown his dedication to his own concept of the music theatre more grippingly than in the third and fourth scenes of *Antigone*. Since Mozart's time, light music has become divorced by degrees from serious composers; in his lighter works, Orff, who is an intelligent but seldom 'intellectual' composer, has attained a possibly viable resynthetisation.

Werner Egk, another Bavarian, is possibly the most obvious aspirant for the mantle of Strauss. His works are always written in diatonic style and generally, however fresh their coloration, for a practical and available consort of instruments. He has composed many operas and ballets; indeed, his recently revised *Die Zaubergeige* seems to have the makings of a new German folk opera. The Bavarian vitality which also —even if in more traditional colours—informs Egk's music has here its aptest and most natural expression. His *French Suite*, a setting of French harpsichord pieces for orchestra, has the advantage of gaiety and brilliance without any faddy adherence to the eighteenth-century originals. The work is boisterous and not unduly portly. Egk has a prehensile and alert sensitivity. This leads him sometimes into less formidable paths where the assimilation of styles is not always fully achieved. But exotic influences will, of necessity, play a large part in Egk's future. Not only his extrovert handling of French tunes in his *French Suite* but also his gay *La Tentation de St. Antoine*, for mezzo-soprano and strings, have charm and resilience. His *Chanson and Romance*, for high soprano and orchestra, adds to his spiritual reaching out for Gallic qualities a probing into Oriental rhythms. Such a juxta-position is by no means strange or wilful. Egk has the skill and sensibility to fuse the most diverse elements. This general intelligence lies behind Egk's sympathetic approach to the theatre as manifested in his numerous operas and ballets.

Boris Blacher, though gifted with the same catholic and witty type of intellect as Egk, shows generally a lighter, more Oriental touch. To a certain extent, he has been influenced by Stravinsky's more aseptic music. He has obviated, as Orff but clearly in quite another style, harmonic problems. His music is, again, thinned of most of the pomp and fatness of nineteenth-century music; and his keen intelligence has led him to concentrate on variable metre, i.e. to vary the rhythm from bar to bar. This involves, in simple words, applying to problems of rhythm the same sequence of rhythms as the tone-row does in so-called serial music in terms of harmony. He has written a very fine dramatic oratorio, *Der Gross Inquisitor*, and numerous ballets, for which his rhythmic gifts predestine him. Although his most successful orchestral works are the *Concertante Musik* and his Paganini Variations, both notable for their superficial brilliance—and in Germany superficial brilliance is not to be found often—probably the achievements of which Blacher would be most proud are the two piano concertos, the *Ornaments,* both for orchestra and for piano (two different sets, each differing specimens of his 'variable metre'), and the Studies in Pianissimo written for Louisville. It is typical of Blacher's mercurial, completely un-German approach to music that he is already aware of the dangers of becoming a prisoner of his own system, and regards his system of variable metres as a guide rather than compulsion to his future development. He is also an important pedagogue.

Wolfgang Fortner has a more academic brand of talent. He is perhaps the most gifted example of the natural musician assuming in turn the varying styles he finds to hand. Thus his early religious music is infused with the cleansed lines prevalent in such music in the first two decades; later his style, which has also attempted to achieve clean and well-defined lines, became more avowedly popular. The collapse of the Nazi régime exposed his sensibilities for the first time to the Schönbergian revolution and gradually, but in no sense slavishly or exclusively, Fortner has adapted the serial technique to his own ends. Fortner's best music, such as the Symphony and the Cello Sonata, has a dry quality; the dryness is that of a wine, not of a book; it shows a fastidiousness and selectiveness which does not allow the banal to supervene in his work. For all his lyric qualities, and his lyricism is never lush or overrich, it remains for Fortner's new *Lorca* opera finally to convince his listeners whether or no he has prolonged dramatic force.

One more Bavarian of a mature generation remains to be considered. Karl Amadeus Hartmann is perhaps the most robust and at the same time the most sentimental of the Bavarian composers. His style is not consistent from work to work nor is he, in the narrow sense of the word, idiosyncratic. The superficial listener can easily detect the shades of Berg, Stravinsky and Bartók wandering through his music; in his piquant Fifth Symphony he has toyed with some aspects of variable metres. Yet the real drive and real feeling behind the music transcend any techniques which may be recognised in his palette. At all events, if a technique is developed and used cogently, who should cast the first stone? If this criterion is to become valid, then early Beethoven is ruled out of court by Haydn and so on. Hartmann is essentially a symphonic composer, though his other works include three concertos and a typically provocative opera. But his six symphonies are perhaps the most recognisable memorial to Hartmann's talents. The contrasts between his boundless *élan* of his quick and frequently fugal movements and the elegiac, lamenting quality of his lyricism is at its clearest in the Third and Sixth Symphonies. Neither as a man nor as a composer is Hartmann concerned overmuch with slimming; his richness of scoring stems from a Mahlerian rather than neo-classic origin. For this reason his Fourth Symphony, scored for strings only, has a more lucid quality than his other symphonies. The quality of tragedy which infuses many of his slow movements derives from Hartmann's violent political sense, notably his anger and misery at the facets of Nazi repression. It is the fiery quality of dynamic passion which in the final instance absolves Hartmann from any slur of eclecticism. The breadth of his conceptions show that he is a romantic symphonist of considerable substance.

Among the older generation of composers there are several who attempt to avoid any tarnishment from post-Schönbergian influences, such as the romantic Karl Hoeller in Munich, Nepomuk David in Stuttgart, and Hessenberg in Frankfurt. Braunfels, too, evolved a fusion of catholicism and full-bloodedness which informed his stage works, in particular his once-famous opera, *The Birds*. A more withdrawn and fastidious talent is that of the Busoni pupil, Philipp Jarnach, whose chamber music in particular shows high seriousness, frequently, too, an elegiac quality which never brims into sentimentality. The fact that he tends to avert current fashions and to write very little music has led to his undeserved neglect. One could catalogue many more figures of the older generation of similar outlook if lesser talents, but that the more absorbing problem of the extremely active younger generation must be examined.

This is not the place to examine the aesthetic which underlay the cultural politics of the Nazi régime. But if we are to understand the phenomena which informed the resurgence of German musical vitality after the war, certain results of the twelve years of Nazi domination come into the picture. First, the actual physical musical tradition carried on and was even encouraged; secondly, and more important, all the trends which bore any signs of innovation were in 1933 deleted from German musical consciousness. For all the discrepancies between the musical aesthetics of Hindemith and Schönberg, both these composers were tarred with the same brush: and although Stravinsky did not suffer the same formal interdict, performances of his works were not encouraged, nor was his importance recognised in any proportion to its actual worth.

After the war, clearly, the idols of the Nazi cave were discredited; but to establish a new and acceptable hierarchy proved more complicated. In view of the thoroughness of all German intellectual processes it is not surprising that the surviving, intellectual mentors of the new generation looked directly back to the Berlin activities of the nineteen-twenties: the cardinal figures of that epoch became, with all their contradictory impulses, the models for the new generation. The radios, albeit under Allied control, began to broadcast the music of Hindemith and Bartók, Stravinsky and Schönberg, as well as a host of other names strange to Germany. Timidly festivals of new music peeped into being, pivoting round the resurgent *Donaueschingen* (where a *succès de scandale* was an annual requisite) and in the Kranichstein Institute summer courses of the music of this century were instituted. Here not only were the masters of twentieth-century music presented with re-furbished glory, but young composers from all over Europe were husbanded together with the young Germans and an admirable synthesis was achieved.

Hans Werner Henze, who studied with Rene Leibowitz and Fortner, was the first talent among the new generation to strike the ear; typical of his generation, however, also was his immediate enchantment first with Stravinsky and then Schönberg. His First Symphony, the ballet music, *Jack Pudding*, and the Concerto for Flute, Piano and Strings are undeniably gifted works, but the composer's genuine admiration for Stravinsky and Hindemith are still a shade too evident for comfort. Somehow the classical moulds his idols imposed obscure Henze's real future, which seems to be the heir of the German romantic tradition. That he possesses the technical and emotional equipment to assume his birthright is manifest, but what is not yet clear (even to Henze himself) are the methods germane to the task. This at first overpraised boy was inevitably lured by the disciplines and fascination of the serial technique of composition, and for many years, though never using it in a hidebound way, he used it to enrich his most amazing gift for tonal colour; whether in the neglected Violin Concerto, the curiously orchestrated cantata, *Apollo and Hyacinthus,* which is for a chamber ensemble, including harpsichord and voice, or in the evocative magnetism of the library scene in his opera, *Boulevard Solitude* (a modern rendering of the Manon story), this quality is paramount. It is therefore with some sense of the correct direction of his talents that for his second major opera, *King Stag,* Henze has turned his attention so skilfully to the world of fairy story.

Because of the dearth of young composers at first evident in the post-war years, Henze has suffered the risks of over-adulation. Sometimes his extraordinary facility leads him into composing too rapidly, with the result that it is not always his best works that appear in foreign countries. It is true to say, too, that his richness of invention and gift for colour are not always matched by an equally compact compositional mould. The same criticism could have been levelled at Schubert. Despite Henze's erstwhile absorption with Stravinsky, he seems well on the way to assuming—in a contemporary garb—the mantle of a protagonist of German romanticism; this matches his profound interest in Schönberg and Webern (cf. Henze's Piano Variations) and must clearly undergo the vagaries of transition. As Henze is a sensitive and rarely cerebral composer, some of these transitional phases will be manifest to his critics.

The other figure in post-war Germany who shows a high promise is Giselher Klebe. As he has come more slowly to the forefront, the dangers of premature fame have in his case been less obtrusive. But even so not all his works are consistent in worth. Although a pupil of Blacher, Klebe too has felt the influence of Anton von Webern. His music has less of the elusive filigree quality of the Austrian composer, but is more robust and admirably composed. While his orchestration lacks the richness of fantasy found in Henze, his probing intelligence leads one into equally stimulating worlds of sound—particularly in his Symphony for Twenty-three Strings. In Germany a composer who does not compose an opera is regarded as in some degree impotent; so it is not surprising to hear that Klebe is at work on one on the theme of Schiller's *Die Rauber*. If his self-criticism marches parallel with the talent shown in the solo violin sonatas, the Symphony for Twenty-three Strings and the Concerto for Violin, Cello and Orchestra, then Klebe can play an important part in the reorganisation of the German musical scene.

The education which Boris Blacher administers to his Berlin pupils is admirably planned; how far they can stray from Blacher's own paths is shown by Klebe, who is intent on exploring a harmonic world which Blacher's more rhythmic experiments tend to eschew. Blacher's pupils are from many nations and so the majority are not relevant to this article. It is clear that when a composer has a strong personality, if his pupils are to achieve anything the umbilical cord has to be broken. Western Europe is, unfortunately, littered with composers who have not dared leave the particular ambit prescribed for them during their artistic infancy by their mentor. The German pupil of Blacher's who, apart from Klebe, seems the most likely to achieve his own resonance is Heimo Erbse. While some of his works smack of midnight oil, the Sonata for Two Pianos and the Piano Trio show a certain vitality and lustiness of invention. All in all, the best of teachers can do no more than give a grounding, and, exceptionally, later encourage the gifted pupil to find his own language; the essence of the matter lies in the composer himself, and here as yet Erbse has to develop.

Bernd Aloys Zimmermann is another figure who has come to the forefront since the war. He has written a Symphony, a Violin Concerto, a Cello Concerto and numerous other quite considerable works. Zimmermann's original point of departure seems to have been Schönberg, though, like the other real talents of his generation, the whole firmament of contemporary music has fascinated him. He has a keen intellect, manifested in his music, without perhaps as yet the spontaneous melodic gifts of a Klebe or Henze; his Cello Concerto is a trifle donnish, but his symphony has a forcefulness and authority which shows that, if Zimmermann can break away from his academic shackles (academic in the most 'contemporary' sense of the word), he may be among the most prominent of German composers. The fascination which the exotic allure of jazz can have is shown by the peacock colours of Zimmermann's Trumpet Concerto entitled *Darkey's Darkness*.

No consideration of the younger German composers would be complete without some attempted reference to the youngest, but by no means least able, figure of prominence, Karl Heinz Stockhausen. Here, as in the case of Pierre Boulez, we approach the thin borderline dividing the extreme extension of Webern's style from the unmapped world of *musique concrète*. The electronic studios attached to the Cologne Radio under the aegis of Professor Eimert, a man already experienced in the ways of radio, have provided a magnet for enquiring minds; and the fact that inevitably 'modernist' snobs have gathered round this particular hive should not blind us to the facts that carrying the bare, exposed tones of Webern's music to their farthest (though not necessarily only logical) extension, the problems of electronic sound are laid before us. This volume is not planned to plot the future; nor is it yet clear whether electronic sound will be satisfied with enriching the palette of radio effects or whether like a Frankenstein's monster it aims at devouring the whole apparatus of music as we see it. Stockhausen has as yet a foot in both worlds; both the *enfant terrible* and the *enfant gâté* of the magnificent hothouse world of radio, the extremely extended and verbose concept of music which Stockhausen has does not always entirely obscure the general musical talent behind his often otiose compositions. The two *Kontrapunkte*, particularly the first for chamber ensembles, show an exotic talent, quite genuine even if, in its mathematical application, of at least as much optical as aural interest. Boulez, for all his own tendency to long-windedness (shades of Webern!), and for all the difficulties involved in performance of his works, has more musical content than Stockhausen, whose second cycle of piano pieces seemed an overlong series of clichés of a modish world. Like Göring when he heard the word 'culture', there is a point where we reach for our (more spiritual) gun; and perhaps in this work Stockhausen threatens, more tediously than heretofore, to scatter his not inconsiderable talents before the glass of fashion. But apart from the problem of squaring Stockhausen's gifts with the techniques which absorb him, he is the outstanding representative of a generation whose rush forward from the limits which were explicit under the Nazis has brought them to the edge of an abyss—across which lies the world of electronic sound with its possible relegation of 'traditional' music to a museum limbo.

There are countless other young figures among composers in modern Germany, all of some potential: Hermann Heiss, whose songs show his real lyric talent, Engelmann, whose light plaintive gifts find their greatest success in work for the radio like his radio opera, *The Wall*, Seidel, Fussan, Zehden and numerous others.

All these composers are encouraged by commissions from the various radio networks; these latter, with their munificent orders, have replaced the electors. As the revivers of a great tradition, their labours have been to the point; the danger is clear—not only the concentration of power in the hands of mannered incompetents (the princelings of the eighteenth century were not always shrewd in their choices), but perhaps a tendency for the composer to imagine he has achieved the bourn of fame too soon. These commissions which preclude young composers from having to seek their living in the more menial walks of musical life are socially conceived, of great worth and contrast happily with the grudging pittances which radios in other countries mete out on far more partisan lines. Nevertheless they account for the frequently orchidaceous compositions produced and also for the ivory tower to which the German composer frequently repairs.

However unclear all futures, and particularly that of German music, may seem, the occupation of German musical youth with Schönberg and Stravinsky, Webern and Hindemith, however academic this frequently becomes, still contrives to liberate German musical life from some of the more crippling fetters which prevail elsewhere. Though it would be prejudiced to imagine that the hegemony once accorded to German composers is again established, certain distinct talents are perceptible and the conditions for their development are propitious. To conclude more at this juncture would involve special pleading and encourage a musical chauvinism which can be as insidious in Germany as elsewhere.

The Soviet Union

BERNARD STEVENS

A<small>LL</small> Russian music during the latter part of the nineteenth century may be considered as broadly national in spirit, the differences between Tchaikovsky and the 'Big Five' being essentially those of method and style rather than indicative of a struggle between nationalism and cosmopolitanism. It is important to remember that Tchaikovsky and the Big Five had mutual respect for each other's works. But the followers of Tchaikovsky, most of whom were associated with Moscow, including Rachmaninov and Medtner, developed away from nationalism towards closer integration with Western and particularly German romantic music. Their spokesman and theoretician was Taneiev, who wished Russian music to acquire classical precision and contrapuntal purity. St. Petersburg, on the other hand, became the centre of the followers of the National school, including Liadov, Glazounov, Stravinsky and Steinberg (who married Rimsky-Korsakov's daughter), and most of them were pupils of Rimsky-Korsakov at the Conservatoire there. (He had refused the offer to become head of the Moscow Conservatoire, presumably because of its domination by the eclectics, although he had great respect for Taneiev as a teacher.) It is interesting to observe that in music the traditional roles of Moscow as the home of 'Mother Russia' and St. Petersburg as the 'window to the West' were reversed.

The 'Moscow' and 'St. Petersburg' schools represented the two dominant trends in Russian music up to the October Revolution in 1917, but they had both developed marked academic tendencies, particularly in respect of harmonic resource, under the influence of Taneiev and Glazounov respectively, so that it is not surprising that, in the early years of the twentieth century, the apparent novelty of

Scriabin's chromatic harmony was eagerly seized upon by those young composers in search of something new and vital. Stravinsky was perhaps the only outstanding young talent to grow up exclusively in the Nationalist school, in which he remained at least until 1917, the year of *Les Noces*. The self-conscious emotionalism of Scriabin is very characteristic of the general mood of the *avant-garde* intelligentsia in the years between the 1905 and 1917 Revolutions. The Soviet poet Pasternak (himself a disciple of Rilke and Scriabin) gives a vivid description of this world in his autobiography, *Safe Conduct,* as also do Miaskovsky and Prokoviev in their correspondence with each other and with the poet Mayakovsky and in their autobiographical writings. The *avant-gardists* in general supported the revolutionary movement both in 1905 and 1917, but in the form of emotional sympathy and self-dramatisation rather than active participation (Gorki and Mayakovsky were, of course, the notable exceptions). But the disillusionment following the failure of the 1905 Revolution caused many of them to take refuge in various forms of mysticism typified by Scriabin's vague theosophy. The emotional and mental climate had much in common with that described so powerfully by Dostoievsky in *The Possessed.*

Like most romantic movements, the *avant-gardist* was vague in its premises and objectives. Nevertheless, it had many positive qualities of which the most valuable was an attitude of wonder towards the world of experience, as shown in the early poetry of Pasternak. In the years immediately preceding the 1917 Revolution, however, the *avant-gardists* developed away from Revolutionary Romanticism with its emotionalism and took what it called a 'Realist' attitude to life under the label of 'Futurism', in which satire and exposure of false sentiment were important elements. Mayakovsky and Prokoviev were the acknowledged leaders of this group. They referred to each other as 'Presidents of the Poetry and Music Sections of the Universe' and, in his autobiography, *I Myself,* Mayakovsky notes how he and a friend 'fled from the unbearable melodised boredom' of a performance of Rachmaninov's *Isle of the Dead.* Gorki, although not himself a Futurist, nevertheless acknowledged Mayakovsky and Prokoviev as the artists who most truthfully reflected the revolutionary spirit of the times.

Dialectical Materialism, which formed the theoretical basis of the policy of the Bolshevik Party when it led the first Soviet Government that took power in October 1917, was first formulated by Marx and Engels and developed by Plekhanov and Lenin as a means of understanding not only social organisation and political economy but also philosophy and aesthetics. In fact, it claims to enable mankind to become conscious of the nature of the world, to control it for the purpose of his development and so win his freedom. Engels defined freedom as 'the consciousness of necessity'. It is important to note that Marxists have always considered the theory to be a guide to action and not a dogma. The various decisions that have been made by the Communist Party of the Soviet Union, on political, philosophical and aesthetic questions must therefore be seen as scientific hypotheses which are neither proved nor disproved in the light of experience. Further, the Party has always asserted its right and duty to make a decision, even on little evidence, if the problem was an urgent one, for, as Lenin said, 'We must not let chaos develop'.

It is true that the Marxist theory of aesthetics is far less developed than that of philosophy or economics. Nevertheless, its basis had been clearly established by 1917. The first formulation of the relationship of art to society on a Realist basis was made by Chernyshevsky, the Russian materialist philosopher, in his *Life and Aesthetics,* published in 1853. In the early nineteenth century, Belinsky, the Russian Nationalist literary critic, established a moral basis of aesthetic criticism which became generally accepted in Russia and to him may be attributed the fact that there is hardly any Russian criticism which claims to be morally disinterested or aesthetically objective, such as that of Coleridge. (It is interesting to note that Matthew Arnold deplored the lack of moral basis in English criticism.) Chernyshevsky attacked the Hegelian view that the advance of science destroyed man's ability to be moved by artistic beauty. He asserted that, on the contrary, any object which expresses life, or reminds us of it, is beautiful. This view was developed in relation to music by Serov, an operatic composer who had considerable influence on Moussorgsky.

Marx and Engels were careful to avoid a mechanical relationship between social and ideological transformations. Man becomes conscious of the latter *through* social consciousness, but these conflicts are fought out on their own terms. Marx considered that 'the exclusive concentration of artistic talent in certain individuals and its consequent suppression in the broad masses of the people is an effect of the capitalist division of labour'. 'In a communist society there are no painters but at most men who, among other things, also paint.' This last point was reaffirmed by Stalin shortly before his death when he said that the aim of socialism should be to reduce man's working day to the point where most of his time could be occupied in cultural activity. Engels warned against the danger of identifying the known views of an artist with what he expresses in his art and instanced Balzac who, in spite of being a Royalist, nevertheless in his *Comédie Humaine* mercilessly exposed the corruption of nineteenth-century bourgeois society. That great creative minds of the past were not aware of the relationship between their consciousness and their social existence does not, of course, from the Marxist point of view, make such an assertion any the less true or in any way reduce the impact of their work. Praise or condemnation of a form of society should also be kept distinct from the assessment of its artistic contribution. 'When therefore Herr Düring turns up his nose at Hellenism because it was founded on slavery he might with equal justice reproach the Greeks with having no steam engines or electric telegraphy' (Engels). The idea that the art of a decadent epoch must also be decadent is false because 'when people speak of ideas that revolutionise society they do but express the fact that within the old society the elements of a new one have been created and that the dissolution of the old ideas keeps even pace with the dissolution of the old conditions of existence' (Marx and Engels, *The Communist Manifesto*). On this basis, Marxists would explain the existence of the vital Russian Nationalist school of Moussorgsky within the thoroughly corrupt and decadent society of nineteenth-century Tsarism.

Plekhanov made a detailed study of the artistic forms of various societies, from the primitive to the most advanced, in development of Chernyshevsky's theory of aesthetic realism. He showed how art forms such as the dance grow directly out of work activity in primitive society because there are no class divisions in which some are unproductive, but the function of the Court minuet in eighteenth-century France, for instance, cannot be explained in terms of economic life because such a dance is the expression of an unproductive class. Plekhanov's work in explaining how every society evolves its own standards of beauty was of great value to musical aestheticians in combating Hanslick's theory of eternal, abstract beauty. Wagner's contribution in this respect is also important.

Lenin applied Engels' definition of freedom to the position of the artist in society by asserting that 'it is impossible to live in society and remain free of it. The freedom of the bourgeois artist, writer or actress is simply secret or hypocritically disguised dependence on the money-bag, on bribery, on maintenance.' (The non-Marxist Swiss composer, Honegger, has recently expressed a similar opinion.) After the Revolution Lenin said: 'Our revolution has freed the artists from the oppression of these all too prosaic conditions. It has made the Soviet State their protector and customer. But of course we are Communists. We must not stand with folded arms and let chaos develop as it will. We must guide the process, following a quite definite plan and mould its results. It is not *our* opinion of art that matters, nor the feeling that art arouses in several hundreds or even thousands among a population of millions. Art belongs to the people. Its deepest roots must lie among the very thick of the working masses. It must be such that these masses will understand and love it. It must voice the feelings, thoughts and will of these masses, must uplift them.' But Lenin warned against the danger of mediocre minds using this policy as a means of achieving domination (a necessary warning in view of certain later developments). 'It goes without saying that literary (or artistic) activity is least of all subject to mechanical equalisation or levelling, to the domination of a majority over a minority. It goes without saying that in this sphere it is absolutely necessary to ensure larger scope for personal initiative and individual inclinations, full play for thought and imagination, form and content.' Lenin is here drawing a distinction between the democratic centralism of the Party itself and the means by which aesthetic problems can be solved.

The Marxist view that science can and does discover objective truth implies that art, too, because it is a part of reality, must reflect this truth. This concept, during the Soviet period, has formed the basis of the study of art in general by Lunarcharsky, a leader in the Department of Art and Education, and of music in particular by Boris Asaviev (1884–1948), composer and musicologist, who had been a leading *avant-gardist* in the immediate pre-Soviet period. In his *Musical Form as a Process* (1930) Asaviev defined music as 'the art of thoughts incorporated in tones'; it owes its origin to emotional experience but, because man has a nervous system of which the brain is the most highly developed part, the experience must be given expression in terms of conscious thought. This comes very near, of course, to Wordsworth's view of poetry as taking its origin in emotion *recollected* in tranquillity, where the recollection must, by definition, be conscious. Asaviev shows the relation between human speech and melody; they both communicate shades of emotion and, from both of them, traits of character, nationality and temperament can be determined. But there are important differences; in speech, tonal inflections are of secondary importance to the communication of meaning, but in melody, even of the simplest, they take on a formal completeness, and with rhythm and harmony, give rise to a musical image. A folksong is the most obvious example of such a formally complete musical image. (It is interesting to see how this idea is expressed also by Schönberg, but he uses it, however, as an argument against composing symphonies based on folk-themes.) Asaviev claims that any musical image, even an instrumental one where there are no words to provide precision of thought, can still be an expression of reality because it is the product of a human being who has not placed himself outside reality and whose feelings are conditioned by his thoughts, themselves conditioned by external reality. Asaviev's assertion that melody is the basis of musical images would be supported by many Western musicians such as Hindemith, but Asaviev sought the content, both emotional and ideological, of the melodic idea and not merely the abstract beauty of its pattern. Further, he was concerned to show that the development of musical images in polyphony and in large musical organisms such as symphony and opera was similarly conditioned by the influence of social consciousness. Beethoven proclaimed and realised 'new paths' in the first movement of the 'Eroica' Symphony not because he wished to invent new abstract patterns and structures but because he was seeking, probably unconsciously, the musical form that would embody the thoughts conditioned by his social existence in early nineteenth-century revolutionary Europe.

V. V. Vanslov developed Asaviev's ideas in his *Reflection of Reality in Music,* published in 1950, particularly in relation to the larger musical forms of the Russian Nationalist and Soviet schools. He considers 'musical representation' to be an important means of making musical images reflect reality; a composer can call up associative ideas by borrowing the inflections of human speech, imitating extra-musical sounds such as those of nature (but as subordinate details in a melodic image), suggesting movements of the human body (as in ballet) and by rhythm in general, with its power to suggest various emotional states, quotations from other kinds of music such as religious or dance and using the stylistic features of other ages. He stresses that such representation must never be an end in itself but must be interwoven in the fabric of music, even in 'programme' music and still more in so-called 'absolute' music, so that it merely recalls reality; otherwise the result will be naturalism, which substitutes external ideas for the language of music itself and is as much a denial of music as formalism (as expounded by Hanslick) in which all association with external ideas is vigorously resisted.

Soviet musical aesthetics, as a science, seems now to have reached the point where a deeper understanding of the nature of music and its influence is possible only after more knowledge has been obtained about those parts of the nervous system of the human personality associated with aesthetic sensibility; the subject will thus become closely linked with neurology and psychology.

The theory of dialectical materialism has always developed in close relation to practical problems and that is as true of musical aesthetics as of political economy. Therefore, there was never any question of developing Soviet musical theory except in relation to the general problem of developing the musical activity of the entire nation and of helping Soviet composers truthfully to reflect the reality of life in the Soviet epoch.

For the first decade after the Revolution the Music Department of the Commissariat of Education of the Soviet Government did not directly concern itself with the aesthetic aspects of music, but confined itself to assisting the development of musical organisations. In fact, the Party urged the greatest tolerance of all methods and styles which might be found acceptable to the working people. Nevertheless, it is not surprising that the leadership and initiative on aesthetic questions was taken by the *avant-gardists* who had been most politically conscious in the immediate pre-Revolution period. They developed two distinct tendencies until about 1930. One group formed themselves into the Russian Association of Proletarian Musicians and were concerned with the creation of an entirely new working-class art form. Old and familiar operas such as Puccini's *Tosca* were presented with new libretti of a revolutionary nature and there was a general lack of tolerance of musical masterpieces of the past except those of an avowed revolutionary significance by Beethoven and Moussorgsky. New operas by leaders of the group, such as Davidenko, Koval and Yudin, were hard-hitting and direct with a crude but vigorous melodic style. These works are now of historical interest only, but the mass songs of such composers as Biely and Davidenko were of more permanent significance, as they formed the basis of an entirely new genre of popular song which has remained a unique and characteristic feature of Soviet music to this day. The larger instrumental forms such as the symphony were considered too characteristic of nineteenth-century decadent romanticism to be of any value to Soviet audiences.

The other group, the Association for Contemporary Music, of which Asaviev was the leader, encouraged experimentation and promoted performances of the most advanced West European music. It will be remembered that the first production of Berg's *Wozzeck* outside Germany took place in Leningrad. At that time the *avant-garde* movement in Europe as represented by the followers of Hindemith and Schönberg was, if not actually socialist in attitude, at least strongly anti-bourgeois. There is no doubt that the work of this group was very beneficial in combating the enervating effect of Scriabin, whom they described as a decadent mystic. Steinberg, Popov, Polovinkin, Lyatoshinsky and Mossolov were, in addition to Asaviev, the leaders of this group. Unlike the 'Proletarians', they did not shun chamber music and symphonic forms, but they were equally anti-romantic. In operas, such as Knipper's *The North Wind*, sustained melodic writing was almost completely replaced by declamation and recitative. The dramatic industrialisation and electrification of the 1920s produced a large number of descriptive works like the famous *Iron Foundry* of Mossolof and Polovinkin's *Telescopes*.

Both groups were anxious to write music that would be understood by the working people and which reflected their lives and aspirations, but they gave little thought to the actual level of musical perception of the masses, to the kind of music they sang themselves in moments of leisure or to differences in tradition and character between the peoples of the various National Republics. The narrow attitude of the 'Proletarians' led to their apparent failure to win wide support among the working people and alienated many composers who were not in agreement with its methods. By the early 1930s the failure of the 'prolet-cult' movement had been generally recognised, particularly in literature, in spite of the great efforts to rally 'shock-brigades' of writers from the ranks of the workers.

Gorki, at the First Congress of Soviet Writers in 1934, and elsewhere, proclaimed the finest and most characteristic Soviet art to be socialist realist, created in the spirit of revolutionary romanticism and imbued with proletarian humanism. It is important to remember that such expressions were not invented by Party leaders but by Soviet creative artists themselves in the process of trying to understand the nature of their problems and to give direction to their work. Gorki was exposing the misconceptions of the advocates of 'prolet-cult', who were really behaving romantically at the very moment they were attacking romanticism (just as neo-classicism in music is itself a romantic attitude, according to Busoni). 'Romanticism tends to provoke a revolutionary attitude to reality—an attitude that changes the world in a practical way.' He showed how proletarian humanism grew out of nineteenth-century humanism as expressed by Tolstoy, but was essentially different because it permeated the whole working people and not merely isolated individuals. Stalin had defined socialist realism as the art which was socialist in content and national in form. The 'Proletarians' had stressed the international solidarity of the working people at the expense of their national characteristics and treated contemptuously their ancient myths and legends. Gorki asserted that the development of the art of the National Republics was quite as important as that of Russia itself.

In 1932 the Union of Soviet Composers was formed, under the presidency of Asaviev, to bring together the various factions that had existed since the Revolution. Sections were established in most of the National Republics and the organisation was entrusted with the responsibility for the economic welfare of composers, the promotion of the performance of Soviet music, publication, assisting in the collaboration of composers with librettists and producers and organising collective discussion of new works.

The general principle of socialist realism adopted by the Union led to the re-assessment of the classical and romantic heritage, to the systematic study of folk music and the stimulating of composition in all the National Republics, particularly the more remote ones. The rise of such figures as Khachaturian belongs to this period. One of the first successes that were claimed for Socialist Realism was in 1935 with the opera, *Quiet Flows the Don*, by Dzerjinsky, based on the famous novel by Sholokhov. In spite of the technical crudity of much of the writing, the combination of a revolutionary story and a melodic, dramatic idiom based on Cossack folksong produced a new art-form that had many followers. The work was not only more popular with working people than any previous large-scale Soviet composition but it also won the approval of many leading musicians of very different styles, such as Shostakovitch, who were captured by its simplicity and vitality. An aspect of Socialist Realism which reflected the sense of economic and political security achieved by the 1930s is that it stressed the positive achievements of socialism rather than the struggle against the remnants of capitalism. But satire, which had been such a powerful weapon in the 1920s, had almost reached the point where humanity itself, not merely bourgeois society, was ridiculed and it is for this reason as well as on aesthetic grounds that Shostakovitch's opera, *Lady Macbeth of Mtsensk*, and, later, the short stories of Zoshchenko were so severely criticised.

In the 1930s economic prosperity made possible the dissemination of Soviet music to vast and eager audiences in performances of a very high standard, and the extent to which the new music satisfied them became of real importance. Many folksong and dance ensembles, such as the famous Piatnitsky, reached a remarkably high standard of skill and artistry and won tremendous popularity. Art music thus found itself in a position where its achievements were being measured by entirely new standards. Since then the relationship of art music and popular music has remained an urgent problem; there has been a consistent refusal to admit the existence or the desirability of a specialised audience for contemporary music such as exists in most other countries. At the same time, although they support Tolstoy's view that the function of art is 'usefulness and virtue', Soviet aestheticians have never shared his hostility to complex, civilised art, as such.

With Shostakovitch's Fifth Symphony in 1937 we come to the first occasion when a work of art by a serious and responsible artist has been acknowledged by him to have been created consciously in the light of public criticism. In criticising *Lady Macbeth* the Party claimed they were voicing the opinion of a very musically experienced society (an opinion, incidentally, shared by many Western musicians). The lasting popularity of the Fifth Symphony is taken as evidence of its power really to satisfy the audience for which it was intended and of the beneficial effects of such criticism.

In the late 1930s, the growing menace of Fascism and the Great Patriotic War itself brought with it the integration of the revolutionary attitude with a re-assessment of the significance of the great figures in Russian history. Artistically this is reflected in a return to the monumental forms which had been contemptuously dismissed as bourgeois romanticism in the 1920s. Shaporin's cantata, *On the Field of Kulikovo*, Prokoviev's *Alexander Nevsky* cantata and Shostakovitch's 'Leningrad' Symphony are characteristic of this phase. It is difficult to separate the emotional associations of the historical events themselves from the musical ideas to which they gave rise, but it is significant that such works as the 'Leningrad' Symphony seem to have lost much of their evocative power now that the historical events are of less immediate impact. This seems to provide additional support to the view that great human experiences can be embodied permanently in art only when they have been fully assimilated and that works created at the time of such experiences are really in the nature of journalism and, as such, generally of temporary value only. It is significant that the great films of

Eisenstein and Pudovkin about the Revolution were, in fact, made long after the events with which they are concerned.

In the meantime post-war period Soviet philosophy and aesthetics, which had been largely neglected during the war, were taken up again on the initiative of the Party, for which Zhdanov was the spokesman, in a series of discussions between 1946 and 1948 with the various professional organisations. The discussion in music was precipitated by criticism of Muradeli's opera *The Great Friendship* by the Party. In the course of the discussion in 1948, it was stated that there had been an alarming falling off of interest in post-war Soviet music among the large concert-going public. The Committee of the Union of Soviet Composers (which consisted of leading composers) was accused of autocratic methods and of being interested only in the propagation of their own works, of stifling criticism of them and of preventing the development of young and unknown composers, particularly those of the remote National Republics. The leaders in popular music, Zakharov and Dzerjinsky, expressed strong condemnation of almost all the leading composers and the young composer, Khrennikov, was frequently contemptuous of his older colleagues. The general level of the discussion, except for the intelligent contributions of Shebalin and Knipper, revealed a marked deterioration in aesthetic criticism. Asaviev, who had been wounded in the siege of Leningrad, was too ill to be present (he died soon after the conference), and had, in fact, made little contribution to the subject since the war. Zhdanov, on behalf of the Central Committee of the Party, wound up the discussion by restating the basic principles of socialist realism, but there were several aspects of his speech that were new. For instance, formalism was given a much wider definition than mere abstraction and pattern-making and made to include all music that did not succeed in directly reflecting Soviet life. At the same time, in his demand that music should contain 'beauty and grace', he implied the existence of abstract and eternal standards for such qualities, a point of view very near that of Hanslick himself and in contradiction to Plekhanov, who had clearly demonstrated the truth that every society evolves its own ideal of beauty. However, his speech, and the decision of the Central Committee that followed the conference, did reflect the urgent desire of the Party and Government that Soviet music should become a mighty force.

The immediate and negative effect of the decision was a spate of mediocre compositions based on folksongs in the nineteenth-century idiom and a bureaucratic 'vetting' of compositions by the new Committee of the Union of Composers (in which Zakharov and Khrennikov were leading members). But the positive aspect was that it did make possible the discovery of a number of young and talented composers from the National Republics such as Taktakishvili, Amirof, Dvarionas, Karajev as well as the Russian, Bunin.

The high quality of the most recent work of the leading composers such as Prokoviev's *Concertante* for Cello and Orchestra (his last work), Miaskovsky's Twenty-seventh Symphony, Shostakovitch's Preludes and Fugues for Piano and the Tenth Symphony and Khachaturian's ballet, *Spartacus*, as well as the critical writing of Vanslov, Khachaturian and Oistrakh, and the reported discussions following performances of new works indicate that, although the fundamental aesthetic basis remains unchanged, it is now being interpreted with much more insight and that the unity of culture that Gorki stressed in 1934 is recognised in the growing interest in Western music that is now developing in the U.S.S.R.

In studying the work of the most significant Soviet composers a clear distinction should be made between those who had already reached a degree of maturity by the time of the 1917 Revolution and those whose development has taken place entirely during the Soviet period.

Of the former category, M. Ippolitov-Ivanov (1859–1935) was the oldest. As a pupil of Rimsky-Korsakov he continued the Nationalist tradition, but he avoided the academicism into which that school had been led by Glazounov. Early in his career he began the systematic study of the folk music of Georgia and Armenia as well as organising musical activity there, including that among children, which he continued indefatigably for the rest of his long life and which was of inestimable value in the creation of the national schools of composition in the remote regions. His most important work as a composer was in opera and symphonic suites based on folk themes. The former, such as *The Last Barricade* (1934), are spacious and noble, rather Moussorgskian in style but less adventurous harmonically and rather slow moving. He completed Moussorgsky's early opera, *The Marriage*, towards the end of his life. The orchestral suites are very rich in orchestration and strong rhythmically, of which the famous *Caucasian Sketches* are typical but by no means the best.

S. N. Vassilenko (b. 1872) was a pupil of Ippolitov-Ivanov. His early works are in the Russian national tradition, but he soon acquired an interest in Debussy and Ravel and later in Eastern mysticism. He arranged much folk music from Japan, Ceylon and India and this led him to an absorbed interest, even before the Revolution, in the folk music of what were to become the Asian Republics of Uzbek and Kurghizia. The influence of this folk music on his own work at this stage was purely in the nature of exotic additions to a basically Russian style, but during the 1930s he collaborated with native Asian musicians, such as the Uzbek Ashrafi, in the development of native operas. *The Snow Storm* (1938), on an Uzbek revolutionary subject, is a remarkable adaptation of the native sonorities and rhythms to the modern orchestra. This work has become of historic importance in the development of large-scale forms in the remote Asian Republics.

R. M. Glier (b. 1875) was also a pupil of Ippolitof-Ivanof and is today the most respected 'elder-statesman' of Soviet music. His early work is representative of the less-adventurous Nationalist school, technically polished and lyrical, but it developed more purpose and direction after the Revolution when he became closely associated with the organisation and development of music in Azerbaijan and, to a lesser extent, in Uzbek and his native Ukraine. His research into the scales of Azerbaijanian music was of great importance in giving authenticity to his own works based on folksongs of the area (collected by him directly from the singers), particularly the opera, *Shah-Senem* (1925), on a mediaeval story. Although he captures the improvisatory and rhythmical character of the folksongs, harmonically it is too European in style. In 1934 he rewrote much of the opera in order to remove from some of the songs the extraneous Persian influence which later research had revealed. This opera is as historically important to Azerbaijan as Vassilenko's *The Snow Storm* was to Uzbek. The *Heroic March* (1936) is said to be the first example of thematically developed Buriat-Mongolian folksongs. Glier's most popular work in his own country is the ballet *The Red Poppy* (1927) and by far the most frequently performed Soviet ballet. Although by no means his most distinguished music, it very successfully combines the traditions of classical ballet and representation of a Chinese revolutionary story. His most recent ballet, *The Bronze Horseman* (1949), based on Pushkin's story, although again not very distinctive thematically, is ideal ballet music owing to its rhythmical strength and elasticity and formal clarity. The large-scale orchestral works, such as the brilliant Concerto for Coloratura Soprano and Orchestra (1942) and the Cello Concerto (published in 1948), although basically nineteenth century in harmonic idiom, are spacious, finely wrought and romantic, with an aristocratic refinement of style.

THE SOVIET UNION

Z. P. Paliashvili (1872–1933) has been called the Glinka of Georgia. His teacher, Ippolitov-Ivanov, encouraged him to collect his native folk music and to establish musical organisations in his country. This activity culminated in his opera, *Abesalom and Eteri*, in 1913, based on a Georgian mediaeval legend of love and patriotism. The work is remarkable for the skilful use of the wonderful choral polyphony found in Georgian folksong and which is claimed by some Soviet musicologists to be the origin of mediaeval liturgical polyphony. He was less successful in the arias which, although very passionate, are too Italianate to blend with the intensely national style of the choruses. This weakness is less obvious, however, in his greatest opera, *Twilight* (1923). These works and his last opera, *Latavra* (1930), are considered to be of historic importance in the development of a Georgian national idiom. His research work in Georgia formed the basis of a fine team of musicologists who are now studying the folk music of the remote provinces of Georgia and the extraordinarily rich mediaeval heritage.

Julia Weisberg (1879–1942) was the leading woman composer. She was a pupil of Rimsky-Korsakov and Glazounov and took an active part in the 1905 Revolution. In her early years she was equally prolific as writer and composer. Most of her work is vocal and dramatic and shows a marked lyrical quality and sense of fantasy. She made a study of Eastern music and her most brilliant work is the opera, *Gulsara*, based on Scheherazade, witty, fast-moving and fantastic. She specialised in children's music and, with *The Wild Geese*, invented an opera-game in which children impersonate the scenery as well as act and sing the roles. The vocal parts are simple and effective, with very skilful and imaginative accompaniment not unlike Prokoviev's *Peter and the Wolf*.

N. I. Miaskovsky (1881–1951) is generally accepted in the Soviet Union as the leading symphonist. His *Autobiographical Notes*, published in 1936, give a vivid description of the musical forces at work in his youth as well as his own struggle in search of musical truth. As a pupil of Glier, he developed not only a sure technical command but assimilated the broad Nationalist tradition from both Rimsky-Korsakov and Tchaikovsky. But he was not content with that. In St. Petersburg he joined a group of poets and musicians who were much influenced by the Russian Symbolists, of whom Alexander Blok was to become the outstanding representative. Miaskovsky's F Sharp Minor Piano Sonata (1912), in one movement, with its turbulent emotionalism and Scriabinesque chromaticism, is characteristic of this influence. It was much admired by Prokoviev and, at the time, was compared with the Hammerklavier and the Liszt sonatas, but today it seems only a very brilliantly executed 'period-piece' and in no way typical of his mature style. This emotionalism pervades all his music until the Sixth Symphony (1923), which was, in his own words, a turning-point in his career, both musically and ideologically. The conflict between emotionalism and discipline gives this work a remarkably powerful impact. The finale, in which the French revolutionary songs as well as the *Dies Irae* and a Russian folksong about death are introduced and combined in a kind of Lisztian metamorphosis, is, however, the least successful movement, for here the directness and strength of the themes are dissipated by the indulgence in harmonic chromaticism. He himself was well aware of this, for his subsequent works reveal a steady clarification and strengthening of harmonic texture together with a more and more successfully realised objectivity.

All his symphonies are consciously associated with his mental and spiritual development and, from the Sixth, this is linked with his personal attitude to the Revolution and the building of Socialism. But they are never 'programme' music; a knowledge of their emotional origin is never necessary for their comprehension. His characteristic method of developing a movement from thematic cells rather than from complete thematic statements has much in common with that of Sibelius, although stylistically they are very different. The Twelfth (1932) is one of the least convincing. The work is intended to symbolise the struggle for the new life implied in the collectivisation of the farms, but it lacks the customary unity of material and development. The Thirteenth (1933), in one movement, is the most enigmatic and has something of the desolation and remoteness of Sibelius's Fourth. It has been suggested with some conviction that its introspective character arose from his disappointment in failing to achieve his aim in the Twelfth. It is a remarkable example of the unity of form and texture so conspicuously lacking in the preceding symphony. The Seventeenth (1937) is perhaps his greatest achievement, for here the thematic material is itself memorable, the highly charged emotion disciplined and the contrapuntal finale a satisfying peroration. Towards the end of his life, from the Twenty-third Symphony (1941), on Kabardinian themes, folksong inflections become more frequent in his melodic ideas, but seldom at the expense of the structural unity. He himself said he was aiming at the orchestral equivalent of folksong.

As a composer and as a man of nobility and integrity he was a great moral force and projected a powerful influence on his many pupils.

M. O. Steinberg (1883–1946) is perhaps more important as an influence than for his actual creative achievement. He was, in effect, a symbolic figure of the *avant-garde* movement from the early 1900s and through the 1920s. He started as a loyal follower of Rimsky-Korsakov, came under the influence of Scriabin's mysticism and after the Revolution led the experimental theatre movement. His work has always the stamp of technical mastery. From the 1930s he studied the folk music of the Central Asian Republics and this is reflected in such works as the Symphony-Rhapsody on Uzbek Themes (1943). In this he succeeds in capturing the atmosphere of primitive life, as does Stravinsky's *Les Noces*, but he never quite lost the somewhat uncontrolled emotionalism of his Scriabinesque phase.

M. F. Gnessin (b. 1883) came from a remarkable family of musicians who established music-training institutes as long ago as 1895 which are the pedagogical basis of teaching throughout the Soviet Union today. From 1905 he took an active part in the revolutionary movement and in the organisation of music for working people. After the Revolution he studied Hebrew music and is today, with A. A. Krein (b. 1883), the leader of Jewish music in the Soviet Union. The melismatic character of Hebrew folk music gives his melodic style its richly ornamented quality, even in instrumental music, and he has some of Bloch's emotionalism, but it is less insistently protesting. His opera, *The Youth of Abraham* (1923), is very characteristic in this respect. But his finest work is the 'Symphonic Monument 1905–1917' (1925), to words by the great Revolutionary poet Yessenin.

B. V. Asaviev (1884–1948) has already been mentioned for his musicological work. He was also a very prolific composer; he wrote four symphonies, nine operas and fifteen ballets in addition to much chamber music. His importance is perhaps more in influence than in creative achievement except for his ballets which, in Soviet opinion, rank with Glier's and Prokoviev's. *The Flames of Paris* (1931) and *The Fountain of Bakhchissarai* (1934) are permanently in the Soviet ballet repertoire. He is a great stylist and in *The Fountain* reflects very subtly the mixture of early-nineteenth-century style and Eastern exoticism that is to be found in the Pushkin poem on which the story is based.

U. Gadzhibekov (b. 1885) is the leading Azerbaijan composer and one of the first composers from the remote Republics to win recognition in the rest of the country. He suffered great economic hardship before the Revolution, but afterwards was appointed head of musical organisation in his native district. He was also one of the first to notate Azerbaijan folk music, a difficult task in view of its great decorative elaboration. When, in 1908, he composed his first opera, *Leili and the Madman,* a kind of Romeo and Juliet legend, he was almost untaught musically. The harmonic treatment of the folksongs is very simple, with plentiful use of pedal-notes, and the native singers are given many opportunities for improvisation. Glier later treated the tunes with more elaborate and chromatic harmony and in an altogether more professional way, but Gadzhibekov's simpler version is probably nearer the original in atmosphere. His most famous work is the opera, *The Blind Man's Son* (1938), based on a sixteenth-century hero. The authenticity of the treatment of the old scales and the genuine sixteenth-century music is not only a testimony to Gazhibekov's scholarship but the work is dramatically very well shaped and alive. The sensitivity of sonorities and the rhythmical decoration do not, however, fully compensate for the harmonic naïvety; in fact, neither he nor Glier really succeeded in evolving a genuine harmonic system out of the folk-material.

S. Prokoviev (1891–1953) was trained in the St. Petersburg Nationalist school but, unlike Stravinsky, he rebelled against it while still a student. His extraordinary precosity is shown in his having written the First and Second Piano Concertos (1911 and 1913 respectively) at the Conservatoire and at the same time reached the position of one of Russia's leading piano virtuosi. His reaction against academicism led him, like Miaskovsky, into the company of the followers of Scriabin, at that time the only independent and progressive group, and this is reflected in the over-chromatic and decadent harmony of the first two piano concertos and the mysticism of the Five Songs (1916). But these works also show qualities that certainly cannot be attributed to Scriabin —a highly developed melodic sensibility and clarity of rhythmical design. The *Scythian Suite* (1914) is a *tour de force* of composition in its deliberate concentration on rhythm and sonority and is one of the most remarkable examples of 'primitivism' ever composed, all the more remarkable in that it deliberately excluded his greatest quality—that of melodic invention. The fact that there are no subsequent works in anything like the same idiom shows that he must have realised that he had already exhausted its possibilities. The extreme contrast provided by his next major work, the 'Classical' Symphony, is thus not surprising. This work is not a parody of Mozart nor is it an early example of 'neo-classicism', but rather a re-affirmation of melody and the classical principles of clarity and precision in texture which were to remain the dominant features of his style, rather than the *enfant terrible* characteristics of his satirical pieces, like *Chout* (1920). Gorki recognised the truly human and compassionate qualities in *The Ugly Duckling* (1914).

His period abroad from 1918 to 1933 was one of great struggle both with himself and with the outside world. His first concert tour in America as a virtuoso, playing his own compositions, was a sensational success, but his return the following year when he had been persuaded to play the 'standard repertoire' was a disaster, and from then he became more and more dissatisfied with the life of a virtuoso (much as did Busoni about the same time). As a composer he found himself more and more in isolation. After the initial sensation of *Chout* and *The Love of Three Oranges* (1919) he was no longer associated with the Parisian *avant-garde* who, later, were estranged by the philosophical and moral basis of *The Flying Angel* opera (1925). At the same time he had never been accepted by the traditionalists, although his work showed real understanding of the importance of tradition. *Le Pas d'Acier* ballet (1925), which he wrote for Diaghilev, was his first work on a Soviet theme (that of industrialisation), but it was directed, with its cold-blooded 'mechanisation', not to the Soviet people but to the sophisticated Paris audience. His failure to find roots in Europe led, inevitably, to his return to his own country.

The first work he wrote in the Soviet Union, the *Symphonic Song* (1933), is a piece of fine sustained lyricism but with a nostalgic quality unusual in Prokoviev and it lacks the characteristic clarity of design and texture. But these qualities returned in full measure in the Second Violin Concerto (1938). The first movement is one of his finest achievements, with its restrained power and melodic distinction which has marked but unselfconscious Russian inflections. In the ballets, *Romeo and Juliet* (1936) and *Cinderella* (1941), the tradition of Russian classical ballet is perfectly matched by the objectivity, restrained lyricism and pathos of the music. In the cantata, *Alexander Nevsky* (1938), the national element is very marked with the Moussorgsky-like desolation of the opening scene and the poignant folksong-like melody of the *Field of the Dead*. His greatest achievement in the post-war period was in symphonic writing. The Fifth Symphony (the first of the Soviet period) is on spacious and noble lines; the Sixth, more subjective and complex but fascinating in its subtleties of rhythm and sonority; the Seventh, light and lyrical but not over-obvious as first impression suggests. His last large-scale work, the *Concertante* for Cello and Orchestra, is one of his very greatest achivements, masterly in its solution of the difficult problem of balance between solo instrument and orchestra, of very great melodic distinction and on a sustained level of impassioned lyricism.

I have seen neither performances nor scores of the last two operas, *War and Peace* (on Tolstoy's novel) and *The Story of a Real Man* (on Polevoy's war novel). He was engaged in revising the former at the time of his death, and, according to his own words, endeavouring to reduce the action in order to leave more room for extended arias, which suggests he had abandoned his former view that opera should not have long arias but should move at the speed of the drama.

The chamber music, particularly the eight piano sonatas and the great F Minor Violin and Piano Sonata (1946), occupy a very special and intimate place in his work. Technically, the piano sonatas are in the great nineteenth-century tradition in that they use the full sonorities of the instrument and not purely percussively or in quasi-eighteenth-century style as in so much contemporary piano writing. But he permits himself more subtlety of harmony and rhythm than in most of the orchestral works and they explore new and often strange psychological regions, as in the first movement of the Eighth, which starts innocently enough but becomes a truly terrifying experience.

Y. A. Shaporin (b. 1889) is the oldest of the leading composers whose creative work belongs entirely to the Soviet period. He completed his musical training at St. Petersburg with Steinburg and others of the National school as late as 1918, having first graduated in Law. In the early 1920s he was closely associated with Gorki and Blok in the Leningrad theatre, where he wrote much incidental music for plays, including Shakespeare, Beaumarchais and Turgenef. The orchestral suite, *The Flea* (1935), based on his earlier music to a play by Leskov (who wrote the novel on which Shostakovitch's opera, *Lady Macbeth*, was based), is the only example of this theatre music that exists in concert form. It is amusing and brilliantly scored. Shaporin has always been a slow and self-critical writer, hence the number of his works is not large. He was never associated with either the 'Proletarians' or the 'Contemporaries' and avoided the conflicts most of his colleagues experienced in the process of integrating themselves with Soviet society. His friendship with Gorki helped him to understand the real relationship between tradition and revolution.

He has remained in the tradition of the 'Big Five' and at first sight he seems to lack individuality, but in his finest work, such as the Pushkin Song Cycle, the *Kulikovo* cantata and *The Decembrists* opera, he shows an originality that is nonetheless real because it is expressed in terms of insight into poetic imagery, the drama of unfolding historical events and the expression of simple but deep human emotions rather than in novelty of idiom. He seems to need the assistance of words to evoke his most imaginative response, hence the Symphony in E minor (1933), although containing much noble music and being finely wrought, lacks precision of musical imagery and dramatic shape necessary in a work of such huge dimensions. The Pushkin Song Cycle (1926), in spite of a rather Brahmsian quality in the piano writing, has great beauty of melodic line and poetic insight. In the *Field of Kulikovo* cantata (1938), to words by his friend Blok, he achieved the real fusion of structure and texture that is lacking in the Symphony. In spite of its great length and the episodic nature (there are eight movements), it retains an almost Tolstoyan sense of historical inevitability, and succeeds in combining symphonic development with vivid expression of the poetic images. With all these qualities, the essentially nineteenth-century character of the idiom seems unimportant.

His most important work, the opera, *The Decembrists*, to a libretto by Alexei Tolstoy, deals with the Russian Army officers' revolt against Nicholas I in December 1825. Shaporin began it in 1925, parts of it were given in concert form in 1937 and it was finally produced in Moscow in 1953 after much revision. In its final form it does seem to have achieved what few Soviet operas have succeeded in obtaining—a permanent place in the repertoire. Those who have seen it say that, in spite of being rather slow moving, it is dramatic and emotionally sustained with noble and spacious vocal writing and very imaginative use of the chorus.

L. K. Knipper (b. 1898) is in every way the antithesis of Shaporin except in that of self-criticism. He strives with determination to find the means by which a bridge could be formed between concentrated musical thought and popular music, in which respect he may be said to epitomise the Soviet composer. Although a native of Georgia and a pupil of Glier, he did not concern himself with nationalism or the folk music of his country until the 1930s. In the 1920s he was active in the 'Contemporary' group, writing satirical, anti-romantic operas and orchestral works of which his Op. 1, *The Legend of the Plaster God* (1925), was the most famous and widely performed. In the opera, *The North Wind* (1930), on a story of the Civil War, the device of speaking against music, much favoured in Central Europe at the time, is used almost to the exclusion of melodic vocal writing. His general harmonic idiom and texture at that time was linear and deliberately dry. In the 1930s, however, he conducted extensive folk-music research in the mountains of Tadjskistan. The direct outcome was the Symphonic Suite, *Vantch* (1932), which is perhaps his greatest work and, with the *Turkmenian* Suite (1934) of B. Shekhter (b. 1900), is one of the most successful examples of symphonically developed folk music from the remote Republic. In this work he evolves a harmonic language out of the folk tunes themselves and avoids the typical 'Oriental' harmony of the Rimsky-Korsakov tradition. The percussion is used with great skill and imagination to provide the rhythmical undercurrent, and the clean counterpoints grow very naturally out of the folksongs themselves. The orchestral sonorities are often extremely original and effective, never complex but always clean and direct. The slow fifth section is of very great poetic beauty.

During the 1930s he wrote several symphonies in which he was concerned in linking his music closely with Soviet life, not only in the titles and general emotional atmosphere but more directly by introducing popular songs such as those of the Red Army and the Youth. He did not succeed in fusing popular Soviet music and symphonic method in these works to anything like the same degree as with folk music, although the symphonies are strong and exciting works. The Third ('Far Eastern') Symphony (1933), for vast resources (large symphony orchestra, brass band, three male soloists and male chorus), grew directly out of his life with the Red Army. Engels had pointed out that the purely musical quality of many revolutionary songs is very poor and that what we are affected by is really their associative qualities. This applies with particular validity in the Third and Fourth ('Konsommol') (1934) Symphonies. The popular songs he introduces are very evocative for the people in whose lives they form an important part, but they are necessarily less so for those who do not share that life (but that would not be considered important from the Soviet point of view). The greatness of the theme of the finale of Beethoven's Choral Symphony lies in its universality (for which he strove many years to achieve); it is doubtful whether even Beethoven's genius could have made much symphonic use of a revolutionary song of his day.

But Knipper's symphonic writing is not exclusively of this type. In the Four Etudes for large orchestra (1933) he explores sonorities with great imagination and technical command, but not for their own sake, in spite of the absence of external association; he is too fine a musician to bother with such abstractions. I have not seen examples of his latest work, but his Thirteenth Symphony received special praise at the Plenary Session of the Union of Soviet Composers in February 1953. Mention should also be made of his popular songs, of which 'Steppe Cavalry' is the most famous; they are obvious and direct but never crude, as are many of the imitations.

V. I. Shebalin (b. 1902) is one of the most gifted pupils of Miaskovsky, with whose later style he has much in common, namely, a basic Russian quality with much folksong influence and an ability to write well-organised and integrated large-scale movements. His music is not sensational, often, like Miaskovsky's, being based on what appear to be themes of no great import, but it has great rhythmical drive and dramatic tension. He is primarily an instrumental composer, his string quartets and symphonies being most representative. The Third String Quartet (1939) is a work of great lyrical beauty and rhythmical elasticity and organic unity. He exploits in an unsensational way and with spontaneity, interesting new scale formations, but the melodic character remains fundamentally vocal. The Sixth Quartet (published in 1946) has similar qualities, but the thematic material shows more marked folksong influence, particularly of a modal type. The Sonata for Violin and Viola (1942) that immediately followed the Sixth Quartet is a masterly exploitation of this fascinating medium, particularly the march-like finale.

One of his finest works is the Third Symphony in C, Op. 17, dedicated to Shostakovitch. (There is some doubt concerning its date, for, in spite of the early opus number, it was not published until 1946; nor must it be confused with the 'Lenin' Symphony of 1934, which is also often described as Number Three.) It is a work of great dramatic power and of fine strong themes, of which one in the slow movement, featuring fourths, is developed with great contrapuntal skill in the finale.

He is an outstanding film composer, one of his recent works being the biographical film of the life of Glinka.

There is little that can be called typically Soviet in his work, but he is important, like Miaskovsky, not only for the actual quality of his musical thinking but also for the moral and intellectual integrity that his work reflects.

D. B. Kabalevsky (b. 1904) was also a pupil of Miaskovsky and is stylistically related to him, but he differs in that his compositions show him to be more spontaneous, less self-critical perhaps, relying on his facile technical command and less concerned with the philosophical content of his work. He is an essentially lyrical composer and seems to know the limits within which he can realise what he has to say. He is an important educative force in the Soviet Union, not only in his charming and very valuable children's music, which is well known in this country, but also in his seeking ways to bring adolescents closer to contemporary music by writing books, such as his fluent and effective Violin Concerto (1948), which are dedicated to them (but not necessarily to be played by them; the Violin Concerto requires an Oistrakh).

His other large-scale works, such as the three symphonies, although finely wrought, are less-compelling examples of Miaskovsky's style. During the war he wrote the cantata, *The People's Avengers*, arising directly from his life with the Partisans in the Ukraine. The choruses of this work are a very successful blending of popular song idiom and Kabalevsky's own style, more successful than Knipper's, because Kabalevsky's own idiom originates in the same tradition as that of Russian popular song. (The cantilena melody in the second movement of the Violin Concerto, although quite typical of the composer, could itself be a Russian popular song.)

Opera is, however, the large form in which he has made his most distinctive contribution. *Colas Breugnon* (1937), based on the novel of Romain Rolland, is one of the few Soviet operas to remain in the repertoire. The episodic nature of the story lends itself to the method of arias, choruses and orchestral *entractes* rather than to the continuous half-recitative favoured by Prokofief. Kabalevsky succeeds in giving the work dramatic shape in spite of this sectional treatment. He also succeeds in preserving the characteristic gaiety of the leading figure, but without losing sight of the fundamental seriousness of the idea of the story. The music, such as the popular Overture, may not seem very distinguished when taken away from the stage, but many fine operas, including some of Verdi's, are unable to survive that treatment. His recently produced *Taras Family*, based on Gogol's story, is reported to be, after its recent revision, very successful.

As mentioned above, A. I. Khachaturian (b. 1904) owes his recognition to the encouragement given to the development of culture in the remote Republics. He was first trained as a cellist, but while in Moscow his talent for composition developed and he became the pupil of Miaskovsky. There is, however, little influence of his teacher to be found, as even his earliest works, such as the Poem for Piano (1927) and the Trio for Clarinet, Violin and Piano (1932), written while still a student, show already his individual characteristics—melismatic thematic material, strongly reminiscent of his native Armenia, harmony with many parallel chords derived from harmonics, as in Debussy and Ravel, and an absence of development of thematic material but rather improvised-like passages in the style of the main themes. The Trio remains one of his best works, for here he avoids the Rimsky-Korsakov-like 'Oriental' harmony which is to be found in some of his later works. The whole work creates the impression of a remarkable piece of sustained improvisation, but is very unified stylistically. The piano part is always kept distinct from the violin and the clarinet, its function being primarily rhythmical and harmonic and to provide a distinctive back-cloth to the melodic designs. The First Symphony (1934) was his diploma work as a student and is very self-confident and mature. The first movement in particular is remarkable for its ability to 'go on' without actual thematic development and needless repetition, while remaining extraordinarily unified rhythmically. It is a similar process to that of the first movement of Walton's Symphony. A weakness in the work as a whole, however, is the limited amount of thematic material (most of which comes from the first movement) in spite of the metamorphosis to which it is subjected.

The Piano and Violin Concertos (1936 and 1940 respectively) are of undoubted technical assurance and have a popular following throughout the world but are in most respects inferior to the First Symphony. Although rhythmically the melismatic and improvised character of Armenian folksong and dance is still present, the structure over whole sections is more rigid and lacking in the flexibility of the first movement of the Symphony. The success of the ballets, *Happiness* (1935) and *Gayane* (1942), causes serious musicians to tend to dismiss them as 'pot-boilers', but they do possess an *élan* and the rhythmical shape and clarity of orchestral tones so essential to this medium. *The Song of Stalin* (1938) has an original structure in that it consists of a long, symphonic poem on folksongs of several Republics culminating in a choral setting of a poem by an Azerbaijan folk-poet; unfortunately the main theme of the choral finale is not strong enough to stand the concentrated attention it receives, but the preceding orchestral section has great beauty.

More recently the Second Symphony (1943) and the Symphonic Poem (1947) exploit sumptuous orchestral sonorities and, in the opinion of some, too much as ends in themselves. His latest work, the ballet, *Spartacus*, to judge by the discussion at the Plenary Session of

227

the Union of Soviet Composers in April 1954, is well thought of by leading musicians, including Shostakovitch, who noted a marked advance in the symphonic character of the music since the earlier ballets.

D. Shostakovitch (b. 1906) is one of the most enigmatic figures in Soviet music. He was a pupil of Steinberg at Leningrad and, as such, brought up in the Nationalist tradition, but there is little evidence of the influence of this on even his earliest works. Leningrad in the 1920's heard performances of the important works of Hindemith, Berg and other Central European composers, and the influence of these is very clear in the remarkable First Symphony (1925), written while he was still a student. Hindemith may be seen in the linear counterpoint of much of the first movement; Mahler and Berg in the almost over-ripe romanticism and fatalistic atmosphere of the slow movement; the nightmarish scherzo and frightening march passages in the first movement suggest the dance-hall and military-band scenes in *Wozzeck*; an occasional hint of Tchaikovsky in the waltz-like second subject of the first movement and in the tragic coda to the whole work and the Russian folksong-like trio of the *scherzo* are the only Russian elements. It might be thought that so much derivation is a denial of Shostakovitch's individuality, but, in fact, the latter is revealed precisely in his sense of stylisation and in the juxtaposition of many clearly recognisable idioms, and is an instance of what Asaviev meant by 'musical representation'. This stylisation, which he probably inherited from Mahler, who had always been popular in Russia, by no means implies that his music is 'pastiche' in character but that he permits himself full use of the associative ideas that arise in stylistic quotation. It also means he is not concerned with the absolute aesthetic quality of the quotation; it could be as easily a cheap dance-hall tune, as in the second movement of the Piano Concerto, or a Bach aria, as in the first movement of the Sixth Symphony. The speed with which these associative ideas succeed each other and the apparent incongruity of some of them give his music, particularly the early works, its neurotic character, and so vivid is the musical imagery that it creates an almost physical reality, as in the music following the murder of Katerina's father-in-law in *Lady Macbeth of Mtsensk* or the 'May-Day in Red Square' atmosphere in the last movement of the Sixth Symphony. It is the psychological and physical realism of his music that has given rise to the violent controversies and the reason why criticism has been so often on moral rather than on aesthetic grounds. *Lady Macbeth of Mtsensk* is really the Soviet *Wozzeck*, but it lacks the compassion of Berg and the moral indignation expressed in the great Epilogue and the objectivity that Berg gives his work by making the occasional naturalism only incidental to the great musical structures.

Shostakovitch's maturity dates from the Fifth Symphony (1937) and is characterised by a growing ability to develop musical images on a larger scale and to rely less on the juxtaposition of musical styles. The Fifth Symphony, the Piano Quintet (1940) and the Tenth Symphony (1953) are the finest examples of this process. They are pervaded with a calm confidence; the high spirits of the finale of the Fifth Symphony are very different from the hysteria of the Second Symphony. The fugue of the Quintet has a wonderful new meditative quality. Only occasionally, as in the tragic Eighth Symphony and the trivial Ninth, does the early neurotic element reappear. *The Song of the Forests* cantata (1949), written to commemorate the great afforestation scheme, fails to communicate much of the dramatic quality of that vast enterprise and is, in general, pervaded by an enervating and complacent lyricism and naïvety of musical language. The Twenty-four Preludes and Fugues (1951) are by no means a 'pastiche' of Bach or an imitation of Hindemith's *Ludus Tonalis*; they possess an intimate and meditative quality (that was first hinted at in the Quintet), of which the F sharp minor is a *tour de force* of technique and imagination.

The Tenth Symphony is an epic work and has none of the Mahlerian sprawling character of the 'Leningrad' or parts of the Fifth. It is at once expansive and closely knit. The first movement is probably his very greatest achievement in the beauty of its thematic ideas and their expansion, combination and development, all contained within an elastic but unifying rhythmical momentum.

The younger generation of Soviet composers has not, so far, revealed a talent of the stature of Prokoviev, Shebalin or Shostakovitch, but there are, nevertheless, several whose work shows imagination, invention and technical brilliance and which give indications of the most likely general development of Soviet music.

V. V. Zhelobinsky (1912–46) was a remarkably precocious young composer. Opera was his principal medium and his first was produced in Leningrad when he was only twenty-one. His most famous was *Mother* (1937), on Gorki's famous novel. His style had much in common with Shostakovitch—brilliant technical command and dramatic power. There was every possibility that, but for his untimely death following a long illness, he would have become of major significance.

T. Khrennikov (b. 1913) was a pupil of Shebalin, and his early works, particularly the First Symphony, written at the age of twenty-two, attracted much attention for its technical command and orchestral imagination. At this time he was much influenced by Shostakovitch, but his later works became much more lyrical in style and more traditional in idiom, as in his most famous work, the opera, *The Storm* (1937), on a story of the peasant struggle against the Counter-Revolutionaries. He is at his best in light, lyrical works such as the incidental music to *Much Ado* (1936). His more recent works, such as the Second Symphony, show a fine melodic sense, but a certain unadventurousness in rhythm and harmony.

Among the young Russian composers who have attracted attention since the war is V. Bunin, whose Second Symphony (1950) is in the Russian tradition of Shebalin and is symphonically well knit and imaginatively scored. The folksong influences are well assimilated, but the rhythms are rather square and inflexible.

B. Dvarionas is a young Lithuanian. His Violin Concerto (1948) is in classical structure. It tends to over-use rhythmical sequence, but the clear and distinctive modal thematic material is treated with harmonic conviction and the orchestration is effective without being sensational.

S. Taktakishvili (b. 1926) is one of the most gifted young Georgian composers. His First Symphony (1952) is quite traditional from the point of view of general structure and is rhythmically rather four-square in its main sections, but the introduction and interludes show he is capable of far more rhythmical elasticity. Harmonically it is derivative of the 'Big Five' except for the influence of Shostakovitch in the finale and in the use of the very distinctive harmony of Georgian polyphonic folk music, particularly in the almost mediaeval-sounding parts of the slow movement. The orchestration is invariably imaginative and telling. The Second Symphony, on Georgian themes (1953), has been highly praised.

Another talented Georgian is A. Matsavariani whose *Choroomi* (1947) for piano is a very successful development of the subtle Georgian rhythms in keyboard writing that has much in common with that of Bartók.

K. Karajef, an Azerbaijanian, is one of the leading young composers of ballet. His *Seven Beauties* Portraits in Music is very rich and colourful. Harmonically it is somewhat derivative of the 'Big Five' but clear and exciting rhythmically.

Babazhdanian is an Armenian and a pupil of Khachaturian. His

Poem for Piano and Orchestra is one of the most popular concert works of the younger composers.

The fostering of creative activity in the Republics has produced in the remote regions many young composers who are concerned with developing folk-instrumental forms in concert works. One of the most interesting and fruitful examples of this is in the Symphonic Mugams that the young Georgian, Armenian and Azerbaijan composers are writing. The mugam in the instrumental folk music of these regions has something in common in method with both the Indian ragas and the formal structure of Negro jazz, that is to say, it is not only a scale which forms a basis for improvisation but also the framework in which concerted improvisation can take place. Something of the mugam process is to be found in Knipper's *Vantch,* but it has only recently been applied more systematically in symphonic music. Its most valuable feature is that it provides an alternative to classical symphonic structure, to which folksong material has never lent itself very willingly. Good and characteristic examples of these Symphonic Mugams are by the Azerbaijan composers, Amirov, Birof and Nyazi. One of these, *Shur* (1950), by F. Amirov, is in one continuous movement of nine sections, each rhythmically distinct. An important element melodically is the systematic use of the elaborate forms of decoration used by the folk-instrumentalists (not unlike those of Scottish and Irish pipers); this is very different from the vague 'Oriental' trills and cascades of Rimsky-Korsakov.

There is no doubt that there are great possibilities in the development of folk-instrumental forms of which the mugam is but one, and it is significant that the most stimulating new music from young Soviet composers comes from those working in this field. It is therefore likely that the most fruitful developments in the Soviet music of the immediate future will come from those regions whose cultural evolution is in its early stages, and that not until these have in their turn revitalised it will there be any real development in the Russian tradition itself.

Modern French Music

DAVID DREW

FOR a tradition to have culminated in so commanding a figure as Debussy, and then to have been robbed of him at a time when he was grappling with the problems inherent in his achievement—this was indeed a heavy blow. In his last years, Debussy realised that the time had come to reaffirm the autonomous nature of music. The preoccupation with literary and pictorial associations had led to a self-indulgent sensuousness of harmony and this in turn had tended to inhibit true formal expansion. It was clear that Debussy could not always rely for his more extended structures on the continuity provided by dance rhythms and associations—a method that had been applied with superb results in the *Images* for orchestra and in many of the relatively quick-tempo piano pieces, but which allowed—even encouraged—a rhapsodic element that was clearly incompatible with the demands of 'pure' music. Significantly enough, Debussy's 'Impressionist' period closes, not with a work involving large forms, but with the twenty-four *Préludes,* the most extreme of which are completely contradictory to traditional conceptions of developing structure. The revolutionary technique was, of course, justified by the expressive aim, but the aim was so specialised that it threatened to lead to sterility. That Debussy was himself aware of this danger is suggested by the work which he wrote immediately after the *Préludes,* namely *Le Martyre de Saint Sebastien.* This score must be regarded as the first-fruit of Debussy's final period, for it shows the composer turning towards a dramatic, as opposed to a passively sensory, conception of harmony. Admittedly, the only unexpected feature of the opening pages of the score, with their very typical organum-like effects, is the austerity with which they are presented—

an austerity that is, in fact, characteristic of all of Debussy's later work. But such things as the *a capella Chorus Seraphicus*, the *andantino* song of the *Virgin Erigone*, and the whole of the final chorus (with its daringly opposed tonalities) reveal in their harmonic writing a directness and purity that is very different in character from anything in Debussy's 'Impressionist' works. The first appearance of *ostinato* as a feature of Debussy's technique is a sign of the extent to which he had pared down his methods of procedure.

Quite apart from its positive qualities, *Le Martyre* seems to have had a purgative function for its composer, and it prepares the way for the extreme cogency of the late sonatas and piano works. But between them and *Le Martyre* stands a most curious and remarkable work—one that at first sight appears to be outside Debussy's main line of development: the ballet score, *Jeux*, of 1912. Superficially, *Jeux* seems to belong to a much earlier stage of Debussy's development. The tremors and swoons, the cries of anguished voluptuousness, which issue from the music arise from that kind of feeling—sensation would perhaps be a better word— which we associate with the Symbolists on the one hand and 'exoticists' like Pierre Louÿs on the other. If at first we note anything unusual in *Jeux* it is likely to be the odd stylistic resemblance to late Scriabin, a resemblance which is by no means confined to the emphasis on the augmented triad. It is at once evident that Debussy's is the keener intelligence and the more refined sensibility, but it is only when one becomes better acquainted with *Jeux* that one appreciates to the full the significance of the doubtless coincidental affinity with Scriabin. The fact is that the harmonic and melodic consistency of *Jeux* arises from a type of modal and motivic control that Scriabin himself used in a more thorough-going form. For Debussy this was an unexpected departure, even though, in retrospect, we can see that it was foreshadowed by the motival working of pieces like *Reflets dans l'eau*. In *Jeux*, Debussy attempts neither the quasi-symphonic development that is typical of *La Mer*, nor the extended dance forms which recur so often in his earlier music. Instead, he allows the structure to evolve from a succession of brief sections whose contrasts of tempo and texture provide the variety that animates the motival unity. Thanks to the sensitivity with which these juxtapositionings are contrived, Debussy succeeds where Scriabin fails. (Indeed, the sectional form of Scriabin's late sonatas and his *Prometheus* is more a harmful by-product than a constructive end.) In rigorously avoiding the conventional melodic period—which, of course, relied on the cadential impulse of traditional harmony—Debussy was taking up a position similar not only to that of Scriabin, but also to that of a much greater revolutionary figure, Arnold Schönberg: the Schönberg of certain of the so-called 'free atonal' works. But there is nothing in the structure of *Jeux* comparable to the great arches of tension in Schönberg's *Erwartung* (1909). The minutely sectional form of *Jeux*—like that of Satie's *Parade* three years later—was prophetic not of early atonal and twelve-note works, and still less of the music of Hindemith, but of much of the 'progressive' music outside the Central European tradition: the music of Stravinsky in particular. In his autobiography, Stravinsky comments as follows on the *Symphonies pour Instruments à vent* which he wrote in 1920 in memory of Debussy: 'I had a distinct feeling that he [Debussy] would have been rather disconcerted by my musical idiom.' Indeed, the Symphonies may be regarded as the final stage in the process of exorcising the ghosts of Debussy which had haunted Stravinsky's early Diaghilev ballets; but, ironically enough, the formal principles underlying the Symphonies are not unlike those of *Jeux*, despite the marked dissimilarity of content. There is, however, one significant feature of form that distinguishes *Jeux* from the *Symphonies* (though not from the later *Capriccio*). The episodes are linked by close intervallic and harmonic relationships. In this respect the most obvious heritage of *Jeux* is to be found in certain works by Messiaen—notably the piano piece, *Cantéyodjayâ* (whose form, like that of *Jeux*, is entirely composed of brief episodes with *ritornelli*).

Formally speaking, *Jeux* had no clear successors in Debussy's own *oeuvre;* but the manner in which the music is derived from a few extremely austere motifs is also typical of Debussy's twelve *Études* for piano, which followed three years later. *Jeux* and the *Études* may fittingly be described as 'experimental', provided that the word is not understood to connote any idea of the tentative or the incomplete. Just as Debussy had sought a new harmonic stability in *Le Martyre*, so in these two works did he establish new structural principles. In the suite for two pianos, *En Blanc et Noire*, and in the three late sonatas, he achieved an impressive synthesis of his harmonic and structural innovations.

There was a time when Debussy's sonatas were cited as proof of his allegedly waning powers. Today the situation has changed for the better, and I do not feel that there is much to be added, within the present limits, to the admirable observations upon these works made by Mr. Wilfrid Mellers in his *Studies in Contemporary Music*. Those who remain unconvinced of the very high place which these sonatas occupy in Debussy's output might profitably compare them with the finest of the earlier piano pieces—say, *La Soireé dans Grenade* and *L'Isle Joyeuse*. It will surely be agreed that although the substance of the sonatas is less luxuriant, their musical and emotional meaning is more complex and ultimately of a higher order. The Debussy of the first movement of the violin sonata, for instance, has completely transcended the limitations which were threatening him in the immediate pre-war years. The argument has become a purely musical one, in which the harmony is the precise and efficient agent of a dramatic-rhetorical idea. Observe how, in the recapitulation of this movement, Debussy withholds the tonic-minor subdominant-major juxtaposition with which the exposition had so dramatically started, in order that he may make it the crux of the magnificent peroration in the coda.

On the evidence of these late works, it is safe to say that had Debussy lived five or ten years longer, he would have continued to write music of the highest significance; and it is certain that the example of a major master steadfastly applying himself to the problems of his musical evolution would have been of incalculable value to the development of French music. But it was not to be. The minor composers—and there were many of them—had to look elsewhere for a lead. Popular opinion would have elected Maurice Ravel to that position, and it is true that he was, and still is, a potent influence. But even on the basis of his achievement up to 1917, one would have good reason to doubt that this influence could be wholly beneficial. To be sure, the Debussy*istes* had made a sorry show, but men like Stravinsky, Bartók, and Kodaly had profited from the example of Debussy's middle period, and there was as much still to be learnt from his later work. Ravel's creative solutions were far less radical that Debussy's; despite the greater astringency of his harmony and a streak of modishness in his sensibility, he always remained closer to the musical sources from which both composers had sprung—Gounod, Massenet and Chabrier. This fundamental traditionalism made it easier for minor composers to imitate his manner, and it became yet more so in proportion as Ravel's interest in surface effect increased—an interest typified, towards the end of his life, by his professed admiration for Saint-Saëns.

The last ten years of Ravel's composing career make an interesting study, for his activities during that time are directly symptomatic of the plight of contemporary French music, a plight that becomes almost tragic when it engulfs an artist of Ravel's stature. The death of Debussy found Ravel in much the same position, artistically, as that occupied by Debussy at the time of the second book of *Préludes*. The suite *Le Tombeau de Couperin* contains some splendid things, but the fugue— a form hitherto unknown in Ravel's music—seems to pose an anxious question. 'What more is there to be said', it seems to imply, 'within the terms of an idiom so scrupulously devoted to the exquisite?' The answer is, of course, 'very little'.

The broad outlines of this type of creative crisis are to be found somewhere in the careers of each of the major French composers of this century—Debussy, Satie, Roussel, Messiaen and Ravel himself. Ravel was intelligent enough to appreciate what was at stake, and vigorous enough to make the effort of reorientation; but what is new in his post-1917 music—the playboy jazziness, the (sometimes) gratuitous bitonality—cannot be compared with the active renunciation and reintegration undertaken by the other major composers. It is not, I think, fanciful to suppose that Ravel's sudden interest in the *trouvailles* of his younger contemporaries arose from a need to find something to replace the stimulus that had been provided by the presence and rivalry of Debussy. The best things in Ravel's late work—for instance the lyrical sections of *L'Enfant et les Sortilèges,* and the sublime slow movement of the G Major Piano Concerto [1]—are those which are frankly retrospective. Together with the less seriously considered passages, they encourage the opinion that Ravel's ultimate place in music will be found to be somewhat similar to that of Puccini, another minor master whose craftsmanship is usually above reproach, whose imagination, though limited,

---

[1] Here, influenced fleetingly by Mozart, Ravel for the first and last time discovered within himself the potentiality of genius. It is impossible to approach this movement, musically, without coming into conflict with Constant Lambert's reference to what he calls its 'synthetic melody'. That Lambert should apply this (dangerously imprecise) term to one of the most beautiful and profoundly creative melodic structures in all music is evidence of how far his opinions are to be trusted. They must, indeed, be challenged at every opportunity, until such time as they no longer influence the impressionable young (to whom Lambert's *Music Ho!* is invariably recommended. I know at least one serious and discriminating musician whose attitude to the Ravel *adagio* was for many years distorted by Lambert's cursory criticism). Those who wish to re-examine their response to this movement would probably be better advised to do so with Fauré, rather than Mozart, in mind. In many ways Fauré must be considered Ravel's equivalent amongst the previous generation of French composers, and there is clear musical evidence that the opening of his *Ballade* for Piano and Orchestra was quite as much in Ravel's thoughts when he wrote the *adagio* of his Concerto as anything in the music of Mozart. Ultimately, the relevant fact is that Ravel here achieved much more than Fauré. It is less interesting that he fell far short of Mozart.

is personal in character and precise in application, but whose artistic incompleteness is revealed in the tendency to seek an easy emotional response by means of an accepted signal rather than by formulating a musical idea in which both substance and expressivity are felt afresh. Like Puccini's 'passionate' climaxes and 'pathetic' reprises, Ravel's insistence on the plangent appeal of the higher diatonic discords and the doubling at the fifteenth of modal melodies sometimes appears scarcely superior, in the moral sense, to the technique of a radio compère controlling the applause of his studio audience. But Puccini, one is inclined to think, knows better than Ravel what his audience is and how he is to reach it.

In certain respects, the most consistent and the most innovatory of Ravel's late works is that much maligned piece, *Bolero*. Because we know that Ravel planned the work merely as an exercise in orchestration, we are apt to assume that its interests extends no farther. The fact is that the specialised technique of *Bolero* represents a violent reaction from harmonic preciosity (and indeed from harmony itself) and thus assures the work a significant place in the history of modern French music. The harmonically meaningless tonic-dominant *ostinato* accompaniment that persists through the work implies that same rejection of vertical correspondence and chord-by-chord progression that later became characteristic of the French post-Webern school—Boulez, Fano, Philippot, and others. More specifically, the reliance on *ostinato* and on the quasi-Oriental technique of varied repetition presages the later work of Messiaen, though with Messiaen the technique is vastly more complex, and is in any case no longer used merely as an instrument of nervous excitement. In its insistence on purely nervous appeal *Bolero* belongs to the artistically unsettled 'Diaghilev era'. The magnificent thirty-four bar melody is a musical *tour de force,* but its extreme sophistication embodies an element of the perverse—which is exemplified by the sensationally emphasised flattened-supertonic of the third melodic sentence. The perversity is made doubly evident (and doubly powerful) through association with the primitive harmonic context. This calculated mating of the sophisticated to the barbaric is the clue to the curiously amoral quality of the music, and thence to the almost hysterical enthusiasm which it sometimes arouses. However, it would be idle to pretend that *Bolero* is characteristic of Ravel's achievement as a whole. Only in the extraordinary precision with which it attains a clearly defined expressive end does the work prove itself worthy of *L'Heure Espagnole, Daphnis et Chlóe,* the piano music, and the songs. These, indeed, contain some of the finest modern French music outside Berlioz and Debussy. But it cannot be denied that even they inhabit a world which, if less restricting than that of *Bolero*, is too small to provide a starting-point for a lifetime of creative work. Music so idiosyncratic and yet so limited is not such as might provide a basis for a healthy 'school', and possibly the only feature of Ravel's style from which later composers could profitably learn was his gift for sustained linear invention. With regard to over-all form, Ravel's music has nothing very valuable to offer, and the works subsequent to *Le Tombeau de Couperin* are particularly unfruitful in this respect. Despite many points of incidental merit, the two sonatas dating from his last period seem very puny when placed beside those of Debussy. They are longer, but their imaginative span is immeasurably less. There is still, as we have seen, evidence of mastery in Ravel's late work, but there are times [1] when a dilettantist strain intrudes upon the musical thought. It was hardly a desirable example for younger French composers at that juncture, especially as the national tradition predisposed them to follow it.

The need for a counterbalancing influence was thus paramount. To some extent it was satisfied by the achievement of Albert Roussel, though some years were to pass before his lead was followed. It is no surprise that Roussel should now be enjoying a period of favour with the critics, at the expense of Ravel, for he is apparently the antithesis of the older composer, and his austerity seems better suited to the spirit of our own day. Yet on the purely musical level it is clear that the antithesis is by no means complete, and that in any case Roussel is certainly not the greater of the two composers.

But before considering how the antithesis between the two composers breaks down, it is necessary to observe that Roussel is almost entirely lacking in those qualities which make Ravel a noteworthy composer, whatever qualities of his own he may possess. His gift for melodic invention is singularly meagre, and were it not for a certain vitality in his handling of asymmetrical phrase-structure, his rhythmic procedures would be quite paralytic. It is perhaps hardly fair to compare the orchestral technique of the two composers, since Ravel was concerned with orchestration *per se* whereas Roussel (except in his early works, such as the *Evocations*, the First Symphony, and *Le Festin*) regarded it, quite legitimately, as an outcome of his musical thought. The result

[1] See, for instance, Concerto in G, *presto* movement, Figs. 11–14, or Violin Sonata, last movement in entirety, or the Fanfare from *L'Eventail de Jeanne*.

is that with Roussel—as with other composers of this kind, notably Hindemith—the quality of the orchestral sound depends to a high degree upon the quality of the musical material. The opaque textures of the Piano Concerto, Op. 36, are a direct result of its melodic nullity. Conversely, such things as the outer movement of the *Suite in F*, Op. 33, and the *Petite Suite*, Op. 39, have a pleasing freshness of sound which arises naturally from the melodic and contrapuntal thought. Yet even in Roussel's best work one is conscious of more sense than sensibility, more integrity than imagination. Where, then, lies the affinity with Ravel that overrides the antithesis?

Of course the antithesis is in itself a kind of affinity, for the apparently opposed qualities of each composer are, in reality, complementary, and derive from the complete synthesis of the French musical genius which we are perhaps nearest to finding in the work of Berlioz. But there is an affinity more positive and fundamental than this. In each case a composer has explored a more or less limited field of expression, only to discover in mid-career that further possibilities are exhausted and that a new departure has become necessary. We have already noted the manner in which Ravel reacted to this necessity. How does Roussel's behaviour compare with that of his senior? Morally speaking, the answer must surely be in his favour. Roussel's integrity was unwavering, and it is nowhere more apparent than in the Fourth Symphony, a work that seems to be specifically directed towards the expansion of the composer's personal idiom. The kind of pseudo-solution to problems of style which Ravel attempted in his last years would never have been acceptable to Roussel. But, on the other hand, his resources were much slighter than Ravel's. Let us pause for a moment and examine the Fourth Symphony in some detail, for in that work Roussel's qualities and limitations stand most clearly in relief. The first movement is a fairly conventional sonata design which seems, like the corresponding movement in the previous symphony, to merit the epithet 'terse'. Such, to be sure, are its intentions. But even before the almost too-typically disjunct first subject is fully exposed, one's suspicions are aroused. The extension of the first strain at Figs. 3-4 is so feeble as to suggest that the initial air of taut vitality was factitious, the innocent artifice of a bankrupt asking his creditors for further grace. We hear much of Roussel's 'lean athleticism', but the leanness of this extension comes from under-nourishment, the athleticism from a forgivable eagerness to return to the initial strain.

This impression might have been dispelled if the second subject

239

were a thing of any substance. But in fact it is a poor affair (self-consciously different from, and manifestly inferior to, the second subject of the Third Symphony). However, disaster is avoided by sheer intelligence and musicianship—the melody accumulates a strength which it never had at the outset. I feel that the exposition of this movement presents in concentrated form the peculiar characteristics of Roussel. The first subject begins promisingly only to lose momentum, whereas the second subject begins half-heartedly only to gather conviction. These two conditions are entirely typical of Roussel's thinking at all periods, the first tending to be most apparent in the fast movement, the second in the slow ones. The *Lento molto* movement of the Fourth Symphony is a case in point. The opening is undistinguished, but interest is aroused by the progress towards the climax (all Roussel's finest slow movements have a climax of this kind), and the climax itself, six bars after Fig. 28, is most impressive. It is characteristic that the success should be harmonic rather than melodic, and equally characteristic that it should not be sustained for long. The Franckian flavour of the continuation of the climax recalls similar influences in the first movement, and reminds us that in this work Roussel is attempting to enlarge his field of expression by returning to a bygone (Romantic) style. But the return does not imply a permanent reorientation. Rather is it in the nature of a series of flying visits interspersed with lengthy spells of self-imitation. The slow movement of the Fourth Symphony seems disturbingly familiar because the second idea is regurgitated from the first idea of the slow movement of the *Petite Suite*, Op. 39, without change of instrumentation or general contour, whilst the first idea is related in feeling to the second idea in the same movement of the Suite. Likewise the jig-like *scherzo*, pleasant enough in itself, adds little of symphonic importance to what has already been said in very similar terms in the final movement of the *Suite in F*, in the *scherzo* of the Third Symphony, and in Bacchus' solo dance in Act Two of *Bacchus et Ariane*.

The *rondo* finale of the Fourth Symphony is certainly the most encouraging movement from the point of view of Roussel's development as an artist. The pastoral lyricism of the *rondo* refrain engages our sympathy at once, and even though the melody is no more consistent idiomatically than any other by this composer, it does at least say something new—new, at any rate, in his music, for it involves a distant echo of Grieg. The first episode is not especially rewarding, but the second episode, upon which the weight of the movement falls, is a remarkable inspiration evolving with witty logic from the refrain itself. The manner in which this leads into, and imposes its rhythm upon, the final statement of the refrain, is almost a stroke of genius. It seems to me to be a finer achievement—because more precise and more efficient in relation to the whole movement—than the combination of refrain and couplet at the conclusion of the *Suite in F*. Here at least Roussel shows himself to be worthy of some of the claims which his admirers make for him.

Unhappily the splendid vitality of the Fourth Symphony's finale did not prove to be an omen for the future. Roussel's only subsequent major work, the choral ballet, *Aeneas*, Op. 54 (1935), confirms that the Fourth Symphony (and the *Sinfonietta*, Op. 52) were transitional stages in the broadening—some would say the 'mellowing' of the composer's style. *Aeneas* completes the process, and in so doing reveals what one had suspected from the somewhat anonymous quality of those parts of the two previous works which might be said to tend towards the new style: namely that Roussel's imaginative reserves could not encompass a new field of expression. *Aeneas* may well be innocent of self-imitation, but it is also innocent of personal ideas of any kind. The ghosts of the composer's heyday hover dimly in the background to remind us of the music's authorship, but of the old fire there is scarcely a glimmer. It is all eminently respectable and eminently uninteresting—something no one could say of Ravel's late works, whatever their faults.

Roussel died in 1937 after a career distinguished by seriousness of purpose. His achievement may not be of the first order, but it merits the respect of those who value the French musical tradition. We may, however, doubt the words of a friend of Roussel's who declared in an obituary that 'there is not a single French musician who would be what he is today if Roussel had not existed'. It would hardly be to Roussel's credit if this were so; but in fact he has had remarkably little influence. The reason for this is not hard to find. Roussel's distinctive achievement lay in his approach to the symphonic problem. The externals of his art—unlike those of Ravel—were not especially remarkable. Now Roussel's contemporaries and juniors showed a marked distaste for symphonic problems, and a dangerous affection for externals. Charm, and its obverse (which Cocteau has called anti-charm), can be faked in music: thoughtfulness and integrity cannot. So most French composers have passed Roussel by. The few that have attempted to follow him have failed to approach, let alone surpass, his achievement. His influence saves the final movement of the Symphony by Henri Dutilleux from falling as low as the other three movements, but although the ideas are Rousselian, the thinking remains sketchy and imprecise. Dutilleux's small talent is shown to best advantage in his theatre music (which includes a score for Roland Petit's *Le Loup*, and ought to include the cheapjack *scherzo* of the Symphony).

A somewhat more considerable figure influenced by Roussel the Symphonist is André Jolivet, to whom I shall return later in this chapter. His Symphony has a coarseness that Roussel would never have permitted, and its argument is as slight in substance as it is insistent in manner. Yet, like much of Jolivet's music, it carries a certain conviction.

The five symphonies of Jean Rivier might charitably be described as Post-Rousselian. In his best-known work, the Third Symphony for strings, the music flows, unruffled and unexciting as the waters of the Seine, through the formal reaches of a bygone age, from whose fastnesses the composer sleepily fishes for ideas, but never catches a single one. In the same composer's Fifth Symphony the activity is a trifle more hectic, but it avails the composer nothing. One discerns, nonetheless, the influence of the best post-Rousselian symphonist, Arthur Honegger. Honegger does not come within the scope of the present chapter, but it is worth observing that the outer movements of one of his more satisfactory works, the Symphony for Strings, are perhaps the only instances of post-Rousselian symphonic writing that are worthy of the model.

On the whole, then, it may be said that Roussel's position as a keyfigure in French music has remained potential rather than actual. Ravel had never legitimately held any such position, potential or otherwise, and Debussy had lived, and died, too early to have afforded much assistance to the younger French musicians who were faced with the revolutionary achievements of Schönberg and Stravinsky. A fourth composer, Charles Koechlin, might—but for a trick of history—have played an important role in the development of modern French music. A fifth, Erik Satie, by another trick of history, did play such a role.

Koechlin, a pupil of Fauré and a pedagogue of some renown, left behind him a vast body of works in almost every form. But of these only a handful of the slighter instrumental and orchestral works are published, and performances of any kind are very rare. In 1942 Mr. Wilfrid Mellers published a sensitive though deliberately uncritical account of what little of Koechlin's music was then available. But the conscience of the musical world has continued to slumber, despite Koechlin's death in 1951.

Like Mr. Mellers, I can only rely, for my judgments, on the few published scores, and one or two scattered performances of orchestral works. With so much of the picture missing, it is impossible to detect the line of development. Thus one is unable, for instance, to determine whether certain revolutionary features were evolved progressively, or whether they sprang from the random inspiration of the moment. The roots from which the idiom has grown are fairly obvious. Even at its most dissonant—as in certain of the tone poems after Kipling's *Jungle Book*—the harmony shows its Ravellian and Debussyan parentage. The orchestral style likewise derives from the practice of these two composers, but the much greater harmonic (or polyharmonic) complexity of certain passages imposes special problems which Koechlin solves in a wholly original way. Composers like Milhaud and Willem Pijper, who all too often attempt a complex texture, could profitably have studied these scores of Koechlin's, for they are at all times models of clarity and precision. (It is not inconceivable that Messiaen, a composer with an even finer ear than Koechlin, has learnt from them). Although, after some years, I cannot recall the details of Koechlin's *Jungle Book* tone-poems, the impression remains with me that Koechlin's mastery of the orchestra is equal to that of any composer of the past fifty years. But I suspect that in the quality of his ideas and in the manner of their formal organisation he is some way behind even Ravel.

The problem of Koechlin's true status is scarcely clarified if one turns from *Le Livre de la Jungle* to the only orchestral work that is generally available—the Partita for Chamber Orchestra. Well written and sometimes quite touching, it is nevertheless a trifle dry and academic. The music is without the richness and justified audacity of the *Jungle Book* pieces, and hardly seems to be the work of the same composer: so delighted was he with his (admittedly great) contrapuntal ingenuity in the Partita that he included a verbal analysis of the two fugal movements at appropriate points between the staves of the printed score. Then again the Partita is hard to reconcile with some of Koechlin's piano pieces, in which the composer might appear to be carrying out a private war against polyphony. Pieces like the 'Chant de Pêcheurs' in *Paysages et Marines*, or 'La Balle' from *Dou-ze Petites Pièces* are of Satiean bareness; and at other times (for instance in *Sur la Falaise*), Koechlin seems content to savour the static impressionistic effect of piled-up fourths and fifths. Apart from the fact that they are beyond doubt the work of a composer who has complete command of the craft of composition, these pieces, and others like them, have almost no perceptible connection with the Schola Cantorum earnestness of the Partita, the colour and variety of the large orchestral works, or the rhetorical assurance of the violin and viola sonatas.

I feel rather strongly that Mr. Mellers attaches too much importance to the two collections of piano pieces entitled *Paysages et Marines*. The complete newcomer to Koechlin's music might well agree that the *Paysages* are the work of an independent-minded and capable musician, but he could equally well be discouraged from further enquiry by the extraordinary monotony of a harmonic style that works to death a number of simple devices—polychordal additions to the major triad that are too reminiscent of the harmonic dabblings of composers like Tansman, and frequent chromatic sideslipping that recall the worst characteristics of the English school of chromaticism. The piano writing, though original enough in itself, is equally lacking in variety.

For my part, I feel that the best introduction to Koechlin is provided by the fourth of the *Sonatines* for piano solo which he wrote for his children, and the second of the *Sonatine Française* for piano duet. To these might be added the *Esquisses* for piano. Taken together, these three works give a fair idea of Koechlin's skill in handling long modal lines of great metrical freedom, and of sustaining them over the simplest harmonic accompaniment. What counterpoint there is arises naturally out of the context—and in the second movement of the *Sonatine Française* reaches considerable complexity (though not of the hyper-chromatic kind which we meet in the orchestral works).

Koechlin's approach to chromaticism can be examined in the curious little sonata for two flutes, and in certain of the pieces in the collection of piano music entitled *Ancienne maison de Campagne*. There is certainly greater precision here than in the *Paysages*, but the chromaticism sometimes appears a trifle forced. The first movement of the Sonata for Two Flutes (1920) opens with a solo phrase of thirteen notes, of which ten are different. The remaining two notes, G and B flat, are added in the second phrase. The third and fourth phrases contain eleven different notes, with only the G lacking. The fifth and sixth phrases also contain eleven different notes, but this time it is the B flat that is missing. However, the mild promise of the opening is not fulfilled when the second flute joins the first. Apparently exhausted by the structural audacity of the opening, the composer introduces a new idea in a dorian E (the implied key of the opening) which develops very tentatively. The systematic chromaticism of the main idea is never justified by the subsequent events. The failure of this movement suggests that Koechlin is at his best in a modal-cum-impressionist style which seems to have resulted from a synthesis of the methods of Fauré and Debussy. It is hard to believe that the twelve-note work, Op. 213, is of more than academic interest.

A marked sympathy with the work of Satie makes itself felt in many of Koechlin's smaller pieces, and a comparison between, say, the sixth of the *Douze Esquisses,* and the chorale from Satie's *Sports et Divertissements* (the unmistakable model for the piece) may help to define at least one aspect of Koechlin's talent. The brevity of the Satie chorale is highly characteristic, in that it is a result of extreme concentration: so much so that one cannot say of the music that it is short-winded, even though one may be aware that Satie would technically have been unable to extend the structure, even had the content required it of him. That the content does not invite any such treatment is evidence of Satie's absolute certainty of aim, his awareness that his talent is that of a miniaturist and that his materials must be moulded accordingly. The Koechlin piece, on the other hand, is three times as long as the Satie chorale, and the invention is successfully sustained throughout, with an assurance that Satie could never have commanded. But, on the debit side, there is a certain lack of intensity in the musical thought (most noticeable in the last stanza), which, combined with the fact that the concept is derivative, shows the limitation of Koechlin's talent.

Several of the instrumental sonatas—notably the flute and the cello sonatas—follow the procedure of the small piano pieces very closely. The illusion of larger structures is maintained by *moto-perpetuo*-like figurations, and even in the more substantial works—for instance the Viola Sonata, which has an impressive finale—there is little *rapport* with the classical sonata-concept. This need not be counted a drawback, but at the same time there is often a disturbing lack of defined and differentiated character—one thinks of the continual preoccupation with the *clair* and the *lumineux*, not to speak of the undistinguished gigue-style into which Koechlin frequently lapses. Although Koechlin's best chamber music amounts to something at least as valuable as Roussel's instrumental works, it is difficult to believe that on their account alone Koechlin deserves to be regarded as a composer of major status. Yet the few works for large orchestra that have been heard indicate that he is an artist of much wider range than the chamber music suggests, and so long as the bulk of his output remains unpublished and unperformed it would be an impertinence to attempt a final estimate of his achievement. One thing is certain: the exceptionally slow rate of harmonic movement often makes the music rather dull, in an individual sort of way. But this is the worst that happens to it. I can find nothing in his work that is bad in the sense that much of the music of his younger compatriots is bad; and there is enough to make it plain that his reputation lags far behind his achievement. Here was a composer who, though manifestly less distinguished than Debussy and less subtly original than Satie, was sufficiently assured in technique and exploratory in impulse to have deserved a more influential position amongst French musicians of our time. However, for the bright young things of the twenties, there would have been much in Koechlin's music that was *vieux jeu*. For them, Satie seemed a much more promising leader. What he had done appeared to be so very easy. Could it not be done again? Events have shown that it could not, for even Satie's greatest admirers had reckoned without, or misinterpreted, his genius; and well they might, for the history of the arts does not record another case of genius invested in so slender a talent. At first one is tempted to decry the Muses for granting to Satie what they had, almost unrelentingly, withheld from Ravel. But was it such a blunder? I do not think so.

Satie's music presents us with a critical problem of the first order. The listener must often make reservations about the musical technique, noting at one moment a faulty harmony, at another a lame conclusion or a loose juxtaposition; yet he must pit these flaws against the sustained evidence of a strikingly original personality. Quite intuitively, Satie evolved means of expression that were so individual and so exactly suited to what he had to say that the incidental weaknesses of execution become of no more importance than they do in, say, the paintings of the Douanier Rousseau or the pottery of Picasso (to cite two artists who otherwise have little in common with Satie). Conceptual originality alone would not be sufficient to support Satie's claim to genius, but the way in which the idea and the execution of a given piece are intimately involved with one another, to the exclusion of anything received from outside the composer's own imagination, is such that his genius seems to me indisputable. It is not something that can be discovered without persistence and many disappointments, though his individuality is immediately apparent—for instance one has only to compare the *Sonatine Bureaucratique* of 1917 with the C major

Sonatine of Clementi upon which it is founded.[1] Broadly speaking, the compositional method of the *Sonatine* is the same as Stravinsky's three years later in his arrangement of Pergolesi for *Pulcinella*. By means of a slight change of harmony or a shift of tonality here, an expansion or contraction of phrase length there, the music becomes wholly Satiean. Stravinsky and Britten are the only contemporary composers who have brought about similar miracles of transformation. This re-creative process demands an absolute certainty of style and a penetrating individuality of vision. These Satie has in full.

Strictly speaking, Satie's early work does not come within the period covered by this chapter; but its relevance to the music of our own day is such that it cannot be passed by without mention. Satie's first important works, the three *Sarabandes* of 1887, are generally regarded as being prophetic of Debussy, but Mr. Martin Cooper attempts[2] to establish that Satie was influenced by Debussy, rather than the other way about. An error in his facts makes this easier for him.[3] But in reality the controversy misses the point, for Satie's technique in the *Sarabandes* is very different from that of Debussy at any time—and the *Sarabande* in Debussy's *Pour le Piano*, which is often cited in this context, is no exception. With Satie the chord movements are dictated by the melodic line, which has a mediaeval contour. Spiritually, too, the music is remote from Debussy's. The older composer was incapable of anything so violent as, for instance, the 'placing' of the chord of the ninth in the fifth bar of the second *Sarabande*. Suspended in time—one notes the use of 'composed'

---

[1] The published score contains no mention of this derivation—an omission that should be repaired at the earliest opportunity.

[2] In his book, *French Music from the death of Berlioz to the death of Fauré* (Oxford University Press).

[3] Satie studied at the Conservatoire in 1879, not in 1883–84, as Mr. Cooper states. Debussy was only fifteen at the time, and there is no evidence whatever that he was then experimenting improvisationally with the kind of harmony that Satie embodied in his *Sarabandes*. And even though we learn from Maurice Emmanuel that Debussy dallied with such chords to shock his companions in the Conservatoire classes of 1883, it was not until long after Satie's 1887 *Sarabandes* that Debussy made compositional use of the new treatment of dissonance. In the interim he was too occupied with the music of Massenet, and later Wagner. Mr. Cooper's implicit suggestion of plagiarism on Satie's part is as insupportable as his contention that Satie angrily accused Debussy of taking the idea of *Pelléas* from him. It is indicative of Mr. Cooper's cursory approach to Satie that he should have stated that Debussy orchestrated two of Satie's *Gnossiennes*, whereas it was, of course, the two (very different) *Gymnopédies*. The lack of critical balance revealed by Mr. Cooper in his discussion of Satie is unworthy of the standards he has preserved elsewhere in his book.

silence that was later to become so prominent a feature of Webern's music—this single chord seems to express some intense yet secretive conflict of spirit. I should like to stress the *violence* that is interior to the event, for it seems to me to underlie Satie's entire output, coming nearest to the surface in *Parade* of 1917, but present still in *Socrate* and the superficially placid little Minuet of 1920. Sometimes it is implicit in a cruel juxtaposition of opposed tonalities, but more often it is indefinable in technical terms. I do not feel that this violence is incompatible with a religious sense which is not to be found anywhere in Debussy (least of all in *Le Martyre*!). If we regard the *Sarabandes* as melodically rather than harmonically conceived, we can rid ourselves of the sensuous associations which Debussy has given to this type of harmony, and are able to see its affinities with the austerer church music of the Middle Ages and Renaissance, and also with that related mode of feeling which informs Stravinsky's Mass and the chorales in his *Historie du Soldat* and Symphonies of Wind Instruments.

The *Gymnopédies* which Satie wrote a year after the *Sarabandes* are quite as remarkable from a technical, emotional and historical point of view, but as they are on the whole better known than the *Sarabandes*, I do not propose to dwell upon them. Likewise we must pass over the works of the Rose Croix period, which, although they contain some profoundly impressive things (notably in the *Messe Des Pauvres*, the Four *Préludes*, and the *Prélude de la Porte Heroique du Ciel*), are less surefooted than the *Sarabandes* and *Gymnopédies*. Their more explicit neo-mediaevalism, and their reliance on a highly dissonant yet static harmony are prophetic of Messiaen, but not of those composers who immediately followed Satie. So, bearing in mind the deftness with which Satie, in his *Jack-in-the-Box*, combined the harmonic discoveries of his Rose Croix period with the spirit of his remarkable café songs, and also taking into account the new disciplines and new conceptions of diatonic harmony which he brought to bear in the two piano-duet works of his post-Schola Cantorum period, we must turn to the nine piano suites (ten, including the *Sports et Divertissements*) which Satie wrote in the years 1912–15.

Those who come to these pieces without prejudice cannot fail to marvel at the skill with which the composer immediately establishes an imaginative and poetic idea that is unique to each piece. Particularly in the astonishing *Sports et Divertissements*, the extreme economy of evocation suggests a parallel with the ideal of film music, and also, more distantly, with the expressionism of Schönberg's Stefan George songs. But despite the immediacy of our response, we found difficulty in defining its precise nature. The music is never explicit—never explicitly gay or explicitly sad, never wholly abstract or wholly descriptive. So we find ourselves in the presence of a mystery that is beyond analysis, as we do with all true art that has the outward appearance of simplicity. (Which of us does not feel that Britten's setting of the Little Sweep's plea to be spared a further climb up the chimney reaches far deeper than anything implicit in the immediate dramatic event, though we are unable to describe just where in our intuitive selves it has lodged?)

It is because this mystery, or magic, in Satie's art is combined with the most radical economy in the musical technique that Satie finds so many of his admirers amongst the literary, who are less likely to be disturbed by the absence of elements familiar to the musician. When the admirers are men like Cocteau or Jacques Maritain, we may be sure that they have apprehended something of Satie's essential nature; but we may be equally sure that they are incapable of defining it in musical terms. Both the best and the worst of the *belle-lettrist* critics talk of the 'purity'[1] of Satie's music, as if good music had to be guaranteed free of imperfections, like a saint or a bottle of olive oil. The purity campaign conducted by Satieists is only another aspect of that recital of Satie's negative virtues to which we are so often treated. Such encomia invite the kind of attack that Mr. Martin Cooper very properly makes in the section on Satie in his book on French music.

The truth is that Satie's music makes the most stringent positive demands upon its listeners, who must be prepared to reorientate themselves completely if they are to arrive at any kind of genuinely musical response. Even the interpreter—as Cortot has pointed out—must do this, learning how to integrate rapid alternations of *secco* and *cantabile*, how to tackle brusque changes of register and texture that often involve close harmonic writing in the extreme bass and metronomic *ostinati* in the extreme treble. The harmonic language incorporates diatonic, modal, whole-tone and ambiguous elements in a manner that has a certain point of contact with Debussyan practice, but which is utterly different in effect. There is, however, *no* affinity with Debussy in the first of the piano suites, the *Préludes* of 1912, or in the last, the significantly entitled *Avant dernières pensées*. The first of the 1912 *Préludes* is a two-part study of almost Hindemithian severity, as prophetic in its

---

[1] See Jacques Maritain on Purity in his *Dialogues*: 'Of the word itself an impure use has been made. It has become an equivocal thing, summoned at every opportunity—at the Marquis de Sade's, at the Tcheka . . .'

way as the *Sarabandes* and *Gymnopédies* had been in theirs twenty-five years before. It is, exceptionally amongst the works of this period, monothematic and through-developing—an example of rhetorical argument that is unique in Satie's music. The *Avant-dernières pensées* are in this respect the complete antithesis of the first *Prélude*. Each consists of an *ostinato* which appears in a number of bitonal contexts, so that it changes continually but never grows. (The method was anticipated by Bartók in certain of his *Bagatelles* of 1908.)

The transitional function of the *Préludes* on the one hand and the *Avant-dernières pensées* on the other is so striking, and the direction of Satie's career so clearly defined, that one is tempted to regard his entire *oeuvre* as a self-ordered musical design. Just as the 1912 *Préludes* lead from the Schola Cantorum pieces to the suites, so do the *Avant-dernières pensées* lead from the suites to *Parade*.

Parade is a masterpiece, one of the rare triumphs of modern French art. If the dangerous disassociation of imaginative and technical content may be permitted, I would say that imaginatively *Parade* is the equal of anything in Debussy and superior to anything in Ravel. Although the work is almost entirely neglected or misunderstood, I believe that it has classic status, and that in years to come it will be as unthinkable to omit it from a survey of twentieth-century music as today it would be to omit *Le Sacre du Printemps* or *Pierrot Lunaire*. Structurally it relies entirely on the cellular method adumbrated in the *Sports et Divertissements* and the *Prélude en Tapisserie*. As in these works (though not as in certain other 'cellular' structures used by Satie), the cellules are never developed, but merely juxtaposed. Technically the work derives from the *ostinato* procedures of the *Avant-dernières pensées*. Structure and technique together offer a significant though distant parallel with *Le Sacre*, and because for once Satie never makes a technical error the work is ideal for assessing his revolutionary status.

Of course, the importance of *Parade* cannot be understood without reference to its expressive content. This is of a very peculiar kind, and in its very different way is as disturbing as the music of *The Rite*. *Parade*, however, is quite without the atavistic traits of that work. It might be compared more profitably with the early paintings of Chirico. Just as Chirico's empty shadow-lined streets are not so much streets as pathways to our inner selves along which stalk, invisible and inexplicable, our profoundest feelings of individual or communal disquiet, so are the dances of *Parade* rid of the function (entertainment) of the *genre* pieces they seem to resemble. It is notable that although the characters in *Parade*—the managers and the performers—are ostensibly human, they are, in fact, more puppet-like, more the victims of sinister and uncontrollable fate, than poor Petrushka. These are the hollow men, the faceless, oval-headed, wooden figures that people Chirico's depeopled world. The normal, perceptible, mechanisms of feeling no longer operate. There is no comic or ironic intent behind the dry biscuits prominently displayed in certain of Chirico's paintings, any more than there is behind the snatches of ragtime and *bal musette* which occur throughout *Parade*. The ideas are divorced from their conventional associations, and are infused with meanings which are the more fearful for our inability to grasp them consciously. If the music for *Parade* remains shockingly apposite to the contemporary situation—and I for one think that it does—the reason is not that it is *topical*, in the sense that the work of Kurt Weill (or Brecht or Georg Grosz) is topical, but that it is unsocial, disengaged, objective—in fact, the product of a spiritual exile that is almost pathological in nature. As such it has central relevance to one aspect of contemporary culture—an aspect which is reflected, in a way that disguises some of its harshness, in the late work of Holst. As ever, Satie has chosen the ideal means of expression. Note, for instance, the cunning with which the only pieces that develop harmonically—the opening and closing fugato and the central ragtime[1]—are designed to establish a norm that sets in relief the abnormality of the remainder. Were it not for the occasional little spasms of pain that cross the surface of the music elsewhere in the score, these three passages would be the only indications that a heart was beating beneath the hard exterior and preserving its flow of life against the creeping numbness of death.

I have tried to suggest that *Parade* is a wholly serious work of art because I believe that the young French composers of the twenties misguidedly took it for something else, and made it the mandate for their frivolities. I have largely avoided discussing the actual text of the music, but I have done so not because I find it uninteresting *per se*—quite the contrary—but because the poetic meaning of the work has a closer bearing on the subsequent history of French music. But, as we

[1] The function of this ragtime seems to me to be precisely the same as that of the figure of a girl bowling a hoop in Chirico's painting, *The Mystery and Melancholy of a Street* (1914—observe the date). The girl is a pathetic fleck of life in the deathly emptiness of the scene, menaced by the cold shadow of a hidden statue that lies ahead of her. As James Thrall Soby has said: 'One has the impression that even if she reaches the light, she is doomed.' The tender spirit of the ragtime is likewise doomed.

have seen, this meaning is veiled in the folds of the subconscious, and for that reason it cannot be defined in such a way as to convert those who feel that the work has no meaning. The response must come from within. It is certain that Satie himself was unaware of the powerful message he was conveying in *Parade*.[1] In answer to a question about its meaning, the composer's subconscious self might have quoted that line of Rimbaud: 'J'ai seul la clef de cette parade sauvage.'

The career of Chirico shows an interesting divergence from that of Satie. During the twenties, Chirico took the curious step of copying his early paintings (whose rich symbolism had been arrived at purely by intuition), with the intention of recapturing the spirit in which they were painted. But he failed; their mystery proved impenetrable. Now Satie was well aware that *Parade* could never be imitated and it is fitting that his career should close with two groups of works that show him continuing his creative progress—the 'classical' *Nocturnes* and *Socrate* on the one hand, and the ballets *Relâche* and *Mercure* on the other. To compare *Relâche* with *Parade* is to realise Satie's amazing ability to renew himself. The unity of *Parade* had been chiefly emotional, but the music progressed in such a way that the recapitulation of the opening *fugato* at the close of the work was wholly convincing and conclusive. In *Relâche* the scenario required a large number of brief dances, and the problem of achieving musical unity was accordingly greater. Satie solved it by a simple kind of variation technique. Despite a certain decline in inspiration towards the end of the second Act— the work was concluded in haste—the total effect is singularly successful. The variation concept necessitated the virtual exclusion of *ostinato* procedures, and in consequence *Relâche* is a particularly good example of Satie's ability as an original harmonist.[2]

Satie is reported to have declared on his deathbed that he had never written a note that he did not mean. In the vast majority of his works this is entirely credible, but one could be forgiven a moment's hesitation over the *Cinq Grimaces* for orchestra and a piano piece like *Les Pantins Dansent*. Yet in the last resort these will be found to be failures not of integrity but of invention. The success of Satie's empirical formal thinking depends upon a microscopically exact calculation of the nature

---

[1] Satie's description of his aims in *Parade* runs as follows: 'I have composed a background of certain noises which Cocteau has deemed indispensable for evoking the atmosphere of his characters.'

[2] *Mercure*, on the other hand, is primarily contrapuntal. From this point of view the most remarkable section is the waltz in double counterpoint.

and quality of material required. If the composer permits his creative concentration to slacken at any point, the disaster is complete. But for the most part Satie's single-minded devotion to his art compels our admiration, and on the strength of his achievement he must be accounted a minor composer of major significance. Milhaud tells us that no less a person than Schönberg had a high regard for Satie. The information should not, I think, be taken at its face value—there are several questions one would like to ask—but even so, our appreciation of Schönberg's genius need not blind us to the slighter genius of Satie.

While I believe that Satie's position as a key-figure should always be insisted upon—perhaps 'skeleton-key figure' would be a better term—we must understand that it is no fault of his that his followers should have used him to open so many wrong doors. Satie was too humble to have wished a school of Satieistes,[1] and he was far from polite concerning the English Satieist, Lord Berners, who, by Satie's lights, was an amateur. But let us now consider those composers who fall within the orbit of Cocteau's famous *Le Coq et L'Arlequin*—a manifesto largely deduced from Satie's work. Poulenc, Sauguet and the now little-known Maxim Jacob[2] were the closest to Satie in spirit and technique. Milhaud and Auric have expressly followed Cocteau's precepts—with occasional deviations—whilst Roland Manuel, Jacques Ibert and Claude Delvincourt have done so intermittently and without consciously attaching themselves to any group. Jean Wièner and his more talented successor Jean Françaix may also be said to share the same ethos.

It is a sobering thought that the work of these composers represents the main-stream of creative musical endeavour in France during the inter-war years. The professional Francophile may rejoice at what he takes to be a return to the traditional French qualities of grace, wit and clarity (poor, dull, heavy-handed Debussy!), but the impertinence of the cheerily dreary inter-war masquerade is exposed when Cocteau holds up the clavecinistes as a model to aspire to. For whilst a member of 'Les Six' might, if he strained every creative muscle, equal the charm of a *Musette de Taverny*, he would get nowhere near the condensed musical

[1] Satie has written: 'There is no School of Satie. There could never be a Satisme. I should be opposed to it. In art there must be no form of slavery.'
[2] Jacob wrote an entertaining Serenade for small orchestra, and a charming little *opéra bouffe*, *Blaise le Savetier*, which amateur groups would find worth reviving. During the late twenties Jacob entered a Benedictine monastery, but has continued to write music—of sacred character. He has also published articles on plainchant (which, one recalls, had been Satie's first musical love).

thought of the major pieces in the later *Ordres*. The fault does not lie in a lack of seriousness and still less in what Lambert has uselessly called 'synthetic gaiety'. Chabrier—another model recommended by Cocteau, and a minor composer if ever there was one—achieved a small masterpiece of gaiety with his Rhapsody *España*, yet there is not one French composer of the inter-war generation who could handle even a simple sectional form as convincingly as Chabrier does here. No, the basic fault is the lack of any real creative drive.

When the heroine of one of Lord Berners' novels declared that 'life is so difficult to cope with that I find that I can only do so by fortifying myself with long periods of respite from thought', she might have been echoing the unconscious motive behind most of the French music written between the wars. Just as Lord Berners' heroine satisfied her desire to match the intense activity of her friends engaged in war-work by laboriously—and to no purpose whatever—unravelling the threads of an ancient and immense tapestry, so did the young French composer seek to do his little bit—when faced with the adamantine creative activity of Stravinsky and Schönberg—by picking to pieces everything he could lay his hands on: eighteenth-century dance forms, nineteenth-century theatre music, twentieth-century popular music, the artistic good manners of all times, and last but not least the very foundations of organic tonal thinking. Darius Milhaud is perhaps the most saddening case in the débâcle, for he was potentially one of the best composers of his generation. Had he written little else beside *Protée*, the little chamber symphonies, the Percussion Concerto, and the ballets, *L'homme et son désir* and *La Creation du Monde*, one would not find it difficult to make a just estimate. Here, one would say, is a composer of individuality and imagination who is sufficiently aware of his limitations to confine himself to small forms and to instrumental ensembles that encourage clarity and colourfulness of texture. But unhappily this is by no means the whole of the picture. Not only do all the works mentioned above date from the early part of Milhaud's career, but even they represent no more than a fraction of the works written at that time. Milhaud, as everyone knows, is an exceptionally prolific composer, and it is as such that he must be judged. But one seeks in vain for any evidence that the prodigality of his output is the result of the pressure of a powerful creative message upon the will-to-expression. On the contrary, it is the extreme paucity of the message that strikes one most often and most forcibly. The prominent quality of Milhaud's eighteen quartets, his seven symphonies, and his copious theatre music recalls something that

H. G. Wells humorously professed to discern in Shaw—'an astonishing knack of fluent inexactitude'. Fluency the music has in abundance, but if one attends to the music, one finds that the activity is undirected, inexact. Nothing—not a chord, not a counterpoint, not a modulation— nothing really *matters*. The piled-up tonalities, the slithering chordal accompaniments, the empirical fugues and canons—all are part of the illusion of bountiful invention, the plastic fruit in the pasteboard cornu-copia. One might suppose that the 'popular' works—those closest to the Cocteau aesthetic—would be free of those flaws which mark the more pretentious pieces. But they are not. Take, for instance, the fantasy on South American airs, *Le Boeuf sur le Toit*. A composer who uses folk-tunes for an extended work—however lightly meant—may reasonably be expected to compensate for the second-hand nature of his melodic material by an intensification of harmonic and formal inventiveness. How does Milhaud meet the challenge?

The work is a kind of *rondo*, in which the refrain appears twelve times in the main section, and three times in the coda. These statements are interspersed with twenty-four episodes, only three of which involve the reprise of foregoing material. The composer seeks to bring order to this thematic profusion by means of his tonal scheme. Although the harmonic 'bricks' are wholly traditional, the tonal plan is typical of Milhaud's essentially nihilistic attitude at this time. The total concep-tion is anti-tonal. Refrain and couplets take their own course through all twelve major keys. The harmonic procedure is very simple. The most elementary four-note groupings of the twelve-note scale consist of the chord of the diminished seventh with its transpositions at the fifth and ninth. Melodically expressed (on G, D and A respectively), they pro-vide the order of the twelve major keys through which the refrain passes during the course of *Le Boeuf sur le Toit*. The couplets modu-late according to the same scheme, but with the starting-point of C. In the case of the couplets, there are repeats of tonal entities, and excur-sions into the minor mode, which accommodate the subsidiary ideas and permit rudimentary modulation from couplet to refrain and back again.

The effect of this purely mechanical scheme is wholly negative. It is not a vital tonal structure, but merely a device for disguising the har-monic poverty of the work. For in truth, the melodies are presented in the crude tonic-dominant harmonies in which they first saw the light of day—it is difficult to see how they could have been treated in any other way—and the polytonal and chromatic decorations do nothing more than obscure the harmonic issue. Like the tonal scheme, they are imposed from without. So far from being graceful, witty and lucid, *Le Boeuf sur le Toit* is, from a purely musical point of view, heavy-handed, boring and confused. The challenge made by the material has been evaded throughout.

Because of its air of cheerful modishness, music of this kind will never fail to appeal to those invertebrate art-fanciers who gather on the fringes of every art, sipping their cocktails and discussing the day's events in the aesthetic stock-exchange. The fact that the music is now a trifle 'dated' is likely to be regarded as something that adds to its charm. The inanity of such judgments hides a trap for the critic. The standard text-book histories will rightly condemn a work like *Le Boeuf sur le Toit*, but for the wrong reason. *Le Bouef sur le Toit* calls for an adverse judgment not because it is dated but because it is bad music. The distinction is vital, as we shall see when we come to consider Poulenc's *Les Biches*, which is greatly superior to *Le Boeuf* in artistic value, as indeed is *La Creation du Monde*, which, despite its distinctly 'period' jazz furniture, is never described as 'dated'. The truth is that the word has no valid critical force. Any work of art that has style and consistency is, in one sense, 'dated'. True criticism is concerned not with fashion and the fluctuation of taste, but with the permanent values inherent in the nature of the art under consideration. To condemn a work on the grounds that it is 'dated' is to accept the same false criteria that govern the opinions of those who follow the fashion of today or patronise the fashion of the day before yesterday. This is the disability that mars the perniciously beguiling criticism of Constant Lambert, which is marked throughout by precisely the same kind of modish superficiality and fashion-consciousness that the writer affects to despise. Thanks to Lambert, *soi-disant* critics will continue to suppose that they have made an illuminating musical judgment if they condemn or approve *Pierrot Lunaire* for being 'ninetyish', just as they will believe they have aptly disposed of *Le Boeuf sur le Toit* if they call it 'twentyish'.

It must be confessed that in discussing a composer like Milhaud, one is sometimes forced to consider extra-musical factors. Thus the pseudo-cerebration of the five *Études* for Piano and Orchestra (1920) can be interpreted not as something disconcertingly divorced from the bland thoughtlessness of *Le Boeuf*, but as its corollary. *Le Boeuf* pretends to *épater le bourgeois*, but at heart it shamelessly courts popularity by concentrating on superficial tunefulness and avoiding anything that resembles a musical argument.[1] By way of compensation—is there not a hint of self-punishment here?—the *Études* court unpopularity, the recognised reward of the successful twentieth-century revolutionary; and if the result happens to *épater* the intelligentsia as well, so much the better. But it is a fleeting success. The club bore may at last make a stir, and will certainly make himself unpopular, if he dresses up as a ragged-trousered philanthropist and declaims passages from *Das Kapital* at street corners, but nobody is likely to be impressed by his radicalism for long. The revolutionary pretensions of the *Cinq Études* (or the Fifth String Quartet) are of a similar order. In the face of such unconstructive thinking, such as sparseness of aural justification, and such nullity of imagination, one may forget any possible arguments in favour of functional polytonality. To the lay ear, the weakly Ravellian opening to the third *Étude* should be the clue to the undistinguished and fundamentally conventional quality of the thought.

Only the third *Étude* makes a distinctive impression, and that is because the composer has confined himself to clear-cut melodic lines. The method is more typical of those works which stand between the would-be intellectual *Études* and theatre music on the one hand, and frankly popular *Le Boeuf* on the other. It has a prominent part to play in a work like the *Serenade* for Orchestra, which takes as its premisses the most simple melodic ideas, founded, as often as not, on baroque formulas (which are the easiest to extend mechanically). To these are added an ever-increasing number of harmonically irrelevant counterpoints, and unless one's ear is deceived by the quickness and profusion of the notes, the result gives only the barest illusion of developing structure.[2] The composer certainly makes a characteristic, identifiable noise—so, after all, does a blacksmith—but the fact that one is able to say 'this is unmistakably Milhaud' is scant compensation for the conceptual poverty of the music. The slow second movement of the *Serenade* makes no pretence of individuality, and is frankly cast in the mould of Massenet's orchestral pieces.

The extremes of false complexity and false simplicity, represented in Milhaud's early instrumental music by the *Études* and *Boeuf sur le Toit*, and the intermediary compromise, represented by the *Serenade*, constitute the three categories into which the majority of his works may

[1] Music that did not have to be listened to at all was, of course, the practical conclusion to Cocteau's famous dictum that there is something wrong with music that has to be listened to with the head between the hands.

[2] The result is a perfect example of what Schönberg has described as 'Rhabarber counterpoint'.

be divided. With the theatre music, however, the lines of demarcation become somewhat blurred, and it is difficult to say, for instance, whether *Les Malheurs d'Orphée* (one of Milhaud's better works) is closer to *Le Boeuf* or the *Serenade*. Or again, one has to distinguish between the complexity of the procedures used in the vast *Oreste* trilogy, and the demagogic, rabble-rousing purpose to which they are put. As a kind of substitute for background noises, the result may be found crudely impressive, but as music it is quite dead. The part-writing in five or six keys has no contrapuntal significance, whether the voices are melodic or thickened chordally, whether they are free or fixed to *ostinati*. A kind of gaseous compound, they arise from within the great corpse of sound and monstrously inflate it. That music so unfelt should ever have found favour whilst the passionately vital music of Schönberg was condemned as mere cerebration is one of the minor freaks of musical history; that even today it should be valued above the deeply expressive counterpoint of Stravinsky[1] is an eccentricity quite as alarming.

In his later dramatic work, the once-famous *Christophe Colomb*, Milhaud discards some of the polytonal paraphernalia. But music which relies to such an extent on a haphazard kind of harmonic ambiguity—the wholly unconsidered and undeveloped conflict between parallel thirds or triads and a 'false' bass—cannot long hold one's interest. Factitious forcefulness should not be confused with dramatic insight. Reading this music, one is reminded by its disastrous heedlessness of a remark of Stravinsky: 'One should tremble at every chord.' If one trembles at *Christophe Colomb*, it is with rage and boredom.

The music which Milhaud has written since the twenties brings into the open a most important fact about his talent: the simpler the texture of thought, the better the music. The almost entirely diatonic *Sacred Service* is outstanding among his later works. The very special occasion for which the music was written has helped to free Milhaud from those inhibitions which elsewhere compel him to decorate and disguise the argument at every turn. The harmonic premises are no different from those of all his works, but because of the greater clarification, the processes are free to develop naturally and expressively. There is nothing, even in the most honest of the early works, to equal the effect of the calmly devotional Amen[2] which emerges at the close

[1] See *Twentieth Century Counterpoint—a Guide for Students*, by Humphrey Searle (Williams and Norgate).

[2] The cadence (tonic minor—sharp submediant major) is a concise expression of the tonal structure of the whole piece: its logic—so rare in Milhaud—is a part of its beauty.

of the Kaddish. The benefits of greater flexibility extend to devices which in earlier works had been worked to death—I am thinking particularly of the dissonant underpinning of plain triadic harmony in the *Adon Olam*.

Although not a work of major stature, the Sacred Service shows just how good a composer Milhaud could be. In this respect, its companion piece amongst Milhaud's lighter works is the deservedly popular *Scaramouche*, which, together with the little Suite for Clarinet, Violin, and Piano, prove that the vein of delicate fantasy that had yielded the charming 'Pastorale' in *Protée* was by no means exhausted. Like the Sacred Service, these two works are composed of short pieces which do not make great demands upon the composer's sense of form. Whereas in the Service, the text acted as a binding force, in *Scaramouche* and the Suite almost everything depends upon the dance rhythms. The result is quite without the subtlety and variety of Debussy's dance pieces, but the technical method is, within its limits, original, and is elaborated with welcome precision. One's feeling that Milhaud's true *métier* is the short *genre* piece is confirmed by the success of these unpretentious works, and is further supported by the failure of a more ambitious essay in the popular style, such as *Kentuckiana*. Here, it would seem, the composer intends the effect to be that of a Quodlibet, but he is quite unable to control the thematic profusion formally, and the contrapuntal superpositions of themes are no more precise and meaningful than a child's game of pat-a-cake. The little *Concertino de Printemps* illustrates another kind of failure to which Milhaud's more popular music is liable (though it is a much better work than *Kentuckiana*, or indeed the other 'Season' Concertinos). Every facet of the music is calculated to contribute to the effect of succinctness—from the laconic themes to the spare, yet unusually felicitous, scoring. But despite the temporal brevity the form is loose to the point of garrulity. Too little comes of too little, and the rhythmic and phraseological uniformity rapidly becomes wearisome. The most notable success is achieved in the *coda*. The wind instruments stutter themselves to silence over a few fragments of one of the themes, whilst the solo violin keeps up a continual meaningless chatter of unadorned C major scale passages and *arpeggios*. This combination of the laconic and the vapid has a curiously comic-pathetic effect in view of what has gone before.

Successes of this kind are all that can be hoped for in Milhaud's later instrumental music, and there is little to be gained from discussing his seven symphonies and his eighteen quartets. The best things in these works—the pastoral *intermezzi* in the symphonies and the Frenchified dance movements in the quartets[1]—are not radically different from anything that we have discussed so far, whilst the worst things— amongst which one must surely count the Seventh Symphony in its entirety—are beneath contempt as examples of symphonic thought. There is nothing in these works that might persuade one that Milhaud's career is anything other than the tragedy of a composer with a huge surplus of energy that he is unable to direct. If his career at any point gave some sign of that self-examination and retrenchment that we have noted in the more-or-less major French composers of the twentieth century, there would be some grounds for viewing his artistic develop- ment in a more favourable light. As it is, one feels that the lack of any guiding principle—whether of faith or aesthetic—accounts for much of its diffuseness. It is, I think, significant that his best work, the Sacred Service, is the one in which he has freely submitted himself both to the Jewish modes of expression to which he is heir, and to the principles of his idol Satie[2] whose lessons of humility, integrity and perseverance he has so loudly praised but so seldom taken to heart.

At the present time, it seems important to give more weight to the faults of Milhaud's music than to its evident and generally appreciated virtues. So long as the badness, the unmusicality even, of Milhaud's pseudo-revolutionary works such as the *Études* and *Oreste* goes un- noticed (in professional or other circles), there is a danger that attention will be distracted both from the more genuinely progressive and from the more valuably conservative music of other composers, making it impossible to obtain an undistorted view of the period. This situation undoubtedly affects the popular estimate of a conservative like Poulenc, who is commonly held to be of less interest and importance than Mil- haud—an estimate which I believe to be unjust, as his career suggests that he is more consistent and (*au fond*) more original, and, again, that he is more seriously dedicated to his art, and quite as musicianly in his service of it. The critical necessity is thus the reverse of that which obtained in the case of Milhaud. The best aspects of his work deserve more attention than its evident and generally appreciated weaknesses. The hostile critic, indeed, has so easy a task that it is hardly worth the effort. Poulenc is the most frank, if not the most reticent, of composers.

[1] The Twelfth Quartet, however, has an unusually good slow movement: the dedication to Fauré has born fruit.
[2] The accompaniment to the *Prière et Response* is clearly influenced by Satie's *Rêverie*.

When he has nothing to say, he says it. There is no sham. The infantile triviality of a work like *Le Bal Masqué*, with its hodge-podge forms and its inept wrong-note harmony, stands naked and undisguised for all to see. That the composer enjoyed writing this music, that it fulfilled a deep pyschological need, is as apparent as the fact that an integrated and adult musical personality would never have committed a note of it to paper. Music such as this—one might also include the early *Rhapsodie Nègre*—represents a deliberate reversion to childhood, the one stage in man's development (apart from senility) when the individual is free from active responsibility and incapable of coherent experience. The *Rhapsodie Nègre* and the *Bal Masqué* belong intimately to that period which Wyndham Lewis has analysed in the chapter of his *Time and the Western Man* entitled 'The Revolutionary Simpleton'. But it would be quite wrong to judge Poulenc from these two works, for they represent an aspect of his art that is far less typical than is generally recognised.

The Rhapsodie and the *Bal Masqué* are settings of virtually meaningless words and syllables, and for that reason may be regarded as instrumental works. The greater part of the remainder of Poulenc's instrumental works—the sonatas for wind instruments, the Sextet and the calamitous *Sinfonietta*—are partialiy, but only partially, weaned from the nursery philosophy. The truth is that Poulenc does not achieve mature expression unless he is setting words or writing ballet music—activities upon which he wisely concentrates. With a firm tradition behind him—Gounod, Chabrier, Debussy, Ravel, Satie, Messager even—he is comparatively sure of himself, and the music is free of the equivocacy that marks even the best passages in the instrumental works. (Much of the Sextet is directly in the *comédie-ballet* tradition, and both the Sextet and the *Aubade* contain recitative-like elements that are purely operatic. Even the *Sinfonietta* resembles the random jottings of a gifted theatre composer.) Only when writing keyboard music—and most notably in the four keyboard concertos—does Poulenc show anything like the assurance that is manifest in his vocal and ballet music. This is doubtless the result of his love for the piano, which he plays very well.

More versatile than Duparc, less accomplished than Fauré, Poulenc has no single ancestor amongst French composers. He is very much a child of our time, and the boundaries of his talent—that of a largely self-taught composer-pianist whose creative successes tend to rely on the inspiration of a text or scenario—suggest parallels with the talent of only one other contemporary artist, George Gershwin. But where-as Gershwin's strength and originality are singularly uninvolved, there is something equivocal about every aspect of Poulenc's music—not least, its originality.

To be sure, the main influences on Poulenc's style are not difficult to discern. The lyrical passages have origins in the late nineteenth-century and early twentieth-century French tradition that are too obvious to require enumeration; one might start, for instance, by comparing almost any of these passages with bars eleven to eighteen of the second of Debussy's *Chansons de Bilitis*. Most of the songs in fast tempi stem from the *opéra comique* tradition, whilst the rapid keyboard pieces derive from the style of French clavecinistes.[1]

These influences are perfectly legitimate, and there is no reason why they should prove irreconcilable. But behind them we find a host of subsidiary stylistic references, jumbled together like the coloured strips of celluloid in a child's kaleidoscope. Reflected and counter-reflected in the composer's imagination, they take on a semblance of style and order. Yet one is all the while disturbed by the feeling that at the other end of the mirrors is the chaotic reality. Is it all just an amusing trick? The music is always identifiable as Poulenc's, but one asks oneself if on that account alone it has any *real* identity. To take a simple example, the famous *Mouvement Perpetuel No. 1* seems at first sight to be quintessential Poulenc; but does it become any the less so when we discover that the main idea is taken directly from the fifth song in Beethoven's *An die ferne geliebte cycle*, Op. 98? Or again, what are we to say of the melody of Diana's variation in the *Aubade*, where the first phrase of the melody is borrowed from Mozart's B♭ *Divertimento*, K.a. 229,[2] while it subsequently veers towards the nineteenth century. (It is not unusual in Poulenc's music to find melodies that change style and back again during the course of a sixteen-bar sentence—a feat that is made easier by the tendency of the music to fall into a succession of self-contained four-bar phrases.) Clearly there

[1] Poulenc also has a marked sympathy for Chopin—to whom he has done homage, explicitly, in a song dedicated to his memory—and this is, of course, most evident in the piano works: see, for instance, the *poco più lento* section of the first movement of the Concerto for Two Pianos.

[2] See the opening of the Larghetto movement. The initial phrase of the melody, with its harmony, its tonality and its instrumentation (for clarinet) are identical with the Poulenc example. The finale of *Les Biches* contains another quotation from Mozart: cf. the finale of the D major Symphony K.504, letter B.

is something profoundly equivocal about the originality of music which *at no single point* gives any sign of originality; music which, moreover, harbours discrepancies of style that would be surprising in the work of a first-year-composition student. The fact is that Poulenc's uniqueness lies solely in the nature of his sensibility. (He is thus even more difficult to discuss than Satie, whose originality extends both to idiom and technique, and is therefore more readily definable.) Possessing, as he does, the ability to juxtapose incongruous elements in such a way that a consistently ironic light is shed upon them, he produces by means of this irony the impression, the illusion if you prefer, of a unified conception. During the course of the imaginative and musical process, ideas that are basically undistinguished acquire a certain poetic refinement, for the irony admits of a certain pathos, and the pathos is an outcome of true feeling. It hardly need be added that without a very considerable musical gift (even if less than assured academically) this creative method would be quite impractical. The first piece by Poulenc to be wholly characteristic of this attitude is the ballet score *Les Biches,* a work that Constant Lambert has suggestively described as Firbankian. The description is worth pondering over, for it may help us to 'place' Poulenc. Firbank's novels rely on very much the same kind of ironic awareness that is present in Poulenc's music, the same precise weighing up of incongruous elements, the matching of the polite with the *risqué,* the courtly with the plebeian, the tender with the grotesque. The means with which Poulenc attains these ends in *Les Biches* may not have been so polished as Firbank's, but they do not exclude a very real musical impulse which is particularly evident in the modulational plan. I am thinking not only of the more-or-less recondite key changes, such as the one that occurs at the *doppio più lento* in the finale, but also the most conventional moves (for instance the turn to the relative major for the first couplet of the *Rondeau*), which have an extraordinary freshness.

Although *Les Biches* is in every way a less powerful achievement than *Parade,* it shares with that work the honour of being the only French ballet score since *Daphnis* and *Jeux* which seems to increase in stature and meaning when divorced from its theatrical setting. The promiscuity of style and the melancholy, godless joviality of *Les Biches* is symbolic of an age in which all sense of belonging together as a community has given way to a meaningless gregariousness. *Parade,* on the other hand, is too hermetic, too aloof in its cold ferocity, to be the expression of a particular place or era; in fact, it stands to *Les Biches,* artistically, much as—shall we say—Rolphe's Hadrian IV stands to Firbank's Cardinal Pirelli.

Since the completion of *Les Biches*, Poulenc's career has been marked not so much by a broadening of his creative personality as by the exercise of greater discrimination and by the growth of a certain measure of technical assurance. One might trace this through the four keyboard concertos, but as I have suggested, it is as a vocal composer that Poulenc has his surest claim to attention. If, at a random selection from Poulenc's fifteen or more song cycles, one happened to hit upon the *Bestiaire* or the *Cocardes* of 1919, and the Eluard cycle, *Tel Jour Telle Nuit* of 1937, one might suppose that Poulenc's art had only acquired seriousness with maturity. (This is a common supposition.) But in fact the seriousness—if that is the right word—was present from the beginning, implicity in the *Bestiaire* and explicitly in the *Poèmes de Ronsard* of 1924. These latter are scarcely distinguishable in style from the *Tel Jour* cycle, even though none of them quite rises to the level of the last song in the Eluard set. In neither collection is there a trace of the style-jumping which we have noted in the instrumental works. The music is directly in the tradition of Gounod's more serious songs, and although Poulenc cannot command the subtlety of phrasing and the distinction of line which sometimes marks Gounod's work as a song writer, his best songs—for instance, *Nous avons fait la nuit*, and *Montparnasse*—are not unworthy of the comparison.

The affinity between Poulenc and Gounod is chiefly one of sensibility; in Poulenc there is nothing of either the scholar or the pedant. But it is not altogether surprising that both composers should have been drawn to pre-classical sources for inspiration. Gounod's lifelong love of Palestrina was founded on close study of the technique, and it bears fruit even in so typically nineteenth-century a work as the Provençal opera, *Mireille*. Listening to Poulenc's illiterate trifling with the music of Claude Gervaise in his *Suite Française*, one feels intensely the lack of Gounod's intellectual discipline, but in the *a cappella* choral works— for instance the beautiful *Salve Regina* or the four *Motets pour un temps de penitence*—a genuine sympathy for the spirit of the vocal composers of the French renaissance controls and guides the music. Had the *Stabat Mater* of 1951 relied more on this guiding influence and less on a debilitated version of Fauréian lyricism, the music would have profited. Perhaps the most imaginative example of Poulenc's return to a modal, neo-liturgical style, is provided by the cantata, *Sécheresses*, where plainchant-like inflections contribute powerfully to the sinister effect of the music.

Sécheresses is a setting of a surrealist text by Edward James. Besides being up to now (1956)[1] the most substantial of Poulenc's 'serious' works, *Sécheresses* is an interesting achievement from the historical point of view. For it is, so far as I know, the only successful translation into musical terms of the surrealist aesthetic which flourished after the First World War. Yet notice the date of its composition—1937. Although Poulenc had been associated with the Parisian surrealist movement almost since its inception, he allowed well over a decade to pass before he embodied his response to surrealist imagery in a large-scale work, and by that time the movement was a long way past its zenith. There would be no cause to attach any particular significance to this immense period of gestation were it not for a similar phenomenon amongst Poulenc's 'lighter' works. It is a striking fact that by far the most successful work to have sprung from Cocteau's *Le Coq et L'Arlequin* (1920) is the *opéra bouffe, Les Mamelles de Tirésias*, which Poulenc completed in 1944. Written at a time when Cocteau's strength-through-jollity maxims had long since faded from the memories of most French musicians—a time, incidentally, when the German invaders were fighting their last desperate struggle on the soil of a ravaged France—*Les Mamelles* may, despite its frivolous exterior, prove to be the most important work that Poulenc has given us. In waiting so long before writing a work that he had doubtless contemplated for many years (whether with reference to Apollinaire or no) Poulenc once again showed himself to be a conscientious artist. In its odd way, the result is a masterpiece.

Whilst being free from the rather self-conscious attitudinising of *Les Biches,* and unflawed by the gaucheness that makes parts of that work sound like an unintentional sequel to the *Musikalischer Spass, Les Mamelles de Tirésias* relies on what might seem to be the flimsiest of techniques—parody. There is scarcely a phrase that does not make some reference to the style of some earlier composer—Richard Strauss,[2] Offenbach, Massenet, Messager, Ravel, even the composer of *Phi-Phi*: but so cunning are the tonal excursions, so perfect the timing and the execution of the transitions, that the multiple references are merged

[1] Poulenc is now reported to have completed a Grand Opera on a story by Bernanos.

[2] The inclusion of Strauss in this assembly is perhaps the wittiest stroke of all.

into a unified and startlingly original whole. Such things as the Ivor Novelloish waltz which accompanies the heavenward flight of Therese's breasts, or the neo-Offenbach tune which announces the two drunkards in the first Act, depend for much of their effect upon the associations aroused by the idiomatic references, but the music would not be creative in the full sense if the parodistic allusions had no markedly personal style as their point of departure.[1] As it happens, the origins of Poulencs' *opéra bouffe* can easily be discerned in four very typical songs written the year previously. The lyrical and nostalgic elements in the opera are foreshadowed in *Montparnasse* and 'C', whilst the comic strain, with its deft prosody, derives from the settings of Louise de Vilmorin's *Paganini*, and Luis Aragon's *Fêtes Galantes*.

In its ultimate effect, *Les Mamelles* is even more Firbankian than *Les Biches*. Apollinaire's original play is already strangely prophetic of Firbank (it dates from 1912) and the serio-comic moral of the story, '*Faîtes des enfants!*'[2] is an explicit statement of the motif underlying almost all Firbank's work, a motif that Edmund Wilson, in an essay on that writer, has described with great solemnity as 'an understatement . . . of the biologically sinister phenomenon of a slackening of the interest in mating on the part of the privileged classes of Europe'. Poulenc's *musical* reaction to the text is in almost every respect parallel to Firbank's literary modes of feeling and procedure. It is thus both possible and useful to sum up Poulenc's most characteristic achievement by quoting an admirable passage from Wilson's essay on Firbank— possible, because the equation is exact at every point, useful because Firbank's known status today is an indication of Poulenc's as yet unknown status in the future:

'The effect of his writing is light, but it differs from the flimsier work of the nineties, which, at first sight, it may resemble, in the

[1] This is the limitation which mars the parodies by so thoroughly professional a composer as Jacques Ibert—see his *Divertissement* and his *Paris*. Ibert is an example of an able musician who has little to offer but his ability. The fundamental anonymity that cripples the parodies has a similar effect (at the other end of the creative scale) in the pseudo-Roussellian Concertos—the Flute Concerto and the Sinfonia Concertante for Oboe. The treatment of Roussel's brand of chromaticised diatonicism in the Sinfonia is particularly unconvincing. Ibert seems to be at his best with the *petits riens* which stand somewhere between the big concertos and the brief parodies—I am thinking particularly of the Saxophone Concertino.

[2] In this respect *Les Mamelles de Tirésias* might be regarded as a companion piece to Strauss's *Die Frau ohne Schatten*!

tension behind it of the effort to find the felicitous or the witty phrase which will render the essence of something. The little dyed twirls of plume and the often fresh sprays of flowers, the half-stifled flutters of laughter and the fusées of jewellery fire, have been twisted and tempered in a mind that is capable of concentration. It is a glancing mind, but it rarely wobbles. Only . . . in a lack of continuity of movement . . . does he betray a certain weakness of syntax. But phrase by phrase, sentence by sentence, paragraph by paragraph, chapter by chapter, the workmanship is not merely exact but of a quality for which the craftsman must gratuitiously tax himself.'

The name of George Auric is often coupled with that of Poulenc, but the two have little in common. Academically Auric is the more proficient: artistically he is far less interesting. The first of his two early ballet scores, *Les Fâcheux,* has a certain forcefulness, a certain continuity and consistency which are hardly characteristic of, say, *Les Biches.* But there is little distinction of style or imagination. The music is couched in that pseudo-contrapuntal style that Constant Lambert used in his ballet, *Pomona,* written two years later. Auric would here seem to be attempting a 'modern' version of the theatrical manner of a composer like Lulli, and if the result is unremarkable, one must concede that the music is hardly less professional than that of the average eighteenth-century Court composer. This is quite evident if one compares *Les Fâcheux* with a work like Germaine Tailleferre's pseudo-classical Overture,[1] a miserably botched affair in which nothing follows from anything, and every idea collapses with a gasp as soon as it has taken its first breath. The superiority of Auric is the more evident because Tailleferre has here modelled herself upon him so closely.

The second of Auric's two early ballets, *Les Matelots,* is a much lighter piece, as innocent and unexceptionable as Milhaud's *Le Train Bleu.* The quality of wit is sometimes not far removed from that of Walton's *Façade.* What one misses particularly in the somewhat attenuated lyrical sections is any evidence of a personal harmonic style. Not only that, but if one makes the effort of attending to the music—it hardly challenges one to do so—one sometimes finds that in straightforward diatonic passages, the harmony does not make sense for bars at a time. The bass parts stagger around without sense of direction,

[1] The classicism, like that of several other French composers, purports to follow on from the kind of thing which Grétry achieved in his Overture to *Céphale et Procris.*

adding nothing to the melody, and lacking even the force to conflict with it. The lack of harmonic purpose is, in a sense, symbolic of the position of the minor composer in the third decade of our century. Failing entirely to comprehend the achievement of the great revolutionary masters, he was left with nothing more definite than a vague idea that strict consonance was a relic of the past which should only be retained in order that it might be mocked. Accordingly, composers like Auric set about enlarging their harmonic vocabularies before they had discovered how to make individual and constructive use of the traditional vocabulary. Poulenc succeeds where Auric fails because, without *partis pris,* he can use the simplest harmony in a personal way, allowing the traditional place for purposeful progression and expressive modulation. Consequently he is able to control a relatively high degree of dissonance without recourse to polytonality, and to invest empirical chord-formations with a meaningfulness that they never have in Auric.

Constant Lambert has remarked—with an inaccuracy that is wholly typical of his critical method—that the 'wrong note' method of composition 'is seen at its worst in the ballets of Auric which consist for the most part of a string of boy scout tunes with an acid harmonic accompaniment'. Besides being totally inapplicable either to the busy counterpoint of *Les Fâcheux* or to the innocuous harmony of *Les Matelots,*[1] this observation misses the main point about composers like Auric: namely that their best music is written for the theatre, and their worst for the concert hall, where they know they will have an audience that concentrates entirely upon what they have to say. If, as is often the case, they have nothing to say, 'modernity' becomes a useful disguise as well as an admired gesture. Take, for instance, Auric's Sonatine for piano, written in 1923. Having turned his back on the tradition of French theatre music, which saves the ballets from disaster, the composer finds himself completely at a loss. The music is quite tonal, in the sense that the composer knows what key he is pretending to be in, but harmonically it is meaningless. There is no distortion here, such as the text-books lead us to expect in French music of the twenties, because there is no norm: the ideas of expectation and fulfilment, of development and relative tension, have vanished without a trace, and one chord will do as well, or rather as badly, as another. The formal working, even on so small a scale, is of unbelievable crudity—witness the transition to the second idea in the *andante.* (Anyone wishing rapidly

[1] If it is true of any music of the twenties, it is true of certain sections of Lambert's own ballet score, *Romeo and Juliet.*

to check the relative merits of Poulenc and Auric could do worse than compare this hopelessly erratic movement with the *andante* in Poulenc's piano-duet sonata, which starts with a similar idea but unassumingly carries it through without a falter.)

The sonatine would be beneath discussion were it not typical of the kind of thing that Auric, Tailleferre, Wièner and others poured forth thirty years ago, and which, in a somewhat more cunning form, is still being written today in many parts of the world. Never before has music so completely lacking in integrity and creative meaning been granted the honour of public presentation; that it should popularly be ascribed to the ideals of Satie is one of the wildest critical blunders to have been accepted in recent years.

Many of Auric's later works seem to be animated by the same desire to atone for indiscretions that we first noted in Milhaud, though the method of doing so is more straightforward and less original. The piano sonata of 1932 is certainly a more serious work than the Sonatine, but the result is unendurably boring and crude. A similar tendency towards 'seriousness' becomes manifest, as we shall see, in Auric's film music, although his activities in that sphere have, by and large, formed his most valuable contribution to modern French music. The discipline is a benefit to him, and he is able both to indulge his native wit and to exploit (to the point of virtuosity) his ability to change the character of his writing radically. As one would expect, the best scores are those written for films like *A nous la liberté* and *Hue and Cry*, where the dramatic content is of the comical-ironic kind most suited to his own talent. But in his score for Cocteau's modern version of the Tristan and Iseult legend, *L'Eternel Retour*, Auric deviates most significantly from his usual style. Written during the German occupation, this skilful and effective music is quite unashamedly Wagnerian. Thus, at a single stroke, the twisted history of post-war French music is turned inside-out and the hollowness of its militant anti-Wagnerism is revealed. It seems not unfitting that the atonement should have been made in the half-light of the film world, and there is something pleasingly ironic about the fact that Auric should have written such music for a film entitled *L'Eternel Retour*. Behind its screen of modishness, Auric's music was always backward-looking, and in the light of his recent work it is no longer mandatory to find anything ironic about such charming pieces of old lavender as the waltz episode from his contribution to *L'Eventail de Jeanne*.

There is certainly little excuse for detecting ironic intention behind the two most ambitious scores that Auric has written since the war, the ballets *Phèdre* and *Le Peintre et son modèle*. The frank traditionalism of the *L'Éternel Retour* score is here confirmed. Although not specifically Wagnerian, *Phèdre* recalls, in an utterly undistinguished way and despite its fairly dissonant idiom, every nineteenth-century attitude that it was once fashionable to decry. The only admirable feature of these scores, their professionalism, is a valuable asset in the purely commercial music which Auric has begun to write in recent years. The musical value of the best-selling *Moulin Rouge* waltz suggests, like its less commercial predecessor, the theme song to *A nous la liberté*, that in defecting to the camp of popular music, Auric has vindicated himself. For in its structure and content[1] the *Moulin Rouge* waltz is perhaps the most original piece that Auric has written, and wholly worthy of the example of Satie, whose own popular songs are supreme examples of the form.

Auric's first attempt at the popular style, the foxtrot, *Adieu, New York*, of 1920, was quite another matter. Despite a standard of invention that would shame a commercial hack, it enjoyed a certain vogue with the smarter dance bands, who were not, however, smart enough to perceive the senselessness of the 'piquant' dissonances with which the music is sprinkled. In spicing up simple jazz formulas for highbrow consumption, Auric was following the lead of Jean Wièner,[2] a pianist and composer who introduced much of the best in modern music to Parisian audiences, but who was also responsible in no small measure for the jazz snobbism which was rife amongst French composers of the twenties. Although wholly uninteresting as a composer, Wièner is not without significance as a representative of the period. In one not-so-honourable respect, he is an 'original'. Having dallied, even more ineffectively than Auric, with a mock-dissonant style,[3] he was astute enough to see that it was a vain enterprise. So, in such works as his first piano sonata, and his *Concerto Franco-Americain,* he turned to the opposite extreme; the *bourgeois* was now to be *épaté* by a 'right-note' style. Instead of adding the insult of meaningless harmonies to the

[1] Needless to say, the harmonic and rhythmic structure of the waltz is almost always obscured in commercial arrangements.
[2] Like Auric, Wièner has recently achieved popular success with a song-hit —*Le Grisbi*. Once again a minor talent finds its proper *métier*: but the inferiority of *Le Grisbi* to the *Moulin Rouge* waltz is a measure of Wièner's inferiority to Auric.
[3] See the *Sept Petites Histoires*, the *Deux Poèmes de Cocteau* and the last of the *Trois Blues Chantées*.

injury of common melodic jargon, he left that same jargon in all its pristine nakedness. The studied rejection of sophistication was itself supremely sophisticated. The finale of the *Concerto Franco-Americain* —whose theme is of unsurpassed and unsurpassable vulgarity—makes its point by suggesting not so much a compromise between the *haute couture* of Paris and New York as between the plebeian joys of Margate pier and the day-trip to Boulogne. The harmony is barrel-organ tonic-dominant, and apart from an occasional added sixth, the necessary spice is provided by 'saucy' cartwheels into remote keys, accented by rapid diatonic scale passages. The method is only worthy of mention in that it was later adopted by Jean Françaix, the youngest of the French composers, to make an international reputation for himself in the years between the two world wars.

Françaix received a thorough musical training from Nadia Boulanger, with results that might well be envied by certain of his more renowned elders. His precision of aim is often exemplary. He limits himself to an astonishingly small harmonic vocabulary, and because his cunning is greater than his gift for extended invention, his most successful pieces are in the nature of brief conjuring tricks. Thus, in the slow movement of the Piano Concertino, the illusion of melody is presented by the simplest homophonic outline to an equally simple harmonic movement. But the illusion is so cunningly contrived, with the aid of neatly asymmetrical phrasing, that the absence of a true melody is not noticed; and even though there is but one structural change of harmony, the *da capo* form of this thirty-one-bar-long piece is not only tolerable but desirable. In the minuet that follows, a similar feat is achieved with a tiny Haydnesque motif[1] (tonic and dominant once again), a scrap of counterpoint, and a daringly high degree of motivic repetition. Sleight-of-hand such as this is not applicable to the composition of *presto* movements, and Françaix' failure to find an equally original method of approach to first- and last-movement form is a serious defect. Take, for instance, the opening *allegro* of the Piano Concertino. The initial figuration and melodic shape is modelled on Czerny's Study, Op. 299, No. 8, in the same key (C major), but a movement such as this requires a stronger contrasting idea than the one Françaix has devised, and the subsequent development by means of scalar or broken-chord figurations is inadequate, despite the general air of brightness. The same faults appear in the *rondo* finale. But in

---

[1] Or even Gounodesque—see the first movement of Gounod's *Petite Symphonie*, four bars before letter E.

both cases brevity makes the weaknesses less apparent. The more extended structures of the Piano Concerto bring these weaknesses into the open, and the interminably chattering passagework is a tawdry foil to the bright little tunes. The music has neo-*galant* pretensions, but in the last resort it is more akin to the empty brilliance of Saint-Saëns. Curiously enough, Françaix achieves a much tauter structure in a work to which he has given the title *Fantasy*—the *Fantasy* for Cello and Orchestra. This beautifully written little work deserves to be heard more often. Françaix has done nothing better.

The distinct musicianship of Françaix' will-o'-the-wisp talent earns him some respect, but like his successor Jean-Michel Damase—whose music combines, most distastefully, the catch-phrases of Françaix and Poulenc with those of commercial *kitsch*—Françaix seems condemned to repeat himself. Occasional attempts at a more ambitious style—as in the *Apocalypse* or the Viola Concerto—need not be taken into account, for the results are without any strongly personal characteristics.

Nonetheless, we must recognise that Françaix' music is free of certain faults of taste and technique that mar the work of many of his seniors. This is no doubt attributable in part to his early training. But in consistency of style and intentness of purpose, Françaix is excelled by a composer who was largely self-taught—Henri Sauguet, the last, and in many ways the most sympathetic (if not the most important), of the 'inter-war' composers whom I shall discuss here. Sauguet is the only one of these composers who was a direct disciple of Satie, and his music, like that of his master, has little or nothing in common with the work of 'Les Six'. A music maker in the humblest sense, Sauguet has shown himself to be indifferent to aesthetic fashion and innocent of any motive of self-advertisement. Unlike those who have proclaimed their allegiance to Satie more loudly, he has always remained faithful to that composer's true ideals—which are to be distinguished from the ideals commonly ascribed to him. He has never attempted to make of Satie an antipope against current heresies—Wagnerism, the picturesque, the sentimental. Content to say of *Socrate* that it moved him '*jusqu'aux larmes*', he has quietly taken from Satie what he needs—a lesson in prosody here, a turn of harmony there, and, above all, the binding principle of sincerity. The lesson learnt, he has followed his own unfashionable course.

Sauguet's debt to Satie, and the gulf that separates the two composers, is most evident in the cantata, *La Voyante*. The melancholy *ostinato* conclusion to the third song, and its indeterminate cadence, is pure Satie, and Satie's influence on the vocal lines and accompanimental figurations can be felt throughout. Typically Satiean, too, are the collage-like allusions to popular rhythms—habanera and polka—in the final song. Yet Sauguet's music is really very different from Satie's. It is at once more conventional and more approachable. This is never more apparent than when Sauguet attempts to emulate his master closely—as in his best-known work, the ballet score *Les Forains* (which is dedicated to Satie's memory). Here the model is *Parade*, but without Satie's intense intellectual and imaginative concentration the simple symmetrical tunes and the bare accompaniments seem flabby and repetitious. *Les Forains* is that equivocal thing, good ballet music—in other words, it is not very good music, or rather, it is incomplete music.

Sauguet's true *spiritual* forebear is Gounod—not the sentimental Gounod that attracts Poulenc, but the relatively 'classical' composer of the *Petite Symphonie pour instruments à vent*. To compare the Symphonie with Sauguet's own *Bocages*, for wind quintet and harp, is to see how very close the two composers are. Gounod is the more precise,[1] Sauguet the more emotional, yet both achieve something that is delicate and pleasing without being trivial. Like Gounod, but unlike all of his own contemporaries, Sauguet is not a humorist. His nearest approach to comedy is the affectionate parody of late nineteenth-century ballet music in *Près du Bal*.

Amiable and well wrought though it may be, music of this kind suffers from a blight that has settled upon so much French art of our century and before. Because it immediately lays everything that it has on the table, and offers no kind of intellectual or imaginative challenge to the public which it addresses, it does not long hold the attention. One no more wishes to return repeatedly to a work like *Bocages* than one does to a painting by Dufy or a novel by Colette. As we have seen, more than one French musician of today has reacted to this danger (and to the prickings of his conscience) by donning the garb of the thinker or tragedian. But although the externals may change, the fundamental texture of thought is as diaphanous as ever. Sauguet, however, is a somewhat different case, and in attempting the dangerous transition to a more substantial idiom for the Symphony recently commissioned by Belgian Radio, he has proved his worth. The natural growth of his harmonic vocabulary since the days of *La Voyante* has made his chances of meeting the symphonic challenge far less remote than they

[1] Formally speaking, Gounod's masterly little symphony is much more closely knit than *Bocages*.

might have seemed twenty years ago. There is nothing about the new Symphony that suggests a deliberate and artificial heightening of the dissonance norm. But harmony alone does not make a symphony, and it is the formal adventurousness of the work that deserves particular attention—especially as Sauguet's earlier symphonic works, such as the *Concerto d'Orphée* are anything but adventurous. In his first movement, *Impetuoso*, Sauguet dares all. Between a highly condensed exposition and a developmental recapitulation, he interpolates a light *fugato* section that acts as the Symphony's *scherzo*. In view of what follows, this procedure is wholly justified. The central, pivotal, position of the second movement, a *passacaglia,* is rightly emphasised, making a dramatic point of its greater consonance. (For technical reasons it seems unlikely that Sauguet could sustain a slow movement at as high a level of dissonance as prevails throughout the outer movements of this Symphony.) The higher degree of harmonic tension in the finale is balanced by a certain relaxation in the form.

It would be foolish to claim that Sauguet's I.N.R. Symphony is intrinsically a work of importance. I discuss it here because of its bearing on Sauguet's status as a minor composer.[1] In the first place, it confirms Sauguet's ability to conduct a symphonic argument that is purposeful and, within its limits, original—virtues notably absent from Milhaud's Seventh Symphony, commissioned by the Belgian Radio for the same occasion. In the second place, the Symphony, if related to Sauguet's abilities and achievement, carries a lesson for his more sensational colleagues: the lesson that however slenderly endowed a composer may be, he has a better chance of developing and renewing himself if he sincerely and conscientiously perseveres with his art than if he trusts to the inspiration, or the whim, of the moment. It is, of course, the lesson of Satie in a new context.

Despite its integrity and ingenuity, the Symphony falls some way short of what is required if such a work is to endure on its own merits. One is prepared to listen because the composer has so bravely challenged us to do so, but the thematic ideas are not such as to make one *deeply* concerned with what happens to them. The musical argument stands on its own feet, but one's admiration is tempered by the knowledge that there is no great richness of ideas within its reach: in other words,

[1] As I have not heard, or been able to examine the score of, Sauguet's earlier symphony, the *Symphonie Expiatoire,* I refer readers to Hans Keller's favourable notice of it under 'First Performances' in the May 1950 issue of *The Music Review.*

the limitations of the work are inherent in its stature, not in its physiology. Thus one must look for Sauguet's most satisfactory achievements in those spheres which contain a greater number of possibilities on the lower levels—particularly, of course, in the field of opera. It is not surprising that Sauguet achieved the most complete fulfilment of his talent in the opera which he based on de Musset's tragi-comedy *Les Caprices de Marianne*. The success of this work is astonishingly far-reaching—indeed, there is only one serious musical failure, the latter part of Act One, scene four, and that perhaps seems more pronounced because the magic suggests a comparison with the much finer *Carillon* in Bizet's *L'Arlésienne*. Sauguet's admiration for the music of Bizet is no less evident, though far more fruitful, throughout the remainder of the opera. By acquiring from Bizet a certain Mediterranean warmth and poignancy, Sauguet has greatly enriched his resources. The fact that he has succeeded in projecting the action through a succession of self-contained numbers is evidence both of the variety of inflection that he can now command, and of the precision with which the music is articulated. Although a less remarkable melodist than Bizet, Sauguet sustains the musical and dramatic invention in a way that stands comparison with anything in Bizet's work apart from *Carmen*. Not that the music is derivative or reactionary. Its roots in the past may be apparent, but the total growth is as personal as it is inimitable. With the exception of our own Lennox Berkeley, Sauguet is perhaps the only contemporary composer who could and would approach this kind of bitter-sweet plot in this kind of way. If *Les Caprices de Marianne* succeeds to an extent that no operatic work of Berkeley's ever could—and I think that it does —the credit may partly be ascribed to Sauguet's peculiar talents, but even more to the power of a tradition that has been absorbed through every fibre of the composer's creative self. Like Charpentier's *Louise*, *Les Caprices de Marianne* sprang from a remarkably propitious conjunction of a particular artist with a particular subject at a particular stage of his own and his culture's evolution. For that reason I am inclined to think that *Les Caprices de Marianne* is one of the very few works by a minor twentieth-century composer that is likely to survive. The Age of the Common Man has also been an age *against* the Common Composer, and the situation in France has been more acute than anywhere else. Deprived of her only major musical genius by the death of Debussy, she was left with a large—too large—group of young composers whose talents were fundamentally similar to those of the *opéra comique* composers who flourished at the end of the nineteenth century.

Instead of following their natural bent, they were forced by the trend of modern culture—which has degraded the popular until it has become synonymous with the commercial—to don the mantle of se:ious composers.

A penetrating remark made by F. R. Leavis in another context seems strangely relevant to the situation: 'A tradition that does not enlist, or make good use of, minor talent [Auric, Ibert, Françaix, etc.] may be suspected of having also confined major talent [Koechlin, Milhaud] to minor performance'. The only successful large works of the period—*Les Mamelles de Tirésias* and *Les Caprices de Marianne*—are precisely those that attempt some kind of reintegration with the tradition to which their composers properly belong, and the less important successes of the period—the songs, choral works and theatre works of Poulenc, and a handful of pieces by Sauguet and Françaix—are equally remote from the distorted 'revolutionary' values that prevailed in the Parisian musical world of the twenties and thirties. Consequently there is nothing to be gained from considering the revolutionary aspects of the scene. The official guide-books to modern music make much of the influence of Stravinsky on French musicians, but whilst it is true that the young French composers professed the greatest admiration for the Russian master, their music contains little evidence of it. There is perhaps a trace of the harmony of *The Rite* in Milhaud's *Protée,* and a few echoes of *Les Noces* and the little song cycles occur in Poulenc's early works, but even when these are combined with a dozen or so less reputable examples,[1] one has no grounds for describing Stravinsky as a major influence. When commentators tell us that Stravinsky's renovation of Pergolesi's music in *Pulcinella* inspired every smart young French composer to spice up eighteenth-century trifles with wrong notes and incongruous harmonies, it is evident that the writer understands no more of Stravinsky's harmonic practice in *Pulcinella* than he supposes Stravinsky does of Pergolesi's. But we are not told what these post-*Pulcinella* works are—for the good reason that they do not exist. If we except Milhaud's refurbishment of the *Beggar's Opera* tunes in the *Carnival de Londres,* and Poulenc's bastardisation of Gervaise in the *Suite Française*—both of which post-date most of the guide-books—we are left with Françaix' arrangement of Boccherini in *Scuola di Ballo,* which is as discreet and tasteful a work as the hardiest academic could wish for.

[1] For instance, the first movement of Wiéner's *Concerto Franco-Americain,* which is a comically inept imitation of Stravinsky's early neo-classicism.

276

What is true of a relatively unimportant work like *Pulcinella* is equally true of Stravinsky's most important achievements. In the whole field of French music, dating from the 1918 War, I have not met with a single work that recalls any significant feature of Stravinsky's style—his unfailingly functional use of characteristic dissonance, his highly original sense of proportion, or his amazing ear for new sonorities. The fact is that for the guide-book writers, 'influenced by Stravinsky' is merely a genteelism for 'discordant' or 'percussive', just as 'influenced by Schönberg' is genteelism for 'partly or wholly incomprehensible'. The so-called revolutionary composers of the post-Cocteau era could never have been influenced by the great revolutionary masters for the good reason that they had no understanding of their constructive achievements. Apart from certain early works of Milhaud, the only things that are likely to survive from this dismal period are those—I repeat—which are most notable for their conservative and regressive qualities. At best it is a very minor achievement, for which the most fitting epitaph might be found in another passage from the poem quoted at the head of this chapter:

> *Our tri-classed life-express carries oh far more*
> *Back-to the engine fares than those face-fore.*

In many respects, French music today is in a more healthy state than it was before the war. This has partly come about through natural reaction—the resilience of a culture in which, even at its most sickly, there remained a flicker of life—and partly through the emergence of the first truly commanding figure since Debussy, Olivier Messiaen. Before discussing Messiaen's achievement, it is necessary to consider the events and personalities attendant upon his development as a major influence.

In June 1936 four French composers—Olivier Messiaen, Yves Baudrier, André Jolivet, and Daniel Lesur—calling themselves La Jeune France, presented a concert of their own works in Paris. Their manifesto, which was printed in the programme, professed their freedom from both revolutionary and academic formulas, and their intention to react in their music against the tendency of modern life 'to become more and more hard, mechanical and impersonal.' Although manifestoes are not in themselves of artistic interest, the event may properly be regarded as closing the period dominated by the Cocteau aesthetic. The fact that a serious, humanistic outlook was now announced as a central feature of the work of the younger generation indicated that the days of camouflaged *Unterhaltungsmusik* were over. Of course, it did not follow that their music would be any better than that of their more light-hearted elders: but the situation was more hopeful.

Of the four members of Jeune France, only one, Yves Baudrier, has failed to make any name for himself (outside the film world, where his score for René Clement's *Bataille du Rail* is highly spoken of). The case of Daniel Lesur is an admirable illustration of the healthier spirit that prevails in French music today. Possessed of only a slender talent, he has neither retreated into academicism—though he is a Professor at the Schola Cantorum—nor advanced, under disguise, into the field of radicalism, where he would have no right to be. His interest in Balinese gamelan music (which links him tenuously with Debussy) and his studies with one of the most original modern French organ composers, Charles Tournemire, helped him to find a harmonic idiom that is consistent and personal. The level of inspiration is not very high, but it is at least a *level*. As one would expect from such a composer, the syntax from phrase to phrase is thoroughly sound, and even, in a mild way, arresting, but the total concept is neither very individual nor as sustained as the original upon which it is modelled. For instance, if one gave half one's attention to Lesur's Piano Concerto, one might think it the work of a composer who has something of his own to say, something that is, within its limits, clearly defined and expressive. But closer observation would reveal that the Concerto is modelled, no doubt unconsciously, on the Ravel G major Concerto. The imagery is different, but the pattern of ideas is the same. In almost every important respect it is a lesser work than its far-from-perfect model. The ternary opening movement is a ridiculously short-winded and naïve version of the discursive form of the corresponding movement in the Ravel, and the melodically impoverished slow movement does not stand a moment's comparison with the wonderful linear movement of Ravel's *andante*.

From the historical point of view, Lesur's finale is the most interesting feature of the work. Ravel's finale, it will be recalled, is a disappointment. An untypically clumsy *rondo*, it rapidly degenerates into the chi-chi chatter characteristic of Ravel's younger contemporaries. When Lesur came to write his Concerto, however, such musical gossip was discredited. In its place, Lesur writes a tinkling, monothematic piece in quasi-gamelan style—a curious little pipe-dream that evaporates almost as soon as it has materialised. Musically the movement is scarcely more adequate as a concerto-finale than Ravel's *rondo*, but artistically it is a more honest and meaningful piece.

I am unable to speak of Lesur's other sympathetic works,[1] but it seems probable that his talents are better suited to a small canvas. In support of this I would cite the success of the unpretentious Sextet. The Sextet is of particular interest in that it relies to some extent on bitonality, and thus provides an opportunity for comparison with the *avant-garde* French music of the inter-war period. How much more musical and sensitive it all is! The lucid polyharmonies of the ternary third movement and the final Tarentella arise naturally out of the false-relations in the *ostinato* accompaniment to the opening Nocturne—a fact that is emphasised (not very subtly) by the return of the Nocturne's idea at the close of the Tarentella. One welcomes the sincerity of the thought whilst being a little disquieted by its lack of depth. Even the *passacaglia* second movement is disconcertingly insubstantial, and the fluent polyphony is without great variety of tension. Delicate and evanescent, it charms the ear but rapidly fades from the mind.

The achievement of André Jolivet, if compared with that of Lesur, might seem complex and weighty. Indeed, in France it is regarded as such. But the variety, and the much-publicised aims, of his music, are deceptive, for he is an essentially simple and unproblematic figure. In so far as his musical career has a Janus-like aspect, Jolivet may be regarded as a latter-day Milhaud; but whereas in Milhaud's case the dichotomy is between the portentous and the frivolous, in Jolivet's it is between the portentous and the unfrivolous. (His one attempt at the street-corner style—the Trumpet Concertino—is unworthy of serious consideration, apart from the fact that it is more logical, harmonically, than its spiritual ancestors of twenty years earlier.) For obvious reasons, Jolivet's 'occasional' music is the simplest to evaluate. It corresponds, in its solemn way, to a work like Milhaud's *Le Boeuf sur le Toit*; that is to say, it is written for a definite event, or as an exercise, and is not meant to carry the composer's most substantial ideas. But if Jolivet is really the original and remarkable composer that he is sometimes made out to be, something of his stature should still be suggested by these works—amongst which one might include the Flute Concerto and the Incantations for solo flute, the children's pieces for piano, and the ballet score, *Guignol et Pandore*. But the small pieces, and the Flute Concerto, are so discreet, so non-committal, that it is difficult to approach them critically. Is there some hidden reason why the composer has thus suppressed his personality? Or is it just that he has no person-

[1] Notably a *Ricercare* for Orchestra and a *Passacaille* for Piano and Orchestra.

ality? *Guignol et Pandore* provides part of the answer, for character, whether original or derived, is a prerequisite of ballet music. Alternating in style between Frenchified Prokoviev and devalued Ravel, *Guignol et Pandore* is effective and highly profesional, yet to all intents and purposes without individuality. Like Dutilleux's *Le Loup*—a work of very similar quality—it is more adult and assured than most French ballet scores of two or three decades previous. But it does no more than suggest French musical culture has recovered its stability.

Jolivet's serious works, such as the Symphony, the Piano Concerto, the *Danses Rituelles,* and the sonata and *Mana* Suite for piano are for the most part governed by his passionate interest in the magical, incantatory properties of music. The challenge this makes upon his technique and imagination has resulted in an accretion of symbolic musical images which cover most (but not all) of the plain ideas beneath, and purport to stand for something powerful and personal. Jolivet's studies with Varèse have both stimulated and disciplined his exploration of the higher chromatic dissonances. After the almost Reger-like thickness of the early *Adagio* for Strings (1934), the colour and flexibility of the harmony in a work like the *Danses Rituelles* (1939) is very welcome. The arched progression towards the climax of the *Danse Nuptuelle* is especially worthy of note.

The harmony of the *Danses Rituelles,* though often extremely dissonant, still retains its contact with traditional practice. In the *Mana* Suite, however, harmonic writing, where it occurs, is of a static kind that permits the continual juxtaposing of opposed sound-complexes. Elsewhere, harmony is replaced by free monody, or by quasi-percussive effects. In any case, these devices are always subsidiary to a rhythmic discourse that often reaches considerable complexity from the linear point of view (though the vertical combinations never involve more than two parts). This deliberate suppression of the conventional proved a stimulating challenge, and within its chosen field—which is wisely limited—*Mana* has something original to say. It seems to me the most interesting of Jolivet's 'advanced' works, and stands in relation to others in this category much as the elegant *Pastorales de Noël* do to his secondary work.

The general ideas underlying *Mana* reappear in a vastly inflated form in the Piano Concerto. During the process of inflation, a substantial element of the conventional is allowed to seep back—as it must with such a composer—and Jolivet's 'advanced' style is seen to be shot through with inconsistencies. But it is not enough merely to condemn the work as pretentious (and it is quite uncritical to do so on the basis of the composer's own literary pronouncements. Such things are not directly relevant—if they were one might, for instance, condemn Elgar's music out of hand, without looking farther than the direction of *Nobilmente*). Before one speaks of pretentiousness, one must try to understand the pretentions, musically speaking, and estimate the force behind them. Whatever else one may say of the Concerto, the music suggests that Jolivet is convinced of the importance of what he has to say—a conviction that may be misguided, but which is certainly sincere. In formulating this judgment one must distinguish between the vitality that is organic, and that which is artificially induced. The nervous energy of the Jolivet Concerto calls to mind Rolf Liebermann's egregious Concerto for Jazz Band, and similarities between certain musical ineptitudes[1] further encourages the comparison. But in the last resort the Jolivet Concerto is innocent of the deadly automatism of the Liebermann work. There is a certain musical life behind such things as the rhythmic development and thematic build-up from the percussion cadenza at Figure 13 of the finale that is manifestly absent from the empty husks of Liebermann's jazz formulae. Yet the vitality of this passage is largely sustained by blood transfusion from the Ravel G major Concerto[2]—that favoured model for the young French composers of our time. The debt which the music owes to Ravel might here pass unnoticed amidst the *tintamarre* of percussion, but in the feeble *cantabile* section (Fig. 11, *et seq.*) of the second movement it is unmistakable. The attempt at Ravellian sensitivity (not forgetting the doubling of the melody at the fifteenth) seems all the more pathetic in the context of the hideously scored *tutti* passages, where the monotonous snarl of the muted trumpets is the only feature that makes itself heard.

The composer's deficiences of aural imagination are equally apparent in his harmonic and contrapuntal writing. Whereas in the music of Messiaen, for instance, similar kinds of polychords and added-note chords have a strangely prismatic effect, seemingly a refraction of sonorities beyond our immediate consciousness, with Jolivet they tend to be leaden and inexpressive.[3] One's sense that the more complex passages are not heard through is confirmed by such things as the C

[1] Cf. the first movement of the Jolivet Piano Concerto, Fig. 2, and the Jump movement of the Liebermann Jazz Concerto, Figs. 7–11.

[2] Cf. Ravel Concerto, first movement, Fig. 12, *et. seq.*

[3] The best example of Jolivet's harmonic writing known to me occurs in the slow section of his Piano Sonata—a work that is otherwise of little value.

major cadence at the close of the Piano Concerto—which is produced like a rabbit from a hat, and has no real meaning in relation to the harmonic context.

The failings of the Jolivet Concerto may be clearly defined in musical terms and there is no excuse merely for dismissing it as pretentious. The danger of this particular blanket-description is twofold; in the first place it is so imprecise that no corroborative evidence can be adduced (with the result that the defence is unfairly deprived of a target); and in the second place it automatically excludes any mitigating factors. Now it so happens that the Jolivet Concerto possesses one characteristic that should to a small extent temper our adverse judgment. The composer's means of expression may well be shoddy and secondhand, but they are controlled by some kind of individual concept (however naïve). Poorly equipped as Jolivet is for these imaginative flights towards the primordial Suns, it is evident that had his ambitions been less his successes would have been fewer. The fate of Icarus is not wholly contemptible. . . .

Commentators who couple the names of Jolivet and Messiaen do so with scant justification, and it is significant that those who begin with this error almost invariably end by committing the far greater error of valuing Jolivet above Messiaen. (This is the official line of prejudice even in France.) The gossip-writers may seize upon the fact that Messiaen has written a highly laudatory, indeed an absurdly laudatory, foreword to *Mana*, and may suppose that they have further support for the pairing of the two composers in the fact that both belong to the *Jeune France* group and have professed ideals that may loosely be described as mystical. But a moment's comparison of their music will show how little the two have in common. It is true—and surprising—that Messian, who is by far the more original of the two, has taken a hint or two from Jolivet; but one only has to compare those parts of Messiaen's *Turangalîla* and *Vingt Regards sur l'Enfant Jésus* that derive from (say) *Mana*, to see that Messiaen has given a clearer and more richly meaningful expression to what he has to say. In regard to the specific character of harmony, melody, rhythm, form and texture, the music of these two composers has nothing in common. And its ultimate value is equally dissimilar.

Messiaen is a crucial figure. Since the pioneering days of Stravinsky and Schönberg, no composer has been subjected to such intensive vilification from all quarters. This, of course, proves nothing, and it would be a rash man indeed who claimed that Messiaen equalled or even approximated these masters in stature. But the impartial observer can hardly have failed to detect something sinister, and also rather familiar, in the general tone of these pseudo-critical reactions. The vulgar facetiousness, the blundering inaccuracies, and the hysterically emotional judgments which marked the British press-notices of *Turangalîla* is a case in point.[1] The stereotyped stone-walling of the official columnists does not give way to such undisguised animus unless some challenge has been made upon their *idées reçues*—and any such challenge must, in the nature of things, be healthy. Is there not a familiar ring about descriptions such as 'indescribable din' and 'a medley of grunts, whistles and pops'? Those who find in Messiaen's music a resemblance to 'Franck at his most sanctimonious' reveal much the same order of perception as enabled their predecessors to say that there was nothing in Schönberg but 'Wagner and Schumann "gone wrong"'. Beyond the journalists there are the technical experts, more sly than their colleagues, who tell us that at the heart of Messiaen's dissonant harmony there lies the simplicity of the common chord. Oh triumph of insight! Schönberg's cerebralism, Stravinsky's time-travelling, Messiaen's naïvety— these labels belong together in the lost-property office of criticism.

The technique of denigrating a newly emerged composer by loosely comparing him to any composer of established ill-repute is much favoured by Messiaen's detractors, who hasten to draw a *trompe 'œil* parallel with Scriabin. Every well-bred musician is expected to take it for granted that Scriabin was a bad composer, and since on that account it is no longer considered necessary to know the music, any argument involving him is freed from strict relevance to the text. The way is thus left open for those whose *métier* is the extra-musical red herring. Problematical composers who happen to subscribe to any brand of mysticism lay themselves open to all kinds of misrepresentation at the hands of such people, and it is no surprise that mysticism has been invoked as the link between Messiaen and Scriabin. When it is discovered that Messiaen, like Scriabin, uses a highly organised and personal language, the case seems complete. Mysticism is conventionally suspect, harmonic methods other than the traditional ones are 'systems' and therefore inartistic: *ergo*, Messiaen may be consigned to the limbo along with Scriabin.

Apart from the irrelevance of the mysticism bogey, there are two

[1] Thoroughly unfavourable though it was, Mr. Desmond Shawe-Taylor's notice in *The New Statesman and Nation* was an honourable exception, by virtue of its seriousness and sincerity.

things wrong with this argument. In the first place, the hypothesis that Scriabin is a worthless composer is contestable, and in the second, even if the hypothesis were true, his music does not resemble Messiaen's in a single detail of procedure, whilst in regard to the general attributes which we look for in good music—coherence, clarity and variety—it is demonstrably inferior.

Analogies with Franck, Massenet and other widely acknowledged sinners are equally valueless, because they can only subsist in the form of extreme generalities. It is true that Messiaen shares certain general characteristics with both these composers, but to make these characteristics the basis of an unfavourable judgment is to distort the issue completely, ignoring as it does the specific features of style and method, upon which Messiaen's claim to originality—like that of any other composer—must rest. We are never told the names of these works by Franck and Massenet which so closely presage Messiaen's own music; and one suspects that our informants are as much in the dark as their readers.

Messiaen would be a very strange composer indeed if he had no *rapport* with any of the traditions of Western music, and in fact the passing reflections of Franck—the fountainhead of the French organ school from which Messiaen has learnt so much—Massenet, Debussy, Satie, Ravel and Fauré are only significant in so far as they prove how deep are his roots in tradition, like those of every other genuine original. So let us have done with this cheap and irresponsible dismissal of an artist by 'proxy'. If a measure of Messiaen's stature and originality is needed, one could do worse than return to Jolivet, whose earliest surviving work, the *Adagio* for Strings (1934), may be compared with the work with which Messiaen first came before the public—the organ piece, *Le Banquet Céleste* (1928). Jolivet was thirty years old when he wrote the *Adagio*: competent and sincere though it is, it says nothing that is very new or original. *Le Banquet Céleste*, on the other hand, dates from Messiaen's twentieth year, and would have been a remarkable achievement for a composer of any age. The point of departure for the solemn hieratic style of this work is perhaps to be found in certain pieces in Tournemire's *L'Orgue Mystique*,[1] but the articulation of the music is wholly individual. In the first place one notes the paradoxical combination of repetition and economy. Without an understanding of Messiaen's 'repetition technique', much of his music will seem non-

[1] See for example *L'Orgue Mystique*, No. 40—the volume for the Fourteenth Sunday after Pentecost.

sensical. One must first distinguish between 'exact repetition' and 'varied repetition'. The former is only met with in Messiaen's *rondo*-like movements, where the *ritornelli* provide points of rest between elaborately discursive episodes. A precise parallel to this procedure may be found in the highly complex work of certain types of Indian classical musicians with whom Messiaen shows a marked sympathy. The principle of 'varied repetition', which plays a much more important role in Messiaen's music, is likewise applied in a manner reminiscent of Oriental practice. Here, the interest lies entirely in the development, not of the thematic idea, but of its ornamentation. The most extreme instance of this technique occurs in the second of Messiaen's *Trois Petites Liturgies*, where one's whole attention should be directed towards the constantly, dramatically, evolving commentary upon the seven-times-repeated theme. The theme itself must be allowed to recede into the background of one's consciousness, for the music is bi-planar, and the non-repetitive, non-thematic, non-tonal commentary is the kernel of the piece. But one cannot be wholly indifferent to the *ostinato* element. What do we mean by repetition? Perceptively, there can be no such thing. An idea repeated cannot evoke in its listeners the *same* experience that it entailed in the first place. The experience will to some extent be a new one, and whether it is more, or less, intense depends upon what has intervened and, of course, upon the nature of the idea itself. Bare repetition is thus the most primitive form of development; but Messiaen has imaginatively translated the fundamental primitivism into something that is singularly adult and developed. If we return to *Le Banquet Céleste*, we will find a simple example of how he achieves this. The opening phrase of the first stanza takes on a new and more powerful meaning when repeated at the start of the second stanza, as a result of the power generated by the first stanza's cadential phrase. This cadential phrase, and the climatic phrase in the second stanza, are the only points of developing harmony in a context that is designedly static. The power and coherence of *Le Banquet Céleste*—so free of tautology despite the high degree of motivic repetition—depends largely upon the placing and nature of these two crucial phrases (though it also owes something to the beautiful change of registration at the second stanza). In this respect, the musical technique reveals an astonishing economy and assurance.

Le Banquet Céleste is so typical of Messiaen's mature work that it offers a useful text for the consideration of something that is intimately connected with the nature of his art, and thence with the violent reaction or aversion which his music inspires in many listeners. It should at once be evident that in Messiaen's music the traditional patterns of harmonic tension and relaxation are no longer operative. Instead we find an extreme form of the procedure favoured by Debussy in certain of his impressionist pieces—the sustained use of unresolved dissonances as a means of subverting the traditional function of the cadence. But a procedure that is primarily of evocative and pictorial significance for Debussy becomes in Messiaen's hands a means of conveying the most intense emotion. It is as if *La lune qui descend sur le temple qui fut* had been infused with the passion of *Tristan and Isolde* (a work which is very dear to Messiaen). I do not wish to suggest that there is anything dispassionate or unemotional about Debussy's impressionist pieces. But the emotion has become so diffused and objectified that it is hardly to be distinguished from the sensual element with which it is associated. In Messiaen's music, the emotion is left bare, and since it is expressed by means of a technique that does not permit a correspondence with the normal trajectory of human emotion from its inception through a climax to resolution or sublimation, the result cannot fail to be disturbing. The harmonic structure of *Le Banquet Céleste* provides a very simple instance of this. The *fons et origo* of the piece is the opening chord, that of the dominant seventh with added sixth. (The added sixth is commonly used as an inhibitory factor in Messiaen's harmony.) The first three phrases of the opening stanza rely entirely on the alternation of V^7 and I, the rhythmic emphasis being placed on the dissonance. The final phrase of the stanza concludes on V^7, but it also carries the music forward to the higher tension of the second stanza, and prepares the way for the climax of the piece. But it is not a climax in the full (physiological) sense of the word. The harmony is denied its proper resolution, and subsides, as it were, into a state of semi-tumescence: the 'climax' has purged the dominant seventh of its 'worldly' added sixth, but at the end of the piece this harmony is left suspended *in vacuo*, denied the relief of a full close.

I think we can find, in this very typical harmonic process, a phenomenon whose essential violence would be immediately apparent if translated into physiological terms. What is true of *Le Banquet Céleste* is true of almost all of Messiaen's works, however simple or elaborate they may be. If we recognise in the technique something bordering on the pathological, we should remember that an element of the pathological is not necessarily incompatible with creative activity. Indeed, rather the contrary.

The fact that *Le Banquet Céleste* is so typical of Messiaen's art should not be taken to mean that the totality of his work is monotonous in character. *Le Banquet* displays a fundamental pattern that is profoundly associated with the composer's aesthetic, but the widest variety of musical ideas are extracted from that pattern. Certain pieces that seem to depart from the pattern by emphasising the cadential impulse or by modulating in a broadly traditional manner—for instance, *L'Apparition de L'Église Éternelle* or the Chorale at the close of the *Trois Petites Liturgies*—do in fact remain close to its basic principles. By adopting an extremely slow tempo and by stressing each and every chord movement, the composer breaks down one's highly conditioned sense of musical time—in other words, one's sense of harmonic expectation and fulfilment. One effect of this method is to equalise the relative importance of real and passing harmonies (together with their melodic adjuncts) and thus to suggest a state of continual flux in which every successive sound is a new and significant event. The slow tempo and block-chord texture of a movement like the *Jardin du Sommeil d'Amour* from *Turangalila* is deceptive, for the demands made upon one's musical responses do not permit any relaxation. Still, the *Jardin du Sommeil* is exceptional in that the cadential impulse, so far from being suppressed, is emphasised. On the other hand, in the great arch-shaped organ piece, *L'Apparition de L'Église Éternelle*, the cadential tendencies which predominate in one's visual impression of the score are broken down in the most astonishing way. By means of the figuration, the organ registration and the extremely slow tempo, the distinction of tension between the dissonant harmonies and the open fifths on which they theoretically resolve is destroyed, and the open fifths become part of what one feels to be a totally dissonant texture.

Ignoring for the moment Messiaen's more controversial late works, one is still faced with a body of music which, for seriousness of purpose, consistency of style and originality of expression has been unequalled by any French composer since the death of Debussy. Whilst profiting consciously from Debussy's example—especially in such works as *Pelléas* and the *Préludes*—Messiaen has also shown a certain affinity with Satie (of which he is no doubt unconscious).

Satie's semi-sacred music of the Rose-Croix period offers a remarkable if somewhat confused prophecy of certain aspects of Messiaen's early works, and the manner in which Satie later attempted to come to terms with the formal problems inherent in his anti-developmental attitude has equally marked parallels in Messiaen's later work. Thus the close *cellule*-with-*ritornello* construction of Satie's *Cinéma* and *Mort de Socrate* reappears in a much more complicated form in Messiaen's *Turangalîla* and *Cantéyodjayâ*, whilst the *ostinato* working of *Parade* and the condensed variation technique of *Relâche*, though primitive, may be regarded as prophetic of two aspects of Messiaen's technique since 1935.

It is fitting that Messiaen should have taken up the threads from Satie and Debussy, for it was the failure to comprehend, or the total rejection of, those two composers that was responsible for much of the futility of French music between the wars. The early works of Messiaen that I have mentioned above represent a kind of reaffirmation in wholly personal terms of the solidity and integrity of the French tradition. Messiaen's development since the completion of *L'Ascension* in 1934 was to be devoted to the exploration of new fields of form and content. For, by that date, he had arrived at the *impasse* which had faced Debussy after completing the *Préludes* and which a few years earlier had faced Satie, at the close of his Rose-Croix period. Only with great risk could Messiaen continue to rely so heavily upon his harmonic invention and his phenomenally sensitive ear. Although the novelty of his harmonic method almost amounted to a minor revolution, it was evident that, without reorientation, he was likely to find it difficult to avoid repeating himself : and it was inconceivable that, as things stood, he could tackle a large form. Debussy had solved *his* peculiar problem by a radical simplification of his harmony and textures, and by a return to a dramatic conception of tonality. Satie had turned to severe counterpoint. Messiaen now gave his full attention to what one can most aptly call the time factor, an element which from the very first he had treated in a most idiosyncratic manner. These experiments, which are conveniently but inaccurately termed 'rhythmic', are concerned with the relationships between varied units or groups of sound-durations. The concepts of metre, and of the association of harmony and rhythm, are overthrown, except where the composer uses added or subtracted fractional time values as a means of intensifying the cadential impulse. But for the most part the rhythmic working is intended to *supplant* the cadential impulse, and to provide, with the aid of polyrhythms, the impressions of expansion and completion that may no longer be inherent in the harmony.

This new departure first becomes apparent in the cycle of organ pieces, *La Nativité du Seigneur*, composed in 1935. Between that work and the *Turangalîla-Symphonie* of 1946–48, Messiaen's researches into the relationships of sound-durations led him ever closer to a position from which he was able to regard rhythm as the predominant factor in the structure of his music. Yet whilst concentrating upon this element, he has continued to extend his abilities in the fields of harmony, melody, timbre and traditional form (which latter he has never lost sight of), so that however little one may respond to Messiaen's rhythmic ideas, much else remains. In Messiaen, France once again has a composer whose seriousness of aim and range of musicianship is that of a master, and whose courageous indifference to the scorn of the *pompiers* is worthy of Berlioz, from whom *Jeune France* took their name.

Like Berlioz, Messiaen is the very type of the highly strung romantic artist, and like Berlioz he will occasionally write music that plumbs the depths of the dull, the foolish and the mechanical. There is nothing in the music of Jolivet, for instance, that is as bad as the worst in Messiaen, but these disasters are the result of taking risks that would be inconceivable to a lesser artist (and to many a greater one). A Romantic of this kind does not know the meaning of discretion; he thrives on hazard, and though his inspiration will sometimes succumb, it will more often emerge, triumphantly justifying every perilous step that it has taken. Because Messiaen, like Berlioz again, is capable at his best of something that is vibrantly new and beautiful, we must accept that his failings qualify rather than contradict his right to the title of genius.

I do not intend to embark here upon a critical examination of Messiaen's later music, or its relation to the composer's aesthetic; the delineation of a balanced view would occupy a space far beyond the scope of the present chapter.[1] In any case, it is sufficient at the present time to establish that Messiaen should be taken seriously. The newcomer to his music would be well advised to forget everything that he has ever read about it, favourable or otherwise, and concentrate at first upon acquainting himself with Messiaen's early works, wherein the composer's originality, though fully evident, is at its least radical. The difficulty of this music, and indeed of the later works, is never one of intellectual complexity. On the contrary, the procedures are remarkably

[1] I have attempted a fuller, though provisional, interpretation and estimate of his work in three articles published in the periodical, *The Score* (1954–55). On that account the relatively unsubstantiated reference in the present instance to 'Messiaen's genius' may be forgiven.

simple, much more so than any literary description of them could be. No, the difficulty lies in ridding oneself of habits of taste that masquerade as aesthetic laws, and of attuning oneself[1] to modes of thought and feeling that are in many ways contrary to the whole trend of modern culture. Having made that effort, and having perhaps been rewarded, one has to face, in the later music, certain challenges to one's conception of the nature and limits of music. It is not an easy task. The student who has open-mindedly listened to the music, or, better still, played it through and observed the meticulous consistency of its processes, might profitably pause before pronouncing too hasty an opinion and clarify his response with the aid of the questions which George Eliot finely posed in her *Judgments on Authors*:

'In endeavouring to estimate a remarkable writer who aimed at more than temporary influence, we have first to consider what was his individual contribution to the spiritual wealth of mankind. Had he a new conception? Did he animate long-known but neglected truths with new vigour, and cast fresh light on their relation to other admitted truths? Did he impregnate any ideas with a fresh store of emotion, and in this way enlarge the area of moral sentiment? Did he, by a wise emphasis here and a wise disregard there, give a more useful proportion to aims or motives? *And even where his thinking was most marked with the kind of mistake that is obvious to the majority, as well as that which can only be discerned by the in-*

[1] I think we must accept as an axiom that 'Genius tends to be a disturbing phenomenon for the critic, for its recognition depends upon new standards of evaluation'. (I quote from an article by Hans Keller in *Music Survey*, March 1951.) As a critical phenomenon, the case of Messiaen is curiously similar to that of Mahler, though in a strictly musical sense they have nothing in common. In either instance it is evident that whenever a critic damns the music of its 'sentimentality', its 'naïvety' or its 'banality' he has not begun to listen to it as a whole.

False emotive interpretations breed false technical observations, and remarks about Messiaen's 'repetitiveness' tend to be as ill considered as those about Mahler's 'rambling forms'. The same is true of criticisms of texture (complexity) and style (inconsistency). Schönberg, in his magnificent defence of Mahler in *Style and Idea*, devotes a section of his argument to the plight of composers. 'At each are fired all those accusations of which the opposite is true. Yes, *all*, and with such accuracy that one must be taken aback by it. For this shows, contrary to one's expectations, that the qualities of an author are really noticed already at the first hearing, but are merely wrongly interpreted. Whenever the most personal of the composer's peculiarities appear, the listener is struck. But instead of recognising immediately that this is a special feature, he interprets the blow as a blow of offence. He believes that there is a mistake, a fault here and fails to see that it is a merit.'

structed, or made manifest by the progress of things, has it that salt of a noble enthusiasm which should rebuke our discrimination if its correctness is inspired with a less admirable habit of feeling?' (My italics.)

If it is Messiaen that we have in mind as our 'writer', the answers to these questions will, for many of us, be in the affirmative.

Whatever one may think of Messiaen as an artist, one fact is irrefutable: his immense technical accomplishment, coupled with his earnestly questing spirit, have made him one of the most sought-after teachers in Europe. Every one of the leading figures of the European *avant-garde*—Boulez, Stockhausen, Goevaerts, Nono, to mention but a few—has either been a pupil of his or attended his classes at the Paris Conservatoire or the Darmstadt Ferienkurse. There is hardly a young French composer of today who has not studied under him, and the fact that the trivia of a minor talent like Marius Constant are of a much higher technical excellence than similar products of the inter-war years may partly be attributed to his instruction. But the young musician is unlikely to model himself on Messiaen's own style. Jean-Louis Martinet has been the only one of the significant talents to have dared to follow his master. His early *Trilogie de Promethée* is at certain points indistinguishable (except in quality) from Messiaen's work. However, even within these borrowed limits, the music is sufficiently creative to warrant the assumption that Martinet would, with maturity, evolve a style of his own. It is said that his later works (in which he has adopted the twelve-note method) fulfil his early promise, on more individual lines.

On the evidence of two hearings of an orchestral work, *Les Cercles des Metamorphoses*, by another Messiaen pupil, Maurice Leroux, it seems possible that Leroux' is a more original and powerful talent than Martinet's. Apart from Boulez' cantata, *Soleils des Eaux* (which I have not heard or seen), the *Cercles des Metamorphoses* is the only work for large orchestra by a member of the Continental *avant-garde* school that has yet been performed in public. It is a most distinguished and encouraging composition. Not only is it informed with the sense of the living beauty of instrumental and orchestral sound that is so manifestly lacking in the work of the less talented if more sensational *avant-gardistes*, but it also develops and progresses as an over-all structure in a way that is immediately comprehensible.

But Leroux has written little and published less, and the fame of the group of post-Messiaen composers largely rests on the achievement of Messiaen's most brilliant pupil, Pierre Boulez. Boulez has withdrawn or (more oddly) partly withdrawn most of his early work. No doubt his disapproval of the *Psalmodies* for piano is due to their rather too obvious debt to Messiaen, but for all that they are very much more imaginative and creative than the juvenilia which some other composers have allowed to stand. The *Psalmodies* are perhaps as characteristic of Boulez' later music as the *Sieben Frühe Lieder* are characteristic of Berg's, and like Berg's *Lieder*, they deserve to survive by virtue of their intrinsic merit rather than for their relevance to the composer's more important work. The case for Boulez' Second Sonata (of which he will permit only the first two movements to be played) is somewhat different. Here the composer's art is in a state of transition from one mode of expression to another, and the stylistic discrepancies are disturbing. Rapid flourishes of almost Lisztian contour seem strangely inconsistent from the textural point of view, whilst the opposition of sections that are fairly regular rhythmically and metrically with others that are quite independent of any metrical feeling does not contribute to over-all unity. The most disconcerting feature of all is the discrepancy between passages founded on a relatively traditional motival technique, and others in which the methods of procedure are less evident, if at all.

On the surface it might seem that the main difference between the Sonata and the *Psalmodies* can be ascribed to the influence of Webern. But whilst certain passages are indeed Webernesque, in a general kind of way, the importance of his influence upon the work as a whole can be over-estimated. Whether one has in mind the whole range of Webern's output, or merely his single work for piano, the Variations, Op. 27, one will find that there are many pages of the Boulez sonata that are not remotely like Webern either in sound or in method. Not only is the texture and rhythmic structure quite different, but the melodic writing has none of that typically Viennese quality that is so important a feature of Webern's style. (One would be very surprised if it had.) On the other hand, when one examines those few passages that do recall Webern, one finds that this resemblance is only half the picture. The general sound of the opening of the second movement is certainly Webernesque, but the intervallic organisation is anything but. Conversely, where the technique derives from Webern, the musical end is in every way dissimilar. Take, for instance, the remarkable passage starting at the tenth bar of the score's twelfth page. The highly compressed canonic procedures upon which this section is founded are developed from the kind of canonic working which Webern used in the second movement of his Piano Variations. But the almost impressionistic effect of these new *Jeux des Vagues*, with their regular undulating swell, could hardly be less like Webern.

The inconsistencies which mar Boulez' second sonata are no longer present in his subsequent works. There can be little question that in *Polyphonie X*, and the *Structures* for two pianos, Boulez is at last sure of what he wishes to do: in that respect his music has attained maturity. But at the same time there is a lack of balance between form and content which indicates that the maturity is not complete. Schönberg has rightly observed that 'the necessity of compromising with comprehensibility forbids jumping into a style which is overcrowded with content', but in these two works, Boulez does not recognise any such necessity. Only one level of his creativity is directed towards communication, and that is the one corresponding to the 'first-level' response—the response to general shapes, textures and sonorities. Across the other levels of his art is stretched a dense web of hidden relationships which do not in themselves have any precise expressive function, though they may contribute to the general impression made by the music (and in the cantata, *Le Marteau sans Maître*, certainly do). The processes are often so complex that it is almost impossible to analyse them without the aid of preliminary data. One is thus faced with a strange anomaly, for *everything* in the music is significant to the composer, in so far as everything is subjected to some kind of serial necessity which he has established, yet *nothing* is significant to the listener, who is incapable of divining that necessity and hence of relating each entity to the morphology of the whole. The music has nothing to offer but its surface; and since the rest is impenetrable, the listener is denied a full musical experience, for such an experience (whether it be offered by Bach or Schönberg, Couperin or Debussy) depends primarily upon the penetrating apprehension and co-ordination of significant musical statements, without which the interplay of the heart and the senses is a shallow thing. Were it not for the vital imagination that informs the surface-level of Boulez' music, the relatively opaque complexity that lies beneath would suggest a parallel with the worst work of Milhaud. As it is, the lack of a perceptible subsoil of meaning seems to give the music a semblance of insubstantiality, of infertility even, that brings it deceptively close to the terrain worked by lightweight composers like Françaix—'deceptively', because even the surface of the music should tell us that at the centre of it all is a serious creative intention.

Obscurity is a serious fault in an artist, but by 'artist' we mean 'mature artist', and I am inclined to think that what one might call the 'inhibitionism' of these Boulez works is merely the negative pole of that pre-adult streak of exhibitionism which we have noted in Poulenc's *Le Bal Masqué*. In *Le Marteau sans Maître* there is already evidence of a new frankness, a dawning consciousness of the value of positive expression; and so far as I can tell from a hearing of part of Boulez' most recent work, the *Livre pour Quatuor*[1], this tendency has now been powerfully consolidated. But rather than discuss the quartet without having heard it in entirety, or having seen the score, I would like to quote an important passage from a recent article by Boulez which seems to point in the same direction as the quartet. It expresses sentiments that other members of the *avant-garde* would do well to take to heart.

'Webern only organised intervallic relationships; now, rhythm, tone colour and dynamics are organised, and all serve as fodder for the monstrous polyorganisation, from which one must break free if one is not to condemn oneself to deafness. Webern never believed that one could equate organisation with composition, and it will soon be agreed that one cannot do so without reducing one's activities to utter senselessness.'

It is clear that Boulez, like many twentieth-century French composers before him, has arrived at a point of crisis in his career from which he must somehow extricate himself. It seems inevitable that he will be forced to simplify his means of expression, but whether he will do so by strengthening his ties with Debussy and early Schönberg, or whether he will be prepared to learn more from the clarity and humanity of Webern remains an open question. In any event, there is already enough evidence to suggest that Boulez may, in the future, produce work of the first importance. There is certainly no French composer of today who shows greater promise. And what of Messiaen? Apart from two works founded on birdsong—experiments which rely

[1] Since writing the above, I have learnt that the *Livre pour Quatuor* is a re-working of material which Boulez composed some time ago. I do not feel that this in any way affects my contention that he is moving towards (or returning to) a greater clarity of form and definition of content.

for their interest on technique rather than creativity—he has written nothing since the *Livre d'Orgue* of 1951. Certain features in his work subsequent to *Turangalîla* suggest that he may be facing another creative crisis, even more crucial than the first. Whatever the outcome of the present situation, we can be thankful that France again has more than one composer who reveres the dignity of his art and understands the meaning of constructive evolution.

Czechoslovakia and Poland

BERNARD STEVENS

Czechoslovakia

$\mathbf{B}$Y the beginning of the twentieth century the Czech national school of composers founded by Smetana, Dvořák, Foerster and Fibich had become generally accepted as an integral part of the European tradition. This integration had been facilitated by the Czech composers developing their national characteristics simultaneously with the assimilation of the powerful influences of Schubert, Schumann, Brahms, Wagner and Liszt. Thus, from the beginning, the movement avoided the provincialism so frequently a feature of some other national schools, such as the Spanish. The founders of the national school were as active in teaching as in composition, thus ensuring continuity of development and preventing academic ossification. The partial autonomy granted by Austria in 1859 and Erben's collection of Moravian folk-poetry and legends gave the national school a political and aesthetic impetus that lasted until further stimulus was provided by the founding of the Czechoslovak Republic in 1918. Although there had not appeared a collection of folk music as comprehensive as Erben's anthology, nevertheless folk music was in the blood of composers of the school, due largely to the peasant origin of so many of its members. The recent research of Racek and Sychra has revealed the remarkable extent to which folk music has conditioned the melodic and rhythmical idiom of the Czech national school.

Suk, Novák, Ostrčil and Janáček were the leading creative figures to reach maturity in the early years of the twentieth century.

Joseph Suk (1874–1935), pupil and son-in-law of Dvořák, asserted his individuality and technical mastery even as a student of eighteen in the Serenade for Strings, Op. 6, still his most frequently performed work. The expansive lyrical melodic shapes and occasional naïvety are characteristic of the old Czech school, but new qualities are seen in the rhythmical elasticity and sustained contrapuntal texture which, however, never deteriorate into mere imitative devices. The vividness of the string sonorities derive from his own experience as a string player; he was for many years a member of the famous Bohemian Quartet. The structure, however, reveals weaknesses due to the difficulty of reconciling classical sonata form and rhapsodic thematic ideas. This problem faced all the early nationalists in their symphonic work, particularly Dvořák, and was, in fact, never solved; rather was it avoided by seeking new forms derived from Liszt's method of thematic metamorphosis. Suk's mental and spiritual experiences always found direct musical expression, but never in a self-dramatised form. His brief but happy marriage is reflected in a series of works permeated by tender lyricism, full of harmonic subtlety and avoiding dramatic conflict, as in the suites from the incidental music to plays based on Slavonic legends, *Raduz and Mahulena*, Op. 13, and *Under the Apple-trees*, Op. 20, and the Fantasy for Violin and Orchestra, Op. 24, in which he combines a sense of remoteness, fantasy and intimacy. The deaths of both Dvořák and his own wife in the space of a year shattered this dream world and was a severe emotional blow which led, however, to the deepening of his musical utterance revealed in the major works of his maturity, the symphonic poem, *Prague*, Op. 26, the *Asrael* Symphony, Op. 27, the symphonic poems, *A Summer Tale*, Op. 29, and *A-growing*, Op. 34, and the *Epilogue*, Op. 37, for orchestra, baritone and bass soli and chorus. The formal weaknesses of the early works are here overcome by the skilful use of thematic motifs. This process is best exemplified in *A-growing*, which is undoubtedly Suk's masterpiece. The life-process of germination, development and maturity implied in the title finds its exact equivalent in the continuously developing thematic elements, the flowering of new counterpoints, all contained in a unifying and free rhythmical process. His last mature work, the *Epilogue*, is his greatest in conception and the clearest exposition of his philosophy of Love, from Mother Love to Divine Love. The dramatic and musical structure is original and convincing in its use of the motif of Mankind and the setting of the twenty-third Psalm, but the quality of musical thought, fine though it is, does not rise to that of *A-growing* except in the powerful opening *Adagio*. The *Meditation on the Chorale St. Wenceslaus*, Op. 35a, for string quartet or string orchestra, arose directly out of the experiences of his country in the First World War and was one of the first works of the Czech national school to succeed in recreating the spirit of the old Hussite chorales. As in a Bach chorale prelude the decorative fantasia texture is assimilated perfectly into the broad spacious metre of the chorale. His subjectivism seldom became introspective as sometimes occurs in Mahler, with whom he has much in common spiritually, and he always retained a Dvořákian spontaneity and wealth of invention, in spite of the philosophical thought that pervades all his mature works. His rich and chromatic, but seldom cloying, harmonic language and rhythmical elasticity had a great influence on the generation that followed, including those who, spiritually, had little in common with him.

The early works of Vítězslav Novák (1870–1949) show only superficial signs of his study with Dvořák and other members of the Czech national school, but rather a disconcerting array of influences from Berlioz to Brahms, mostly in piano works and songs. His national and individual qualities did not, in fact, begin to assert themselves until his chance discovery of Moravian and Slovak folk music. It is not without significance that, unlike so many other Czech national composers, he was not of peasant origin and thus did not grow up in an atmosphere permeated with folk music. The remarkable rhythms and unfamiliar scales and the drama, mystery and irony of Moravian folk-tales stimulated all the works of his middle period. He arranged numerous Slovak folksongs for voice and piano in which the counterpoint of the accompaniment is idiomatically derived from the melodies themselves. Several chamber works for strings and piano and the Sonata, *Eroica*, Op. 24, for piano, retain the romantic passion of the early works but in terms of the rhythms and melodic characteristics, particularly fourths and fifths, of Slovak folksong. The large-scale orchestral works of this period are frankly programmatic, such as *In the Tatra*, Op. 26, and *Eternal Longing*, Op. 33, but he is never content with typical late nineteenth-century orchestration; the orchestra is used always with great restraint and reserved passion. In the *Slovak Suite*, Op. 32, the decorative devices of Slovak fiddlers and cymbalo players are suggested with great vividness. In his last period he turned to patriotic themes for his operas, *Karlstein*, Op. 50, and *The Lantern*, Op. 56. Only the comic opera, *The Imp of Zvikov*, Op. 47, retains the irony characteristic of his earlier work. His last large work, 'The May Symphony', celebrated the liberation of his country in 1945. He was always a frank and unashamed romantic, but his romanticism was always restrained and controlled by an almost aristocratic refinement of language. His originality in forging an individual language of expression from Moravian and Slovak folk music is comparable with that of Janáček but is less obvious because he avoided the blunt realism of the latter.

Otakar Ostrčil (1879–1935) was important both as composer and as conductor at the National Opera in Prague from 1920 until his death. In both capacities he was a consistent champion of the new tendencies in European music, particularly those of Mahler and Schönberg, without in any way abandoning basically national qualities. He was a man of very wide culture, in fact, a professor of modern languages in Prague, studying music privately with Fibich and only later devoted his whole life to composition and conducting. His technical mastery, in spite of his amateur status, revealed itself in his earliest works such as the opera, *The Death of Vlasta*, but the influence of Fibich, particularly the latter's melodramatic characteristics, are overpowering. Gradually, however, his individuality asserted itself, largely through his growing interest in folk-poetry and mysticism. The influence of Mahler was as much psychological as musical. The fascination that Chinese philosophy had for Mahler is matched by Ostrčil's interest in Indian mysticism as in the opera, *Kinala's Eyes*. Purely musically, however, Mahler showed him how to develop a rich chromaticism of harmony in terms of clear contrapuntal lines. The Suite in C Minor from this point of view is his finest achievement in instrumental music. But his instrumental works are, in general, marred by a rhythmical stiffness and a sectional rather than organic treatment of larger forms. The symphonic poem, *Summer*, suffers in this respect in spite of the vividness of the orchestral imagination. His operas and oratorios are remarkable not only for their dramatic power but more particularly for the precision with which he captures the spiritual atmosphere and psychological states of mind of the characters—the comedy of modern life in *The Bud*, the optimistic simplicity of *Jack's Kingdom*, the combination of religious naïvety and irony in *The Legend of St. Zita*.

Suk, Novák and Ostrčil, in spite of their individual characteristics, are all in a direct line of development from the older school of Czech nationalist composers, and their work, taken as a whole, can be said to be part of the general West European tradition. Leoš Janáček (1854–1928), however, stands apart from his contemporaries in both attitude and methods. Like Dvořák and Suk, his first acquaintance with music came from the choir and band of his native village, where his father was the last of a long line of poor schoolmasters. At the age of eleven he was sent to the choir-school of the Austin Friars at Brno, capital of Moravia, where the director of music was Křížkovský. The latter was a remarkable musician both as choir-trainer and composer of powerful dramatic part-songs for male voices, developed from folksongs and stories, which became famous throughout the country, having a decisive influence on Smetana and hence on the whole development of the Czech school. The importance of Janáček's training under Křížkovský can hardly be exaggerated, as it embedded in his as yet unformulated mind the principles on which his whole artistic life would develop. It is fortunate from this point of view that his father's poverty prevented his entering the Leipzig Conservatoire until his twenty-fifth year, by which time his artistic character was already formed. It is thus not surprising that his period of study with Reinecke in Leipzig was of little value to him. Apart from his work in Vienna, where he hoped to become a pianist (a project abandoned through lack of money), and occasional visits to foreign countries for performances of his works, the rest of his life was spent in his native Moravia, particularly Brno, which he built up into a vital musical centre. Only his apparently unlimited mental and physical energy can explain how he succeeded in combining this vast organisational work with his stupendous creative output, not to mention his theoretical writing and systematic researches into folk music. Apart from the handful of pieces he wrote during his study abroad, his whole output is remarkably homogeneous. It is not surprising that his first compositions were modelled on those of Křížkovský and were mostly male-voice part-songs. His choral writing received a tremendous stimulus from his acquaintance with the poems of the folk-bard Bezruč and reached its highest point in his setting of the latter's *The Teacher Halfa*, *Maryčka Magdanová* and *The Seventy Thousand*, a trilogy characterised by suffering at the hands of social injustice. They are virtually operatic choral scenes, anticipating his great operatic achievement, just as Monteverdi's madrigals anticipate his *Ulysses* and *Poppea*.

Meanwhile, his acquaintance with the folklorist Bartoš led him to a systematic study of Moravian folk music, not only the collection of material but also theoretical analysis of its character. His work in this field is of comparable value with that of Bartók and Kodály, and as important to his creative development as to that of the two Hungarian masters. In many ways his analysis went deeper than theirs in that he was more alive to the mental and social conditions that give rise to folk-art forms, for he never analysed the tunes in the abstract, detached from their words, as Bartók does. His realisation of the bond between the words and melodic inflections of folksong and his close observation of the speaking voice in various emotional states led him to the formulation of his theory of the 'melodic curves of speech'. The full implications of this theory were later to be realised in the great operas and the song-cycle, *The Diary of One who Disappeared,* but it also conditioned the whole character of his thematic invention, both vocal and instrumental, leading him towards short evocative motifs and away from the long themes with several balanced phrased of European romantic music. His assimilation of folk instrumental style is shown in his habit of keeping distinct the function of each instrument in an ensemble and in exploiting extremes of compass, particularly those of the wood-wind, in order to achieve the maximum heightening of expression, just as a folksinger habitually sings at a pitch that would be considered by a concert singer to be uncomfortably high. The late *Concertino* for Seven Instruments and the *Sinfonietta* for Full Orchestra are particularly vivid examples of both characteristics as well as of his daring use of repetition as a means of heightening intensity. The early *Lachian Dances,* the first work to derive directly from his folkloristic studies and the first to be published in Prague, are, in spite of their popularity in his own country today, only a partial realisation of his methods. The work has great rhythmical power and the structure of the original Moravian dances is dramatised by the daring key relationships, but the orchestra is in general that of the usual late nineteenth-century type except for the very original use of the harp, which is here more usually rhythmical than harmonic in function. All folk music relies to a considerable extent on the cumulative effect of rhythmical and melodic repetition. In general, it may be said that it has been reintroduced into advanced composed music only where a consciously primitive effect is required, as in Ravel's *Bolero* or Stravinsky's *Les Noces.* This kind of primitivism is quite foreign to Janáček. In abandoning thematic development he rediscovered the power with which an apparently slight melodic or rhythmic motif gradually but inexorably by repetition establishes and maintains an emotional or psychological condition. This use of motifs is quite distinct from that of Wagner where the function lies primarily in the dramatic relationship between leitmotifs.

Janáček's genius reaches its full stature in his operas. They give the most comprehensive view of his artistic methods as well as of his attitude to humanity. This attitude is unmistakable in the texts that he set from his early male-voice part-songs to his last large-scale work, the opera, *The House of the Dead,* and it is even explicit in such instrumental works as the Piano Sonata '1.X.1905', originating from the death of a worker in a demonstration, and the First String Quartet, based on Tolstoy's *Kreutzer Sonata.* He was for ever concerned with the human personality in its struggles for freedom against the forces of religious superstition, hypocritical bourgeois morality, jealousy and social and economic oppression.

Janáček's first opera, *Sarka,* based on the well-known legend of Vlasta and the revolt of the women, was admired by Dvořák and is the only work that shows his influence. Owing to copyright difficulties it was not performed until 1925. The second, in one Act, *The Beginning of a Novel,* was destroyed by the composer after its first performance in Brno. The third, *Jenůfa,* marks the beginning of his operatic maturity. Whereas the story of *Sarka* might well have been chosen by any of the Czech national schools and was in fact by both Smetana and Fibich, that of *Jenůfa,* with its jealousy between the half-brothers, the passionate love of Jenůfa and the middle-class respectability of the foster-mother, is highly characteristic of Janáček. It was composed during the darkest period of his life, 1896-1903, when he was exhausted physically and emotionally by overwork at teaching and by the deaths of his daughter and little son. Its idiom was so misunderstood in Prague that it was refused performance at the National Opera; the Brno production was of only local success. It seems surprising that, whereas personal suffering brought forth from him what is perhaps his greatest masterpiece, lack of recognition induced in him a condition of indecision, for he followed *Jenůfa* by a series of tentative efforts in opera which remained either in manuscript or were never completed, including sketches for *Anna Karenina.* Only after *Jenůfa* was at last performed in Prague in 1916, with tremendous success, did he acquire the self-confidence to complete *The Excursions of Mr. Brouček,* begun in 1908. The delay in public recognition, as well as the extraordinary originality of his work, explains the curious fact that, in spite of his having been born as early as 1854, Janáček must be regarded as a modern composer. *Jenůfa* is remarkable for its power of characterisation, in which respect it is comparable with Moussorgski's *Boris,* and for the precision of its dramatic timing. The chorus is never used for mere 'crowd scenes' but to add emotional power, as in the erotic symbolism of the choral dances in the fifth scene of Act One: 'On a high hill there stands a castle with a tower made of fine young fellows.' *The Excursions of Mr. Brouček* is an ironic satire on middle-class philistinism presented in witty but eccentric humour, helped by the apparently inconsequential sequence of events in which Mr. Brouček, a property owner, is carried away in his alcoholic dreams first to the moon and then to fifteenth-century Prague. The work is remarkable for the subtle mixture of realism and fantasy in the musical texture and for maintaining an essential seriousness beneath the satire. Janáček's visit to Russia shortly before he wrote *Jenůfa* stimulated the interest in Russian literature reflected in several of his later works, the operas, *Kaťa Kabanova*, *The House of the Dead*, the *Kreutzer Sonata* String Quartet, the symphonic poem *Taras Bulba*. *Kaťa Kabanova*, completed in 1921, has something in common with *Jenůfa* in its emotional content, but the sense of frustration and doom pervading the whole opera is nearer to the Verdi of *Othello* or the Puccini of *Tosca*, but Janáček is always far too committed to his characters to permit himself the lyricism of those masters. Perhaps in no other work of art, with the possible exception of Berg's *Wozzeck*, have the depths of human misery and degradation been plumbed than in *Kaťa* and *The House of the Dead*.

The Sly Vixen, completed in 1923, is a charmingly light-hearted comedy, again with an underlying seriousness in the contrast between the freedom and spontaneity of animals in love and the frustration and conflicts of human relationships. The work is really a highly developed form of the anecdotal folk dance of the type common in many Slav countries. The *Makropulos Affair*, completed a year later, is from Capek's play about a girl who drinks an elixir which keeps her alive in all her beauty for three hundred years, ordaining her to a life of boredom. The abstract nature of the story is matched by a correspondingly disinterested quality in the music where, for perhaps the only time, there is hardly any discernible influence of folk music. His last opera, *The House of the Dead*, completed in the last year of his life, was never performed in his lifetime. It is to his own libretto from Dostoevski's novel about his experiences in prison. The structure is most original; by selecting an isolated episode for each Act, with no development from one Act to the next, Janáček succeeds in creating a static atmosphere which perpetuates the sense of hopelessness in the day-to-day existence of 'Life's disinherited'.

Janáček achieved as has no other composer the conscious civilised artist's equivalent of a perfectly integrated folk-art. His work is complete in itself, it left no unsolved problems to be taken up by other composers. That is why he left no musical heirs and why he had very little direct influence on the generation that followed him.

With Alois Hába (born 1893) we come to the most original of a long line of brilliant pupils of Novák. Like so many of his colleagues, his first musical experience was in the village band. He had already studied Moravian and Slovak folk music in great detail before becoming a pupil of Novák, who encouraged his composition in the spirit of folksong. But he was searching for a more systematised method in which the science of sound was an important element. This process was facilitated by his long period of study with Schreker in Vienna and Berlin. From Schreker he learned also to master the early twentieth-century German atonality that we associate with Mahler and early Schönberg. The Symphonic Fantasy for Piano and Orchestra, Op. 8, is a characteristic example of this phase. It also illustrates the beginning of his athematic method, for which there were, in his view, philosophical as well as aesthetic reasons. At this time he was developing an interest in Oriental philosophy and the anthroposophy associated with Rudolf Steiner. The direct influence of the latter on his composition is seen in his opposition to thematic repetition and development as characteristic of primitive 'animalistic' remnants in the human mind which must be discarded if he was to develop his full potentialities.

Hába's athematism is a testimony to the fertility of his invention and he achieved a stylistic unity through harmonic and rhythmical means. But the absence of clearly defined themes necessarily gives his music an abstract and remote character at variance with his avowed philosophical intentions. Hába renewed his study of Moravian and Slovak folk music, but this time from the athematic standpoint, that is to say he was more concerned with the improvised decoration and counterpoints than with the melodies themselves. He paid particular attention to the use of micro-tones as melodic inflections in Moravian folksongs from which he evolved his system of quarter-tone and sixth-tone composition. The important difference, however, between Hába's use of micro-tones and that of Moravian folk music lies in the fact that in the latter they are always incidental to the main melodic line, whereas Hába uses them as notes of equal melodic importance with the tones and semitones. He maintains that this is a logical development involving new divisions of the tetrachord, but many others, including Hindemith, dispute this on the same acoustical grounds as they dispute the validity of atonality itself. It is indisputable that in Hába's arrangements of folksongs for women's voices with *obbligato* for quarter-tone clarinet and in much of the vocal writing in his opera, *Mother*, where he uses quarter-tones to heighten the evocative power of the melody, he achieves imaginatively convincing results. In the Fantasias for quarter-tone and sixth-tone piano and the string quartets, however, it is difficult to dissociate the micro-tones from the sensation of false intonation. Hába's followers, including the young composer Karel Reiner, would claim that that is explained by lack of familiarity. But my own experience of frequent hearings on gramophone records brings me no nearer acceptance of systematic micro-tone music, but does confirm the first impression of rhythmical obviousness and even complacency. It is here that the fundamental difference between Hába and Janáček is to be found. The rhythmical vitality and subtlety of the latter explains the extraordinary evocative power of his music in spite of the apparent naïvety and even crudity of his harmonic and structural methods. Nevertheless, Hába stands as a figure of great integrity and historical importance, and it is likely that composers in the future will find possibilities of development in many of his ideas.

Bohuslav Martinů (b. 1890) is the most internationally famous and widely performed of living Czechoslovak composers. This can be explained not only by the intrinsic qualities of his work but also by his success in fusing national and cosmopolitan elements and his long period of residence in France and America in the *milieu* of Western musical activity. His career is in many respects similar to that of Prokofiev: both grew up in the nationalist movement of their countries, found academic training irksome, joined the neo-classical movement in Paris and rediscovered their nationalism in the Second World War. That Prokofiev returned to his country while Martinů remained in France and America is of less importance than might at first appear, since Martinů is recognised and accepted in his own country as the leading national composer. He has always been remarkably prolific, composing continuously since the age of ten. He was already technically mature when he attended Suk's class in Prague after having been dismissed from the Organ School, so that it is not surprising he found it of little value. By 1923, when he went to study with Roussel, his musical personality was already formed, but Roussel's advice, even if not always taken, was valuable in establishing classical principles of clarity of texture and form which prevented his succumbing completely to the fashion of neo-classicism in the 1920s.

Martinů's artistic maturity dates from the 1930s and he is today at the height of his powers. His extraordinary fluency is reflected in the mere catalogue of his works; at sixty-five he has produced over one hundred and fifty major works, including twelve operas, eleven ballets, twenty orchestral works, including six symphonies, twenty concertos for various solo instruments, fifty chamber works, including seven string quartets. He has forged for himself a very personal idiom in which he thinks freely and spontaneously. Melodically it is derived from Moravian folksong, with its strong intervals, and more recently from the Hussite chorales, harmonically generally clear and simple, avoiding chromaticism but finding new associations of simple chord structures and with a taste for the parallel sixths characteristic of Czech folk ensembles; rhythmically the influence of the neo-classical movement is strongest with its balanced formal sentences and consistency of figuration. In the structure of large-scale movements Martinů generally avoids the development of thematic ideas, preferring the *ritornello* and episode principle of the classical *concerto grosso*. He is predominantly a serious composer, in spite of the number of witty and satirical works he has written for opera and ballet. The latter are brilliant and effective, but seem less spontaneous than the similar works of Prokofiev. Martinů is at his greatest in large-scale works, where he has room to explore a wide range of experience, controlled by the classical precision of his structures. The six symphonies composed since 1941 are the culmination of his development. Here he successfully adapts the *ritornello* principle to the symphony without becoming enslaved by Bachian 'Brandenburg Concerto' rhythms which are such a restricting influence in some of his neo-classical works such as the Sinfonietta Giocosa. They achieve a remarkable degree of sustained intensity without ever degenerating into emotionalism. Recognition of their qualities has been slow for the same reason as with Prokofiev's symphonies, namely unwillingness to take seriously a composer whom public opinion has labelled a satirist. They are genuinely national works which only a composer who felt deeply the experiences of his country from 1938 to 1945 could have written.

The establishment of the independent state of Czechoslovakia led to a remarkable outburst of creative activity in the 1920s and 30s, most of it intended for home consumption. It is therefore not surprising that few of the composers to be mentioned now are known to the rest of Europe. Most of them were pupils of Novák and Suk. Otakar Jeremiáš (b. 1892) made few technical innovations, but he achieved considerable dramatic power and psychological insight in his opera, *The Brothers Karamazov*. Emil Axman (1887-1950) was one of the few composers directly influenced by Janáček. Ladislav Vycpálek (b. 1882) is an impressive master of polyphony and his music is permeated with religious and moral strength. Pavel Bořkovec (b. 1894) is essentially a lyrical composer. His ballet, *The Pied Piper*, is his most popular work.

One of the most colourful and versatile personalities among the composers born in the early years of the twentieth century is Emil Burian (b. 1904). He is equally gifted as playwright and producer of satirical plays and reviews; a kind of Czech Offenbach. But he has also composed much impressive serious music, particularly chamber music. Jaroslav Ježek (1906-42) was also a satirist and like Burian had his own theatre in Prague. He was much influenced by jazz in the style of the early Milhaud and Poulenc. Isa Krejči (b. 1904) has the distinction of having composed the most successful Czech comic opera, *The Revolt in Ephesus*, based on *The Comedy of Errors*.

The Nazi occupation was a severe testing time for Czechoslovak composers. Many fine creative spirits perished as a result of hardships experienced during this period—such as Rudolf Karel, Dvořák's last pupil, and several gifted young composers, particularly Vítězslava Kaprálová at the age of twenty-five. Her 'Military Symphonietta', heard in London in 1938, and her Partita for Piano and Strings reveal an outstanding talent in the Martinů style. There is no doubt that had she lived she would have become one of the greatest women composers in Europe. Vítek Nejedlý, son of the great authority on Smetana, was a very promising and prolific talent in symphony, choral works and opera. But the war years were by no means entirely negative in effect. The necessity for giving artistic expression to the desire for national survival and regeneration was enthusiastically accepted by most composers, forging them into a unity that was carried forward into the post-war years. They were not slow to realise their responsibilities to the Czechoslovak people and this found expression in dramatic cantatas on historical periods that had a contemporary relevance, in popular songs of resistance and in satirical cartoon films, subtly disguised to avoid offending the enemy, but making their point to those for whom they were intended.

The Union of Czechoslovak Composers, formed at the end of the war, was given by the Government the task of developing the musical life of the whole nation and not merely that of creating the conditions for the healthy development of serious composition. Popular music was considered an important sphere of activity, and many composers who had hitherto worked exclusively in serious music devoted much time and energy to the development of popular songs that were based on the folksong tradition, but contemporary in spirit, easy to remember and of the highest artistic quality. Joseph Stanislav (b. 1897), who had been a pioneer in this field since the 1920s, was joined by others of his generation such as Alois Hába and by many gifted younger men such as Vaclav Dobiáš (b. 1909) and Jan Seidl (b. 1908). At the same time composers were urged to remember the vast new potential audience for serious music that had come into being with the organisation of concerts for working people in the big industrial centres. Frequent national and international conferences to discuss the means by which composers can reach this new audience have been organised by the Union. The necessity for attempting to solve these problems is recognised by all composers, if only because they are provided by the Union with very favourable economic conditions and given opportunities for frequent performances of their works. The vast quantity of music being composed and performed in Czechoslovakia today makes for great difficulty in assessing what is most valuable. However, the following composers are perhaps the most talented from the point of view of intrinsic quality of imaginative thought, irrespective of their success or otherwise in the solution of the problems they have set hemselves.

Miloslav Kabeláč (b. 1908) is primarily a symphonic composer on spacious Sibelian lines. He wrote a very powerful cantata, *Do Not Retreat,* at the beginning of the war. Václav Trojan (born 1907), although a pupil of Hába, no longer uses micro-tones. His music for the magnificent puppet colour cartoons of Trinka is outstanding for its subtlety of orchestration and sense of fantasy, the Czech equivalent of Ravel's *L'enfant et les sortilèges.*

Vaclav Dobiáš (b. 1909) is the indefatigable president of the Union and vitally concerned with the problem of composers in relation to their audience. He has a rare lyrical charm in his chamber music, of which his Nonet is a fine example. His more recent work, such as the very popular cantata, *Build your Country to defend Peace,* is brilliantly written but rather obvious in idiom and content. Jan Seidl (born 1908), a pupil of Hába, in addition to his very successful popular songs, has recently composed a very fine cantata, *People, be on your guard!*—a setting of the prison diary of Julius Fučik, the great Czech Resistance hero, murdered by the Nazis.

Klement Slaviký (b. 1910) writes very intense and rhythmically subtle works, often derived from Moravian folksong, many of which have aroused much controversy. He has much in common stylistically with Szymanowski. His *Rhapsodic Variations on a Moravian Folksong* is very exciting rhythmically, but perhaps rather over-rich in instrumentation.

Jan Kapr (b. 1914) is generally considered the leader of the younger composers. His work is characterised by powerful rhythms and richness of texture, notably in his cantata, *Song of my Native Land*. His early works such as the Fantasia for Viola and Piano are rather 'overripe' harmonically, but latterly his harmonic idiom has become simpler and stronger. He has written much popular music that is both simple and distinguished.

Jan Hanuš (b. 1915) has made a speciality of children's music, of which his Suite for children's choir and chamber orchestra, *Czech Year*, is outstanding for its directness and sensitivity. He is also a fine symphonist.

Jiří Pauer (b. 1919), although not a pupil of Hába, wrote, nevertheless, at one time in the micro-tone system, as in his Concerto for Quarter-tone Clarinet and Small Orchestra. More recently he has worked in the field of Mass-Song, of which those for youth choir have won a well-deserved popularity. His greatest work, the cantata, *I call you, People*, is ardent, noble and dramatic.

Stěpán Lucký (b. 1919) is a master of instrumental sonorities as in his Divertimento for Three Trombones, Strings and Percussion and his incidental music for many films.

An important post-war development has been the rise of the Slovak school of composers. They now have their own section of the Union and publishing house. Slovak folk music shares most of the Balkan characteristics that we associate with Hungary, Bulgaria and Jugoslavia —exciting, uneven rhythms, elaborate *melisma* and frequent use of the Phrygian and Lydian modes. These qualities are reflected in most of the contemporary Slovak composers. Jan Laroslav Bella, a priest, collected many Slovak folksongs long before Bartók, and these have been of inestimable value to the younger generation.

Alexander Moyzes (b. 1906) is generally considered the founder of the modern Slovak school. His early work such as the Piano Sonata, brilliant and dramatic though it is, anticipates none of the Slovak qualities of his later works, particularly the Suite for Full Orchestra, with its clear but rich orchestration and subtlety of rhythm.

Eugen Suchoň (b. 1908) has written what is certainly the most sensational opera of post-war Czechoslovakia, *The Whirlpool*, based on a Slovak folk-drama of love and revenge. Its sense of the stage, brilliant characterisation, psychological insight and dramatic power place it in the category of *Kat'a Kabanova* and *Wozzeck*. It is undoubtedly one of the masterpieces of contemporary opera in spite of a certain limitation of harmonic language. His *Psalm of the Sub-Carpathian Country*, for chorus and orchestra, is a deeply moving lament for the sufferings of his country during the German occupation.

Ján Cikker (b. 1911) is also at his best in opera. His *Juro Janošik*—the Robin Hood of Slovakia—is characterised by vivid orchestration and skilful use of melodic melismatic decoration derived from Slovak folksong.

Simon Jurovský (b. 1912) has made fine folksong arrangements. His most important recent work is a Peace Symphony, for piano concertante and orchestra, of which the faster movements have strong, clean and almost classical lines and the slow movement very imaginative string figuration and sonorities.

Of the youngest Slovak composers, Ján Zimmer has specialised in work for piano alone and with chamber groups and orchestra. He writes on broad, spacious and romantic lines. So far, typically national elements from folksong sources are less apparent in his work than in the other Slovak composers, but he shares with them a typically Slovak passionate quality which contrasts with the more meditative and thoughtful characteristics of the composers from the Czech lands.

The general attitude of most of the young Czechoslovak composers reveals more concern with the content than with the idiom and structure of musical forms. In this respect they are in sharp contrast with most of their colleagues in Western Europe; this may be explained by their understandable reaction against the over-concern with methods of composition that featured so largely in Central Europe in the 1920s and 1930s and by their passionate desire to identify their work with the mental and spiritual life of their own people.

Poland

The national cultural movement in Czechoslovakia dates from the granting of partial independence by Austria in 1859; in Poland, however, the failure of the insurrection against Russian occupation in 1830, with the consequent large-scale emigration of most of the leading intelligentsia, prevented the possibility of a corresponding united cultural renaissance on Polish soil. Nevertheless, the great example of Mickiewicz, both as poet and as revolutionary leader, continued to stimulate the leading creative minds throughout the nineteenth century.

Lithuania and this is reflected in his ballad, *Lilje*. Otherwise his work was not, until recently, much influenced by folk music. His recent opera, *The Students' Revolt*, based on a true episode in mediaeval Polish history, although rather old-fashioned in some of the vocal parts, makes effective use of folk music and mediaeval harmonic progressions in the choruses and dances. It is by far the most successful post-war Polish opera and has had many productions outside Poland. His ballet, *The Peacock and the Girl*, also uses folk-material very successfully. He is at present very active as chairman of the Union of Polish Composers.

Jan Maklakiewocz (b. 1899), like Szymanowski, is interested in the Orient, but in his case his interest takes the form of a special study of Japanese music. He wrote a number of pieces in Japanese scales (including quarter-tones) and rhythms as preliminary studies for his Japanese Songs for Soprano and Orchestra (1930). These songs reveal remarkable sensitivity to delicate orchestral sonorities and the vocal part captures the strange Japanese melodic style with its decoration and *portamento*. His largest work is a mystical oratorio, *Oh Holy Lord*. His work may be described as a rarified development of Szymanowski's middle period style.

Boleslau Woytowicz (b. 1899) is also one of Poland's leading pianists. He writes on spacious, romantic lines, and folksong influence, particularly of a modal kind, is very strong. His finest work is the Second Symphony, published in 1947. It is on a vast scale, for a very large orchestra. The whole work is derived from a modal motif first announced by the horns and is very convincing in its structural unity and dramatic power, particularly the third movement, a fugue with recitative interludes. The finale makes effective use of bi-tonal and bi-rhythmical methods. He has received much praise for his recent 'Warsaw' Symphony and for the *Cantata in Praise of Work*.

Of the generation of composers born in the early years of the twentieth century, Artur Malawski (b. 1904) is one of the most important. Unlike many of his colleagues he studied exclusively in Poland, and his work shows none of the customary French influence; nor for that matter are Polish characteristics, except in his recent work, very pronounced. His work is characterised by strong lines, powerful rhythms and logically convincing harmony and he is at his best in orchestral writing. The Symphonic Studies for Piano and Orchestra (1947), which made a strong impression at the 1948 I.S.C.M. Festival, is perhaps his finest work, rhythmically powerful, rich in texture, the harmony basically tonal but arresting because of the clear contrapuntal means by which it is obtained. In the six movements of this work he achieves a remarkable diversity within unity. The stylisation within each movement is maintained with classical consistency, although he is always free from neo-classical mannerisms. The Toccata for Small Orchestra (1947) achieves much subtlety of cross-rhythms with deliberately restricted patterns and counterpoints. More recently his melodic style has become influenced by folk-themes as in the suite for orchestra, *Heights*. He has also, with other composers, been concerned in the revival of eighteenth-century music as in his Sonata on themes by Janiewicz (1951).

Roman Palester (b. 1907) is one of the best-known Polish composers outside his own country. His work is not noticeably Polish in character, nor has he been much influenced musically by his living in France. His String Quartet (1936) is remarkable for its brilliant exploitation of the sonorities of the instruments and the wide range of moods from subtle impressionism to strong dance rhythms. The Sonata for Piano Duet (1940) is more classical in rhythmical style, with little of the former impressionism. It is frequently very dissonant but is logical harmonically and contrapuntally strong. The Serenade for Two Flutes and Strings (published in 1948) is a delicate and elaborately contrapuntal piece. The Nocturne has something of his older impressionistic style with its intricate figuration. His most impressive recent work is the cantata, *The Vistula*, evoking various aspects of the great Polish river, nostalgic and full of the most imaginative and convincing sonorities.

Tadeuz Kassern (b. 1904) is a fine vocal composer. His arrangements of Polish Folksongs from the Reclaimed Western Regions (1948) have very sensitive piano accompaniments that owe something to Szymanowski with subtle harmony and counterpoints that merge with the melodies. His Concerto for Soprano and Orchestra is a very successful example of this difficult medium.

Michal Spisak has much in common with Palester in that his style is European rather than national. His Suite for Strings, published in 1948, is effective, powerful writing, but rather square and rigid rhythmically.

Anton Szalowski (b. 1907) shows marked French influence. His Overture, published in 1947, has many neo-classical features in the Toccata-like figuration, but it is strong rhythmically with a very poetic middle section. The Third String Quartet, published in 1947, has simple, clear texture but is a little mechanical in rhythm in the faster movements; the slow movement, however, is very imaginative.

Andrzej Panufnik (b. 1914) is one of the most remarkable composers of his generation. He has unlimited audacity and conviction in his exploitation of novel sonorities. His melodic style is deeply rooted in folksong. In his Five Popular Songs for child's voice or soprano chorus, two flutes, two clarinets and bass clarinet (1940) the wind accompaniments have what can be described only as a sophisticated naïvety, and the series of rising semitonal modulations in the second song is most skilfully and unobtrusively effected. The *Lullaby*, for Twenty-nine Strings and two harps (1947), is an extraordinary study in *glissando* effects almost completely devoid of thematic material, relying entirely on the succession of sonorities and the gently lilting rhythm. The Tragic Overture, commemorating the Warsaw Rising of 1942, is a *tour de force* of thematic concentration, based entirely on a single short motif. This work is, in fact, an extreme example of his very characteristic device of achieving tremendous cumulation by means of rigid consistency of figuration. The Symphony of Peace (1951), for orchestra, with children's, women's and men's voices, is of great emotional power expressed in the most direct terms. Only a composer of consummate mastery could achieve such simplicity and at the same time avoid banality. The first movement, Lament, is slow and sustained with the children's and women's voices used without words. The second movement, Drammatico, a *scherzo*, has much in common with the Tragic Overture in its thematic and rhythmical consistency, based entirely on a rocking figure and a slow chorale-like theme heard against it, the middle section being in march rhythm. The last movement, Solenne, is a steadily moving march in which the voices are heard with words for the first time in a diatonic tune of great nobility and simplicity. One of his most recent works, the Rustic Symphony, in three movements with two *intermezzi*, skilfully exploits sonorities associated with folk-music ensembles but in general suffers from over-obviousness of content. Like Malawski, he has arranged works of eighteenth-century Polish composers, notably the *Divertimento* for strings on themes by Janiewicz. During and since the war he has written many mass songs for amateurs. They are often of an unbelievable naïveté and even banality in their melodies, frequently with extraordinarily dissonant accompaniments; it is difficult to take them as serious attempts to achieve a genuinely popular idiom, having nothing in common with the deeply moving simplicity to be found in the Symphony of Peace.

Witold Lutoslawski (b. 1913) is probably the most widely popular living composer in Poland today. He lacks the startling originality of Panufnik, but he has a genuinely personal melodic gift with its roots in

Polish folk music, combined with a refined, clear and subtle harmonic idiom. There is French influence in his style, but it is free of the mannerisms of the 1920s to be found in some other Polish composers. His best early work, the Symphonic Variations (1938), for large orchestra with piano, has an original and convincing structure of four movements. The simple and short folksong-like theme is treated very freely, but the work is harmonically unified and delicately orchestrated. His finest recent works, the *Silesian Tryptych*, for orchestra and solo voice, and the Miniature Suite for Orchestra very successfully combine the Polish folk-idiom with sensitivity and directness of expression. On a smaller scale his settings of poems by Tuwim, the greatest modern Polish poet, are amongst the finest children's songs of modern times.

Grazyna Baciewicz, who graduated from the Warsaw Conservatoire in 1932, is the most outstanding woman composer of Poland. She is also a leading violinist. Her work is well known in Paris, where she studied with Nadia Boulanger and Carl Flesch and was awarded a prize for her Wind Quintet in 1933. Her work shows marked French influence, particularly that of the Paris neo-classical school, as in the Overture for Full Orchestra published in 1947. This work contains brilliant string writing and strong rhythms held together by consistent figuration against flowing counterpoints. She has concentrated mostly on chamber and orchestral writing and concertos—three for violin and one for piano; so far she has written little vocal music. Her Fourth String Quartet was awarded first prize at Liège in 1952. The neo-classical element remains strong in her later work, but the melodic ideas are less abstract and contain far more characteristically Polish inflections.

Jan Ekier (b. 1913) is a leading pianist and has written mostly piano music which is very fluent and with a strong folksong influence, but more recently he has answered the growing demand for choral and orchestral cantatas as in his *Colourful Melodies*.

Kazimerz Serocki (b. 1922) is the most outstanding young composer in Poland. He was a pupil of Nadia Boulanger, but the French influence is not marked except in his highly developed sense of sonority, which suggests Stravinsky rather than the French school itself. His Suite for Four Trombones (1953) is a masterly exploitation of the medium, with brilliant counterpoint and a very beautiful harmonisation of a chorale-like theme. His Suite for Piano (1954) is a series of remarkable studies in concentrated melodic and rhythmical patterns. Latterly he has composed much film-music and a large-scale cantata, *Symphony of Songs*, based on folksongs and the *Symphony of Struggle*.

Tadeus Baird (b. 1928) is another talented young composer. His Symphony in C, awarded a State Prize in 1951, and the Suite, *Colas Breugnon*, show less obvious originality than Serocki, but he has achieved much success in linking contemporary thought and language with the ancient Polish tradition.

Tadeus Paciorkiewicz, one of the youngest, has a charming lyrical talent, as shown in his piano pieces and Violin and Piano Sonata, but it is rather complacent and not very adventurous at present.

The large number of amateur song-and-dance ensembles that have been formed since the war has presented Polish composers with the problem of arranging folk music in a way that preserves its original character but also makes it effective when performed before large audiences. In addition, the growing demand for songs about everyday life gives composers the opportunity to extend the folk-idiom into a modern popular style, replacing the commercialised type of popular song. The leader of the movement was Tadeuz Sygietynski, whose Mazowsze group was the first of many such remarkable ensembles. Today there exists a very healthy situation in which leading composers of opera, symphony and chamber music are devoting much of their imaginative thought to popular songs, not in an attitude of 'writing down' to the people but directing their skill towards simplicity and clarity of expression. Lutoslawski and Serocki have been markedly successful, as well as composers like Gradstein and Szpilman, who have made popular music their speciality.

In general, it may be said that Polish music has now overcome the slavish subservience to foreign influences, particularly French, that arose from the peculiar historical conditions in Poland during the last hundred and fifty years. The work of the present generation of composers suggests that they are beginning to realise the potentialities that exist in a country no longer torn between rival claimants to its territory and where there exists an audience for their work much larger and keener than at any other time in its history.

Nikos Skalkottas

JOHN G. PAPAIOANNOU

A UNIQUE case in the history of contemporary music is that of the Greek composer, Nikos Skalkottas, who died in 1949 completely unknown, leaving behind him an imposing *oeuvre* of which many even of his closest friends were unaware. Up to his death practically all his works remained unpublished and, apart from a few early compositions, unperformed.

His life pursued a somewhat dull course, containing few points of real interest. Yet the development of his creative career, on an entirely different plane, reveals a powerful personality which was able to conceive and define its goal in the highest terms and proceed towards it along an unfailingly personal and original road. This uncompromising attitude towards his task, together with the fact that during the fully mature years of his life he worked in complete isolation, account to a considerable extent for the intrinsic autonomy and independence of his style. This is one of the main reasons why so much difficulty is encountered when an attempt is made to relate his contribution to the main course of contemporary musical thought in Europe. Nevertheless, he had in fact proceeded from foundations which show an assimilation of the important elements of most of the chief modern styles (the impressionists, Busoni, Schönberg, Stravinsky and, to some extent, Bartók) gained after mastering the styles of Bach, Mozart and Brahms, to name only those composers to whom his language seems most indebted.

Before attempting to outline his style, however, and to assess the importance of his output, a brief survey of his life is essential.

Nikos Skalkottas was born on the 8th March, 1904, in the small town of Halkis (population about 20,000), capital of the island of Euboea. His paternal ancestry shows several musical connections (flute-playing, conducting, teaching, etc.); the composer's sister is a pianist and singer. He showed musical aptitudes very early in life, and when he came to Athens with the family at the age of five, he was already able to play tunes on a small violin of his own manufacture. Later he studied the violin at the Athens Conservatoire, graduating in 1920, winning a gold medal. During his student days he also developed his literary gifts, and some of his poems were published by the leading Athenian magazine, *Numas*.

Having won the 'Averof Scholarship', which ran for two years, he went to Germany in 1921 and remained there until 1933. From 1923 on he relied mainly on another scholarship, offered by M. Benaki, which enabled him to study independently. Practically all his stay in Germany was spent in Berlin. At first he continued his violin studies under Willy Hess at the Hochschule there. Although he reached an exceptional level of virtuosity,[1] he decided in 1925 to abandon a virtuoso career in favour of composition. By that time he had produced, apart from various unpretentious works based on Greek folk music, a number of daring and original compositions in which he had already forsaken tonality (e.g. a remarkable sonata for unaccompanied violin). When in 1927 he went to study with Schönberg at the *Akademie der Künste* he can be said to have been an accomplished composer. For Schönberg he had a profound respect and affection. He worked under him until 1931, and the two kept in contact until Schönberg left Germany in May 1933. Schönberg thought very highly of Skalkottas and once publicly declared him the most talented student of the 'younger generation' (i.e. after Berg and Webern) in his class. Although they lost touch with each other after Schönberg left for the U.S.A., in Schönberg's book, *Style and Idea* (1951), Skalkottas is one of the few names among the hundreds of his pupils who is given the exalted label of 'composer', and Schönberg was unaware at that time of Skalkottas' subsequent and more important output.

Skalkottas had also previously studied composition with Paul Kahn at the Hochschule with Philip Jarnach from 1925 to 1927, and for a short period in 1931 with Kurt Weill, being by this latter doubly con-

---

[1] His most unusual way of playing the violin was characterised by an exceptionally pure and disembodied sound, with almost no *vibrato*. Yet it was especially warm and always mathematically precise, even in the wildest passages in his own works.

nected with the Busoni school. Some imprints of these contacts may be found in his later works, such as Jarnach's refined feeling for form and Weill's witty rhythms which made a strong impression on some of his works, particularly those written around 1940. These, however, have to be considered only as incidental influences. The main influence was Schönberg. This he affirmed himself. It must be stressed, however, that the works written before he knew Schönberg are already characteristic of the main traits of his style which had thus crystallised very early in his career and was only partly reorientated under Schönberg.

Skalkottas was of a very lively, ironic and combative character up to about 1932. He was well acquainted with the main contemporary tendencies and open to the many influences which reached the central capital of Germany. He possessed a large musical library, including full scores bound in gold of practically all the operas of Wagner and Strauss (a fact partly due to his protector's—M. Benaki—fondness for these composers). For a long time he led a string quartet which played a considerable amount of 'new music'. Finally a number of his early works were performed with great success at the *Singakademie* concerts (especially 1929–31) and he came to be considered a most promising young composer.

A curious and rapid change in his whole attitude ensued, caused by material difficulties of life, in 1931–33, and he felt compelled to leave Germany, returning to Athens where he settled until his death. Lack of understanding here and financial problems made him more detached from everyday life, so that all his mature creative period in Athens (1933–49) can be said to have evolved in complete isolation. Although he earned his living without too much difficulty as a violinist in the State and Opera orchestras and elsewhere, he became utterly indifferent to everything around him, especially in music, where he felt that nobody in his country understood his aims. He never discussed serious music or his work, even with friends; he completely lost touch with any new music after 1933 and he certainly never heard any major work composed abroad after then or saw its score (except that of Schönberg's Piano Concerto, which he borrowed from the writer shortly before his death; he was keenly interested in it).

His evolution after 1933, therefore, took place entirely apart from any happenings in Europe in a completely secluded world of his own. His only outlet was composition. He was writing almost continuously, often during the long hours of the night, producing one important work after another as if compelled to complete his message before his premature death.

In 1946 he married a Greek pianist, Maria Pangali; they had two sons. His sudden death on the 19th September, 1949, from a strangulated hernia (typical of his extreme carelessness in practical matters), cut short his career at what may well have been the eve of a new flowering.

During the twenty-five years of his composing career, however, Skalkottas had been able to produce an impressive quantity of works consisting of more than a hundred and fifty compositions[1] (collections like the *Thirty-six Greek Dances* or the *Thirty-two Piano Pieces* being counted as one). Of these, some seventy-five are of comparatively large dimensions (average duration twenty to thirty minutes), including, but rather as an exception, a few unusually large ones; these comprise some sixty works in sonata or allied (suite) forms and some fifteen collections and works in other large forms. The remaining seventy-five or so are usually short (two to six minutes)—mostly songs and short choruses.

Purely in bulk, this output is one of the largest in our time, exceeding, for example, the combined output of Schönberg, Berg and Webern. It contains about a dozen major symphonic works, including a monumental thirty-minute symphony in one movement for large orchestra (overture to a projected opera, *The Return of Ulysses*); the gigantic *Second Symphonic Suite* in six movements, lasting some ninety minutes; at least fourteen concertos (nine of large dimensions, tending towards concertante symphonies); a very great deal of chamber music (more than fifty works)—one of his most cherished fields, including more than six string quartets and at least eight works in sonata form for violin and piano; piano music, e.g. the large collection of thirty-two pieces, four suites, etc.; songs; choruses, a 'fairy drama', *With the Spell of May*; a work for chorus and orchestra, *The Unknown Soldier* (R. Stein), and many others, apart from the numerous arrangements, orchestrations and other subsidiary work. He also left a treatise (in Greek), *The Technique of Orchestration* (1940).

After the already mature, pre-Schönberg years (1925–27), three main periods in his compositional career can be distinguished. The first

---

[1] Of these, one hundred and thirteen have been identified so far in the Skalkottas Archives in Athens; the others are known from collective descriptions in Skalkottas' own catalogues or other sources. In the Skalkottas Archives manuscripts of ninety-four works, comprising most of his major compositions, have been gathered so far.

period (1928–38) is characterised by a more transparent, sharp, somewhat disconnected style, pronouncedly Schönbergian and using exclusively his 'strict serial technique'. This can be subdivided into the Berlin years (1928–33), with a fuller, more spacious style, and the Athens years (1934–38), more daringly incisive and uncompromising. Three peaks of increased output can be found: 1928–30, 1935 and 1937–38. The middle period (1938–1945) is the richest in output (especially 1940–43) and the most diversified in its experimentation with various new techniques. Writing becomes more compact and yet more free, works grow larger in dimensions, tending towards the monumental. The last period (1946–49), apart from some unpretentious tonal music (probably written as a sideline), contains only a handful of chamber music, but of the highest quality, very concentrated and usually gloomy in colour. In 1949, however, just before his death, there was a considerable increase in output (including the orchestration of earlier scores) which seems to indicate that a new surge of creative activity was imminent.

In spite of experiment and constant evolution of style, Skalkottas seems after 1927 to have adhered to a more steady and unified conception of his approach to composition. This approach, however, seems at first rather difficult to define in direct relation to that of the main contemporary European schools. The probable explanation of this may lie in the fact that, despite his immediate contact with most of them, and his critical appreciation of their essential merits and shortcomings, he had at the same time pursued an independent and personal path. This accounts for the often surprising novelty of his idiom. At the same time, nevertheless, he worked out a synthesis between this new idiom and the stream of historical tradition in a manner at once natural and unexpected, so that the listener is puzzled when he attempts to define its concrete characteristics. The impact of his music is of such power, however, that it leaves no margin for any doubt of its genuineness and authenticity. The perplexing dualism of novelty and tradition in his works is certainly not a compromise—much less a retrogression or a capitulation to 'easier' goals; on the contrary, it should be considered a fusion on a higher level of two only seemingly conflicting paths into a new, original entity. Skalkottas' compositional technique proceeds in its essentials from Schönberg's teaching in 1928–30 (about five years after Schönberg had definitely formulated his 'serial' system). Skalkottas, however, imposes on the 'classical' serial technique a number of significant modifications of his own, which are not conceived with a view to relaxing its requirements, but mainly to adapt it to the desiderata of his own style. His version of serial technique, more or less uniform throughout his first period (1928–38), disperses from 1938 onwards into a considerable number of variants, so that it is probably no exaggeration to say that practically every serial work of his middle or last period uses its own serial technique, this technique being often a highly evolved, particular new 'system' of twelve-tone writing. At the same time, in the last two periods, Skalkottas also uses what seems to be a non-serial system, where nothing like a tone-row seems to be present, although many other techniques used in his strictly serial works are also used here. It is not yet clear whether this system should be considered a free one (from the serial point of view), or whether, in some cases at least, groupings having the *function* of a row (although *not* consisting of the twelve notes of the chromatic scale) are also present here. Pending a final assessment of the technique used in this group of works, the system (or systems) used here may be provisionally termed 'figurative', in view of the strong role usually played by specifically melodic figurations or contours in them, which are not attached to definite intervallic relations. At any rate, Skalkottas' serial compositions far outweigh his 'figurative' (and, of course, his plainly tonal) output, in number, volume and over-all importance. At the same time, his constant struggle with technique shows firstly his deep understanding of the problems pertaining to the foundations of his writing, and, secondly, the flexibility with which he faced them, always remaining within the framework provided by his own style.

One can point to certain constant features in the main line of evolution of his serial works, which show the following chief differences from the 'classical' twelve-tone system:

(*a*) The unique basic row is replaced by a basic complex of two, three, four, six, eight or even twelve, sixteen or eighteen independent twelve-tone rows, which are correspondingly associated with each other within this complex, either in horizontal juxtaposition or in 'counterpoint' with each other (up to four rows heard together, in extreme cases).

(*b*) The usual rules for repetition of notes and variation techniques for the rows are used more strictly than in late Schönberg, but the rows are usually presented in the original position. Inversion and especially transposition are usually avoided, in order, as he said, 'to keep rows more easily recognisable'. They are used only in exceptional cases for special reasons; retrograde forms of rows are used more frequently.

(*c*) The main variation technique used by Skalkottas for his rows is what could be termed 'group variation': the subdivision of rows into equal or unequal groups of usually three to five (sometimes two or six) notes is important and determines a 'neighbourhood relationship' of the notes within the respective group; this neighbourhood relationship being strictly maintained, every conceivable technique of variation, regular or irregular, is used within each group.

It will be noticed that Skalkottas disdained processes of variation that are too mechanical (inversion, use of mathematically regular combinatorial devices, etc.) and concentrates on what preserves relationships created by the 'audible vicinity' of sounds. At the same time, the use of more than one row as a basis provides not only a greater richness and variety in writing, but also additional articulation to his language, making use of the specific role or physiognomy usually attached to each one of the rows of the basic complex. Moreover, this basic complex acquires a greater 'thematic' significance than the single row of classical twelve-tone works. The composition appears as a series of variations on it, superimposed over the traditional form of the piece (e.g. sonata, suite), and this interplay of two forms (e.g. sonata, plus variations) provides an additional interest to its structure.

This approach to musical structure seems also to confer a more flowing unity on the formal complexes: whereas in 'classic dodecaphony' difficult, bold, structural leaps (note—row—entire movement) are presented to the perceptive powers of the listener, Skalkottas subdivides this whole range into shorter, closer steps (e.g. note—note-group (within row)—row—complex of rows—entire movement), so that it becomes easier to grasp the gradual growth of the form from its consecutive elements, consciously or subconsciously.

In his subdivision of the complex into rows, and of each row into groups, and in the way he uses, varies and combines them, Skalkottas comes very near to the techniques used, for example, in the renaissance *cantus firmus* masses; his highly polyphonic writing, moreover, is also more closely related to renaissance (and partly to late baroque) counterpoint conceptions, than to those of any other musical era.

To relate him to or compare him with any specific modern school of thought or composer is, however, very difficult, even on a superficial basis. One would be tempted perhaps to place him in a line of descent proceeding from somewhere midway between Schönberg and Berg were it not for the considerable number of individual characteristics that defy any attempt at really rewarding comparisons. There are a few points of similarity with Webern—an intense refinement of writing

and a structural use of multiple group relationship are the most obvious
—and he has often been bracketed with Berg. Passionate warmth, a
predominantly gloomy palette, iridescent and veiled richness of sound,
are certainly common to both. But for all its intensity, Skalkottas'
music sounds less exuberantly romantic than Berg's and here the comparison must break down. At various times J. M. Hauer (harmony and
orchestration), Stravinsky of the early twenties (harmony, rhythm and a
characteristic, rather ironic, quality) and even Kurt Weill and Krenek
have been cited, but in the last instance perhaps it is a less tangible
feeling for a country and landscape—Greece and the Mediterranean—
that really imbues Skalkottas' music with its personality, transparency
and light, its singing lyricism and its joy in rich sonority. Curiously
enough, Skalkottas only occasionally used Greek folk music and then
in simple, tonal harmonisation (as in the *Thirty-six Greek Dances*, for
orchestra) or by incorporating folk tunes, usually as themes for variation.

What seems to be one of the most outstanding features of Skalkottas'
contribution to post-Schönbergian thinking (and one of the most per-
suasive justifications for it is his elegant approach) is the synthesis,
already referred to, of a truly novel language with conceptions incorporating a real sense of tradition.

Skalkottas seems to devote only a small proportion of his efforts
in creating entirely new formal structures. Then they are usually found
in very short pieces based on some sort of mathematical predetermina-
tion of events, as used by the earlier Schönberg or by Webern. What
chiefly absorbs his interest is a revaluation of classical forms, mainly
of the sonata type, which he often subjects to (*a*) a recasting of the
outward scheme, (*b*) a change of accepted proportions within it and
(*c*) a refinement of details in internal formal relationships that often
produces extremes of elaboration. His satisfaction that the serial system,
as he uses it, can serve this reorientation of traditional forms is shown
by his insistence on them throughout his career, as if he were proving
that they do not belong only to the past but that they still have the
power to feed new musical idioms.

Melody is another field in which this synthesis seems most valuable.
Skalkottas can create real, long melodies that 'sing' as classical ones
and yet which are based on serial principles. Even the over-expressive
wide intervals ('dissonant' intervals over more than one octave) are
melodically exploited so that they never disrupt the unity of the line
(such as *pointilliste* writing would often do).

In harmony also his imagination reaches far and wide. Here the loss occasioned by the deliberate rejection of tonal functions is more than compensated by richness of articulation, by the creation of the most diverse 'families of chords', each of which has its own characteristic colour. The unusual variety provided by this constant change of 'harmonic colour' is used also as a powerful means of supporting and clarifying formal structures. Tonality in the traditional sense is, of course, totally absent from his music; yet two special instances might be mentioned: (a) in certain cases a kind of tonal centre is established by emphasis and frequent repetition, and (b) in his last years (from 1943 onwards) a peculiar 'tonal quality' seems present, even in his most violently atonal works. This curious contradiction is usually created by the use of melodies with a strong tonal feeling harmonised by every means possible to belie their tonality. Although harmonically no trace of tonal functions, polytonality or even tonal centres can usually be found, the over-all impression, despite the grating dissonances, comes curiously near that of tonal music.

Considering his facility of melodic invention, it is not surprising that contrapuntal writing appears as another hallmark of his style. He indulges in it with effortless ease and despite the astonishing mobility and independence of his parts, the sum total is at the same time harmonically controlled. It may be mentioned, moreover, that in his manuscripts the vertical alignment of simultaneous notes is not always very precise, because he was not writing, so to speak, bar by bar, but line by line, part by part.

Rhythm in his works is never a play of mathematical formulas, never an artificial experiment. It is an elemental power, explosive in quick movements, flowing in wide, co-ordinated waves in the slow ones, full of vitality and alert in supporting the *Urlinie* and form, in the virile tradition of Handel, Schumann and Brahms. In his metrical structures, moreover, originality again is allied to traditional conceptions, akin to Schubert in their relation to form.

Finally his style, in its over-all aspects, stands far from the *pointilliste* post-Webern ideals, and (increasingly towards his later years) reaches towards a more familiar, traditional, simpler scheme of note-grouping on the score. This writing persists at a much more daringly progressive level than that of many newer tendencies.

The lack of sketches, note-books and the like among his manuscripts, which he appears never to have destroyed or mislaid, seems to show that he put a work on paper only when having practically finished its composition in his mind. This fact is confirmed by other evidence, including the almost complete lack of erasures and errors in his scores, which were written at an incredible speed, despite all their complexity. As well as perfect pitch and a phenomenal memory (he remembered practically all his works and actually rewrote by heart his entire first orchestral suite six years after it was composed), an unequalled power of imagination helped him to achieve his aims, without ever sacrificing directness and spontaneity.

But over and above these technical aspects of his work, its main importance lies in the inherent, direct power of his utterance, and in its profound message, so masterfully presented and conveyed in the most original language. His hundred and fifty-odd compositions stand as a monument of true creative power that needed no other outlet, incentive, reward or justification than their formulation. This seems one of the finest achievements of our time.

Index

INDEX

INDEX

INDEX

Reger, Max, 62, 79, 80, 82, 167, 168, 313
Respighi, Ottorino, 170, 173–4
Rieti, Vittorio, 187
Riisager, Knud-Aage, 118, 119–20
Rimsky-Korsakov, N. A., 40, 41, 43, 47–8, 54, 204
Ringbom, Nils-Eric, 123
Rivier, Jean, 242
Rosenberg, Hilding, 126, 127, 129
Roussel, Albert, 120, 238–42
  Aeneas, 241
  Bacchus et Ariane, 240
  Concerto, Piano, Op. 26, 239
  Evocations, 238
  Festin, Le, 238
  Petite Suite, Op. 39, 239, 240
  Sinfonietta, 241
  Suite in F, Op. 33, 239, 240, 241
  Symphonies, 1st, 238; *3rd*, 240; *4th*, 239–41
Rozycki, Ludomir, 312
Rubbra, Edmund, 133–4
  Missa in honorem Sancti Dominici, 134
  Symphonies, 1st–6th, 134

Sacher, Paul, 33, 155, 159
Saeverud, Harald, 125
Satie, Erik, 245, 246–53, 272
  Avant dernières pensées, 249, 250
  Cinq Grimaces, 252
  Gymnopédies, 48, 248
  Jack-in-the-Box, 248
  Mercure, 252
  Messe des Pauvres, 248
  Minuet, 248
  Nocturnes, 252
  Pantins Dansent, Les, 252
  Parade, 248, 250–2
  Prélude de la Porte Héroïque du Ciel, 248
  Prélude en Tapisserie, 251
  Préludes, 248, 249
  Relâche, 252
  Sarabandes, 247, 248
  Socrate, 248, 272
  Sonatine Bureaucratique, 246–7
  Sports et Divertissements, 245, 248, 251
Sauguet, Henri, 272–6
  Bocages, 273
  Caprices de Marianne, Les, 275

  Concerto d'Orphée, 274
  Forains, Les, 273
  Pres du Bal, 273
  Symphony, I.N.R., 274–5
  Voyante, La, 272–3
Schenker, Heinrich, 76–7
Scherchen, Hermann, 100, 185, 186
Schoeck, Otmar, 167–8
Scholes, Professor Percy, 64
Schönberg, Arnold, 2–3, 7, 9, 11–12, 51–2, 69, 76–93, 94, 96, 97, 102, 129, 158, 192–3, 209, 234, 253, 290n, 293, 321, 322
  A Cappella Pieces, Op. 27, 145
  Erwartung, Op. 17, 81, 86, 88–91
  Five Orchestral Pieces, Op. 16, 81, 83, 88
  Glückliche Hand, Die, 83, 86
  Moses and Aaron, 92, 93
  Ode to Napoleon, 92
  Orchestral Variations, Op. 31, 92
  Pelleas and Melisande, 82
  Pierrot Lunaire, 83, 86
  Quartets, String, 86; *2nd*, 81
  Serenade, Op. 24, 82
  Six Little Piano Pieces, Op. 19, 88
  Songs, Four Orchestral, Op. 22, 86
  Structural Functions of Harmony, 97
  Suites, Piano, 86; *Piano, Clarinet and Strings*, 70
  Survivor from Warsaw, A, 92
  Symphonies, 1st Chamber, Op. 9, 80, 84, 87; *2nd Chamber*, 92
  Theory of Harmony, 97
  Three Piano Pieces, Op. 11, 81, 109
  Verklärte Nacht, 80
Schultz, Svend F., 120
Scriabin, Alexander, 58, 205, 233, 283
Searle, Humphrey, 146–7
  Concerto, Piano, in D Minor, 146
  Gold Coast Customs, 146
  Intermezzo, 146
  Poem, 146
  Put Away the Flutes, 146
  River-run, The, 147
  Shadow of Cain, The, 146
  Symphony, 147
Sechter, Simon, 79
Seiber, Matyas, 15, 71, 130, 146
Seidl, Jan, 308

338

INDEX

INDEX

INDEX

Webern, Anton—(*Cont.*)
 Six Pieces for Orchestra, Op. 6, 110
 Songs, Five, Op. 15, 111; *Four, Op. 12*, 111; *Four, with Chamber Orchestra, Op. 13*, 111; *Six, Op. 14*, 111; *for Soprano and Piano, Op. 3*, 109; *Three, Op. 17*, 111–12; *Two Rilke, Op. 8*, 110
 Symphony, Op. 21, 106, 107, 112–13
 Trio, String, Op. 20, 112
Weill, Kurt, 29, 251, 321–2
Weis, Fleming, 120
Weisberg, Julia, 217
Wellesz, Egon, 146
Wiechowicz, Stanislav, 314
Wienawski, 311
Wièner, Jean, 270–1

Wiesengrund-Adorno, T., 83
Williams, C. F. Abdy, 86
Williams, R. Vaughan, 133, 149, 150
Wilm, Wilm, 63
Wirén, Dag, 120, 128
Wolf, Hugo, 77
Wordsworth, William, 150
Woytowicz, Boleslau, 315

Yudin, 210

Zafred, Mario, 190
Zakharof, 214, 215
Zelenski, 311
Zhdanof, A. A., 214
Zhelobinsky, V. V., 229
Zimmer, Ján, 310
Zimmermann, Bernd-Aloys, 201

341